YUGE!

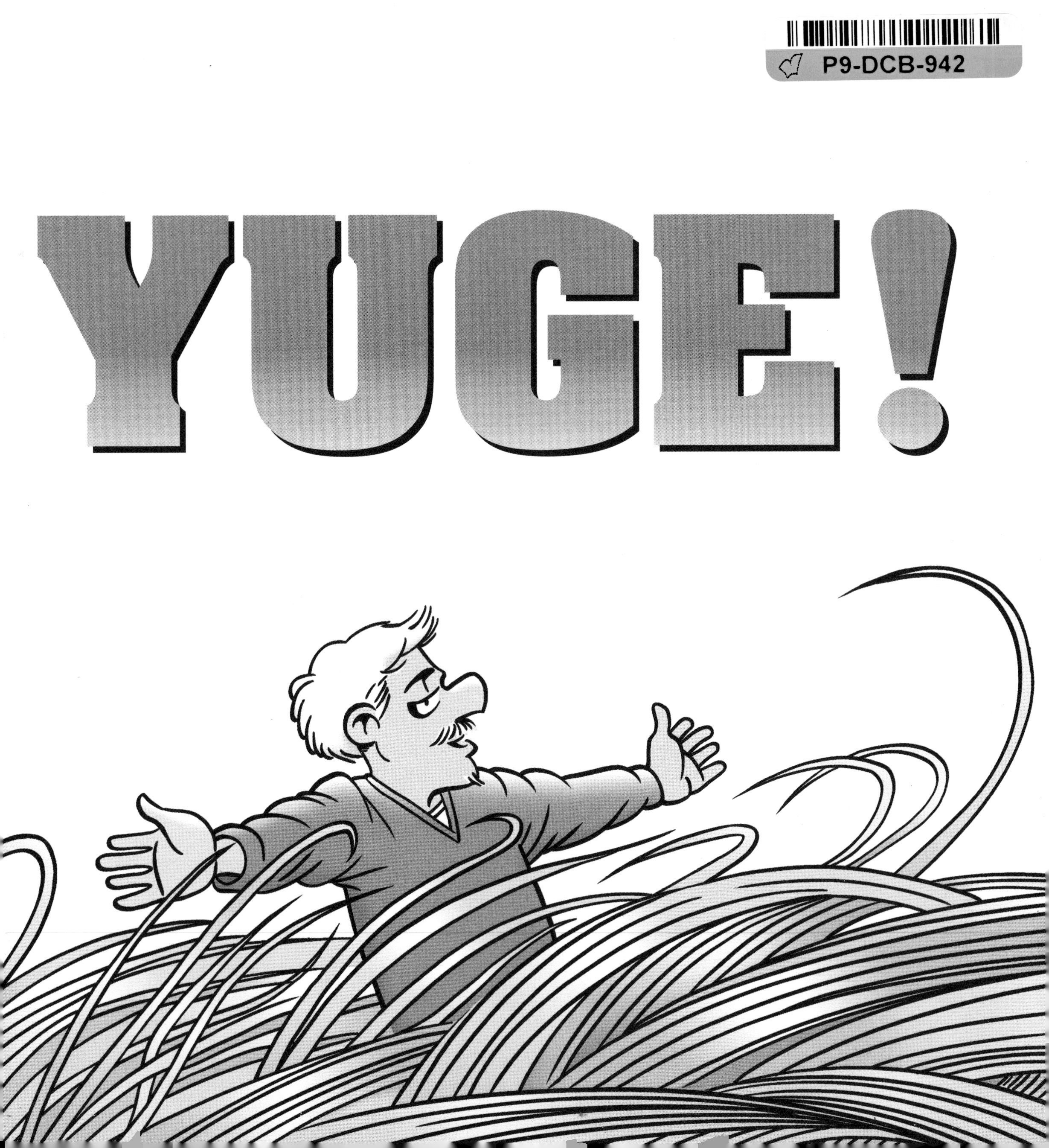

Recent Collections

Virtual Doonesbury
Planet Doonesbury
Buck Wild Doonesbury
Duke 2000: Whatever It Takes
The Revolt of the English Majors
Peace Out, Dawg!
Got War?
Talk to the Hand
Heckuva Job, Bushie!
Welcome to the Nerd Farm!
Tee Time in Berzerkistan
Red Rascal's War
Squared Away
The Weed Whisperer

Anthologies

The Doonesbury Chronicles
Doonesbury's Greatest Hits
The People's Doonesbury
Doonesbury Dossier: The Reagan Years
Doonesbury Deluxe: Selected Glances Askance
Recycled Doonesbury: Second Thoughts on a Gilded Age
The Portable Doonesbury
The Bundled Doonesbury
40: A Doonesbury Retrospective

Special Collections

Action Figure!: The Life and Times of Doonesbury's Uncle Duke
Dude: The Big Book of Zonker
Flashbacks: Twenty-Five Years of Doonesbury
The Sandbox: Dispatches from Troops in Iraq and Afghanistan
The War in Quotes
"My Shorts R Bunching. Thoughts?": The Tweets of Roland Hedley

Wounded Warrior Series

The Long Road Home: One Step at a Time
The War Within: One More Step at a Time
Signature Wound: Rocking TBI
Mel's Story: Surviving Military Sexual Assault

YUGE!
30 YEARS OF DOONESBURY ON TRUMP

A DOONESBURY BOOK
by G. B. TRUDEAU

Andrews McMeel
Publishing®
a division of Andrews McMeel Universal

DOONESBURY is distributed internationally by Universal Uclick.

Andrews McMeel Publishing
a division of Andrews McMeel Universal
1130 Walnut Street, Kansas City, Missouri 64106

www.andrewsmcmeel.com

16 17 18 19 20 RR3 11 10 9 8 7 6 5

ISBN: 978-1-4494-8133-9

Library of Congress Control Number: 2016936954

DOONESBURY may be viewed on the Internet at
www.doonesbury.com and www.GoComics.com.

ATTENTION: SCHOOLS AND BUSINESSES

Andrews McMeel books are available at quantity discounts with bulk purchase for educational, business,
or sales promotional use. For information, please e-mail the Andrews McMeel Publishing
Special Sales Department: specialsales@amuniversal.com.

PREFACE

"A third-rate talent trying to get publicity on my back."

His message, conveyed through the tabloids, boiled down to this: Get off my cloud, loser. Which is not, of course, how satire works. The target, having set himself up, doesn't get a say over the incoming. Besides, Trump had already become the gold standard for big, honking hubris, and to ignore him would have been comedy malpractice. In New York City, he practically owned the '80s, rocketing to the top as the Big Apple's loudest and most visible asshole, knocking off big-league rivals like Ed Koch, Julian Schnabel, and Steve Rubell. To those of us in the ridicule industry, the man *Spy* dubbed "a short-fingered vulgarian" was a gift beyond imagining, and we made him a permanent part of our business plans.

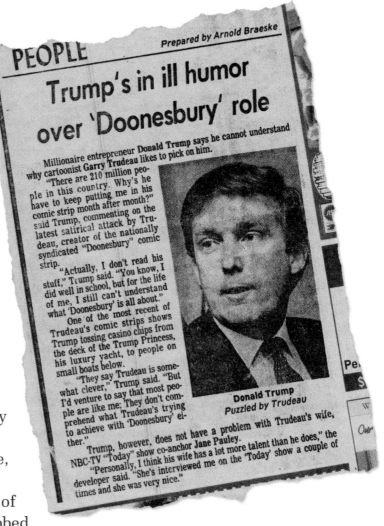

Prepared by Arnold Braeske

PEOPLE

Trump's in ill humor over 'Doonesbury' role

Millionaire entrepreneur Donald Trump says he cannot understand why cartoonist Garry Trudeau likes to pick on him.

"There are 210 million people in this country. Why's he have to keep putting me in his comic strip month after month?" said Trump, commenting on the latest satirical attack by Trudeau, creator of the nationally syndicated "Doonesbury" comic strip.

"Actually, I don't read his stuff," Trump said. "You know, I did well in school, but for the life of me, I still can't understand what 'Doonesbury' is all about."

One of the most recent of Trudeau's comic strips shows Trump tossing casino chips from the deck of the Trump Princess, his luxury yacht, to people on small boats below.

"They say Trudeau is somewhat clever," Trump said. "But I'd venture to say that most people are like me: They don't comprehend what Trudeau's trying to achieve with 'Doonesbury' either."

Trump, however, does not have a problem with Trudeau's wife, NBC-TV "Today" show co-anchor Jane Pauley.

"Personally, I think his wife has a lot more talent than he does," the developer said. "She's interviewed me on the 'Today' show a couple of times and she was very nice."

Donald Trump
Puzzled by Trudeau

The earliest strips (mocking Trump's first presidential trial balloon) began in the fall of 1987. "People tell me I should be flattered," he told *Newsweek*. But as there was nothing remotely flattering about the portrayal, he soon became confused, then irritated—all the more as I was drawing him in a way that suggested I was unaware of how good-looking he was. By the end of the week, it was game on: Trump had someone new to wail on, and I had a new recurring character, one whose real-life counterpart could be counted on to react in real time.

I was one lucky tar baby, and remained so for years. Of course, I've had plenty of company. Google "Trump" and "third-rate," and you'll come across the names of most of the country's first-rate comedians. And no matter how many wise guys wanted a piece of him, there was always more than enough of the big fellah to go around—an embarrassment of follies. After that first presidential head fake, there was the *Trump Princess*, a luxury yacht whose owner's fear of ocean travel kept it moored off his various failing casinos. Then came the extramarital affairs, both real and imagined, conducted under klieg lights, followed in rapid succession by the high-profile bankruptcies, his attempts to tear down a family restaurant to build a parking lot for limos, his various televised spectacles (the most storied of which featured him firing celebrities who were already out of work), his creepy sexual fantasies about his own daughter, the Truther debacle, his failed product lines, and on and on. Like you wouldn't believe.

But the best was yet to come. As Trump bore down on his seventieth year, he needed a new neighborhood to ruin, so after thirty years of lusting after a certain teardown at 1600 Pennsylvania Avenue, he made good on his threat and actually ran for president. Tan, rested, and ready? Not so much. More like orange, hyperactive, and breathtakingly unprepared. When his physician Harold Bornstein declared that Trump would be "the healthiest individual ever elected to the presidency," Trump publicly thanked Jacob Bornstein, his doctor's father, who'd been dead since 2010.

You can't make this stuff up, so why try? Some people feel that Trump is beyond satire, but we professionals know he *is* satire, pure and uncut, free for all to use and enjoy, and for that we are not ungrateful. For our country, though, we can only weep.

Garry Trudeau
April 14, 2016

"Analysis: Donald Trump talks to voters at a fourth-grade level."

–*USA Today* headline

"I know words. I have the best words."
–Donald Trump

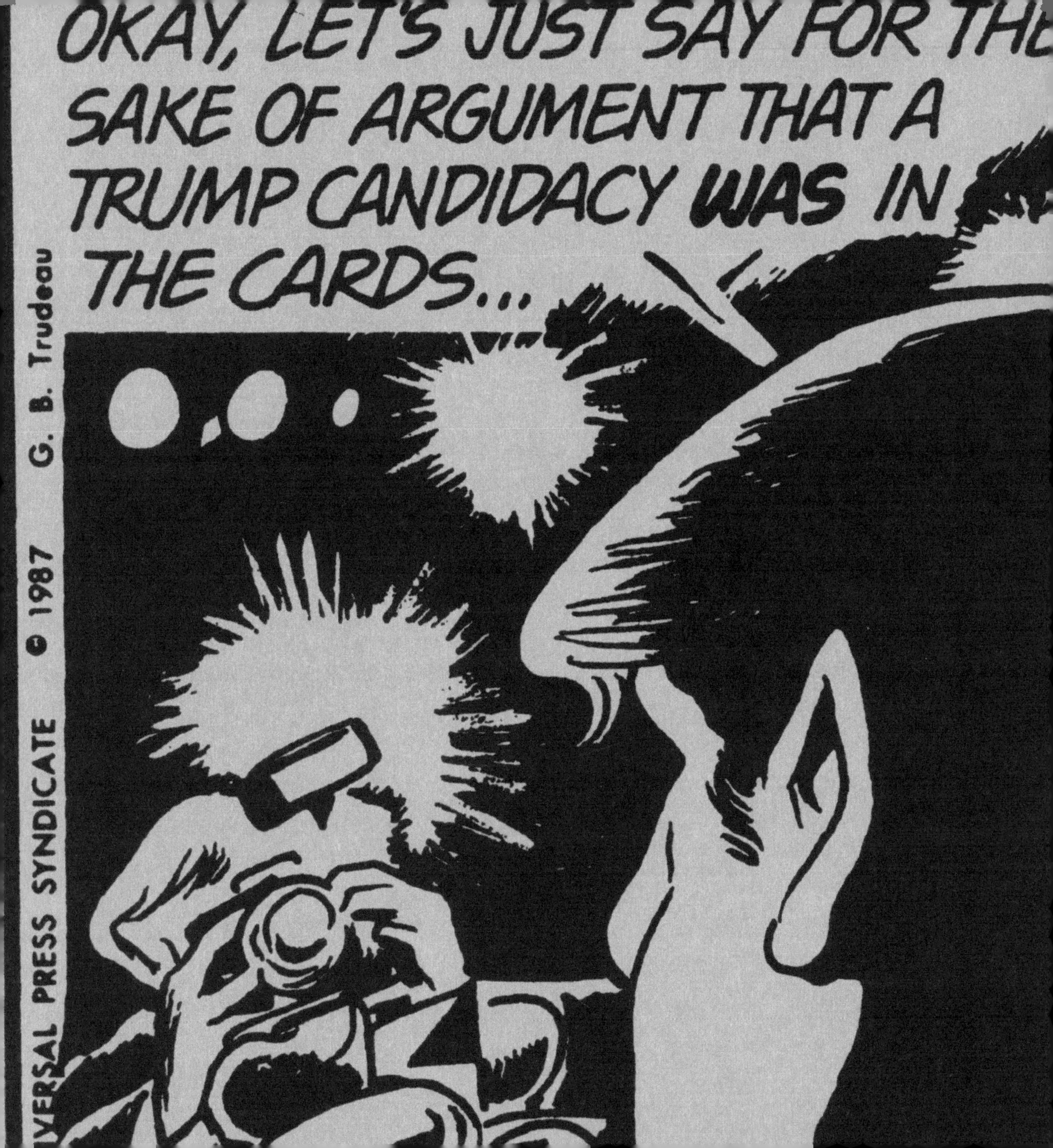
OKAY, LET'S JUST SAY FOR THE SAKE OF ARGUMENT THAT A TRUMP CANDIDACY WAS IN THE CARDS...
VERSAL PRESS SYNDICATE © 1987 G. B. Trudeau

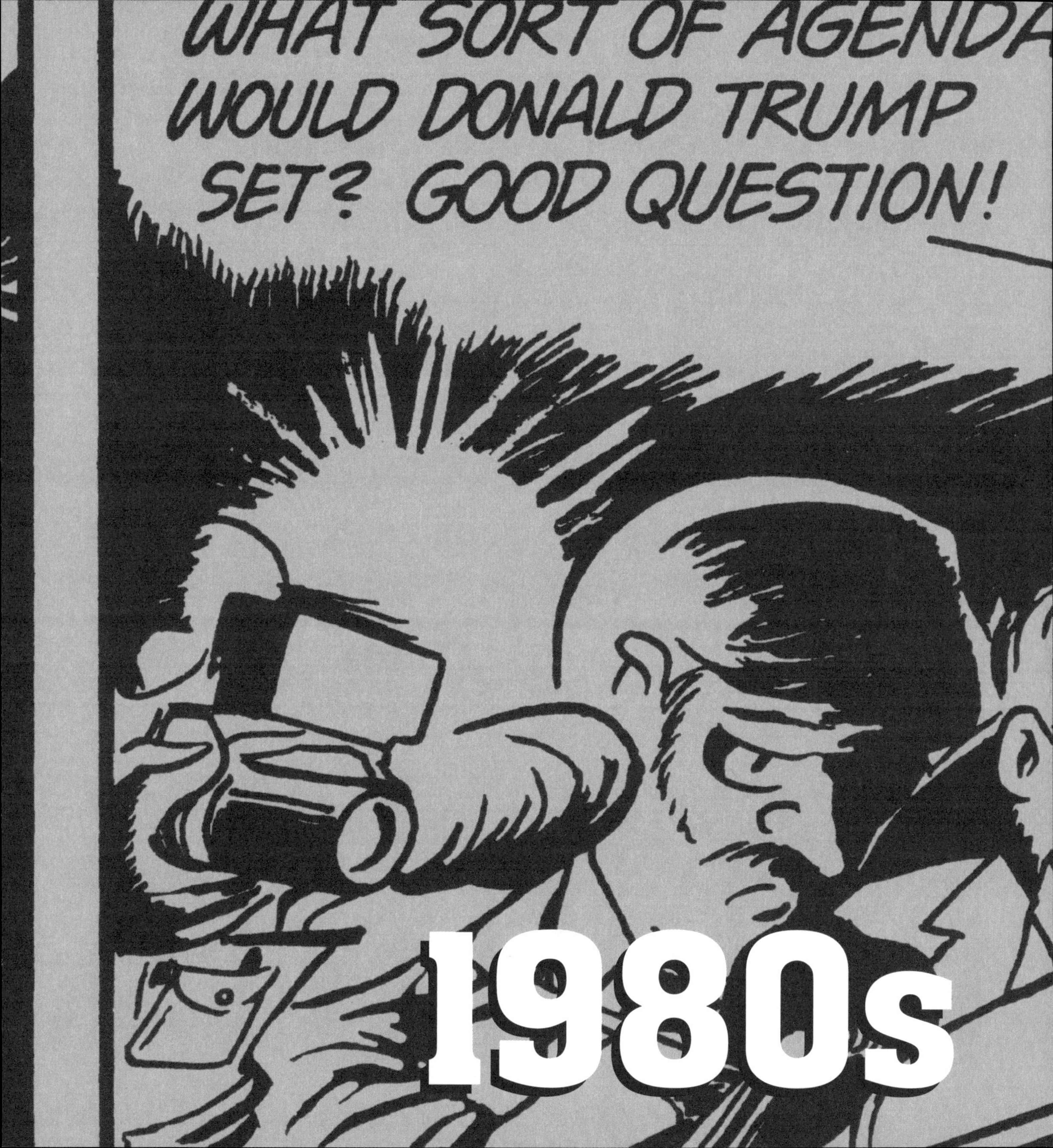
WHAT SORT OF AGENDA WOULD DONALD TRUMP SET? GOOD QUESTION!

1980s

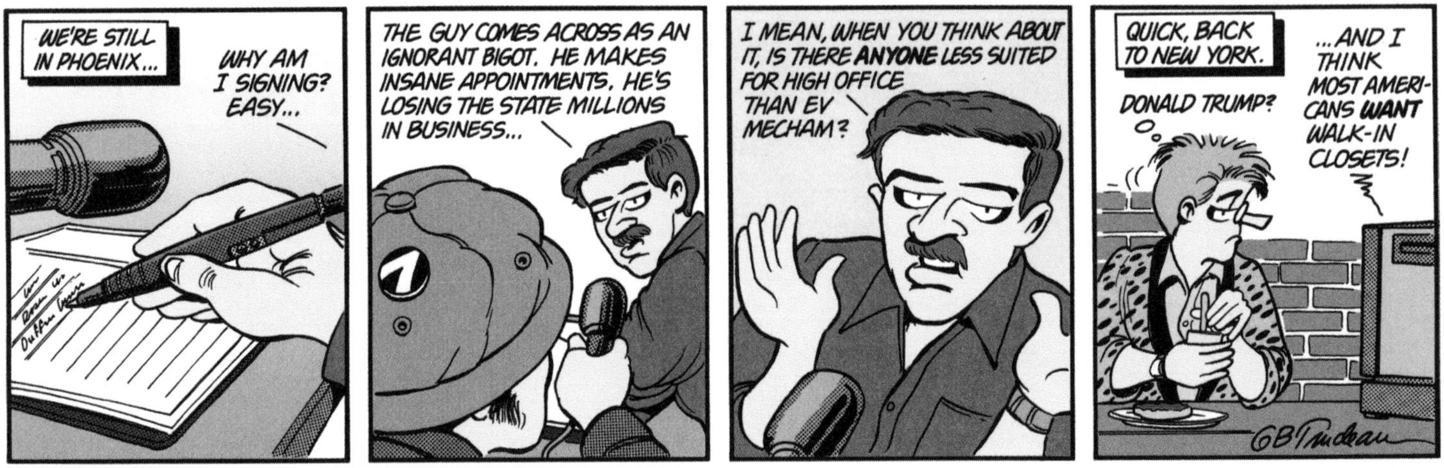
WE'RE STILL IN PHOENIX...
WHY AM I SIGNING? EASY...
THE GUY COMES ACROSS AS AN IGNORANT BIGOT. HE MAKES INSANE APPOINTMENTS. HE'S LOSING THE STATE MILLIONS IN BUSINESS...
I MEAN, WHEN YOU THINK ABOUT IT, IS THERE **ANYONE** LESS SUITED FOR HIGH OFFICE THAN EV MECHAM?
QUICK, BACK TO NEW YORK.
DONALD TRUMP?
...AND I THINK MOST AMERICANS **WANT** WALK-IN CLOSETS!

September 14, 1987

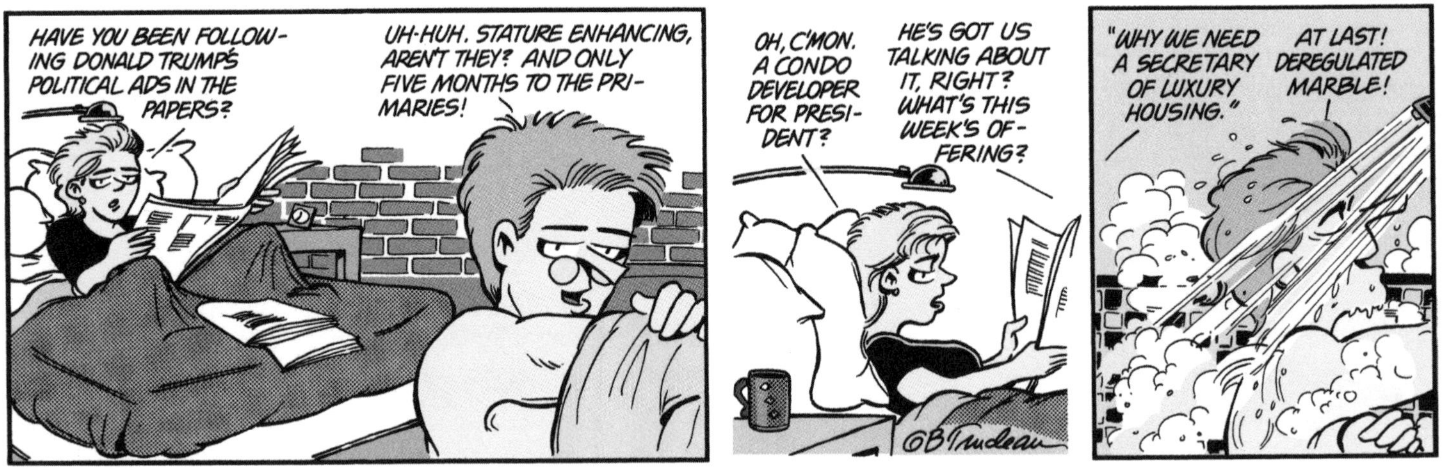
HAVE YOU BEEN FOLLOWING DONALD TRUMP'S POLITICAL ADS IN THE PAPERS?
UH-HUH. STATURE ENHANCING, AREN'T THEY? AND ONLY FIVE MONTHS TO THE PRIMARIES!
OH, C'MON. A CONDO DEVELOPER FOR PRESIDENT?
HE'S GOT US TALKING ABOUT IT, RIGHT? WHAT'S THIS WEEK'S OFFERING?
"WHY WE NEED A SECRETARY OF LUXURY HOUSING."
AT LAST! DEREGULATED MARBLE!

September 15, 1987

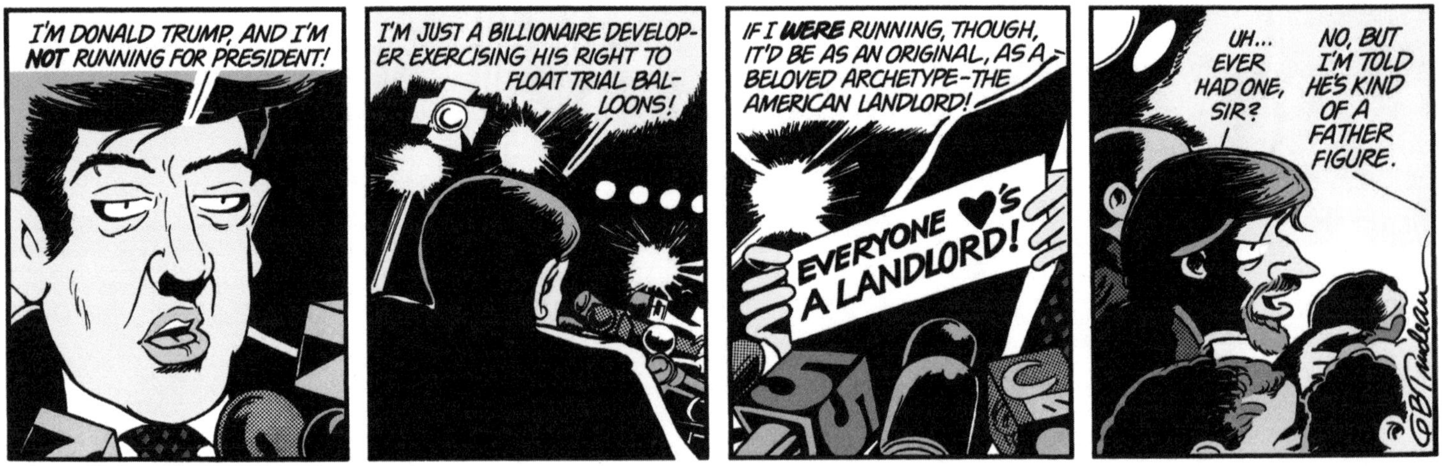
I'M DONALD TRUMP, AND I'M **NOT** RUNNING FOR PRESIDENT!
I'M JUST A BILLIONAIRE DEVELOPER EXERCISING HIS RIGHT TO FLOAT TRIAL BALLOONS!
IF I **WERE** RUNNING, THOUGH, IT'D BE AS AN ORIGINAL, AS A BELOVED ARCHETYPE—THE AMERICAN LANDLORD!
EVERYONE ♥'S A LANDLORD!
UH... EVER HAD ONE, SIR?
NO, BUT I'M TOLD HE'S KIND OF A FATHER FIGURE.

September 16, 1987

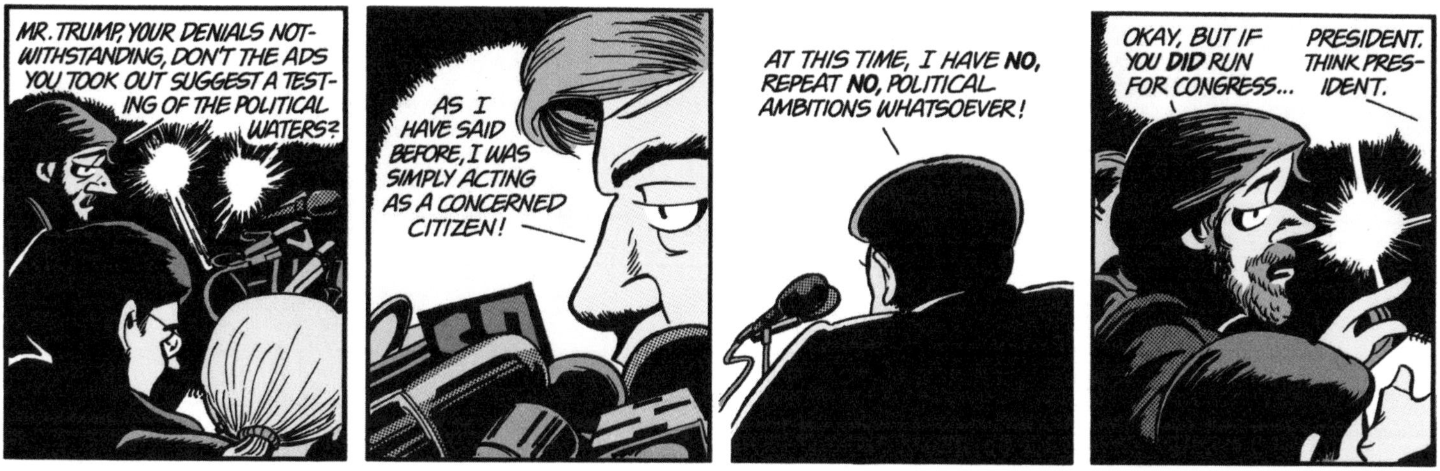
MR. TRUMP, YOUR DENIALS NOTWITHSTANDING, DON'T THE ADS YOU TOOK OUT SUGGEST A TESTING OF THE POLITICAL WATERS?
AS I HAVE SAID BEFORE, I WAS SIMPLY ACTING AS A CONCERNED CITIZEN!
AT THIS TIME, I HAVE NO, REPEAT NO, POLITICAL AMBITIONS WHATSOEVER!
OKAY, BUT IF YOU DID RUN FOR CONGRESS...
PRESIDENT. THINK PRESIDENT.

September 17, 1987

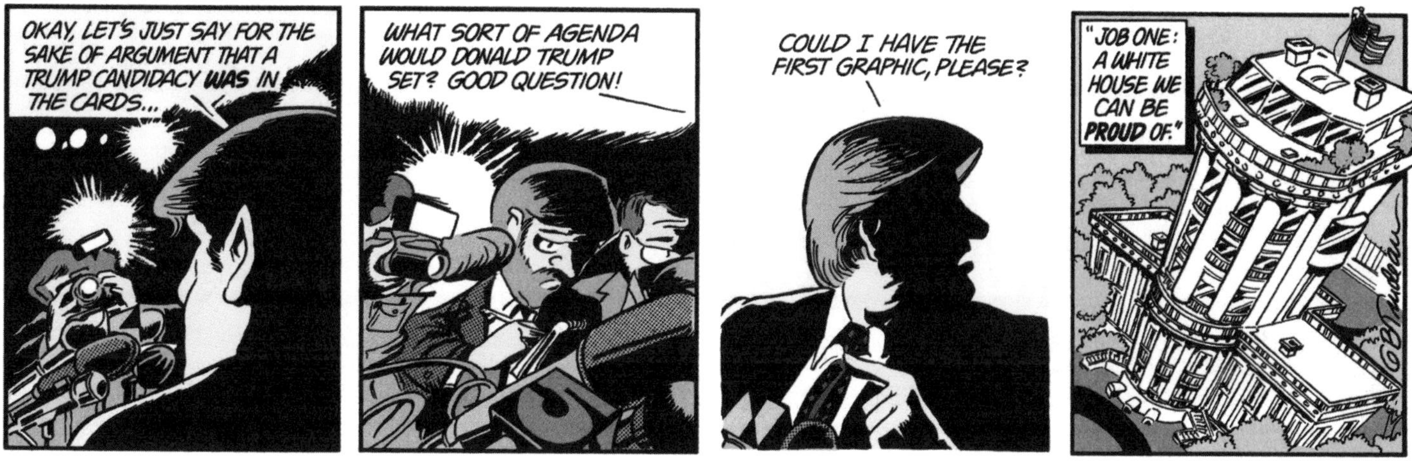
OKAY, LET'S JUST SAY FOR THE SAKE OF ARGUMENT THAT A TRUMP CANDIDACY WAS IN THE CARDS...
WHAT SORT OF AGENDA WOULD DONALD TRUMP SET? GOOD QUESTION!
COULD I HAVE THE FIRST GRAPHIC, PLEASE?
"JOB ONE: A WHITE HOUSE WE CAN BE PROUD OF."

September 18, 1987

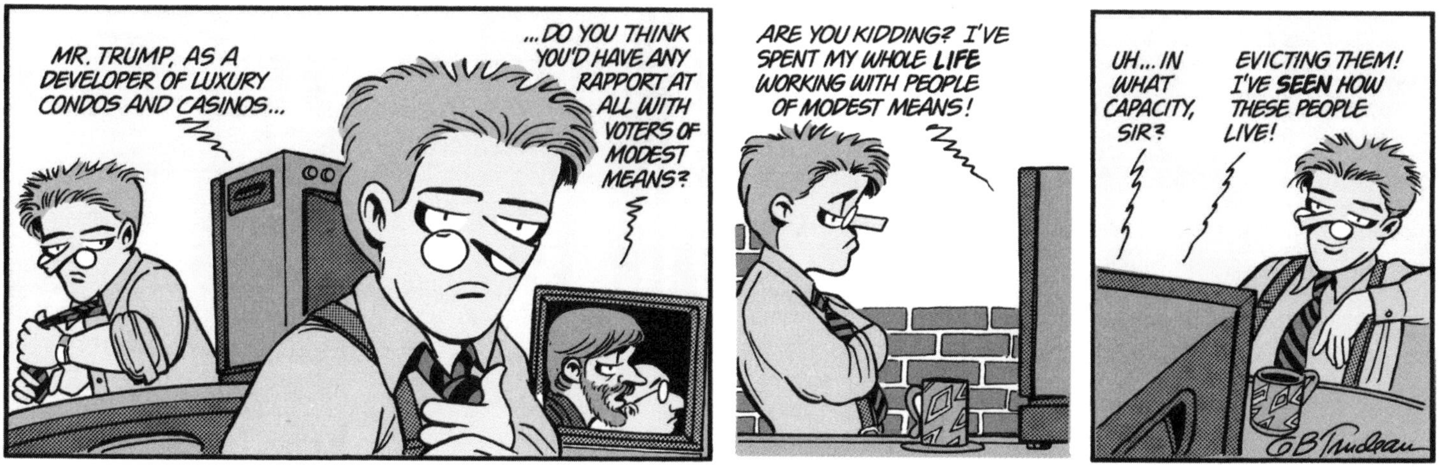
MR. TRUMP, AS A DEVELOPER OF LUXURY CONDOS AND CASINOS...
...DO YOU THINK YOU'D HAVE ANY RAPPORT AT ALL WITH VOTERS OF MODEST MEANS?
ARE YOU KIDDING? I'VE SPENT MY WHOLE LIFE WORKING WITH PEOPLE OF MODEST MEANS!
UH... IN WHAT CAPACITY, SIR?
EVICTING THEM! I'VE SEEN HOW THESE PEOPLE LIVE!

September 19, 1987

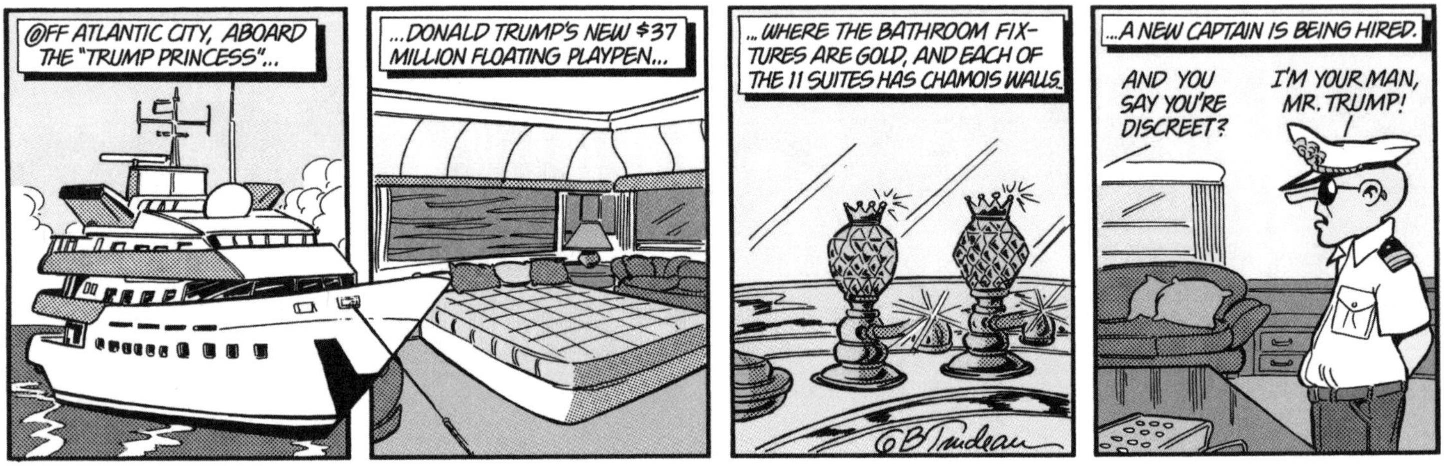
OFF ATLANTIC CITY, ABOARD THE "TRUMP PRINCESS"...
...DONALD TRUMP'S NEW $37 MILLION FLOATING PLAYPEN...
...WHERE THE BATHROOM FIXTURES ARE GOLD, AND EACH OF THE 11 SUITES HAS CHAMOIS WALLS.
...A NEW CAPTAIN IS BEING HIRED.
AND YOU SAY YOU'RE DISCREET?
I'M YOUR MAN, MR. TRUMP!

July 25, 1988

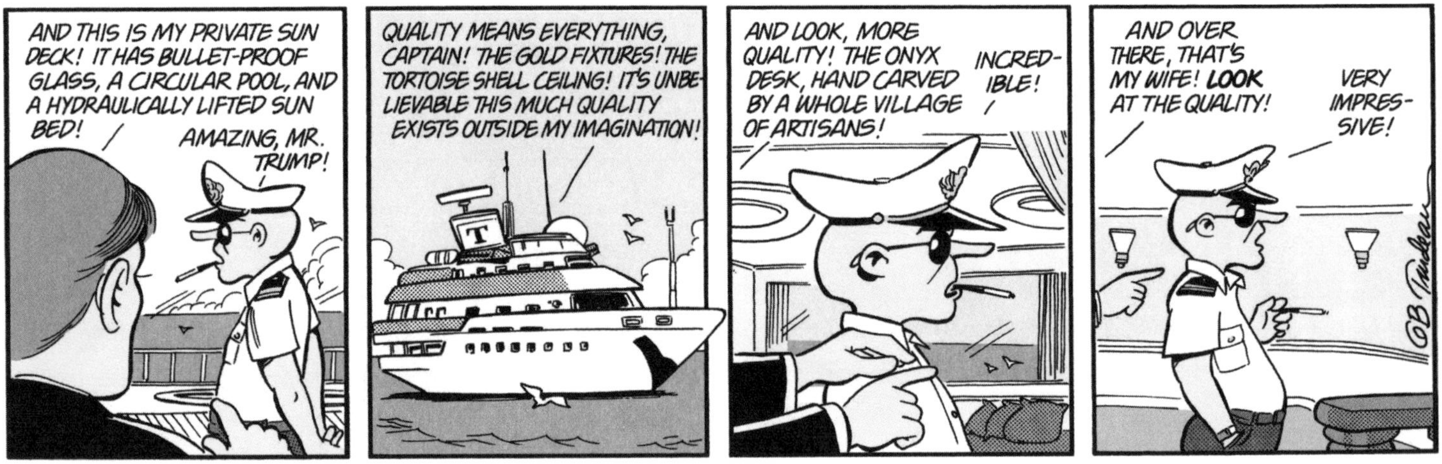
AND THIS IS MY PRIVATE SUN DECK! IT HAS BULLET-PROOF GLASS, A CIRCULAR POOL, AND A HYDRAULICALLY LIFTED SUN BED!
AMAZING, MR. TRUMP!
QUALITY MEANS EVERYTHING, CAPTAIN! THE GOLD FIXTURES! THE TORTOISE SHELL CEILING! IT'S UNBELIEVABLE THIS MUCH QUALITY EXISTS OUTSIDE MY IMAGINATION!
AND LOOK, MORE QUALITY! THE ONYX DESK, HAND CARVED BY A WHOLE VILLAGE OF ARTISANS!
INCREDIBLE!
AND OVER THERE, THAT'S MY WIFE! LOOK AT THE QUALITY!
VERY IMPRESSIVE!

July 26, 1988

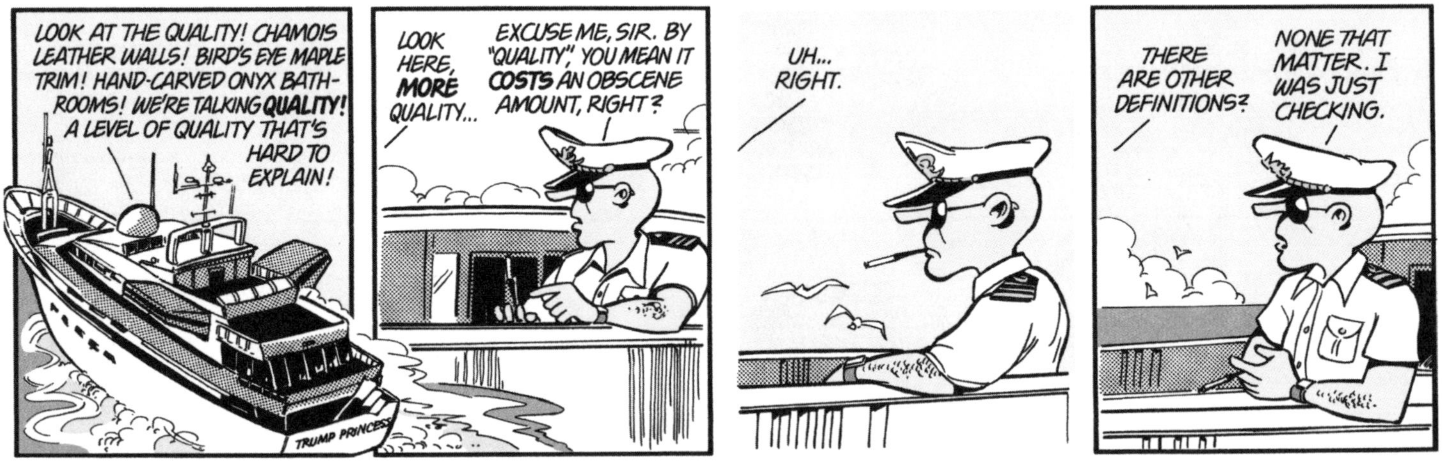
LOOK AT THE QUALITY! CHAMOIS LEATHER WALLS! BIRD'S EYE MAPLE TRIM! HAND-CARVED ONYX BATHROOMS! WE'RE TALKING QUALITY! A LEVEL OF QUALITY THAT'S HARD TO EXPLAIN!
TRUMP PRINCESS
LOOK HERE, MORE QUALITY...
EXCUSE ME, SIR. BY "QUALITY," YOU MEAN IT COSTS AN OBSCENE AMOUNT, RIGHT?
UH... RIGHT.
THERE ARE OTHER DEFINITIONS?
NONE THAT MATTER. I WAS JUST CHECKING.

July 27, 1988

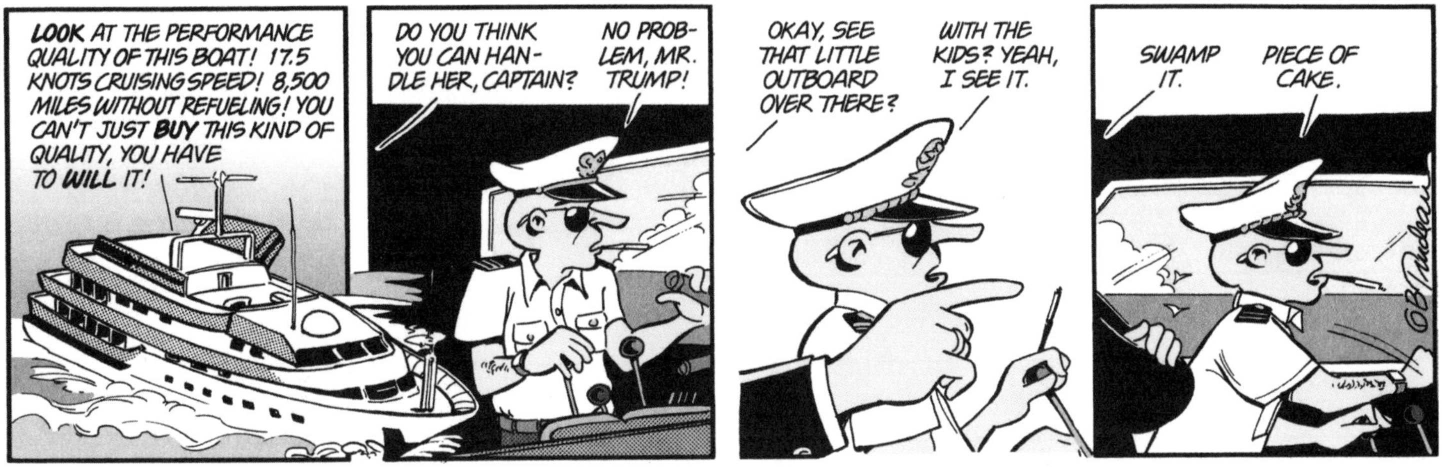
LOOK AT THE PERFORMANCE QUALITY OF THIS BOAT! 17.5 KNOTS CRUISING SPEED! 8,500 MILES WITHOUT REFUELING! YOU CAN'T JUST BUY THIS KIND OF QUALITY, YOU HAVE TO WILL IT!
DO YOU THINK YOU CAN HANDLE HER, CAPTAIN?
NO PROBLEM, MR. TRUMP!
OKAY, SEE THAT LITTLE OUTBOARD OVER THERE?
WITH THE KIDS? YEAH, I SEE IT.
SWAMP IT.
PIECE OF CAKE.
©B Trudeau

July 28, 1988

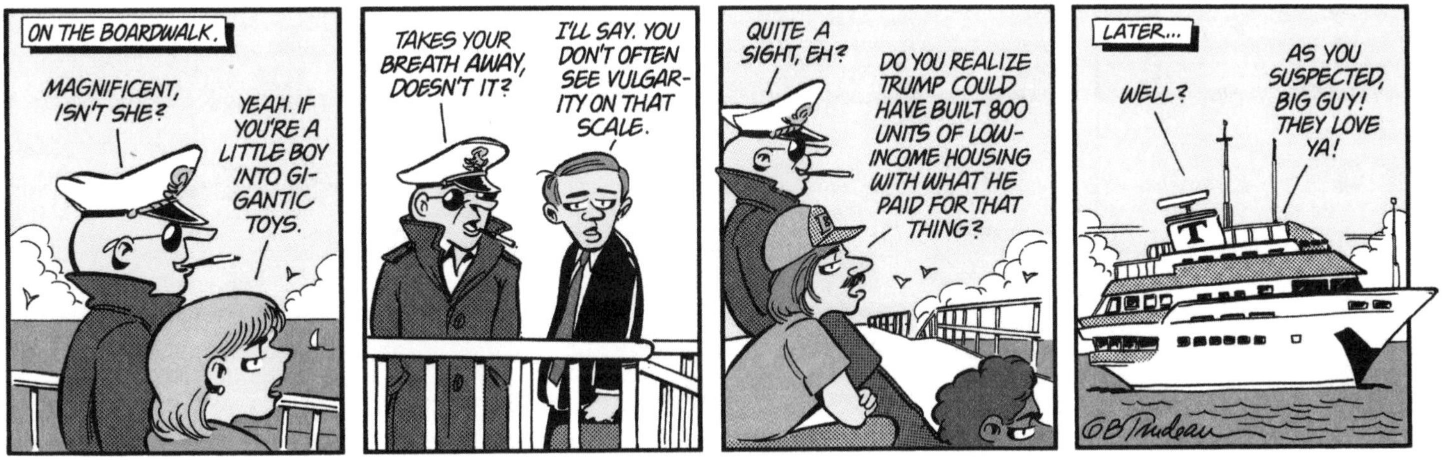
ON THE BOARDWALK.
MAGNIFICENT, ISN'T SHE?
YEAH. IF YOU'RE A LITTLE BOY INTO GIGANTIC TOYS.
TAKES YOUR BREATH AWAY, DOESN'T IT?
I'LL SAY. YOU DON'T OFTEN SEE VULGARITY ON THAT SCALE.
QUITE A SIGHT, EH?
DO YOU REALIZE TRUMP COULD HAVE BUILT 800 UNITS OF LOW-INCOME HOUSING WITH WHAT HE PAID FOR THAT THING?
LATER...
WELL?
AS YOU SUSPECTED, BIG GUY! THEY LOVE YA!
T
©B Trudeau

July 29, 1988

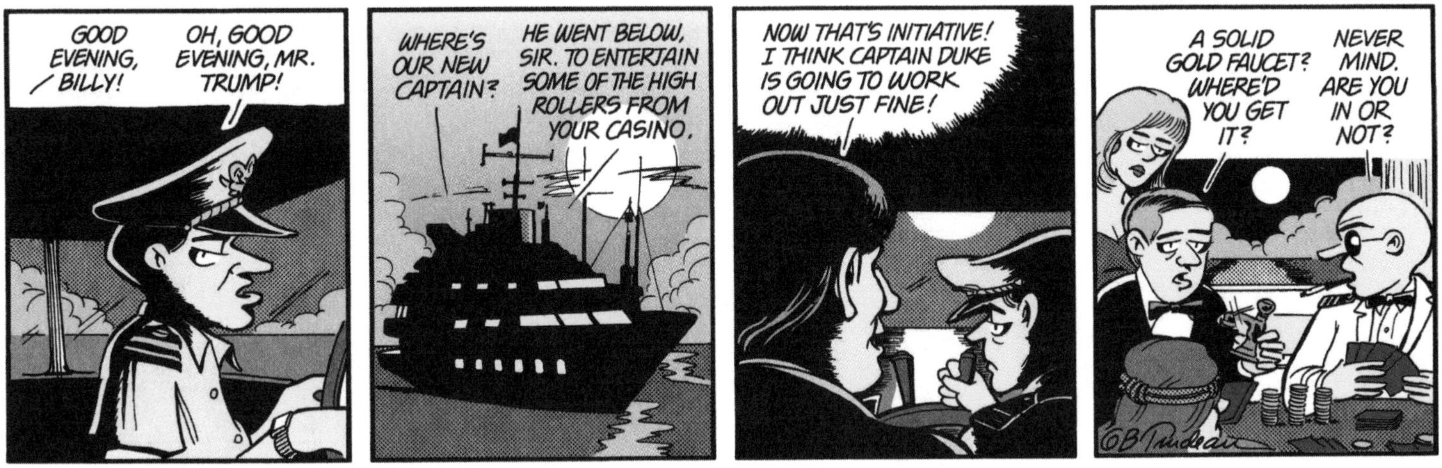
GOOD EVENING, BILLY!
OH, GOOD EVENING, MR. TRUMP!
WHERE'S OUR NEW CAPTAIN?
HE WENT BELOW, SIR. TO ENTERTAIN SOME OF THE HIGH ROLLERS FROM YOUR CASINO.
NOW THAT'S INITIATIVE! I THINK CAPTAIN DUKE IS GOING TO WORK OUT JUST FINE!
A SOLID GOLD FAUCET? WHERE'D YOU GET IT?
NEVER MIND. ARE YOU IN OR NOT?
©B Trudeau

July 30, 1988

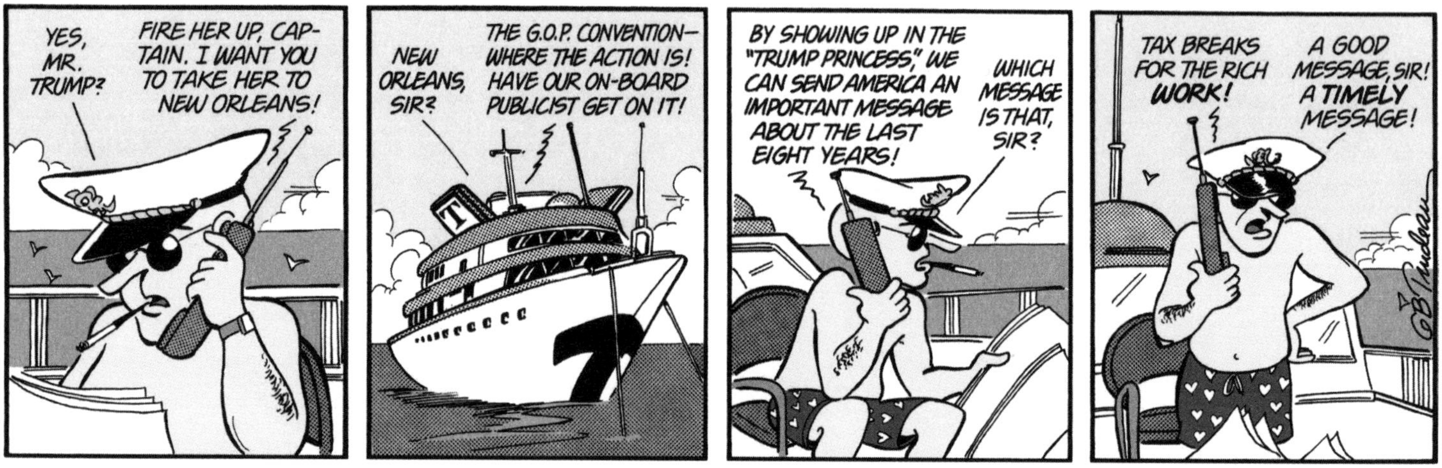
YES, MR. TRUMP?
FIRE HER UP, CAPTAIN. I WANT YOU TO TAKE HER TO NEW ORLEANS!
NEW ORLEANS, SIR?
THE G.O.P. CONVENTION— WHERE THE ACTION IS! HAVE OUR ON-BOARD PUBLICIST GET ON IT!
BY SHOWING UP IN THE "TRUMP PRINCESS," WE CAN SEND AMERICA AN IMPORTANT MESSAGE ABOUT THE LAST EIGHT YEARS!
WHICH MESSAGE IS THAT, SIR?
TAX BREAKS FOR THE RICH WORK!
A GOOD MESSAGE, SIR! A TIMELY MESSAGE!

August 8, 1988

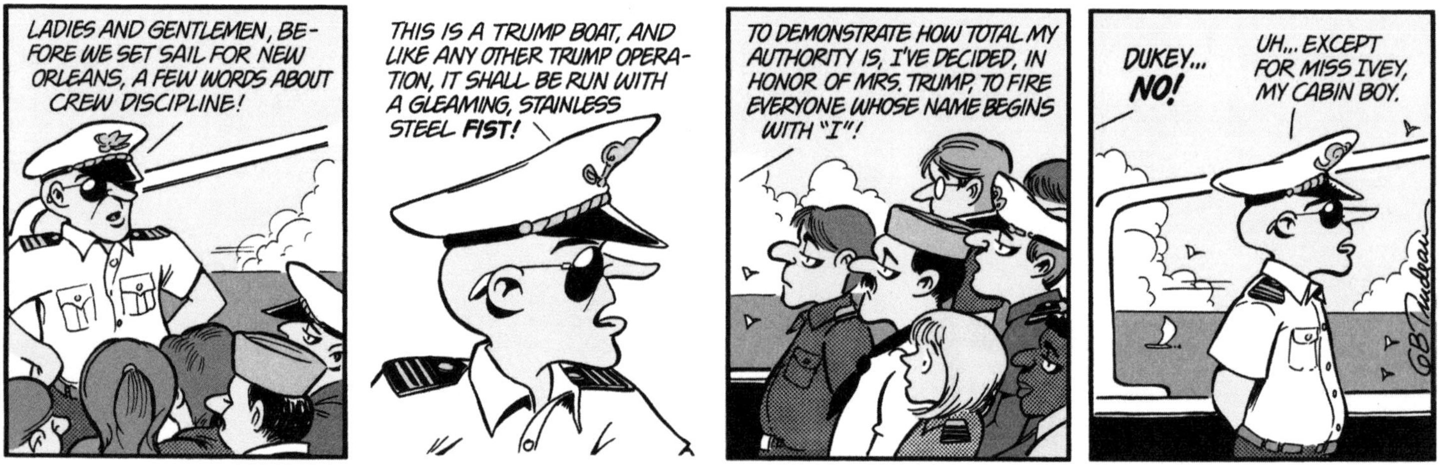
LADIES AND GENTLEMEN, BEFORE WE SET SAIL FOR NEW ORLEANS, A FEW WORDS ABOUT CREW DISCIPLINE!
THIS IS A TRUMP BOAT, AND LIKE ANY OTHER TRUMP OPERATION, IT SHALL BE RUN WITH A GLEAMING, STAINLESS STEEL FIST!
TO DEMONSTRATE HOW TOTAL MY AUTHORITY IS, I'VE DECIDED, IN HONOR OF MRS. TRUMP, TO FIRE EVERYONE WHOSE NAME BEGINS WITH "I"!
DUKEY... NO!
UH... EXCEPT FOR MISS IVEY, MY CABIN BOY.

August 9, 1988

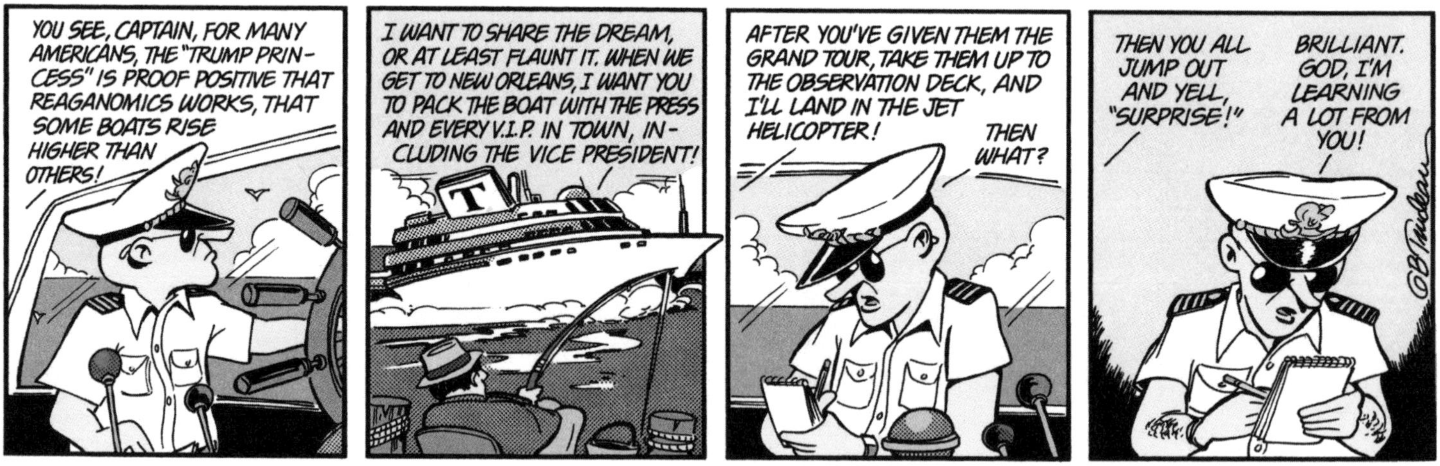
YOU SEE, CAPTAIN, FOR MANY AMERICANS, THE "TRUMP PRINCESS" IS PROOF POSITIVE THAT REAGANOMICS WORKS, THAT SOME BOATS RISE HIGHER THAN OTHERS!
I WANT TO SHARE THE DREAM, OR AT LEAST FLAUNT IT. WHEN WE GET TO NEW ORLEANS, I WANT YOU TO PACK THE BOAT WITH THE PRESS AND EVERY V.I.P. IN TOWN, INCLUDING THE VICE PRESIDENT!
AFTER YOU'VE GIVEN THEM THE GRAND TOUR, TAKE THEM UP TO THE OBSERVATION DECK, AND I'LL LAND IN THE JET HELICOPTER!
THEN WHAT?
THEN YOU ALL JUMP OUT AND YELL, "SURPRISE!"
BRILLIANT. GOD, I'M LEARNING A LOT FROM YOU!

August 10, 1988

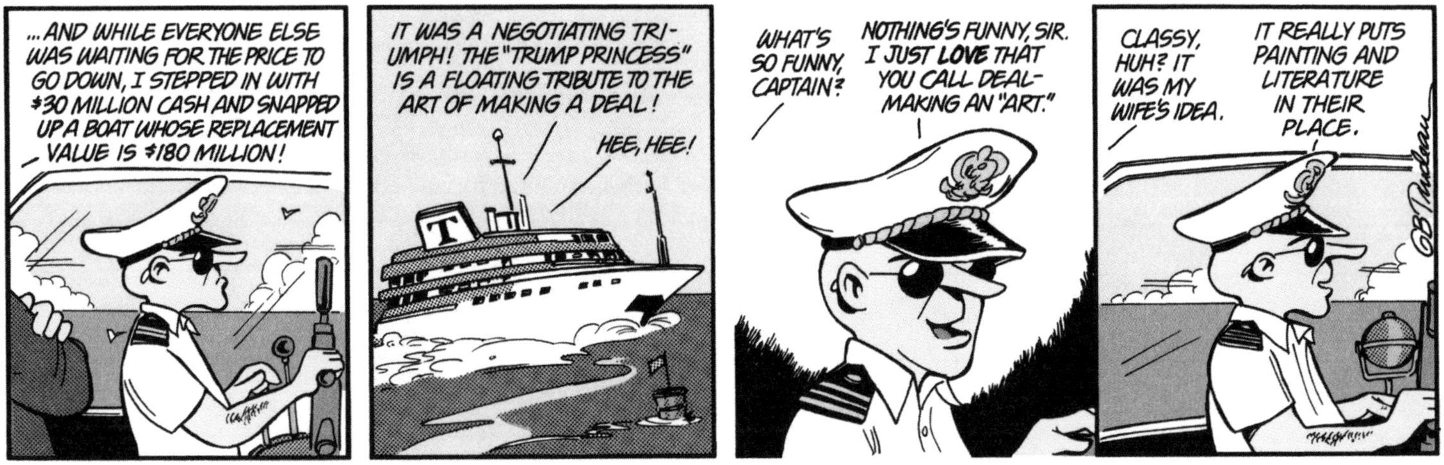
...AND WHILE EVERYONE ELSE WAS WAITING FOR THE PRICE TO GO DOWN, I STEPPED IN WITH $30 MILLION CASH AND SNAPPED UP A BOAT WHOSE REPLACEMENT VALUE IS $180 MILLION!
IT WAS A NEGOTIATING TRIUMPH! THE "TRUMP PRINCESS" IS A FLOATING TRIBUTE TO THE ART OF MAKING A DEAL!
HEE, HEE!
WHAT'S SO FUNNY, CAPTAIN?
NOTHING'S FUNNY, SIR. I JUST LOVE THAT YOU CALL DEAL-MAKING AN "ART."
CLASSY, HUH? IT WAS MY WIFE'S IDEA.
IT REALLY PUTS PAINTING AND LITERATURE IN THEIR PLACE.

August 11, 1988

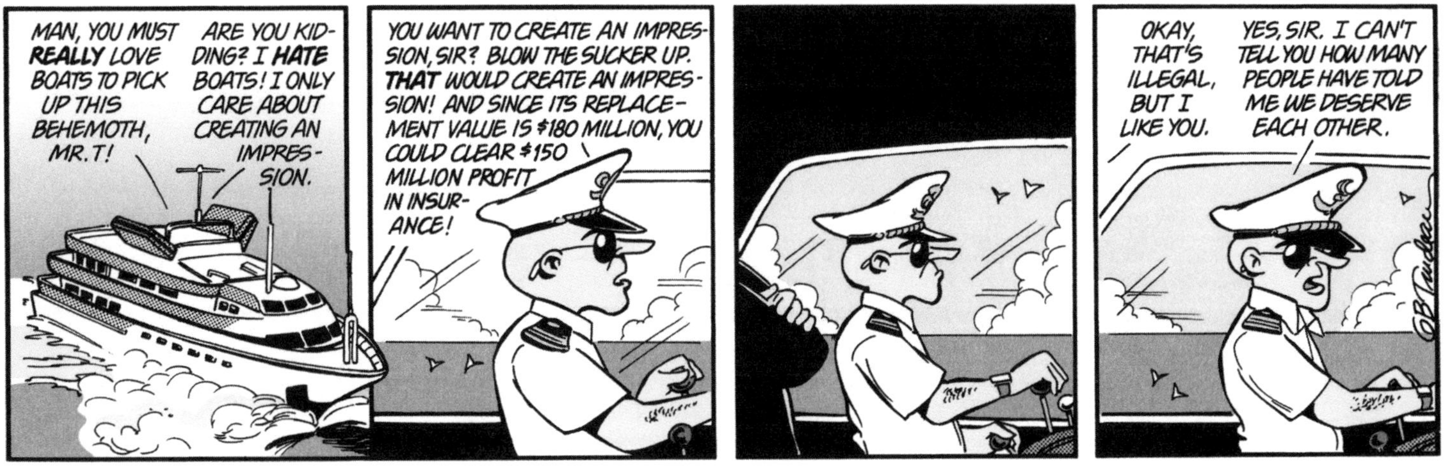
MAN, YOU MUST REALLY LOVE BOATS TO PICK UP THIS BEHEMOTH, MR. T!
ARE YOU KIDDING? I HATE BOATS! I ONLY CARE ABOUT CREATING AN IMPRESSION.
YOU WANT TO CREATE AN IMPRESSION, SIR? BLOW THE SUCKER UP. THAT WOULD CREATE AN IMPRESSION! AND SINCE ITS REPLACEMENT VALUE IS $180 MILLION, YOU COULD CLEAR $150 MILLION PROFIT IN INSURANCE!
OKAY, THAT'S ILLEGAL, BUT I LIKE YOU.
YES, SIR. I CAN'T TELL YOU HOW MANY PEOPLE HAVE TOLD ME WE DESERVE EACH OTHER.

August 12, 1988

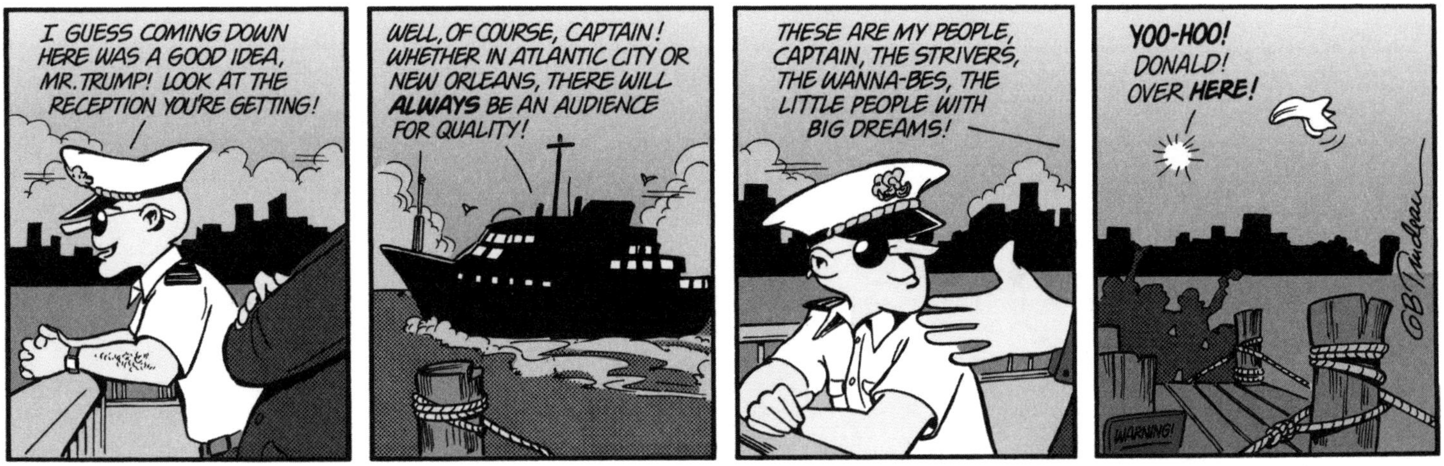
I GUESS COMING DOWN HERE WAS A GOOD IDEA, MR. TRUMP! LOOK AT THE RECEPTION YOU'RE GETTING!
WELL, OF COURSE, CAPTAIN! WHETHER IN ATLANTIC CITY OR NEW ORLEANS, THERE WILL ALWAYS BE AN AUDIENCE FOR QUALITY!
THESE ARE MY PEOPLE, CAPTAIN, THE STRIVERS, THE WANNA-BES, THE LITTLE PEOPLE WITH BIG DREAMS!
YOO-HOO! DONALD! OVER HERE!
WARNING!

August 13, 1988

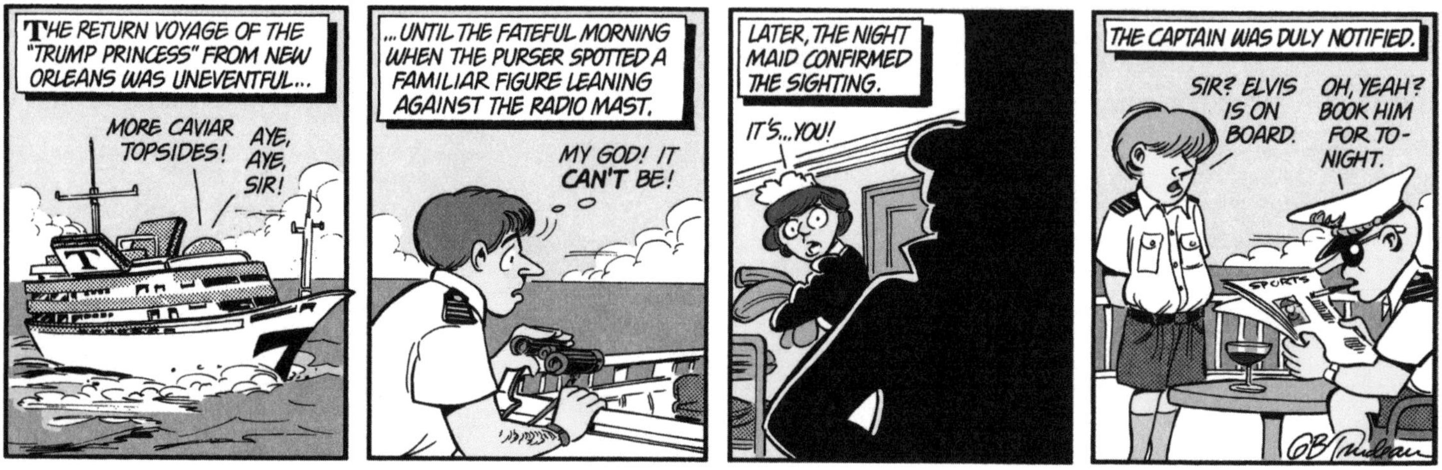
THE RETURN VOYAGE OF THE "TRUMP PRINCESS" FROM NEW ORLEANS WAS UNEVENTFUL...
MORE CAVIAR TOPSIDES!
AYE, AYE, SIR!
...UNTIL THE FATEFUL MORNING WHEN THE PURSER SPOTTED A FAMILIAR FIGURE LEANING AGAINST THE RADIO MAST.
MY GOD! IT CAN'T BE!
LATER, THE NIGHT MAID CONFIRMED THE SIGHTING.
IT'S...YOU!
THE CAPTAIN WAS DULY NOTIFIED.
SIR? ELVIS IS ON BOARD.
OH, YEAH? BOOK HIM FOR TO-NIGHT.
SPORTS

August 29, 1988

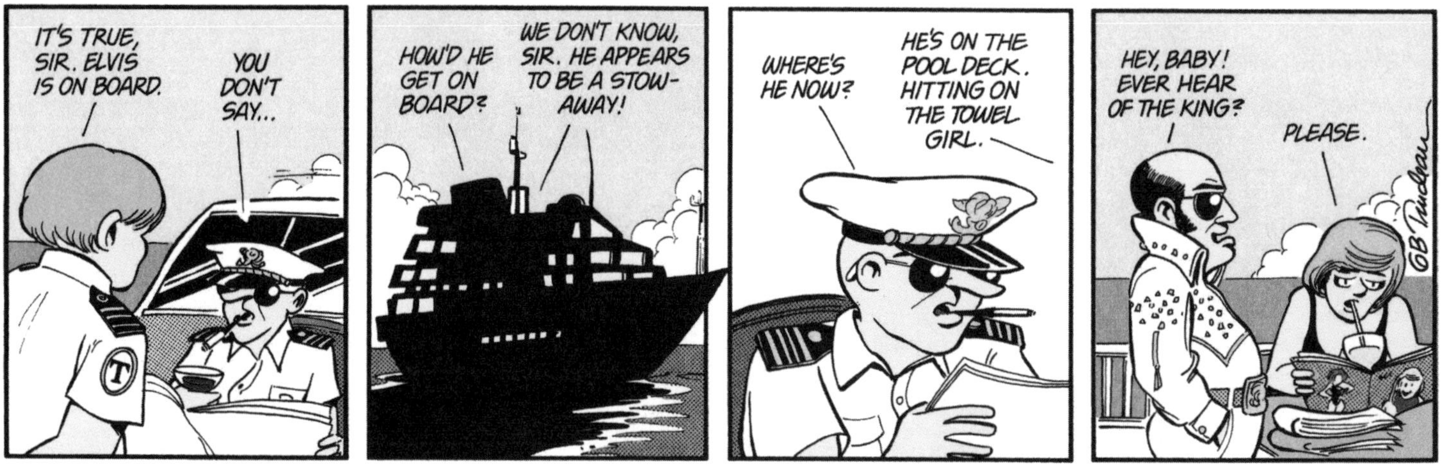
IT'S TRUE, SIR. ELVIS IS ON BOARD.
YOU DON'T SAY...
HOW'D HE GET ON BOARD?
WE DON'T KNOW, SIR. HE APPEARS TO BE A STOW-AWAY!
WHERE'S HE NOW?
HE'S ON THE POOL DECK. HITTING ON THE TOWEL GIRL.
HEY, BABY! EVER HEAR OF THE KING?
PLEASE.

August 30, 1988

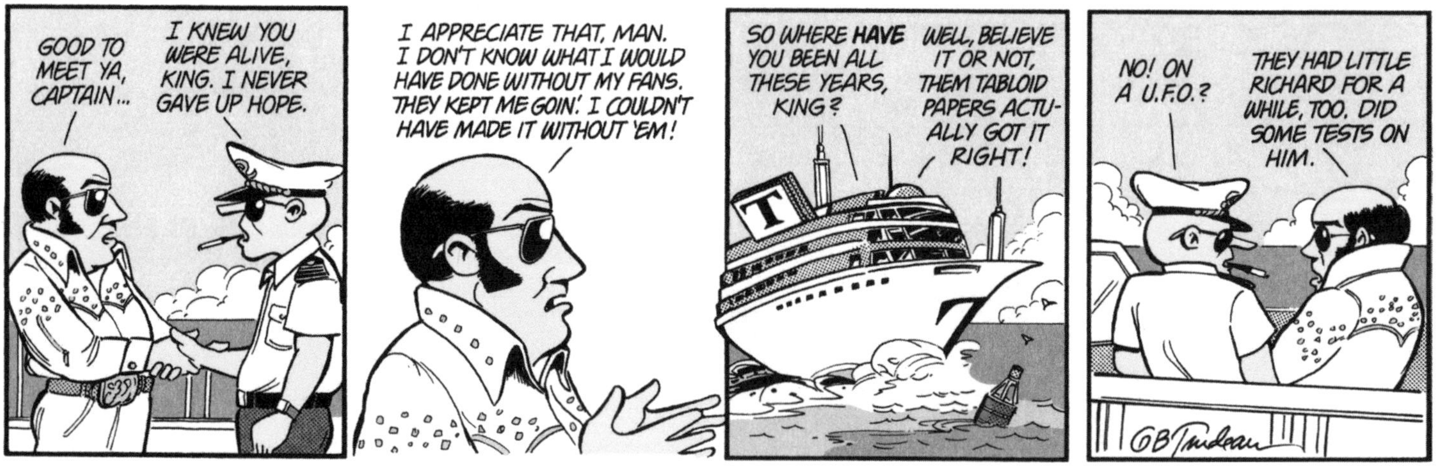
GOOD TO MEET YA, CAPTAIN...
I KNEW YOU WERE ALIVE, KING. I NEVER GAVE UP HOPE.
I APPRECIATE THAT, MAN. I DON'T KNOW WHAT I WOULD HAVE DONE WITHOUT MY FANS. THEY KEPT ME GOIN'. I COULDN'T HAVE MADE IT WITHOUT 'EM!
SO WHERE HAVE YOU BEEN ALL THESE YEARS, KING?
WELL, BELIEVE IT OR NOT, THEM TABLOID PAPERS ACTU-ALLY GOT IT RIGHT!
NO! ON A U.F.O.?
THEY HAD LITTLE RICHARD FOR A WHILE, TOO. DID SOME TESTS ON HIM.

August 31, 1988

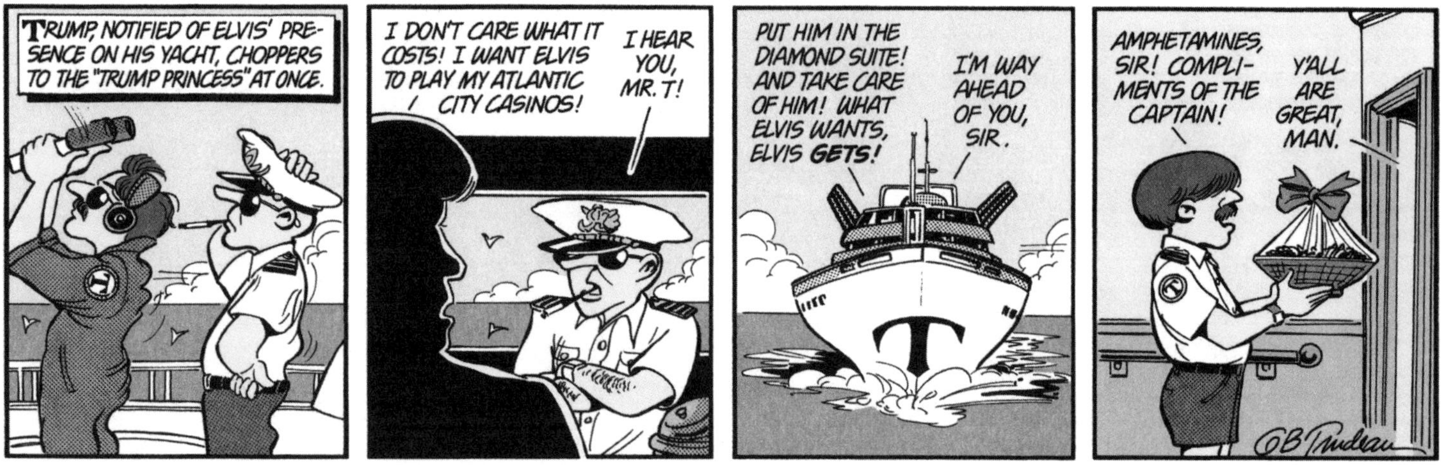
TRUMP, NOTIFIED OF ELVIS' PRESENCE ON HIS YACHT, CHOPPERS TO THE "TRUMP PRINCESS" AT ONCE.
I DON'T CARE WHAT IT COSTS! I WANT ELVIS TO PLAY MY ATLANTIC CITY CASINOS!
I HEAR YOU, MR. T!
PUT HIM IN THE DIAMOND SUITE! AND TAKE CARE OF HIM! WHAT ELVIS WANTS, ELVIS GETS!
I'M WAY AHEAD OF YOU, SIR.
AMPHETAMINES, SIR! COMPLIMENTS OF THE CAPTAIN!
Y'ALL ARE GREAT, MAN.
GB Trudeau

September 1, 1988

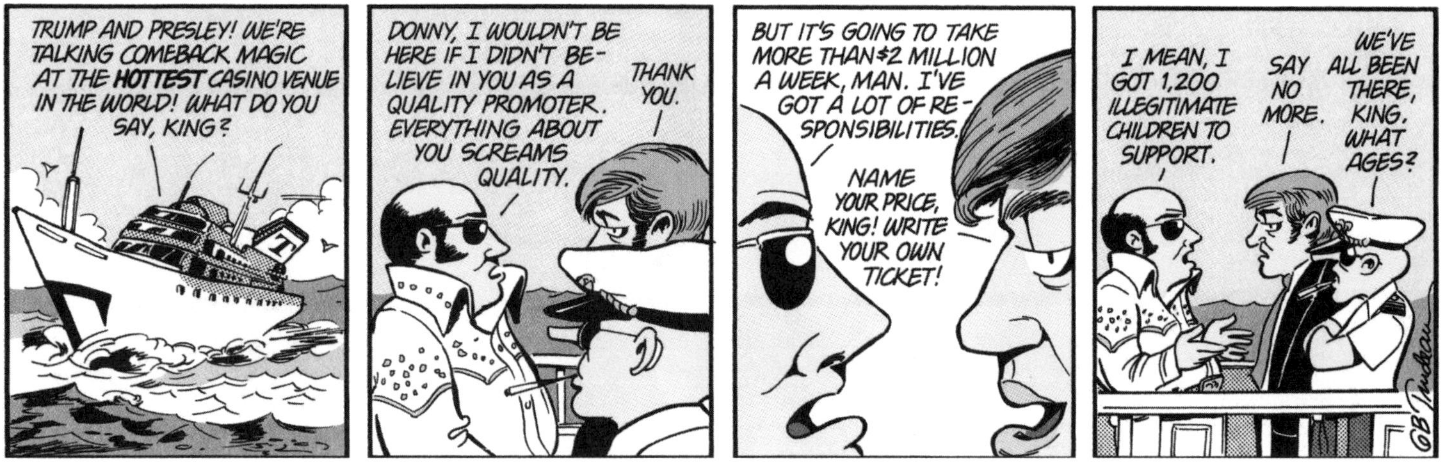
TRUMP AND PRESLEY! WE'RE TALKING COMEBACK MAGIC AT THE HOTTEST CASINO VENUE IN THE WORLD! WHAT DO YOU SAY, KING?
DONNY, I WOULDN'T BE HERE IF I DIDN'T BELIEVE IN YOU AS A QUALITY PROMOTER. EVERYTHING ABOUT YOU SCREAMS QUALITY.
THANK YOU.
BUT IT'S GOING TO TAKE MORE THAN $2 MILLION A WEEK, MAN. I'VE GOT A LOT OF RESPONSIBILITIES.
NAME YOUR PRICE, KING! WRITE YOUR OWN TICKET!
I MEAN, I GOT 1,200 ILLEGITIMATE CHILDREN TO SUPPORT.
SAY NO MORE.
WE'VE ALL BEEN THERE, KING. WHAT AGES?
GB Trudeau

September 2, 1988

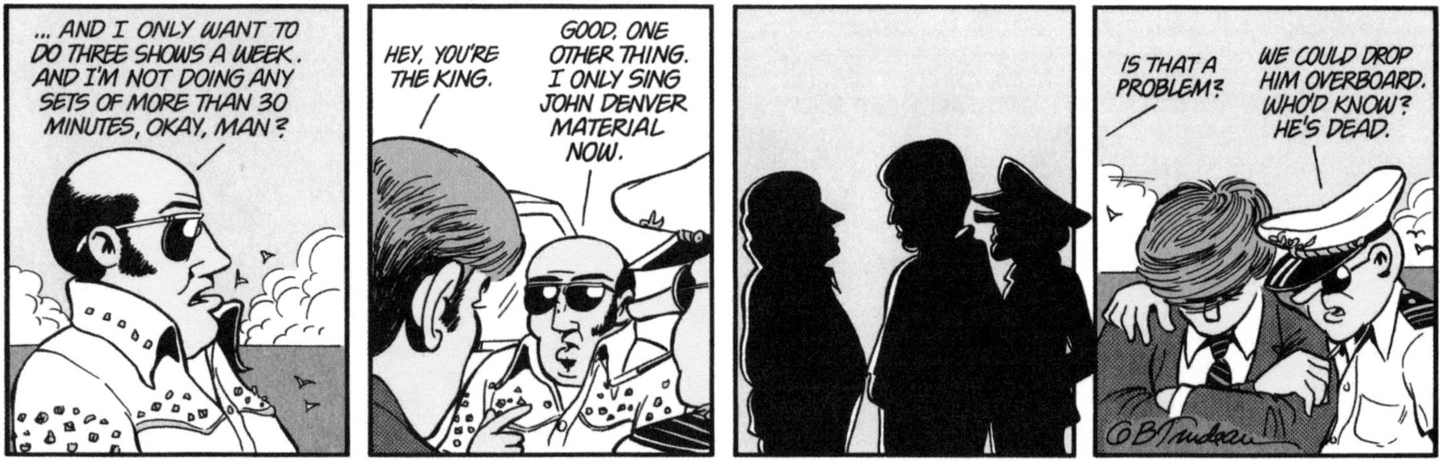
... AND I ONLY WANT TO DO THREE SHOWS A WEEK. AND I'M NOT DOING ANY SETS OF MORE THAN 30 MINUTES, OKAY, MAN?
HEY, YOU'RE THE KING.
GOOD. ONE OTHER THING. I ONLY SING JOHN DENVER MATERIAL NOW.
IS THAT A PROBLEM?
WE COULD DROP HIM OVERBOARD. WHO'D KNOW? HE'S DEAD.
GB Trudeau

September 3, 1988

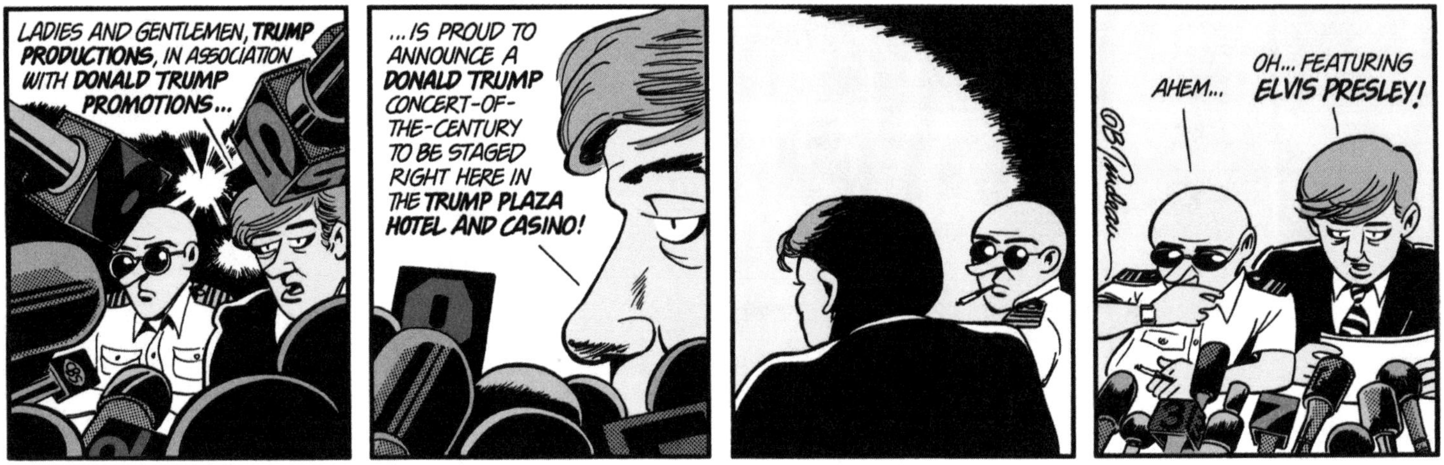
LADIES AND GENTLEMEN, **TRUMP PRODUCTIONS**, IN ASSOCIATION WITH **DONALD TRUMP PROMOTIONS**...
...IS PROUD TO ANNOUNCE A **DONALD TRUMP** CONCERT-OF-THE-CENTURY TO BE STAGED RIGHT HERE IN THE **TRUMP PLAZA HOTEL AND CASINO!**
AHEM...
OH... FEATURING **ELVIS PRESLEY!**

September 12, 1988

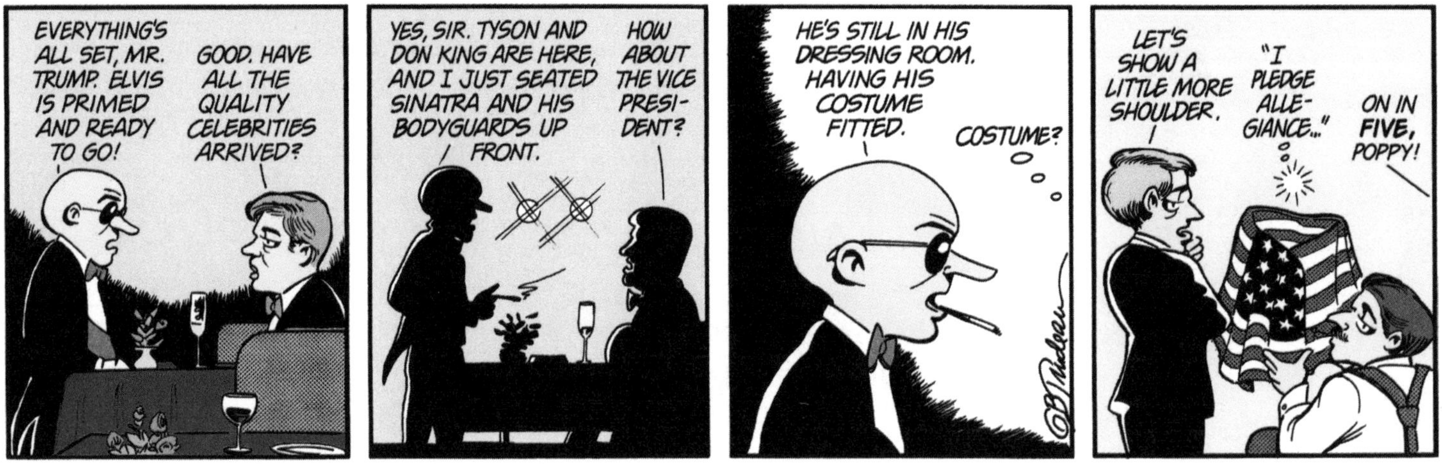
EVERYTHING'S ALL SET, MR. TRUMP. ELVIS IS PRIMED AND READY TO GO!
GOOD. HAVE ALL THE QUALITY CELEBRITIES ARRIVED?
YES, SIR. TYSON AND DON KING ARE HERE, AND I JUST SEATED SINATRA AND HIS BODYGUARDS UP FRONT.
HOW ABOUT THE VICE PRESIDENT?
HE'S STILL IN HIS DRESSING ROOM. HAVING HIS COSTUME FITTED.
COSTUME?
LET'S SHOW A LITTLE MORE SHOULDER.
"I PLEDGE ALLEGIANCE..."
ON IN **FIVE,** POPPY!

September 13, 1988

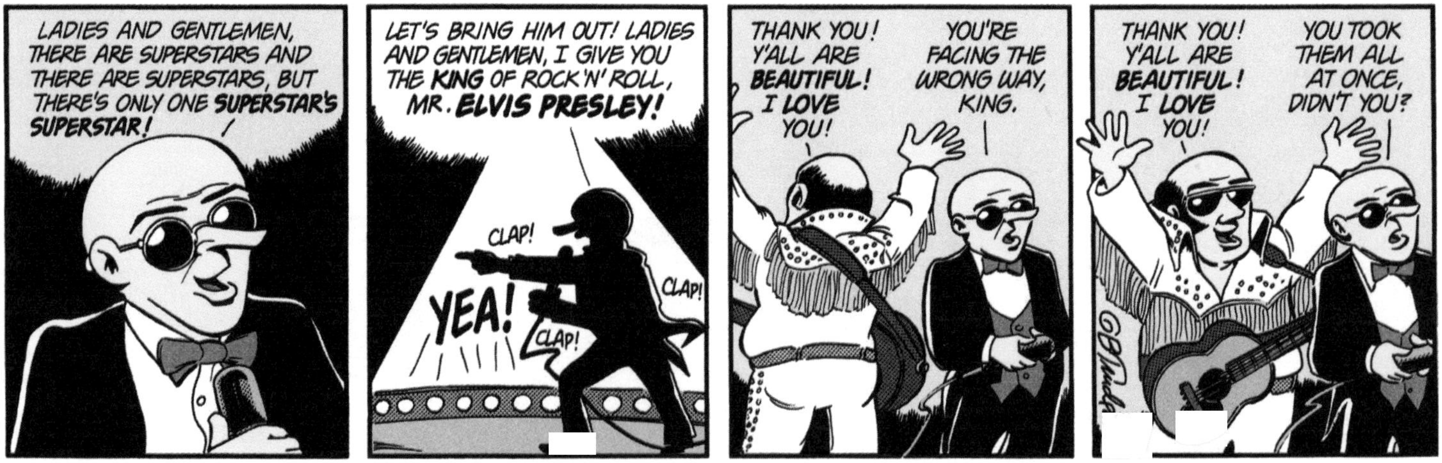
LADIES AND GENTLEMEN, THERE ARE SUPERSTARS AND THERE ARE SUPERSTARS, BUT THERE'S ONLY ONE **SUPERSTAR'S SUPERSTAR!**
LET'S BRING HIM OUT! LADIES AND GENTLEMEN, I GIVE YOU THE **KING** OF ROCK 'N' ROLL, MR. **ELVIS PRESLEY!**
CLAP!
CLAP!
YEA!
CLAP!
THANK YOU! Y'ALL ARE **BEAUTIFUL!** I **LOVE** YOU!
YOU'RE FACING THE WRONG WAY, KING.
THANK YOU! Y'ALL ARE **BEAUTIFUL!** I **LOVE** YOU!
YOU TOOK THEM ALL AT ONCE, DIDN'T YOU?

September 14, 1988

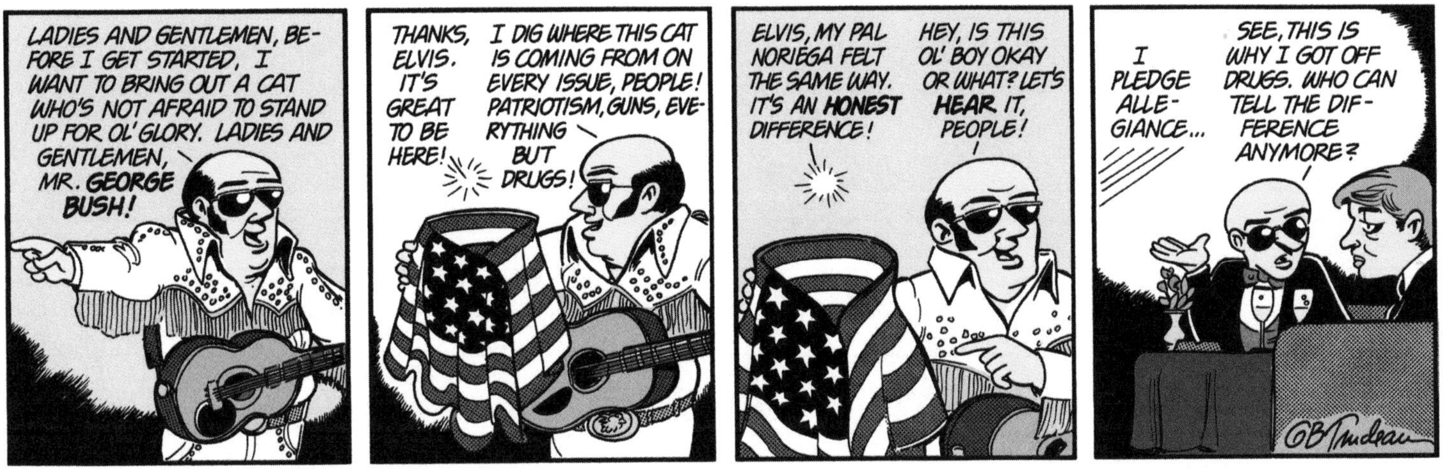
LADIES AND GENTLEMEN, BEFORE I GET STARTED, I WANT TO BRING OUT A CAT WHO'S NOT AFRAID TO STAND UP FOR OL' GLORY. LADIES AND GENTLEMEN, MR. GEORGE BUSH!
THANKS, ELVIS. IT'S GREAT TO BE HERE!
I DIG WHERE THIS CAT IS COMING FROM ON EVERY ISSUE, PEOPLE! PATRIOTISM, GUNS, EVERYTHING BUT DRUGS!
ELVIS, MY PAL NORIEGA FELT THE SAME WAY. IT'S AN HONEST DIFFERENCE!
HEY, IS THIS OL' BOY OKAY OR WHAT? LET'S HEAR IT, PEOPLE!
I PLEDGE ALLEGIANCE...
SEE, THIS IS WHY I GOT OFF DRUGS. WHO CAN TELL THE DIFFERENCE ANYMORE?
GBTrudeau

September 15, 1988

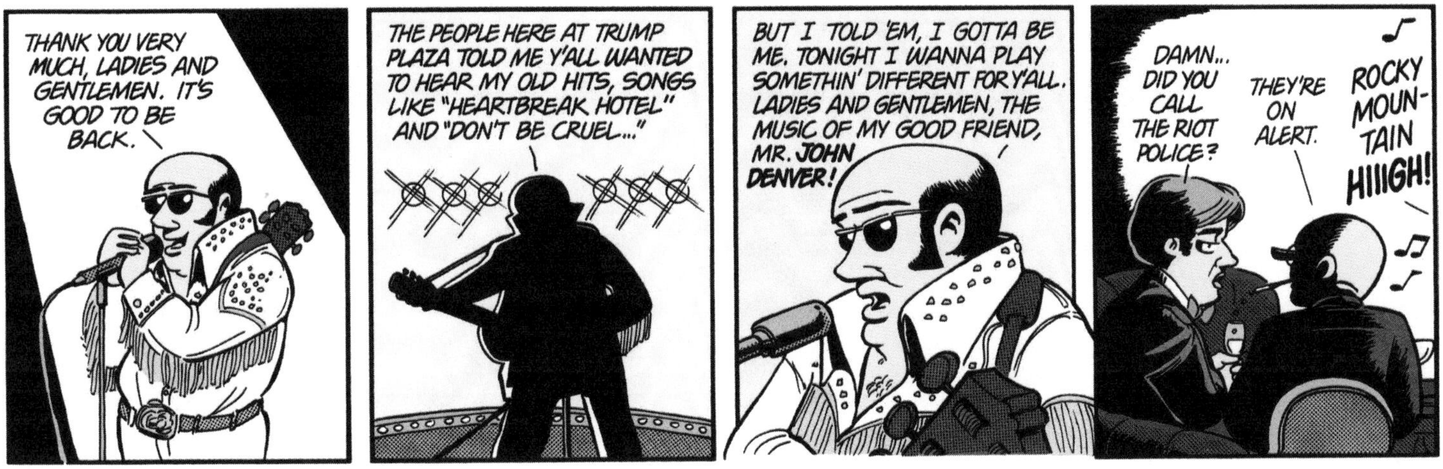
THANK YOU VERY MUCH, LADIES AND GENTLEMEN. IT'S GOOD TO BE BACK.
THE PEOPLE HERE AT TRUMP PLAZA TOLD ME Y'ALL WANTED TO HEAR MY OLD HITS, SONGS LIKE "HEARTBREAK HOTEL" AND "DON'T BE CRUEL..."
BUT I TOLD 'EM, I GOTTA BE ME. TONIGHT I WANNA PLAY SOMETHIN' DIFFERENT FOR Y'ALL. LADIES AND GENTLEMEN, THE MUSIC OF MY GOOD FRIEND, MR. JOHN DENVER!
DAMN... DID YOU CALL THE RIOT POLICE?
THEY'RE ON ALERT.
ROCKY MOUNTAIN HIIIGH!

September 16, 1988

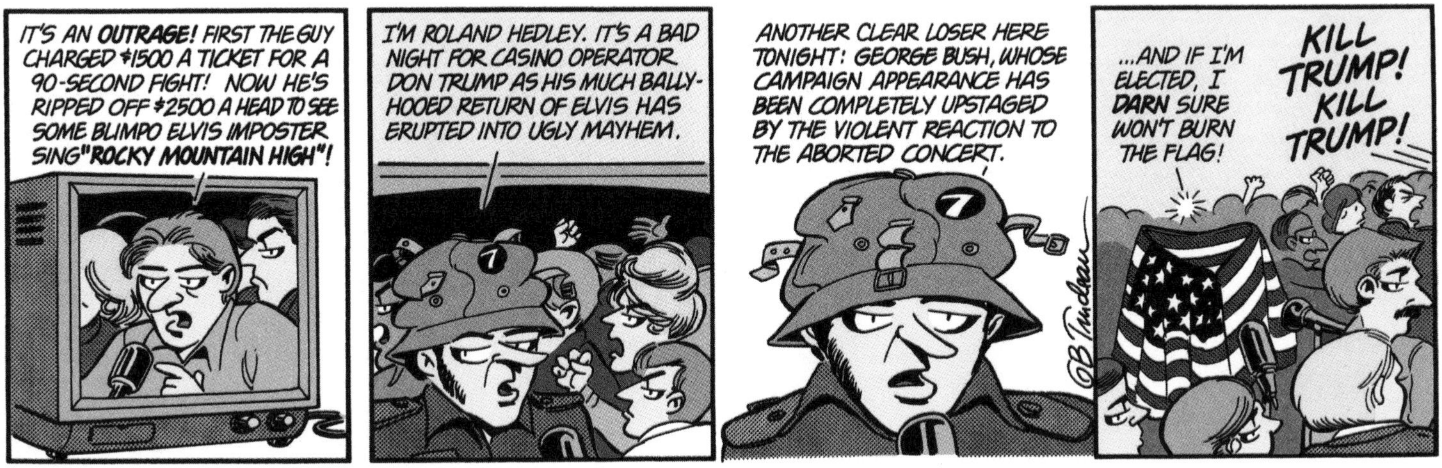
IT'S AN OUTRAGE! FIRST THE GUY CHARGED $1500 A TICKET FOR A 90-SECOND FIGHT! NOW HE'S RIPPED OFF $2500 A HEAD TO SEE SOME BLIMPO ELVIS IMPOSTER SING "ROCKY MOUNTAIN HIGH"!
I'M ROLAND HEDLEY. IT'S A BAD NIGHT FOR CASINO OPERATOR DON TRUMP AS HIS MUCH BALLYHOOED RETURN OF ELVIS HAS ERUPTED INTO UGLY MAYHEM.
ANOTHER CLEAR LOSER HERE TONIGHT: GEORGE BUSH, WHOSE CAMPAIGN APPEARANCE HAS BEEN COMPLETELY UPSTAGED BY THE VIOLENT REACTION TO THE ABORTED CONCERT.
GBTrudeau
...AND IF I'M ELECTED, I DARN SURE WON'T BURN THE FLAG!
KILL TRUMP! KILL TRUMP!

September 17, 1988

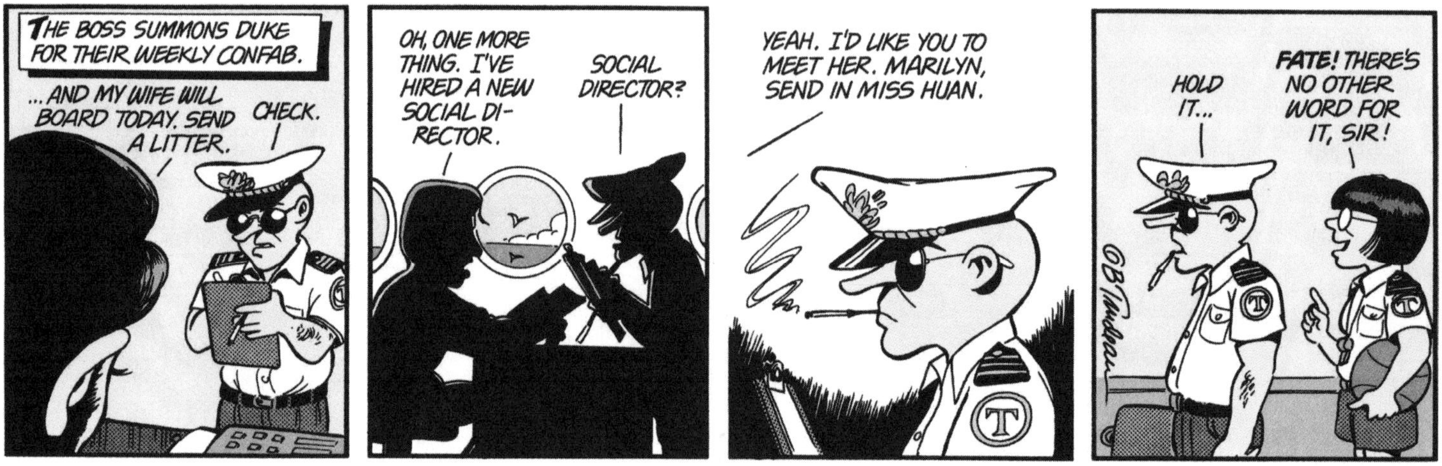
THE BOSS SUMMONS DUKE FOR THEIR WEEKLY CONFAB.
...AND MY WIFE WILL BOARD TODAY. SEND A LITTER.
CHECK.
OH, ONE MORE THING. I'VE HIRED A NEW SOCIAL DI- RECTOR.
SOCIAL DIRECTOR?
YEAH. I'D LIKE YOU TO MEET HER. MARILYN, SEND IN MISS HUAN.
HOLD IT...
FATE! THERE'S NO OTHER WORD FOR IT, SIR!

October 3, 1988

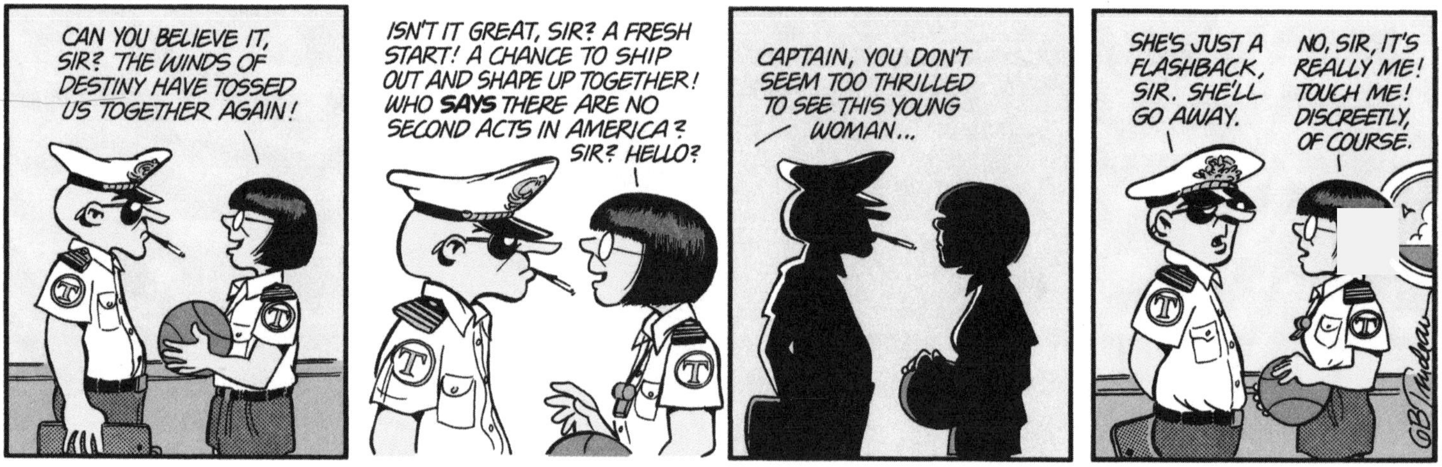
CAN YOU BELIEVE IT, SIR? THE WINDS OF DESTINY HAVE TOSSED US TOGETHER AGAIN!
ISN'T IT GREAT, SIR? A FRESH START! A CHANCE TO SHIP OUT AND SHAPE UP TOGETHER! WHO SAYS THERE ARE NO SECOND ACTS IN AMERICA?
SIR? HELLO?
CAPTAIN, YOU DON'T SEEM TOO THRILLED TO SEE THIS YOUNG WOMAN...
SHE'S JUST A FLASHBACK, SIR. SHE'LL GO AWAY.
NO, SIR, IT'S REALLY ME! TOUCH ME! DISCREETLY, OF COURSE.

October 4, 1988

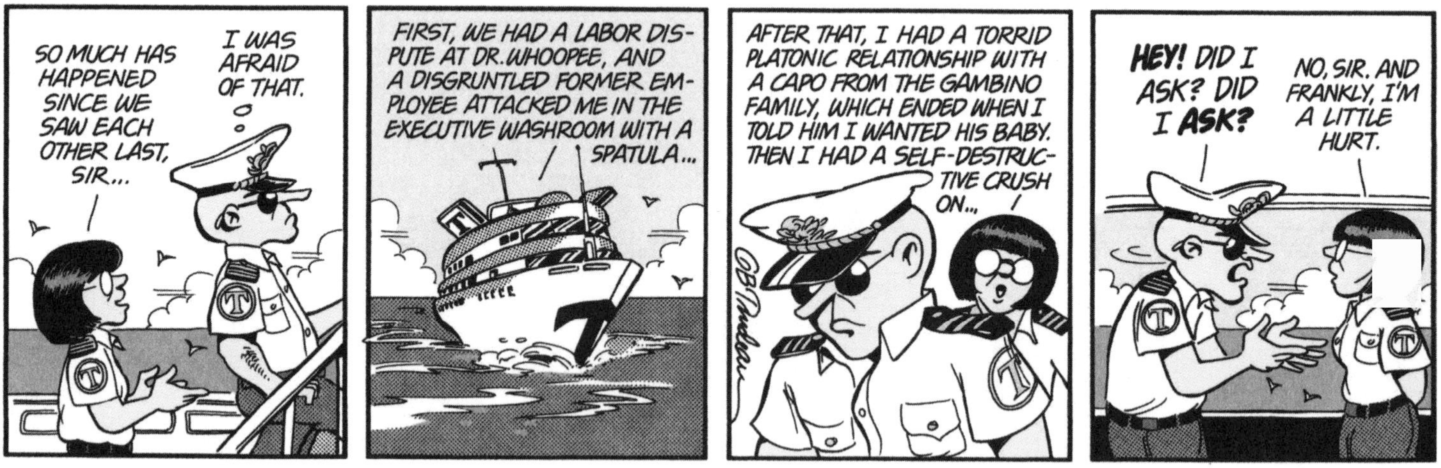
SO MUCH HAS HAPPENED SINCE WE SAW EACH OTHER LAST, SIR...
I WAS AFRAID OF THAT.
FIRST, WE HAD A LABOR DIS- PUTE AT DR. WHOOPEE, AND A DISGRUNTLED FORMER EM- PLOYEE ATTACKED ME IN THE EXECUTIVE WASHROOM WITH A SPATULA...
AFTER THAT, I HAD A TORRID PLATONIC RELATIONSHIP WITH A CAPO FROM THE GAMBINO FAMILY, WHICH ENDED WHEN I TOLD HIM I WANTED HIS BABY. THEN I HAD A SELF-DESTRUC- TIVE CRUSH ON...
HEY! DID I ASK? DID I ASK?
NO, SIR. AND FRANKLY, I'M A LITTLE HURT.

October 5, 1988

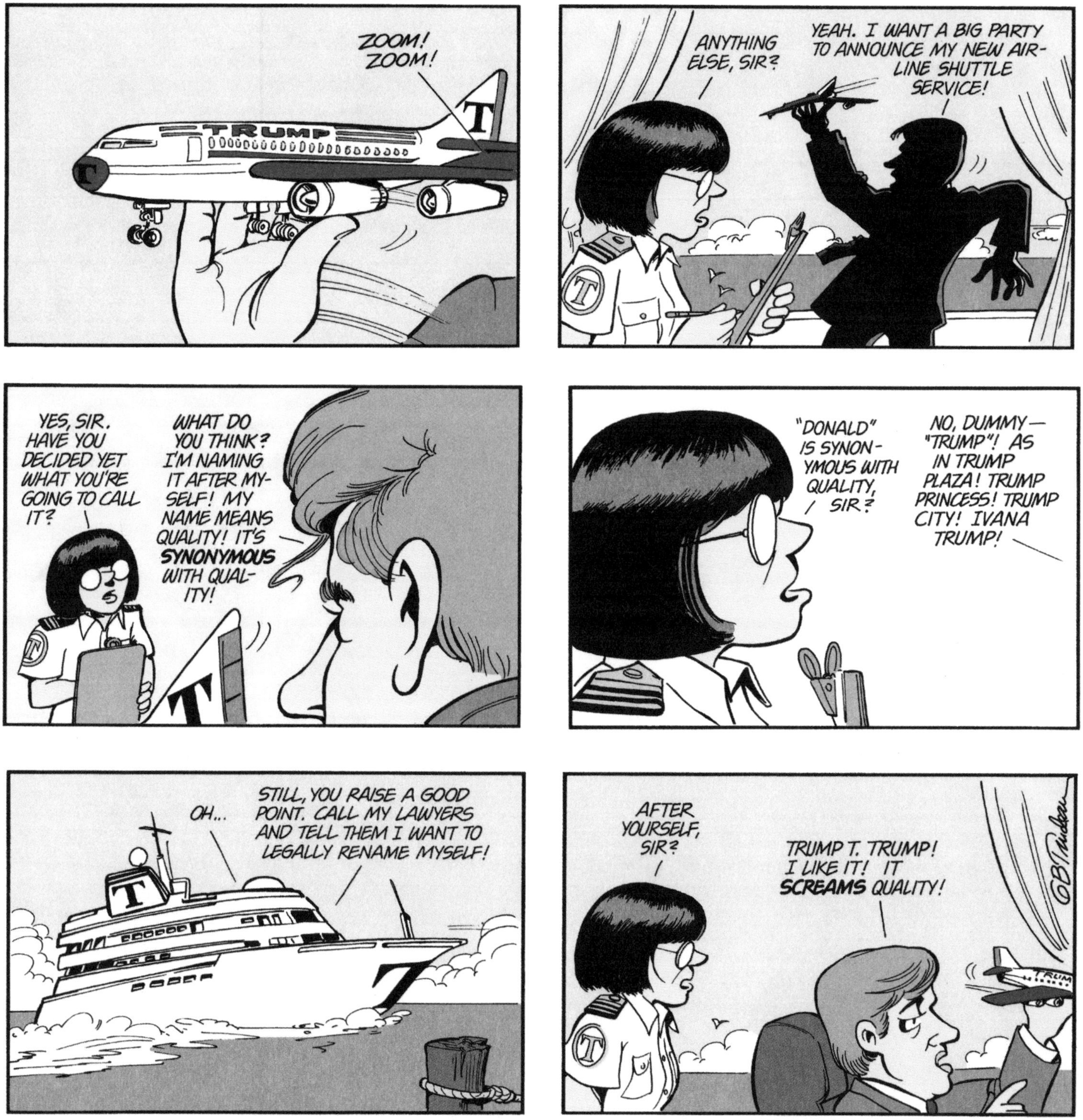

ZOOM! ZOOM!
TRUMP
ANYTHING ELSE, SIR?
YEAH. I WANT A BIG PARTY TO ANNOUNCE MY NEW AIR-LINE SHUTTLE SERVICE!
YES, SIR. HAVE YOU DECIDED YET WHAT YOU'RE GOING TO CALL IT?
WHAT DO YOU THINK? I'M NAMING IT AFTER MY-SELF! MY NAME MEANS QUALITY! IT'S **SYNONYMOUS** WITH QUAL-ITY!
"DONALD" IS SYNON-YMOUS WITH QUALITY, SIR?
NO, DUMMY— "TRUMP"! AS IN TRUMP PLAZA! TRUMP PRINCESS! TRUMP CITY! IVANA TRUMP!
OH...
STILL, YOU RAISE A GOOD POINT. CALL MY LAWYERS AND TELL THEM I WANT TO LEGALLY RENAME MYSELF!
AFTER YOURSELF, SIR?
TRUMP T. TRUMP! I LIKE IT! IT **SCREAMS** QUALITY!
©B Trudeau

November 20, 1988

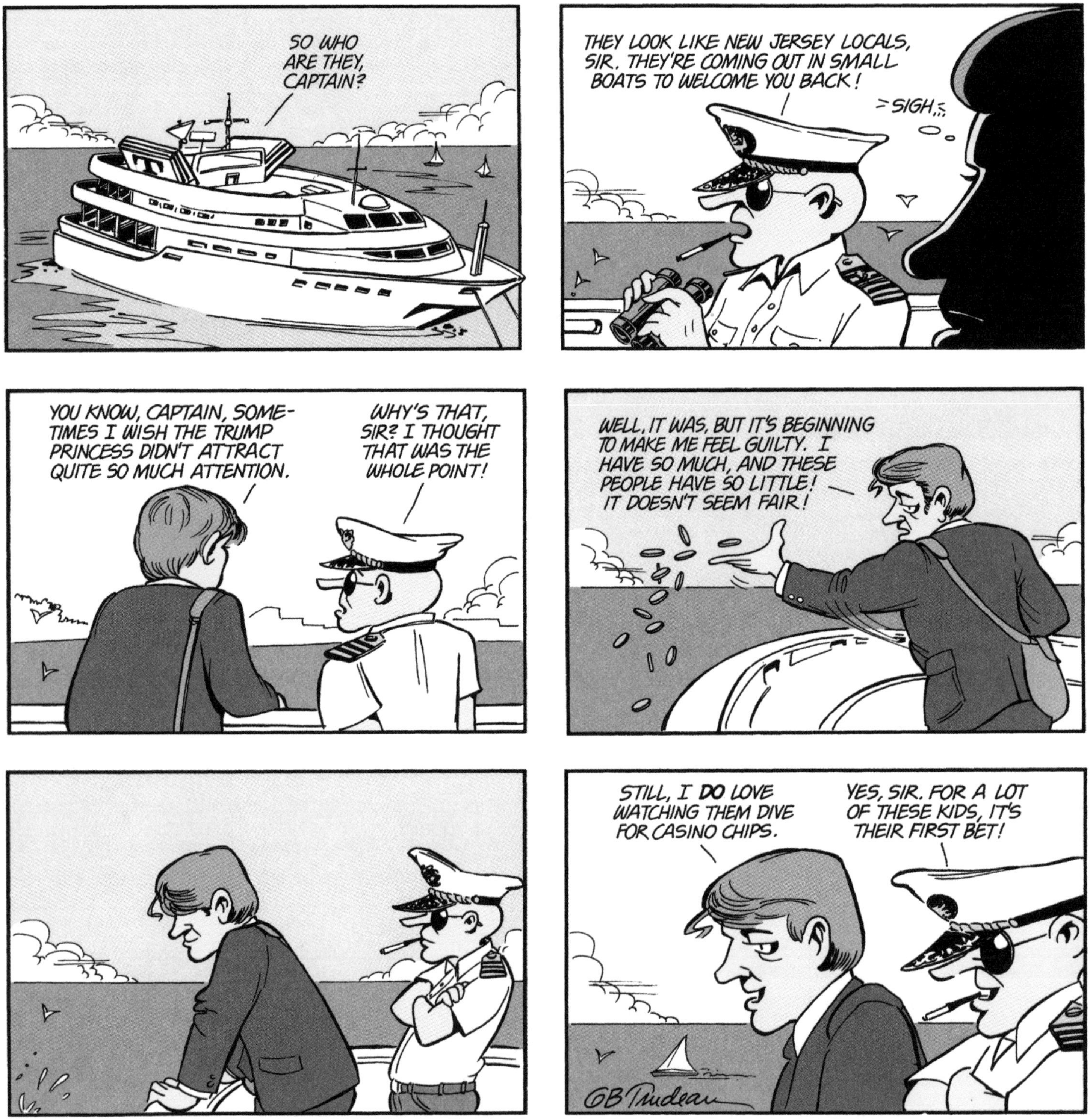
SO WHO ARE THEY, CAPTAIN?
THEY LOOK LIKE NEW JERSEY LOCALS, SIR. THEY'RE COMING OUT IN SMALL BOATS TO WELCOME YOU BACK!
SIGH..
YOU KNOW, CAPTAIN, SOMETIMES I WISH THE TRUMP PRINCESS DIDN'T ATTRACT QUITE SO MUCH ATTENTION.
WHY'S THAT, SIR? I THOUGHT THAT WAS THE WHOLE POINT!
WELL, IT WAS, BUT IT'S BEGINNING TO MAKE ME FEEL GUILTY. I HAVE SO MUCH, AND THESE PEOPLE HAVE SO LITTLE! IT DOESN'T SEEM FAIR!
STILL, I **DO** LOVE WATCHING THEM DIVE FOR CASINO CHIPS.
YES, SIR. FOR A LOT OF THESE KIDS, IT'S THEIR FIRST BET!
GB Trudeau

December 25, 1988

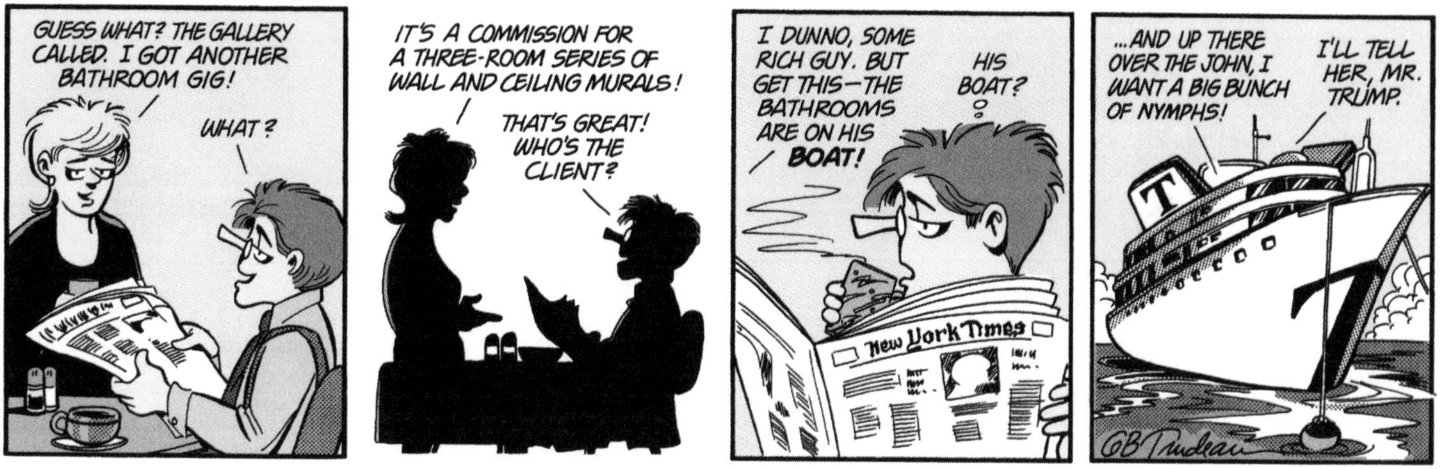
GUESS WHAT? THE GALLERY CALLED. I GOT ANOTHER BATHROOM GIG!
WHAT?
IT'S A COMMISSION FOR A THREE-ROOM SERIES OF WALL AND CEILING MURALS!
THAT'S GREAT! WHO'S THE CLIENT?
I DUNNO, SOME RICH GUY. BUT GET THIS—THE BATHROOMS ARE ON HIS **BOAT!**
HIS BOAT?
New York Times
...AND UP THERE OVER THE JOHN, I WANT A BIG BUNCH OF NYMPHS!
I'LL TELL HER, MR. TRUMP.

March 13, 1989

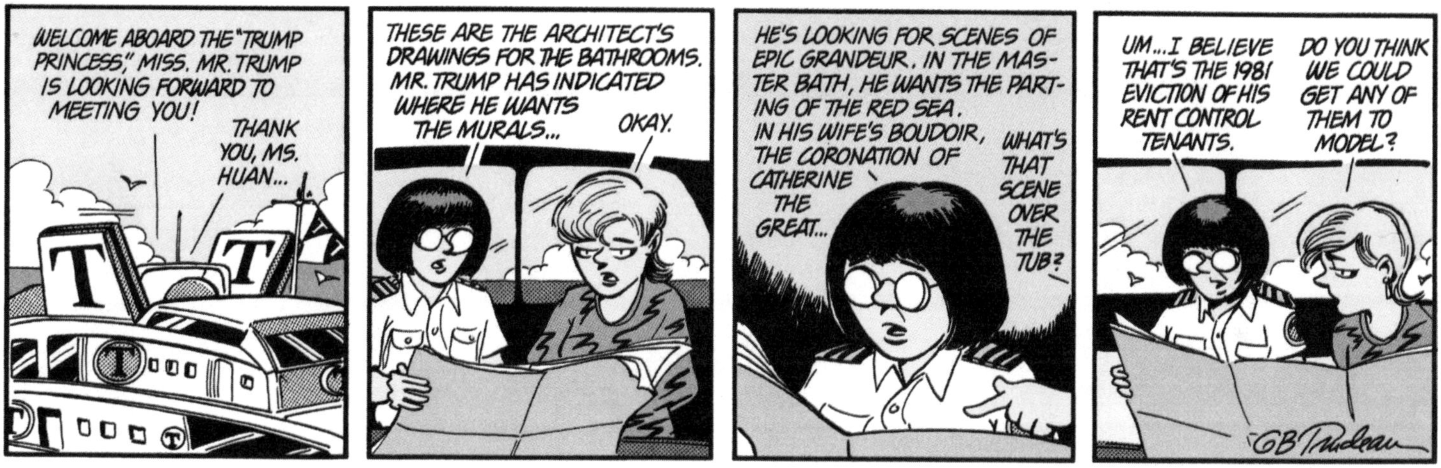
WELCOME ABOARD THE "TRUMP PRINCESS," MISS. MR. TRUMP IS LOOKING FORWARD TO MEETING YOU!
THANK YOU, MS. HUAN...
THESE ARE THE ARCHITECT'S DRAWINGS FOR THE BATHROOMS. MR. TRUMP HAS INDICATED WHERE HE WANTS THE MURALS...
OKAY.
HE'S LOOKING FOR SCENES OF EPIC GRANDEUR. IN THE MASTER BATH, HE WANTS THE PARTING OF THE RED SEA. IN HIS WIFE'S BOUDOIR, THE CORONATION OF CATHERINE THE GREAT...
WHAT'S THAT SCENE OVER THE TUB?
UM...I BELIEVE THAT'S THE 1981 EVICTION OF HIS RENT CONTROL TENANTS.
DO YOU THINK WE COULD GET ANY OF THEM TO MODEL?

March 14, 1989

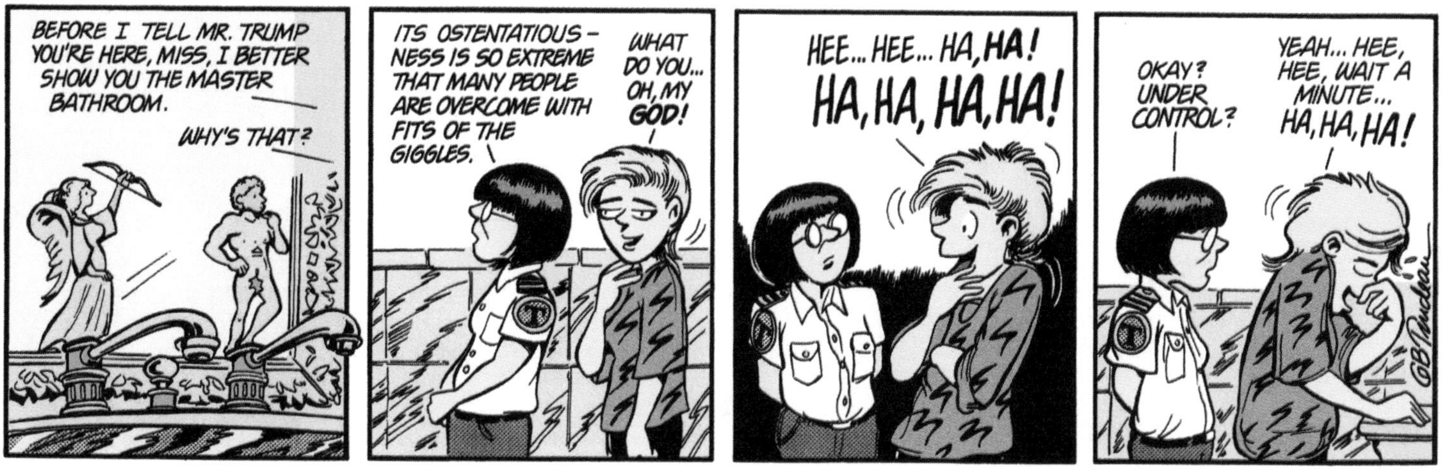
BEFORE I TELL MR. TRUMP YOU'RE HERE, MISS, I BETTER SHOW YOU THE MASTER BATHROOM.
WHY'S THAT?
ITS OSTENTATIOUSNESS IS SO EXTREME THAT MANY PEOPLE ARE OVERCOME WITH FITS OF THE GIGGLES.
WHAT DO YOU... OH, MY **GOD!**
HEE... HEE... HA, HA!
HA, HA, HA, HA!
OKAY? UNDER CONTROL?
YEAH... HEE, HEE, WAIT A MINUTE... HA, HA, HA!

March 15, 1989

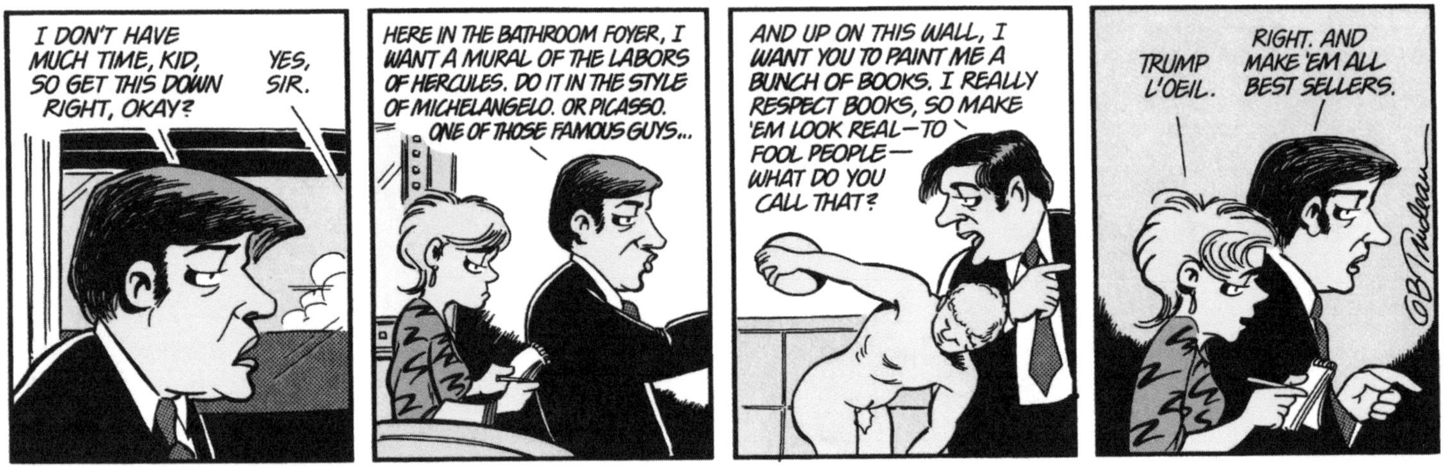
I DON'T HAVE MUCH TIME, KID, SO GET THIS DOWN RIGHT, OKAY?
YES, SIR.
HERE IN THE BATHROOM FOYER, I WANT A MURAL OF THE LABORS OF HERCULES. DO IT IN THE STYLE OF MICHELANGELO. OR PICASSO.
ONE OF THOSE FAMOUS GUYS...
AND UP ON THIS WALL, I WANT YOU TO PAINT ME A BUNCH OF BOOKS. I REALLY RESPECT BOOKS, SO MAKE 'EM LOOK REAL—TO FOOL PEOPLE—WHAT DO YOU CALL THAT?
TRUMP L'OEIL.
RIGHT. AND MAKE 'EM ALL BEST SELLERS.

March 16, 1989

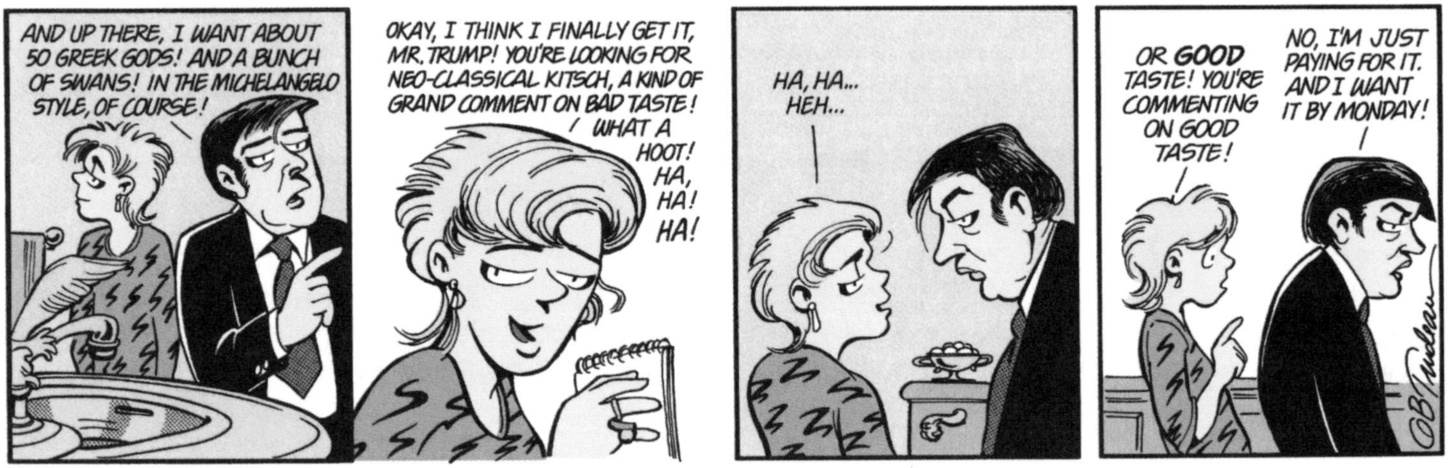
AND UP THERE, I WANT ABOUT 50 GREEK GODS! AND A BUNCH OF SWANS! IN THE MICHELANGELO STYLE, OF COURSE!
OKAY, I THINK I FINALLY GET IT, MR. TRUMP! YOU'RE LOOKING FOR NEO-CLASSICAL KITSCH, A KIND OF GRAND COMMENT ON BAD TASTE!
WHAT A HOOT! HA, HA! HA!
HA, HA... HEH...
OR GOOD TASTE! YOU'RE COMMENTING ON GOOD TASTE!
NO, I'M JUST PAYING FOR IT. AND I WANT IT BY MONDAY!

March 17, 1989

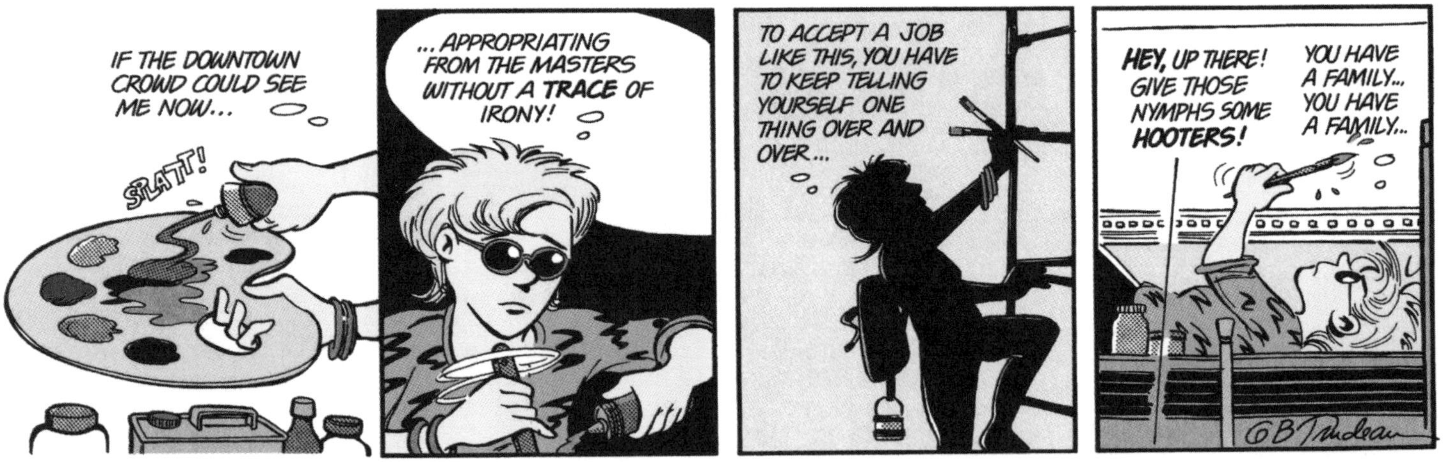
IF THE DOWNTOWN CROWD COULD SEE ME NOW...
SPLATT!
...APPROPRIATING FROM THE MASTERS WITHOUT A TRACE OF IRONY!
TO ACCEPT A JOB LIKE THIS, YOU HAVE TO KEEP TELLING YOURSELF ONE THING OVER AND OVER...
HEY, UP THERE! GIVE THOSE NYMPHS SOME HOOTERS!
YOU HAVE A FAMILY... YOU HAVE A FAMILY...

March 18, 1989

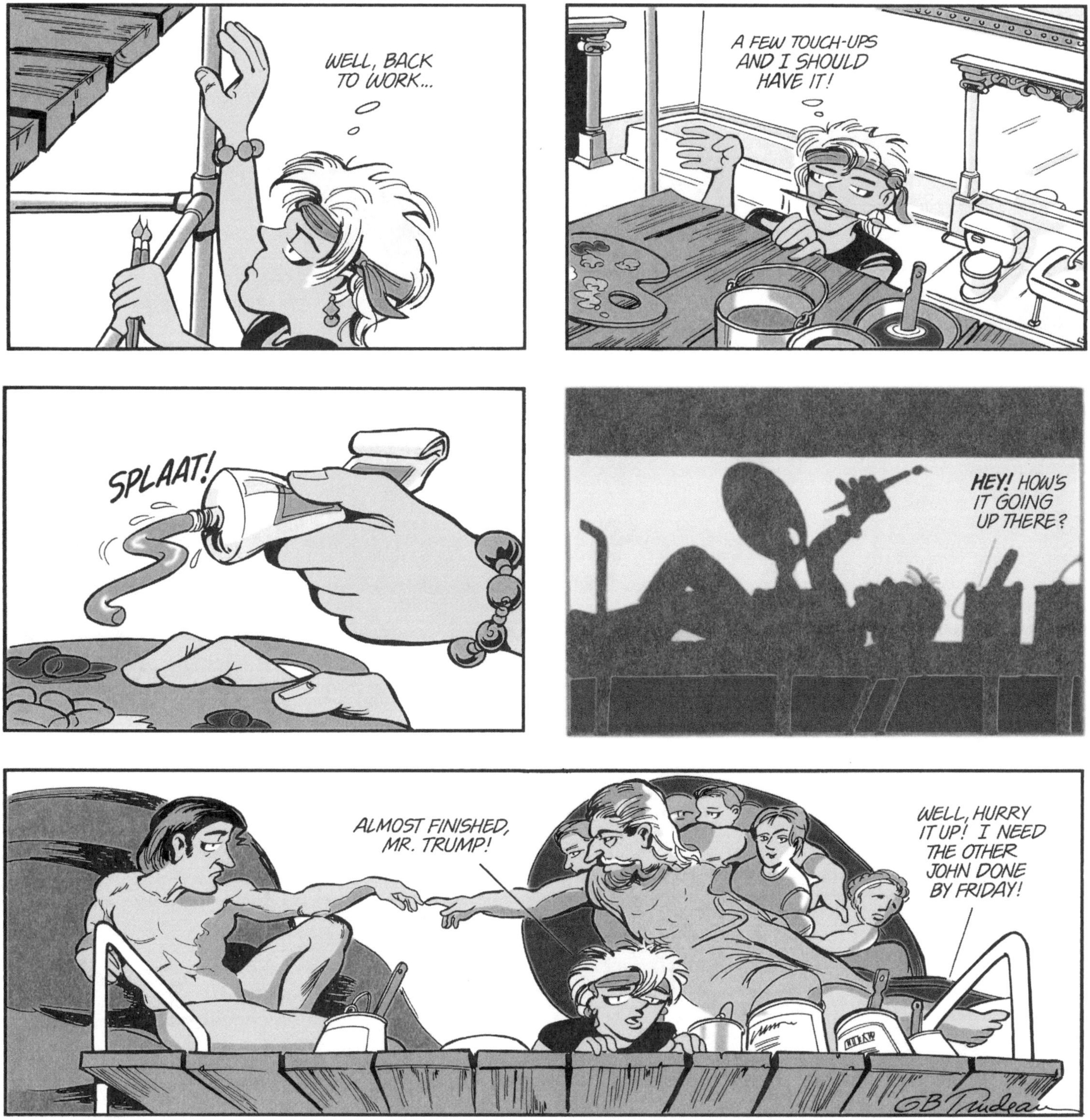
WELL, BACK TO WORK...
A FEW TOUCH-UPS AND I SHOULD HAVE IT!
SPLAAT!
HEY! HOW'S IT GOING UP THERE?
ALMOST FINISHED, MR. TRUMP!
WELL, HURRY IT UP! I NEED THE OTHER JOHN DONE BY FRIDAY!
GB Trudeau

March 19, 1989

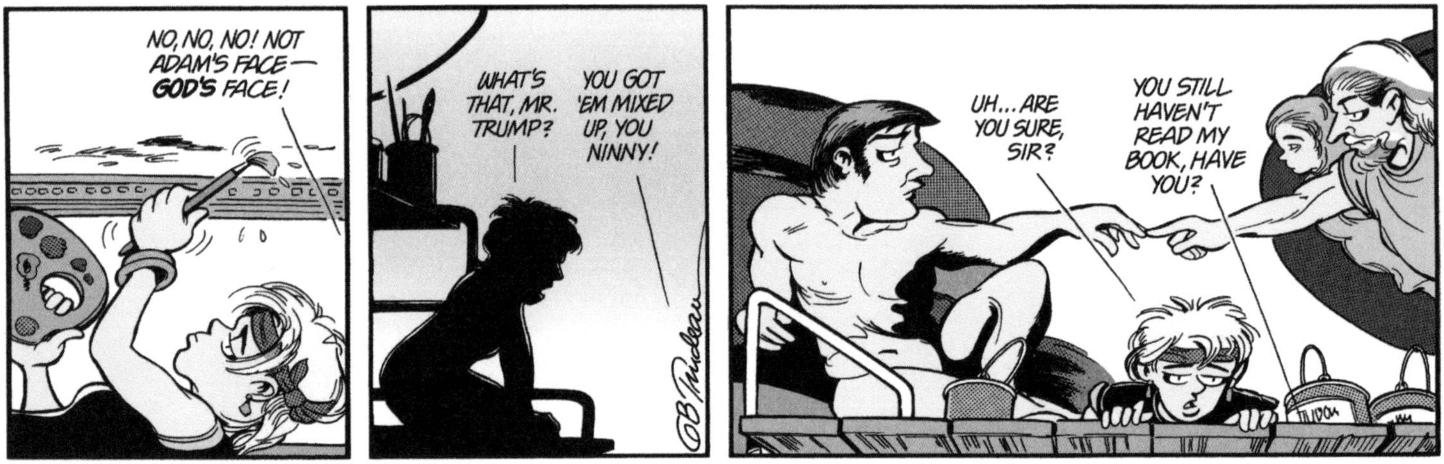
NO, NO, NO! NOT ADAM'S FACE— GOD'S FACE!
WHAT'S THAT, MR. TRUMP?
YOU GOT 'EM MIXED UP, YOU NINNY!
UH... ARE YOU SURE, SIR?
YOU STILL HAVEN'T READ MY BOOK, HAVE YOU?

March 20, 1989

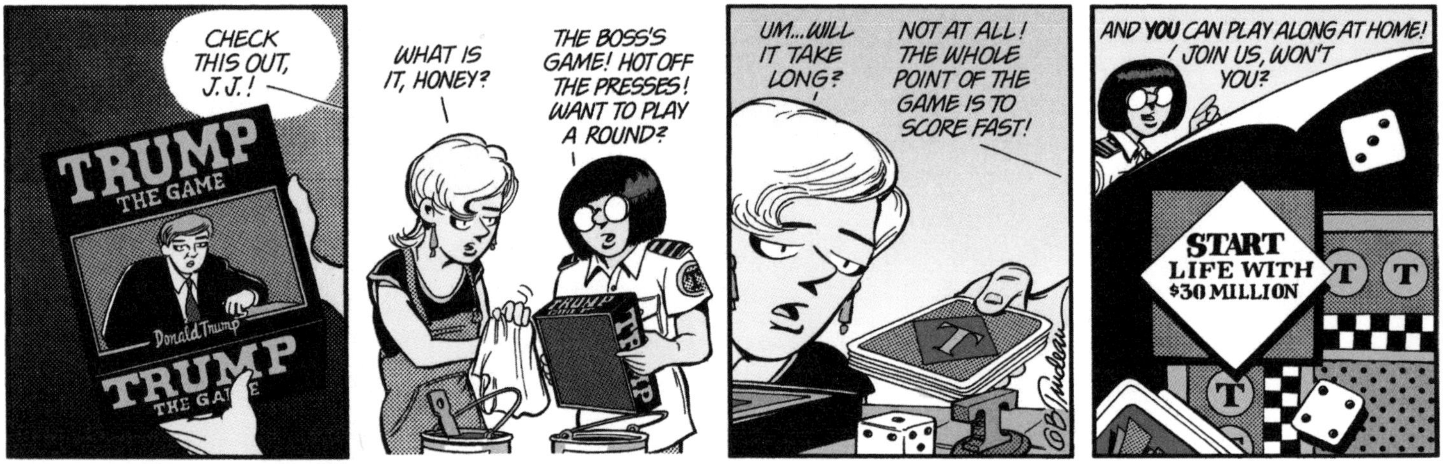
CHECK THIS OUT, J.J.!
TRUMP THE GAME
Donald Trump
TRUMP THE GAME
WHAT IS IT, HONEY?
THE BOSS'S GAME! HOT OFF THE PRESSES! WANT TO PLAY A ROUND?
UM...WILL IT TAKE LONG?
NOT AT ALL! THE WHOLE POINT OF THE GAME IS TO SCORE FAST!
AND YOU CAN PLAY ALONG AT HOME! JOIN US, WON'T YOU?
START LIFE WITH $30 MILLION

March 21, 1989

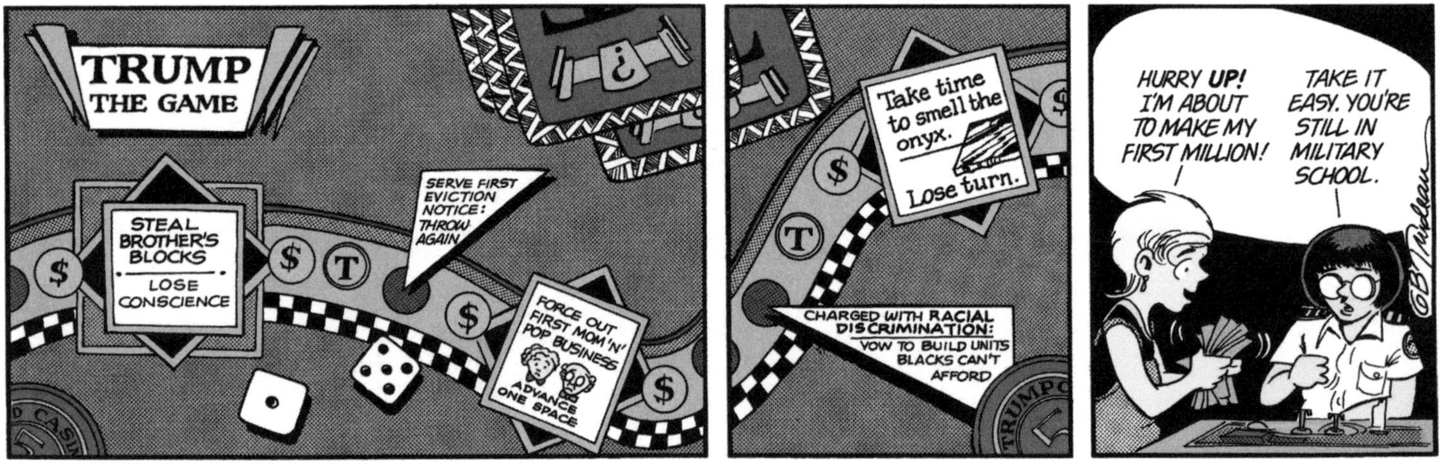
TRUMP THE GAME
STEAL BROTHER'S BLOCKS
LOSE CONSCIENCE
SERVE FIRST EVICTION NOTICE: THROW AGAIN
FORCE OUT FIRST MOM 'N' POP BUSINESS
ADVANCE ONE SPACE
Take time to smell the onyx.
Lose turn.
CHARGED WITH RACIAL DISCRIMINATION:
VOW TO BUILD UNITS BLACKS CAN'T AFFORD
HURRY UP! I'M ABOUT TO MAKE MY FIRST MILLION!
TAKE IT EASY. YOU'RE STILL IN MILITARY SCHOOL.

March 22, 1989

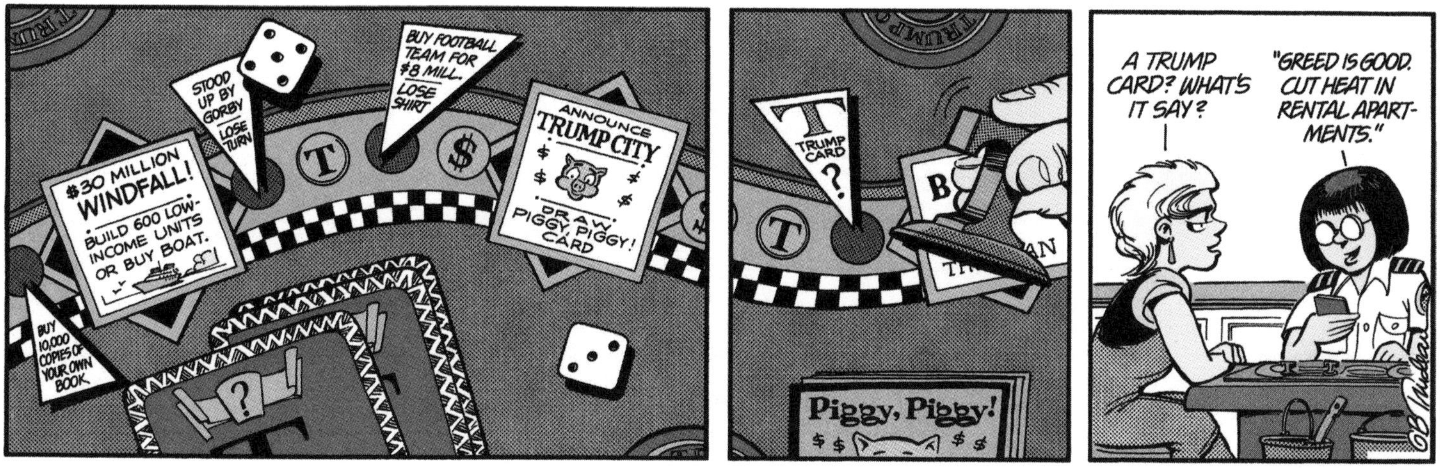
STOOD UP BY GORBY
LOSE TURN
BUY FOOTBALL TEAM FOR $8 MILL.
LOSE SHIRT
$30 MILLION WINDFALL!
BUILD 600 LOW-INCOME UNITS OR BUY BOAT.
ANNOUNCE TRUMP CITY
DRAW PIGGY, PIGGY! CARD
BUY 10,000 COPIES OF YOUR OWN BOOK
TRUMP CARD
?
Piggy, Piggy!
A TRUMP CARD? WHAT'S IT SAY?
"GREED IS GOOD. CUT HEAT IN RENTAL APARTMENTS."

March 23, 1989

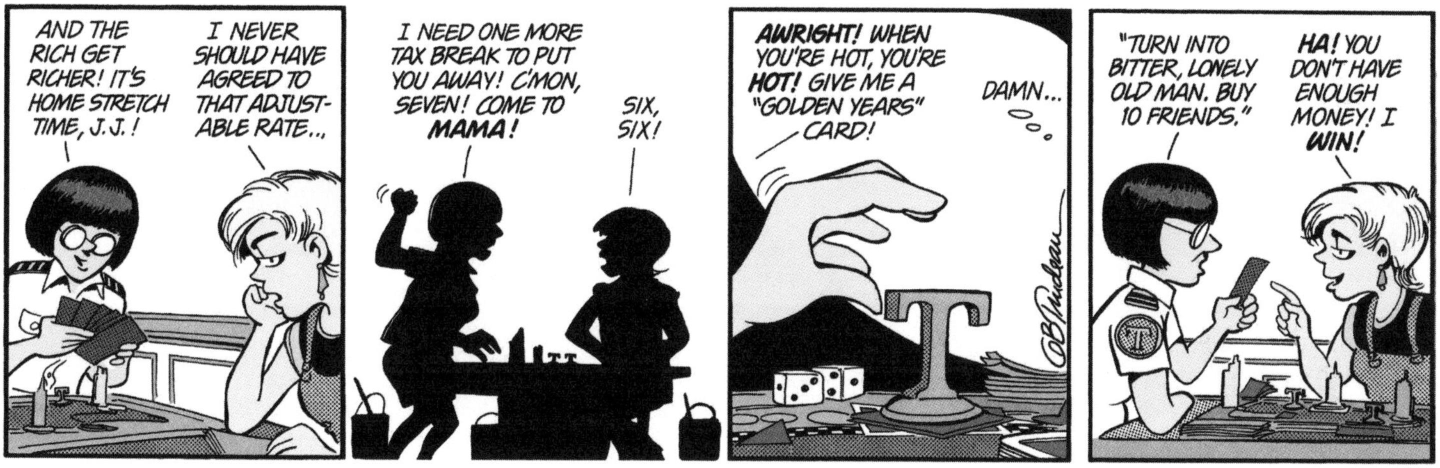
AND THE RICH GET RICHER! IT'S HOME STRETCH TIME, J.J.!
I NEVER SHOULD HAVE AGREED TO THAT ADJUSTABLE RATE...
I NEED ONE MORE TAX BREAK TO PUT YOU AWAY! C'MON, SEVEN! COME TO MAMA!
SIX, SIX!
AWRIGHT! WHEN YOU'RE HOT, YOU'RE HOT! GIVE ME A "GOLDEN YEARS" CARD!
DAMN...
"TURN INTO BITTER, LONELY OLD MAN. BUY 10 FRIENDS."
HA! YOU DON'T HAVE ENOUGH MONEY! I WIN!

March 24, 1989

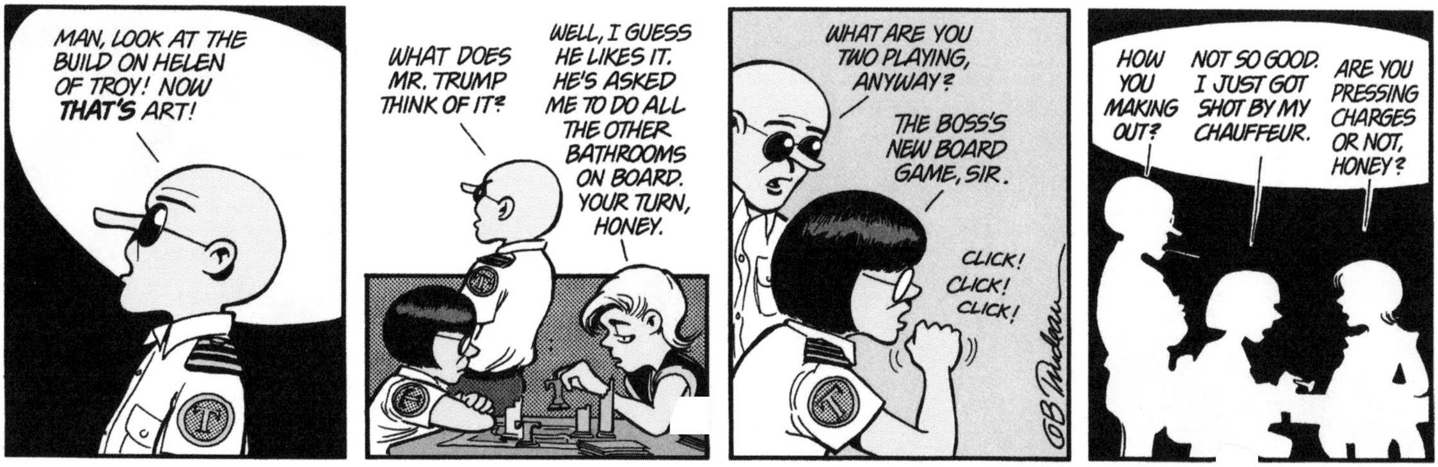
MAN, LOOK AT THE BUILD ON HELEN OF TROY! NOW THAT'S ART!
WHAT DOES MR. TRUMP THINK OF IT?
WELL, I GUESS HE LIKES IT. HE'S ASKED ME TO DO ALL THE OTHER BATHROOMS ON BOARD. YOUR TURN, HONEY.
WHAT ARE YOU TWO PLAYING, ANYWAY?
THE BOSS'S NEW BOARD GAME, SIR.
CLICK! CLICK! CLICK!
HOW YOU MAKING OUT?
NOT SO GOOD. I JUST GOT SHOT BY MY CHAUFFEUR.
ARE YOU PRESSING CHARGES OR NOT, HONEY?

March 25, 1989

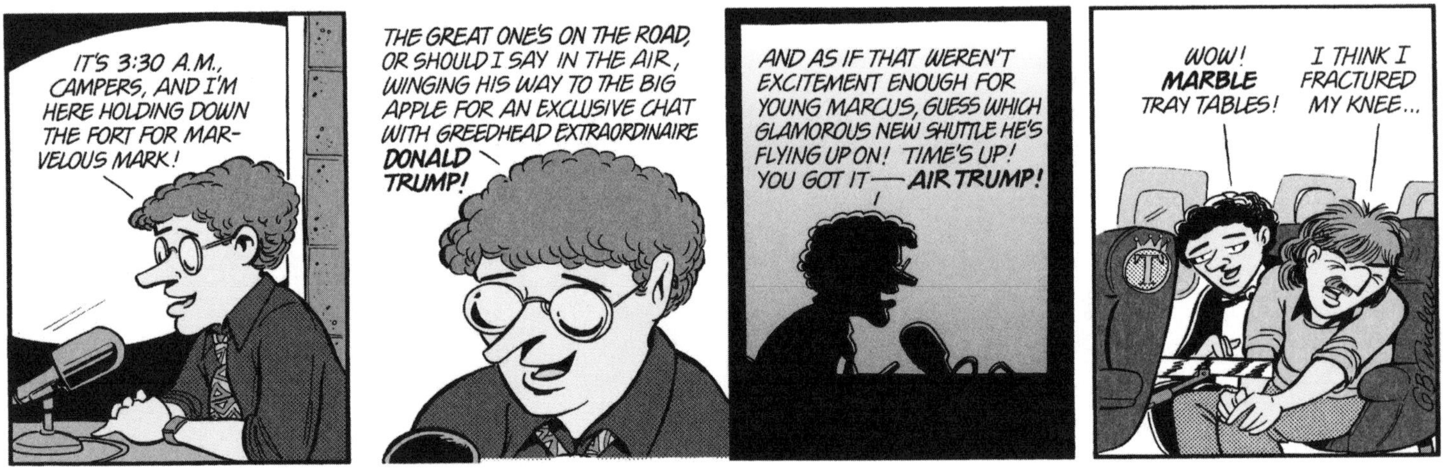
IT'S 3:30 A.M., CAMPERS, AND I'M HERE HOLDING DOWN THE FORT FOR MARVELOUS MARK!
THE GREAT ONE'S ON THE ROAD, OR SHOULD I SAY IN THE AIR, WINGING HIS WAY TO THE BIG APPLE FOR AN EXCLUSIVE CHAT WITH GREEDHEAD EXTRAORDINAIRE **DONALD TRUMP!**
AND AS IF THAT WEREN'T EXCITEMENT ENOUGH FOR YOUNG MARCUS, GUESS WHICH GLAMOROUS NEW SHUTTLE HE'S FLYING UP ON! TIME'S UP! YOU GOT IT — **AIR TRUMP!**
WOW! **MARBLE** TRAY TABLES!
I THINK I FRACTURED MY KNEE...
T

July 10, 1989

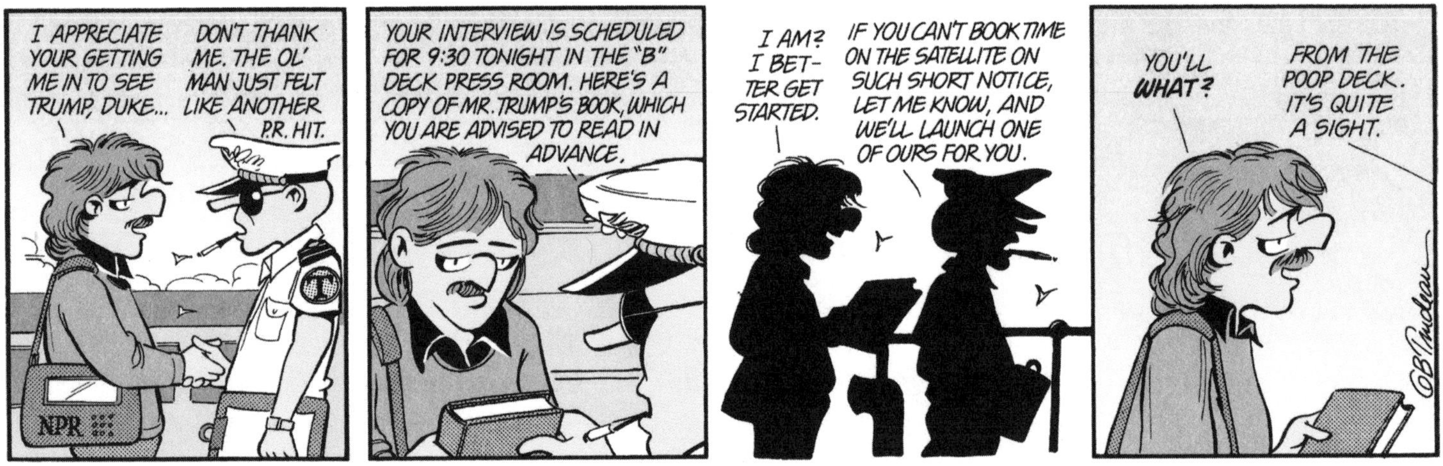
I APPRECIATE YOUR GETTING ME IN TO SEE TRUMP, DUKE...
DON'T THANK ME. THE OL' MAN JUST FELT LIKE ANOTHER P.R. HIT.
NPR
YOUR INTERVIEW IS SCHEDULED FOR 9:30 TONIGHT IN THE "B" DECK PRESS ROOM. HERE'S A COPY OF MR. TRUMP'S BOOK, WHICH YOU ARE ADVISED TO READ IN ADVANCE.
I AM? I BETTER GET STARTED.
IF YOU CAN'T BOOK TIME ON THE SATELLITE ON SUCH SHORT NOTICE, LET ME KNOW, AND WE'LL LAUNCH ONE OF OURS FOR YOU.
YOU'LL **WHAT?**
FROM THE POOP DECK. IT'S QUITE A SIGHT.

July 11, 1989

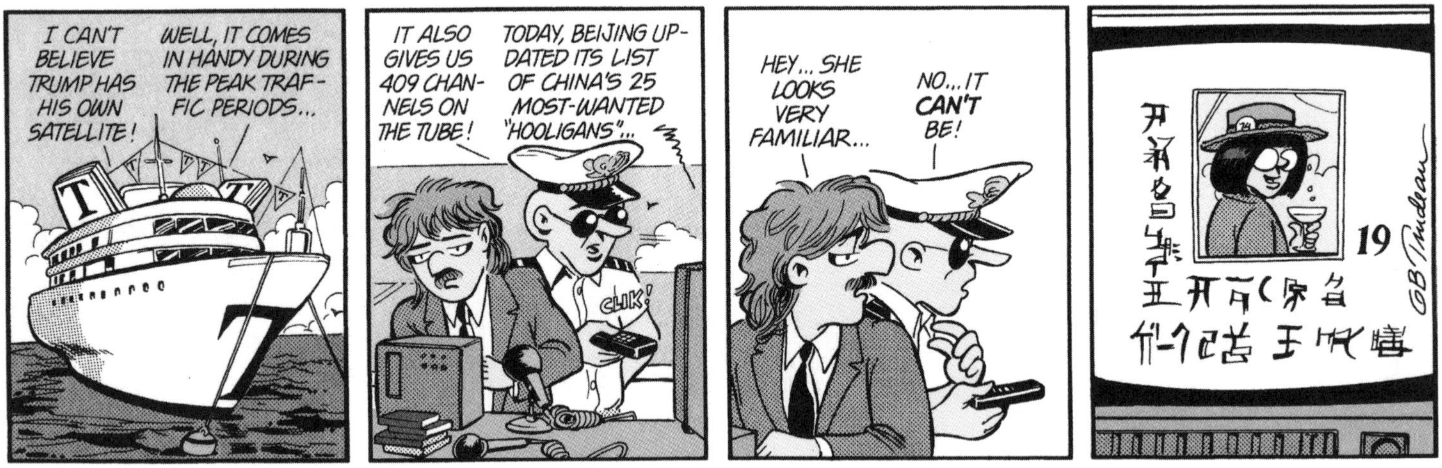
I CAN'T BELIEVE TRUMP HAS HIS OWN SATELLITE!
WELL, IT COMES IN HANDY DURING THE PEAK TRAFFIC PERIODS...
T
IT ALSO GIVES US 409 CHANNELS ON THE TUBE!
TODAY, BEIJING UPDATED ITS LIST OF CHINA'S 25 MOST-WANTED "HOOLIGANS"...
CLIK!
HEY... SHE LOOKS VERY FAMILIAR...
NO... IT **CAN'T** BE!
19

July 12, 1989

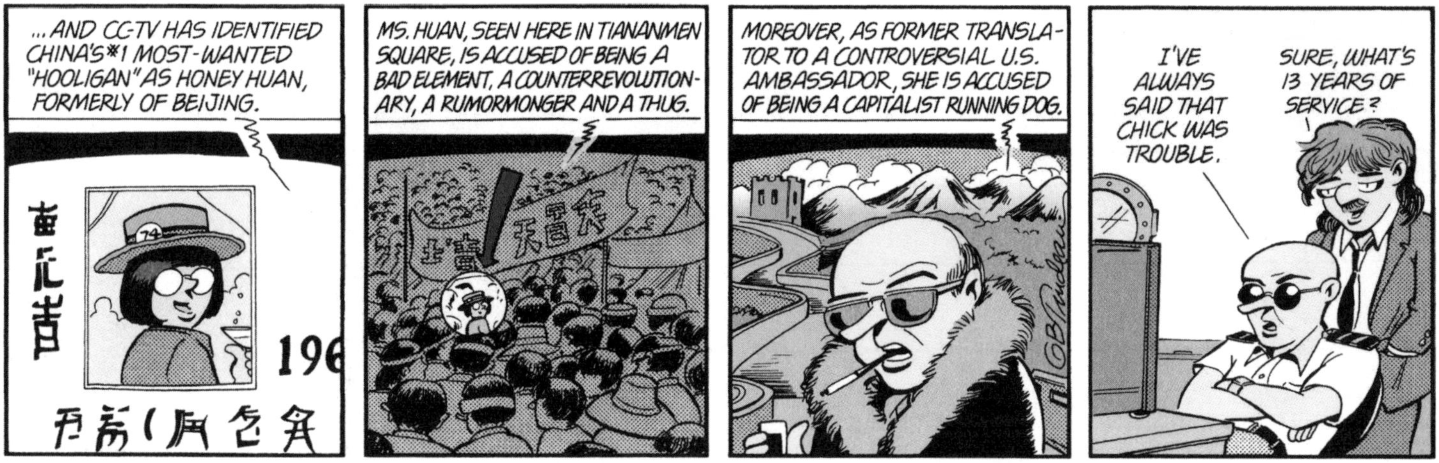
...AND CC-TV HAS IDENTIFIED CHINA'S *1 MOST-WANTED "HOOLIGAN" AS HONEY HUAN, FORMERLY OF BEIJING.
196
MS. HUAN, SEEN HERE IN TIANANMEN SQUARE, IS ACCUSED OF BEING A BAD ELEMENT, A COUNTERREVOLUTIONARY, A RUMORMONGER AND A THUG.
MOREOVER, AS FORMER TRANSLATOR TO A CONTROVERSIAL U.S. AMBASSADOR, SHE IS ACCUSED OF BEING A CAPITALIST RUNNING DOG.
I'VE ALWAYS SAID THAT CHICK WAS TROUBLE.
SURE, WHAT'S 13 YEARS OF SERVICE?
GB Trudeau

July 13, 1989

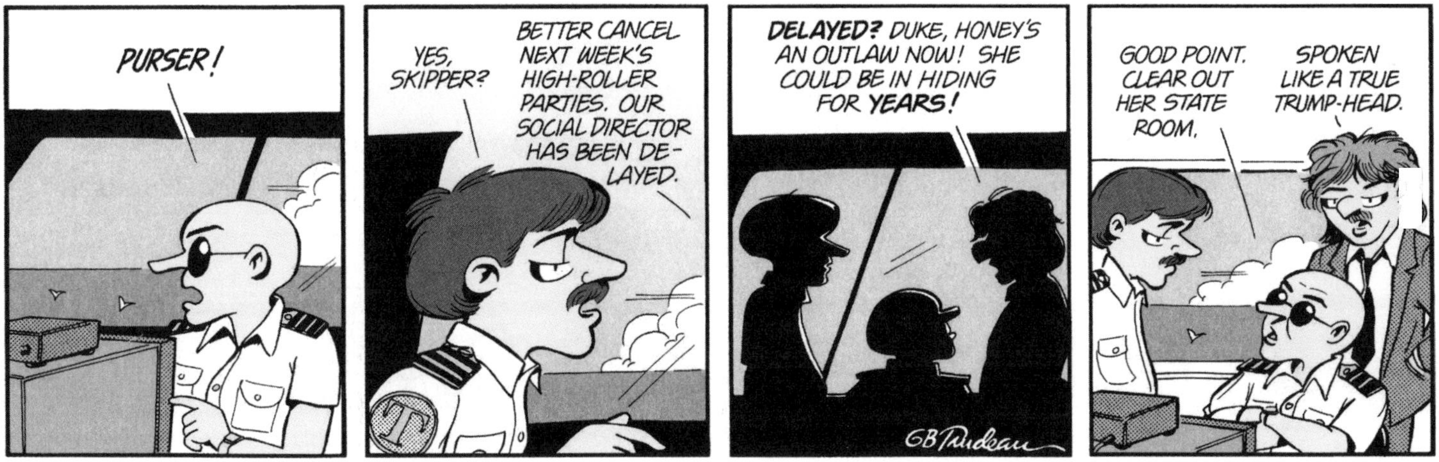
PURSER!
YES, SKIPPER?
BETTER CANCEL NEXT WEEK'S HIGH-ROLLER PARTIES. OUR SOCIAL DIRECTOR HAS BEEN DELAYED.
DELAYED? DUKE, HONEY'S AN OUTLAW NOW! SHE COULD BE IN HIDING FOR YEARS!
GOOD POINT. CLEAR OUT HER STATE ROOM.
SPOKEN LIKE A TRUE TRUMP-HEAD.
GB Trudeau

July 14, 1989

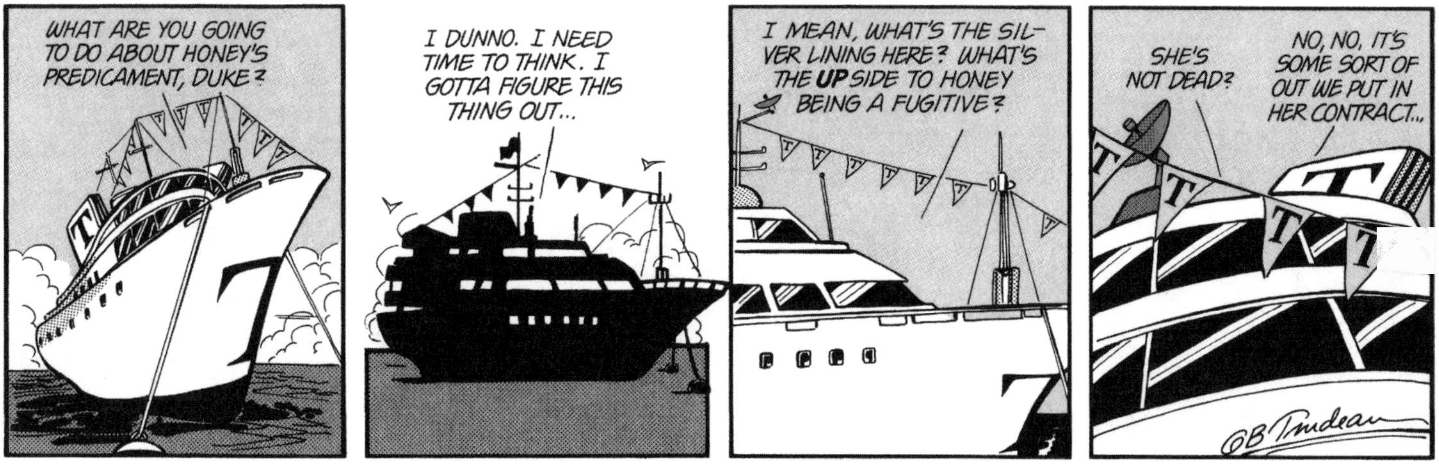
WHAT ARE YOU GOING TO DO ABOUT HONEY'S PREDICAMENT, DUKE?
I DUNNO. I NEED TIME TO THINK. I GOTTA FIGURE THIS THING OUT...
I MEAN, WHAT'S THE SILVER LINING HERE? WHAT'S THE UP SIDE TO HONEY BEING A FUGITIVE?
SHE'S NOT DEAD?
NO, NO, IT'S SOME SORT OF OUT WE PUT IN HER CONTRACT...
GB Trudeau

July 15, 1989

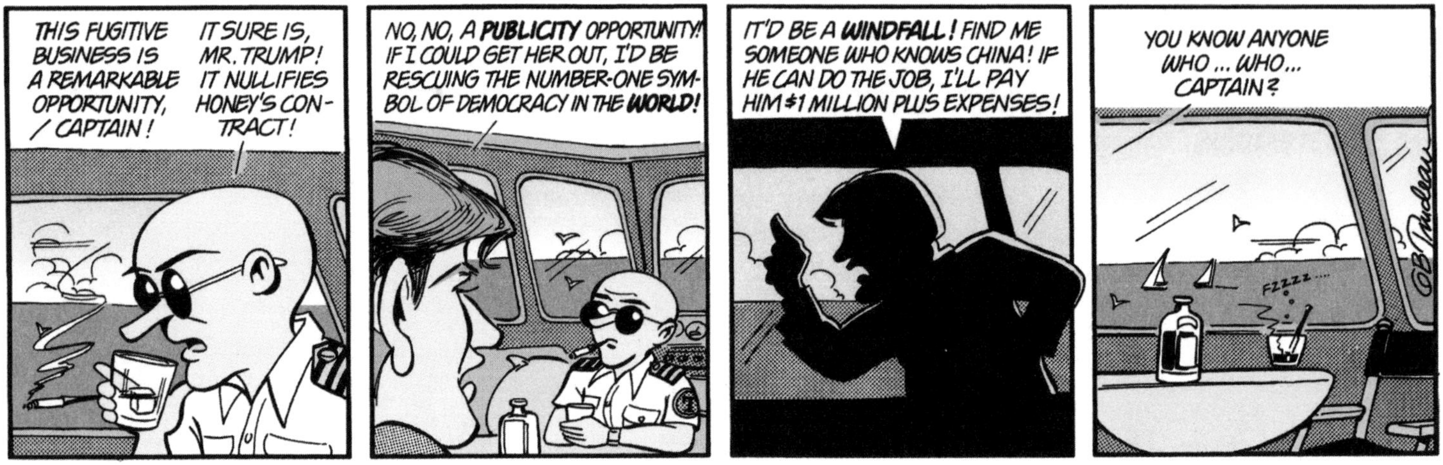
THIS FUGITIVE BUSINESS IS A REMARKABLE OPPORTUNITY, CAPTAIN!
IT SURE IS, MR. TRUMP! IT NULLIFIES HONEY'S CONTRACT!
NO, NO, A **PUBLICITY** OPPORTUNITY! IF I COULD GET HER OUT, I'D BE RESCUING THE NUMBER-ONE SYMBOL OF DEMOCRACY IN THE **WORLD**!
IT'D BE A **WINDFALL**! FIND ME SOMEONE WHO KNOWS CHINA! IF HE CAN DO THE JOB, I'LL PAY HIM $1 MILLION PLUS EXPENSES!
YOU KNOW ANYONE WHO ... WHO... CAPTAIN?
FZZZZ....

July 17, 1989

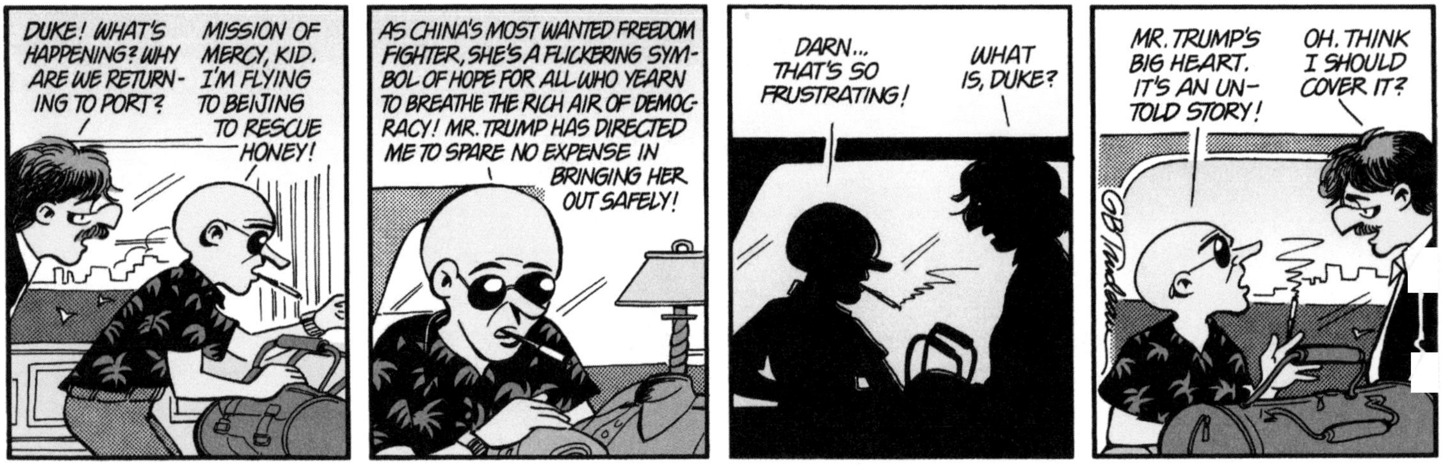
DUKE! WHAT'S HAPPENING? WHY ARE WE RETURNING TO PORT?
MISSION OF MERCY, KID. I'M FLYING TO BEIJING TO RESCUE HONEY!
AS CHINA'S MOST WANTED FREEDOM FIGHTER, SHE'S A FLICKERING SYMBOL OF HOPE FOR ALL WHO YEARN TO BREATHE THE RICH AIR OF DEMOCRACY! MR. TRUMP HAS DIRECTED ME TO SPARE NO EXPENSE IN BRINGING HER OUT SAFELY!
DARN... THAT'S SO FRUSTRATING!
WHAT IS, DUKE?
MR. TRUMP'S BIG HEART. IT'S AN UNTOLD STORY!
OH. THINK I SHOULD COVER IT?

July 18, 1989

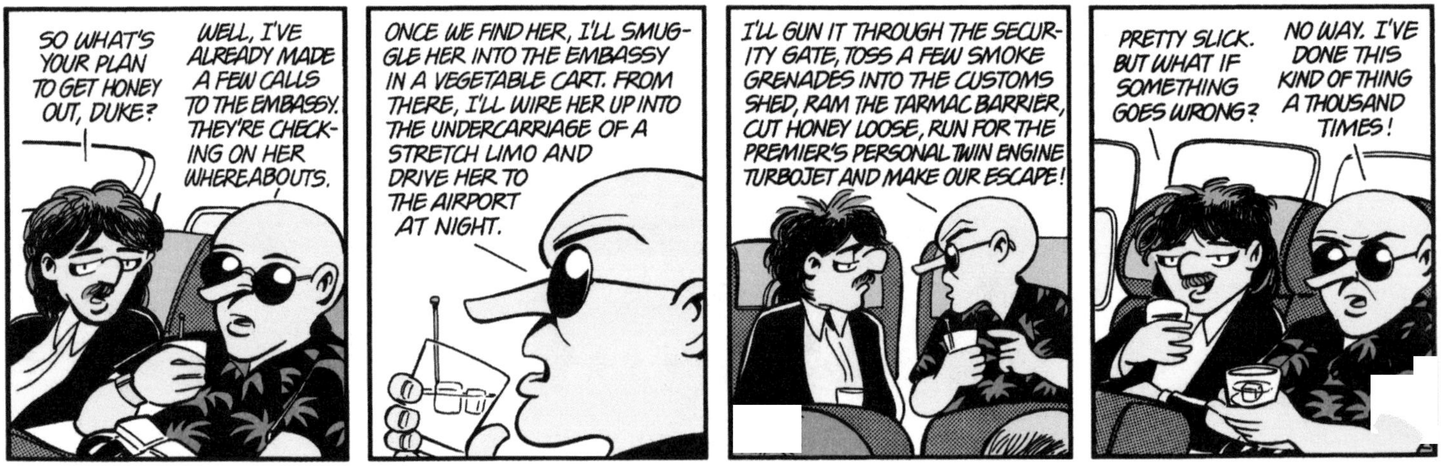
SO WHAT'S YOUR PLAN TO GET HONEY OUT, DUKE?
WELL, I'VE ALREADY MADE A FEW CALLS TO THE EMBASSY. THEY'RE CHECKING ON HER WHEREABOUTS.
ONCE WE FIND HER, I'LL SMUGGLE HER INTO THE EMBASSY IN A VEGETABLE CART. FROM THERE, I'LL WIRE HER UP INTO THE UNDERCARRIAGE OF A STRETCH LIMO AND DRIVE HER TO THE AIRPORT AT NIGHT.
I'LL GUN IT THROUGH THE SECURITY GATE, TOSS A FEW SMOKE GRENADES INTO THE CUSTOMS SHED, RAM THE TARMAC BARRIER, CUT HONEY LOOSE, RUN FOR THE PREMIER'S PERSONAL TWIN ENGINE TURBOJET AND MAKE OUR ESCAPE!
PRETTY SLICK. BUT WHAT IF SOMETHING GOES WRONG?
NO WAY. I'VE DONE THIS KIND OF THING A THOUSAND TIMES!

July 19, 1989

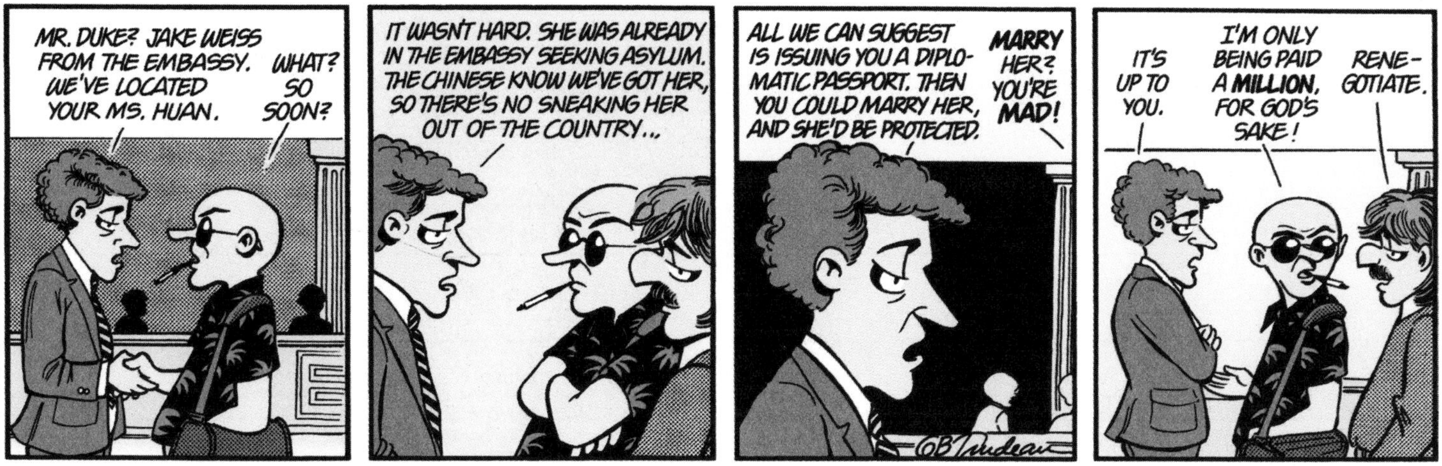
MR. DUKE? JAKE WEISS FROM THE EMBASSY. WE'VE LOCATED YOUR MS. HUAN.
WHAT? SO SOON?
IT WASN'T HARD. SHE WAS ALREADY IN THE EMBASSY SEEKING ASYLUM. THE CHINESE KNOW WE'VE GOT HER, SO THERE'S NO SNEAKING HER OUT OF THE COUNTRY...
ALL WE CAN SUGGEST IS ISSUING YOU A DIPLOMATIC PASSPORT. THEN YOU COULD MARRY HER, AND SHE'D BE PROTECTED.
MARRY HER? YOU'RE MAD!
IT'S UP TO YOU.
I'M ONLY BEING PAID A MILLION, FOR GOD'S SAKE!
RENEGOTIATE.

July 20, 1989

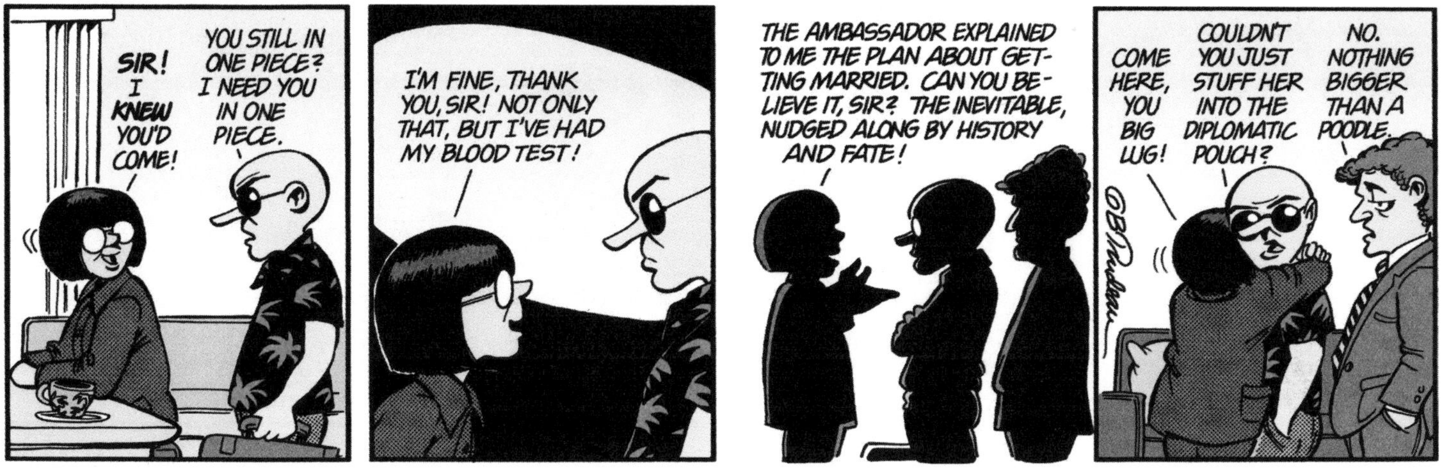
SIR! I KNEW YOU'D COME!
YOU STILL IN ONE PIECE? I NEED YOU IN ONE PIECE.
I'M FINE, THANK YOU, SIR! NOT ONLY THAT, BUT I'VE HAD MY BLOOD TEST!
THE AMBASSADOR EXPLAINED TO ME THE PLAN ABOUT GETTING MARRIED. CAN YOU BELIEVE IT, SIR? THE INEVITABLE, NUDGED ALONG BY HISTORY AND FATE!
COME HERE, YOU BIG LUG!
COULDN'T YOU JUST STUFF HER INTO THE DIPLOMATIC POUCH?
NO. NOTHING BIGGER THAN A POODLE.

July 21, 1989

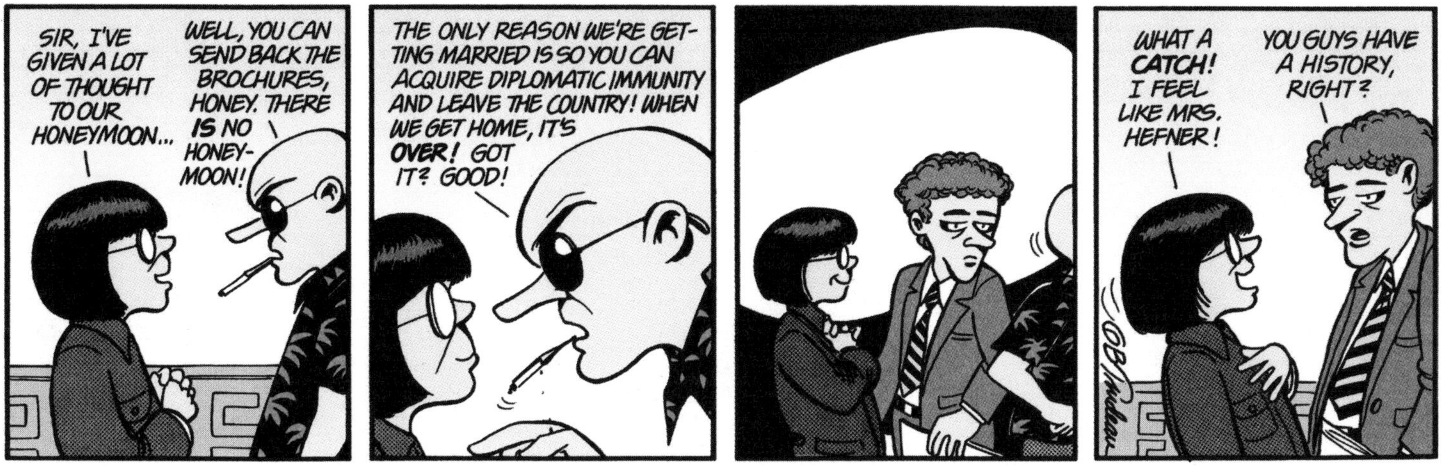
SIR, I'VE GIVEN A LOT OF THOUGHT TO OUR HONEYMOON...
WELL, YOU CAN SEND BACK THE BROCHURES, HONEY. THERE IS NO HONEYMOON!
THE ONLY REASON WE'RE GETTING MARRIED IS SO YOU CAN ACQUIRE DIPLOMATIC IMMUNITY AND LEAVE THE COUNTRY! WHEN WE GET HOME, IT'S OVER! GOT IT? GOOD!
WHAT A CATCH! I FEEL LIKE MRS. HEFNER!
YOU GUYS HAVE A HISTORY, RIGHT?

July 22, 1989

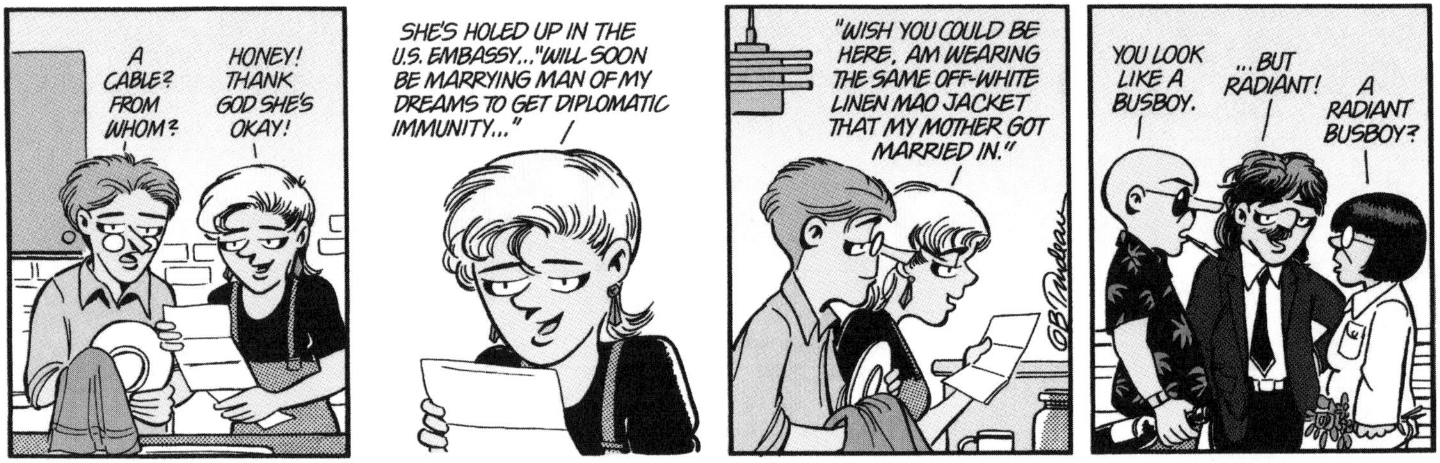
A CABLE? FROM WHOM?
HONEY! THANK GOD SHE'S OKAY!
SHE'S HOLED UP IN THE U.S. EMBASSY..."WILL SOON BE MARRYING MAN OF MY DREAMS TO GET DIPLOMATIC IMMUNITY..."
"WISH YOU COULD BE HERE. AM WEARING THE SAME OFF-WHITE LINEN MAO JACKET THAT MY MOTHER GOT MARRIED IN."
YOU LOOK LIKE A BUSBOY.
...BUT RADIANT!
A RADIANT BUSBOY?

July 24, 1989

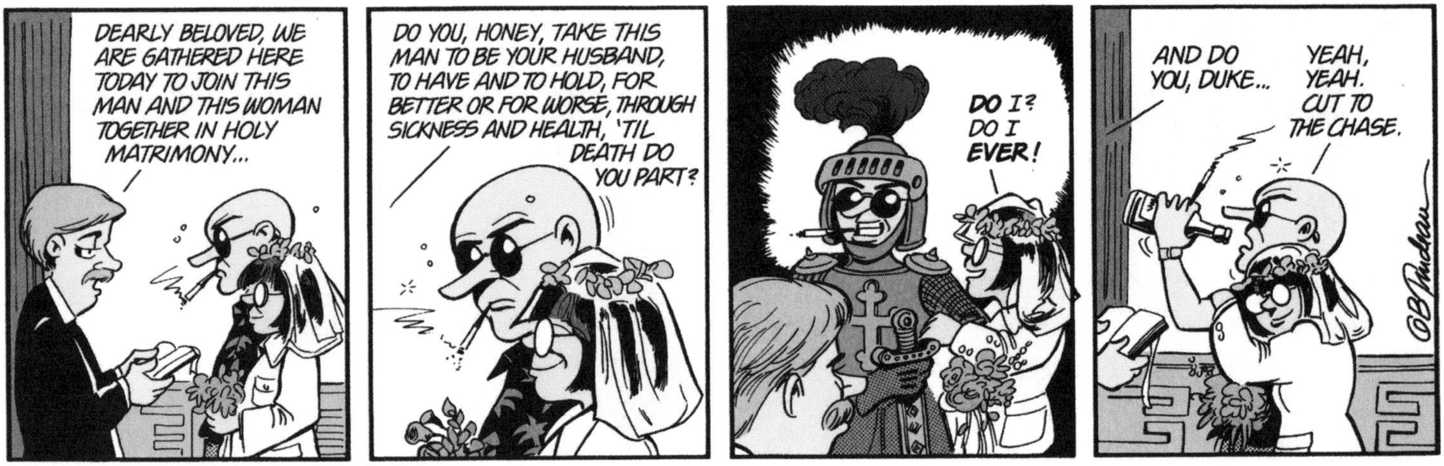
DEARLY BELOVED, WE ARE GATHERED HERE TODAY TO JOIN THIS MAN AND THIS WOMAN TOGETHER IN HOLY MATRIMONY...
DO YOU, HONEY, TAKE THIS MAN TO BE YOUR HUSBAND, TO HAVE AND TO HOLD, FOR BETTER OR FOR WORSE, THROUGH SICKNESS AND HEALTH, 'TIL DEATH DO YOU PART?
DO I? DO I EVER!
AND DO YOU, DUKE...
YEAH, YEAH. CUT TO THE CHASE.

July 25, 1989

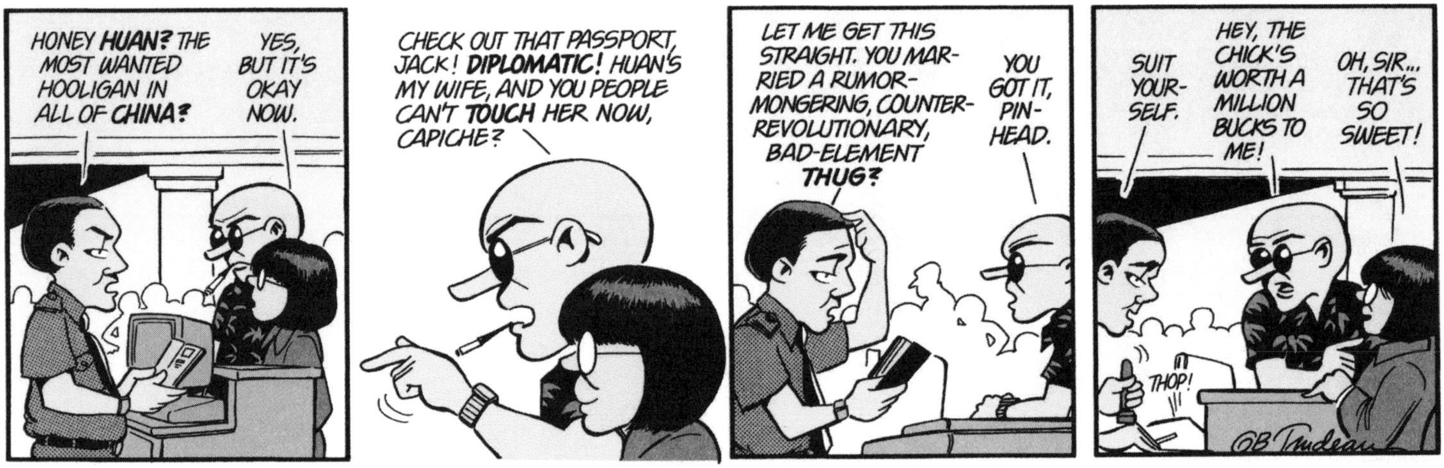
HONEY HUAN? THE MOST WANTED HOOLIGAN IN ALL OF CHINA?
YES, BUT IT'S OKAY NOW.
CHECK OUT THAT PASSPORT, JACK! DIPLOMATIC! HUAN'S MY WIFE, AND YOU PEOPLE CAN'T TOUCH HER NOW, CAPICHE?
LET ME GET THIS STRAIGHT. YOU MARRIED A RUMOR-MONGERING, COUNTER-REVOLUTIONARY, BAD-ELEMENT THUG?
YOU GOT IT, PIN-HEAD.
SUIT YOURSELF.
HEY, THE CHICK'S WORTH A MILLION BUCKS TO ME!
OH, SIR... THAT'S SO SWEET!
THOP!

July 26, 1989

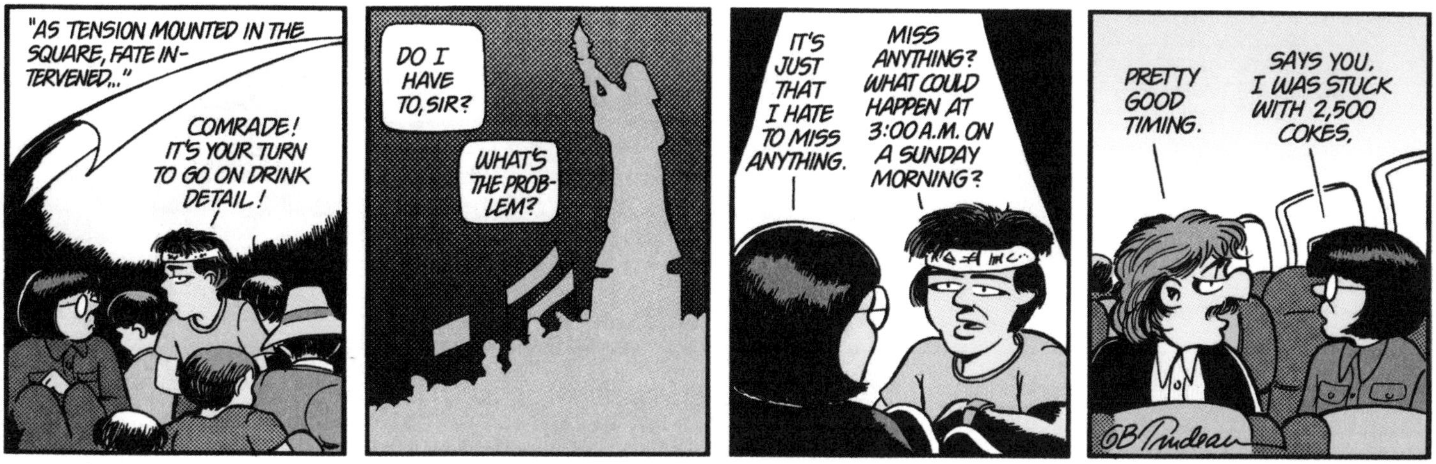
"AS TENSION MOUNTED IN THE SQUARE, FATE INTERVENED..."
COMRADE! IT'S YOUR TURN TO GO ON DRINK DETAIL!
DO I HAVE TO, SIR?
WHAT'S THE PROBLEM?
IT'S JUST THAT I HATE TO MISS ANYTHING.
MISS ANYTHING? WHAT COULD HAPPEN AT 3:00 A.M. ON A SUNDAY MORNING?
PRETTY GOOD TIMING.
SAYS YOU. I WAS STUCK WITH 2,500 COKES.

July 31, 1989

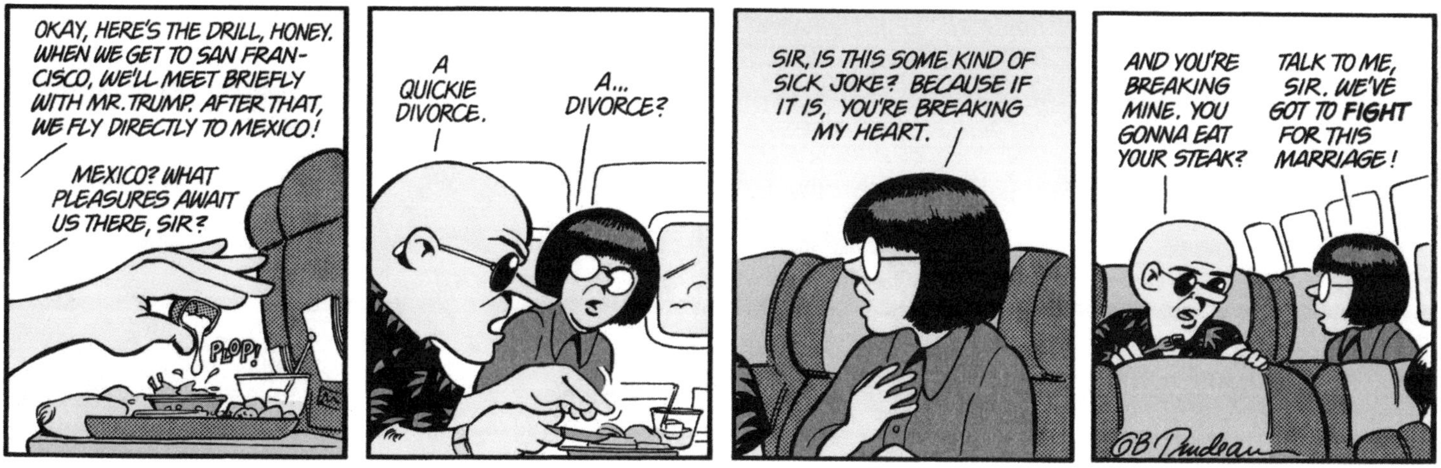
OKAY, HERE'S THE DRILL, HONEY. WHEN WE GET TO SAN FRANCISCO, WE'LL MEET BRIEFLY WITH MR. TRUMP. AFTER THAT, WE FLY DIRECTLY TO MEXICO!
MEXICO? WHAT PLEASURES AWAIT US THERE, SIR?
PLOP!
A QUICKIE DIVORCE.
A... DIVORCE?
SIR, IS THIS SOME KIND OF SICK JOKE? BECAUSE IF IT IS, YOU'RE BREAKING MY HEART.
AND YOU'RE BREAKING MINE. YOU GONNA EAT YOUR STEAK?
TALK TO ME, SIR. WE'VE GOT TO FIGHT FOR THIS MARRIAGE!

August 1, 1989

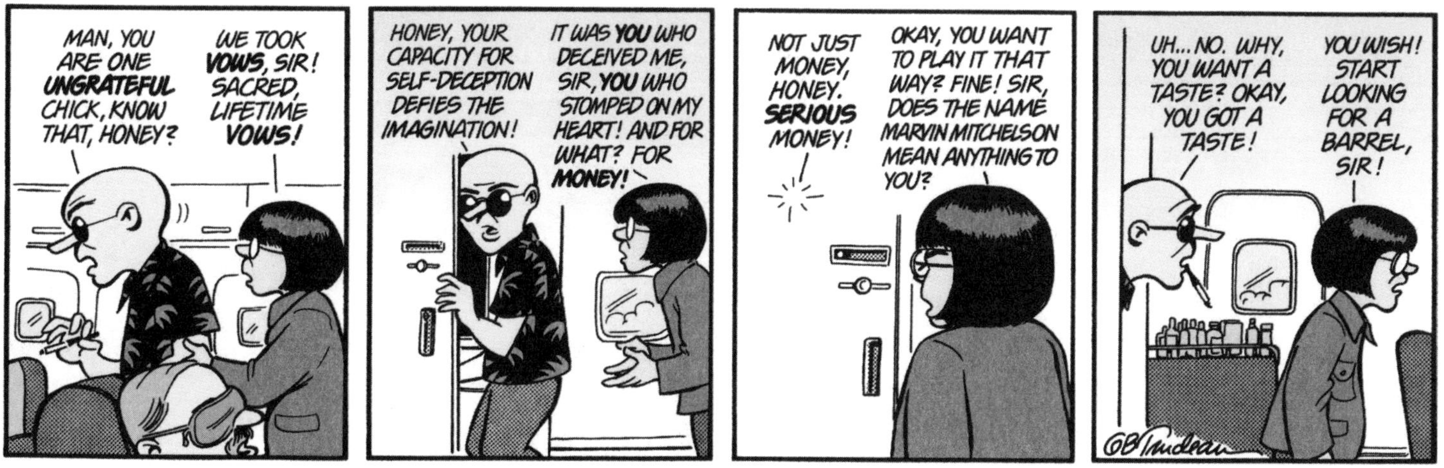
MAN, YOU ARE ONE UNGRATEFUL CHICK, KNOW THAT, HONEY?
WE TOOK VOWS, SIR! SACRED, LIFETIME VOWS!
HONEY, YOUR CAPACITY FOR SELF-DECEPTION DEFIES THE IMAGINATION!
IT WAS YOU WHO DECEIVED ME, SIR, YOU WHO STOMPED ON MY HEART! AND FOR WHAT? FOR MONEY!
NOT JUST MONEY, HONEY. SERIOUS MONEY!
OKAY, YOU WANT TO PLAY IT THAT WAY? FINE! SIR, DOES THE NAME MARVIN MITCHELSON MEAN ANYTHING TO YOU?
UH... NO. WHY, YOU WANT A TASTE? OKAY, YOU GOT A TASTE!
YOU WISH! START LOOKING FOR A BARREL, SIR!

August 2, 1989

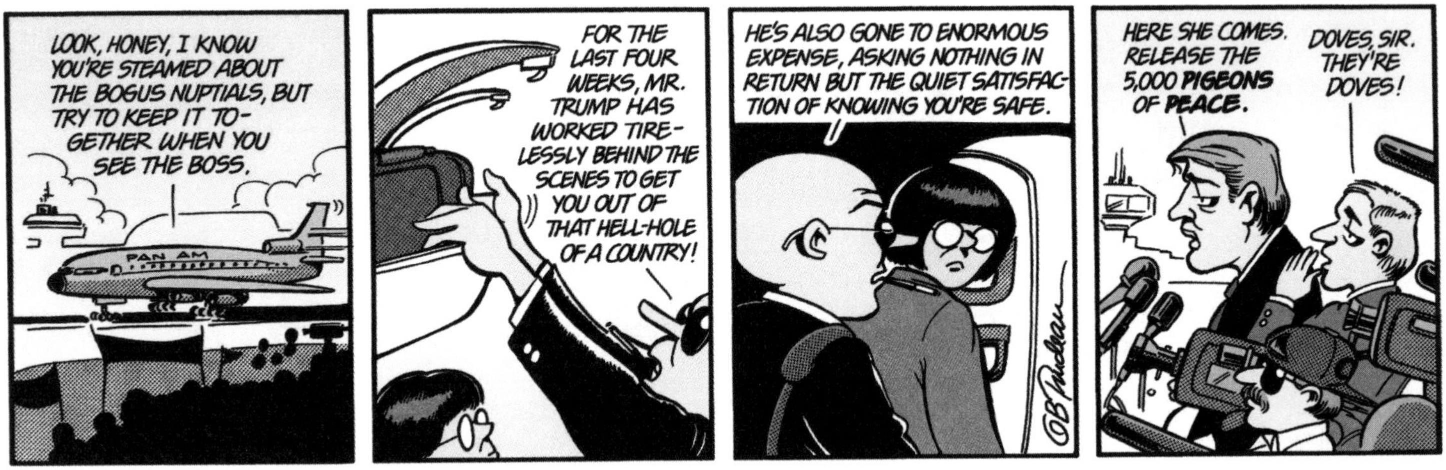
LOOK, HONEY, I KNOW YOU'RE STEAMED ABOUT THE BOGUS NUPTIALS, BUT TRY TO KEEP IT TOGETHER WHEN YOU SEE THE BOSS.
PAN AM
FOR THE LAST FOUR WEEKS, MR. TRUMP HAS WORKED TIRELESSLY BEHIND THE SCENES TO GET YOU OUT OF THAT HELL-HOLE OF A COUNTRY!
HE'S ALSO GONE TO ENORMOUS EXPENSE, ASKING NOTHING IN RETURN BUT THE QUIET SATISFACTION OF KNOWING YOU'RE SAFE.
HERE SHE COMES. RELEASE THE 5,000 **PIGEONS** OF **PEACE**.
DOVES, SIR. THEY'RE DOVES!

August 3, 1989

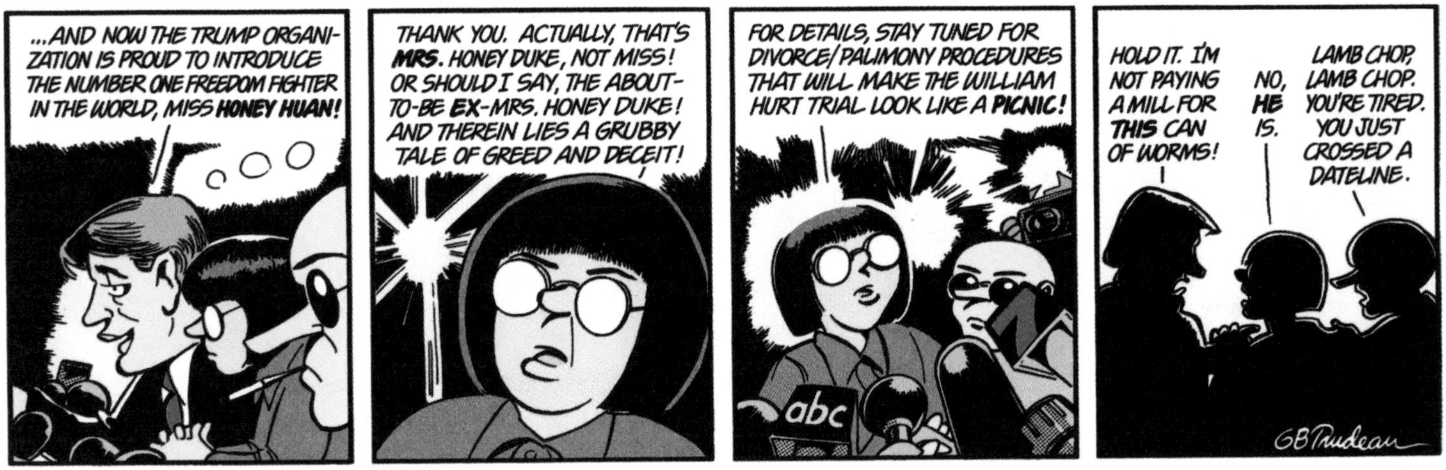
...AND NOW THE TRUMP ORGANIZATION IS PROUD TO INTRODUCE THE NUMBER ONE FREEDOM FIGHTER IN THE WORLD, MISS **HONEY HUAN!**
THANK YOU. ACTUALLY, THAT'S **MRS.** HONEY DUKE, NOT MISS! OR SHOULD I SAY, THE ABOUT-TO-BE **EX**-MRS. HONEY DUKE! AND THEREIN LIES A GRUBBY TALE OF GREED AND DECEIT!
FOR DETAILS, STAY TUNED FOR DIVORCE/PALIMONY PROCEDURES THAT WILL MAKE THE WILLIAM HURT TRIAL LOOK LIKE A **PICNIC!**
abc
HOLD IT. I'M NOT PAYING A MILL FOR **THIS** CAN OF WORMS!
NO, **HE** IS.
LAMB CHOP, LAMB CHOP. YOU'RE TIRED. YOU JUST CROSSED A DATELINE.

August 4, 1989

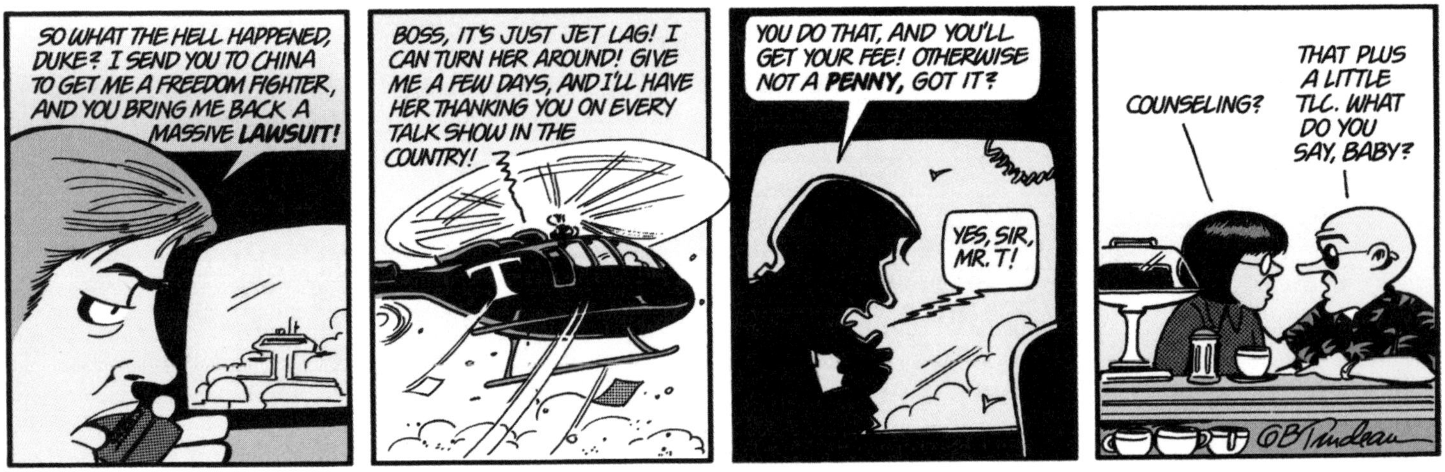
SO WHAT THE HELL HAPPENED, DUKE? I SEND YOU TO CHINA TO GET ME A FREEDOM FIGHTER, AND YOU BRING ME BACK A MASSIVE **LAWSUIT!**
BOSS, IT'S JUST JET LAG! I CAN TURN HER AROUND! GIVE ME A FEW DAYS, AND I'LL HAVE HER THANKING YOU ON EVERY TALK SHOW IN THE COUNTRY!
YOU DO THAT, AND YOU'LL GET YOUR FEE! OTHERWISE NOT A **PENNY,** GOT IT?
YES, SIR, MR. T!
COUNSELING?
THAT PLUS A LITTLE TLC. WHAT DO YOU SAY, BABY?

August 5, 1989

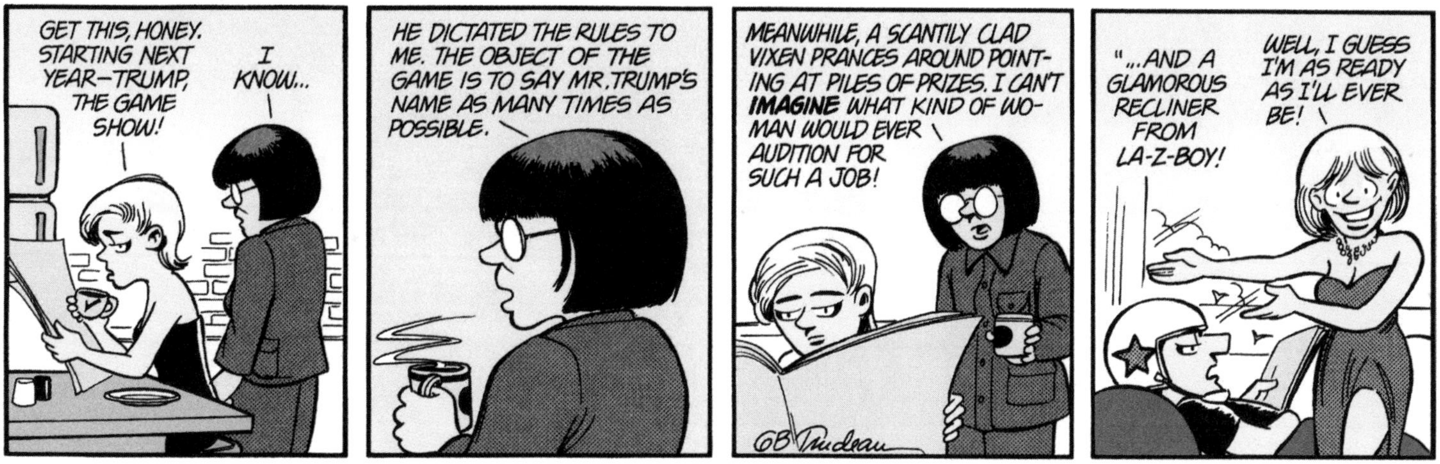
GET THIS, HONEY. STARTING NEXT YEAR—TRUMP, THE GAME SHOW!
I KNOW...
HE DICTATED THE RULES TO ME. THE OBJECT OF THE GAME IS TO SAY MR. TRUMP'S NAME AS MANY TIMES AS POSSIBLE.
MEANWHILE, A SCANTILY CLAD VIXEN PRANCES AROUND POINTING AT PILES OF PRIZES. I CAN'T IMAGINE WHAT KIND OF WOMAN WOULD EVER AUDITION FOR SUCH A JOB!
"...AND A GLAMOROUS RECLINER FROM LA-Z-BOY!
WELL, I GUESS I'M AS READY AS I'LL EVER BE!

September 18, 1989

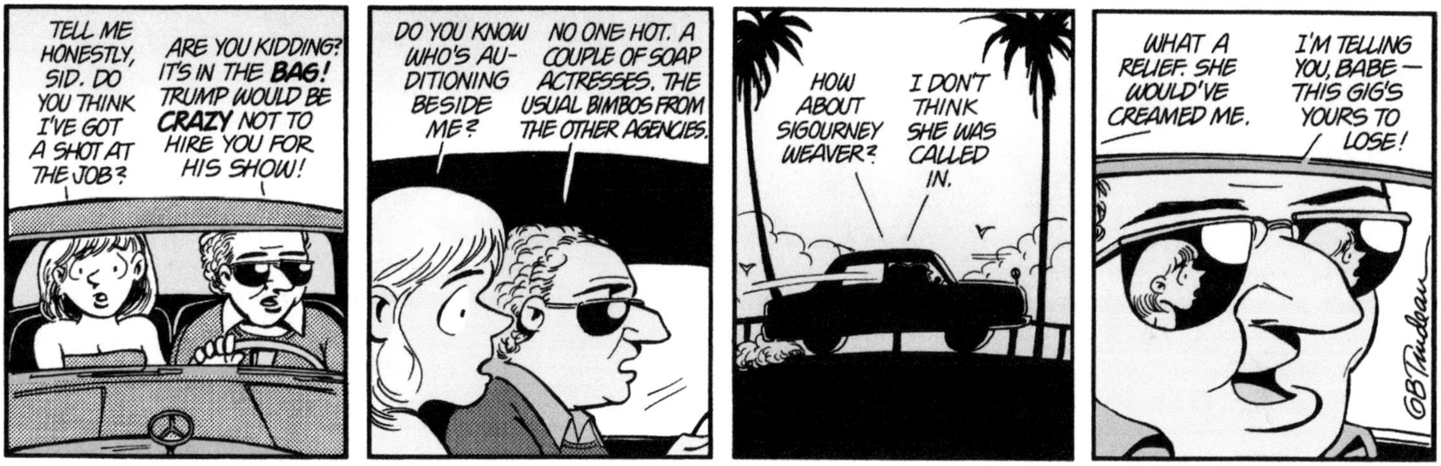
TELL ME HONESTLY, SID. DO YOU THINK I'VE GOT A SHOT AT THE JOB?
ARE YOU KIDDING? IT'S IN THE BAG! TRUMP WOULD BE CRAZY NOT TO HIRE YOU FOR HIS SHOW!
DO YOU KNOW WHO'S AUDITIONING BESIDE ME?
NO ONE HOT. A COUPLE OF SOAP ACTRESSES. THE USUAL BIMBOS FROM THE OTHER AGENCIES.
HOW ABOUT SIGOURNEY WEAVER?
I DON'T THINK SHE WAS CALLED IN.
WHAT A RELIEF. SHE WOULD'VE CREAMED ME.
I'M TELLING YOU, BABE—THIS GIG'S YOURS TO LOSE!

September 19, 1989

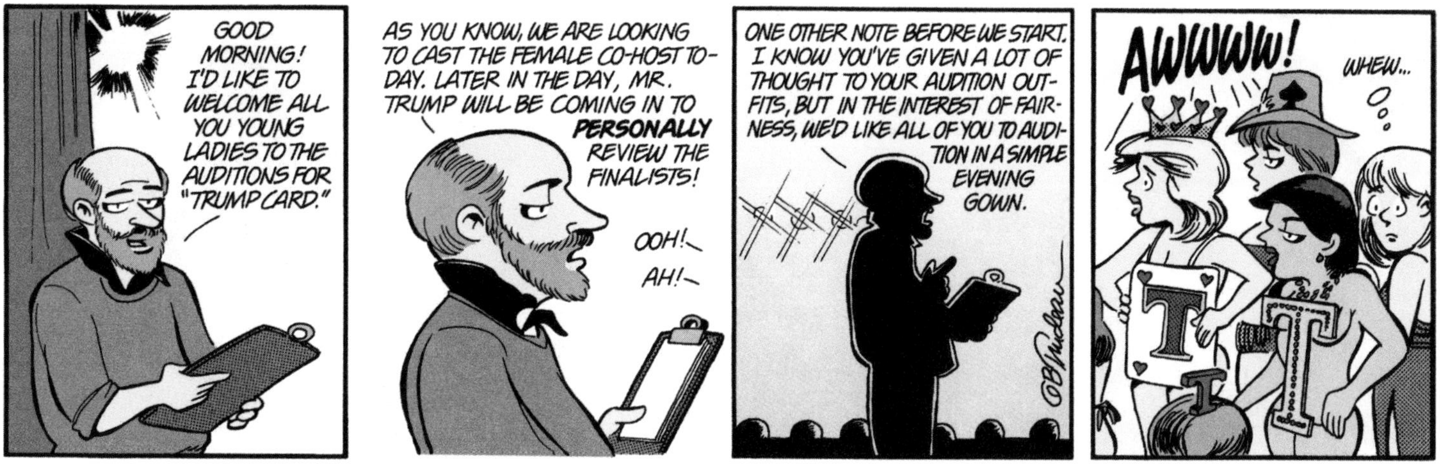
GOOD MORNING! I'D LIKE TO WELCOME ALL YOU YOUNG LADIES TO THE AUDITIONS FOR "TRUMP CARD."
AS YOU KNOW, WE ARE LOOKING TO CAST THE FEMALE CO-HOST TODAY. LATER IN THE DAY, MR. TRUMP WILL BE COMING IN TO PERSONALLY REVIEW THE FINALISTS!
OOH!
AH!
ONE OTHER NOTE BEFORE WE START. I KNOW YOU'VE GIVEN A LOT OF THOUGHT TO YOUR AUDITION OUTFITS, BUT IN THE INTEREST OF FAIRNESS, WE'D LIKE ALL OF YOU TO AUDITION IN A SIMPLE EVENING GOWN.
AWWWW!
WHEW...

September 20, 1989

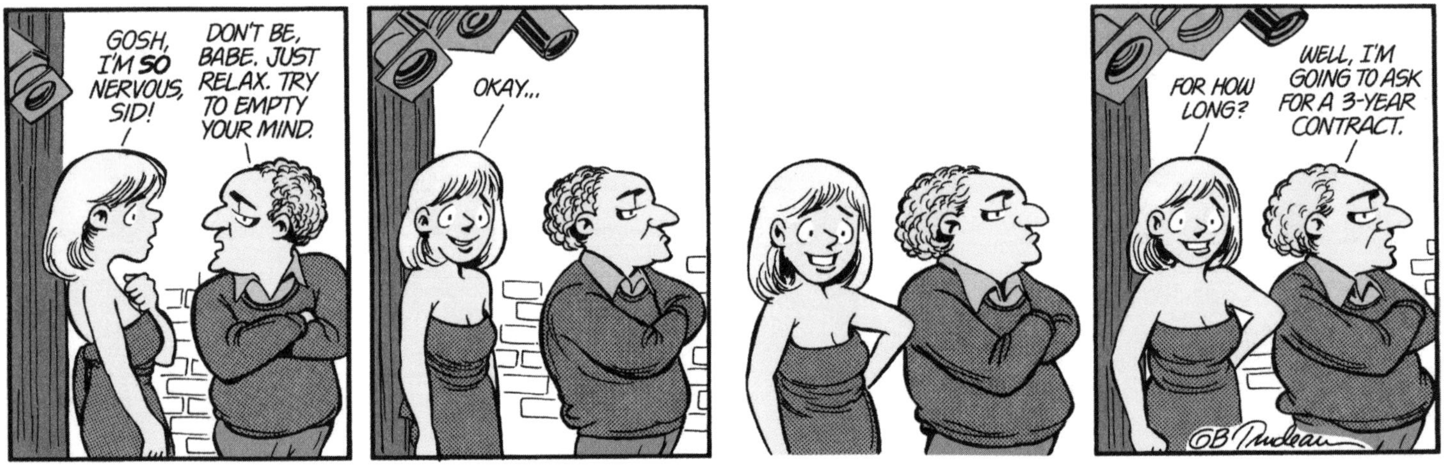
GOSH, I'M SO NERVOUS, SID!
DON'T BE, BABE. JUST RELAX. TRY TO EMPTY YOUR MIND.
OKAY...
FOR HOW LONG?
WELL, I'M GOING TO ASK FOR A 3-YEAR CONTRACT.
GB Trudeau

September 21, 1989

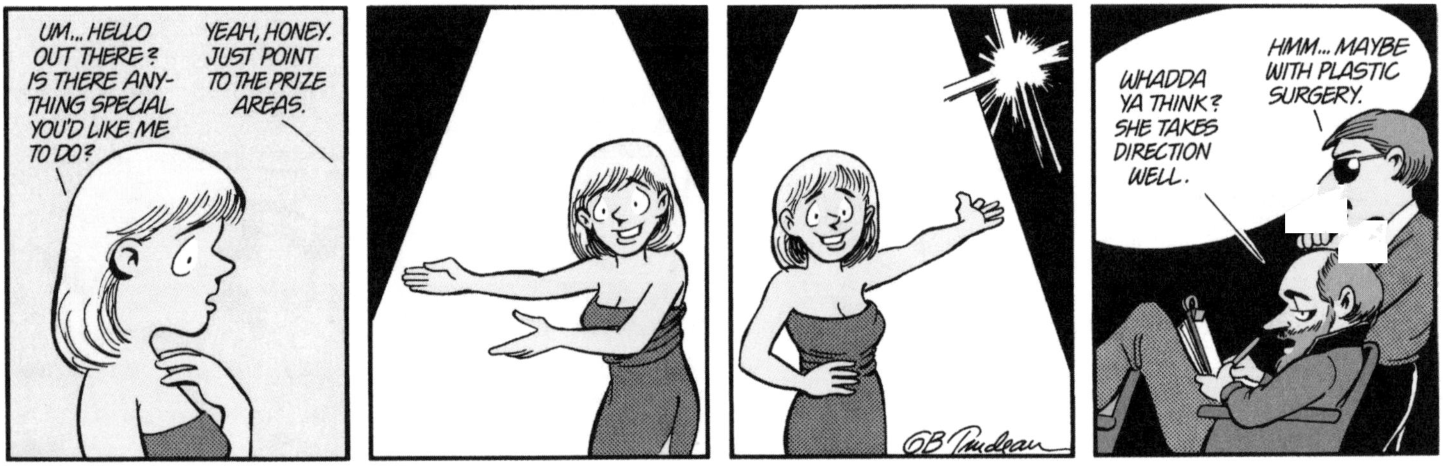
UM... HELLO OUT THERE? IS THERE ANYTHING SPECIAL YOU'D LIKE ME TO DO?
YEAH, HONEY. JUST POINT TO THE PRIZE AREAS.
GB Trudeau
WHADDA YA THINK? SHE TAKES DIRECTION WELL.
HMM... MAYBE WITH PLASTIC SURGERY.

September 22, 1989

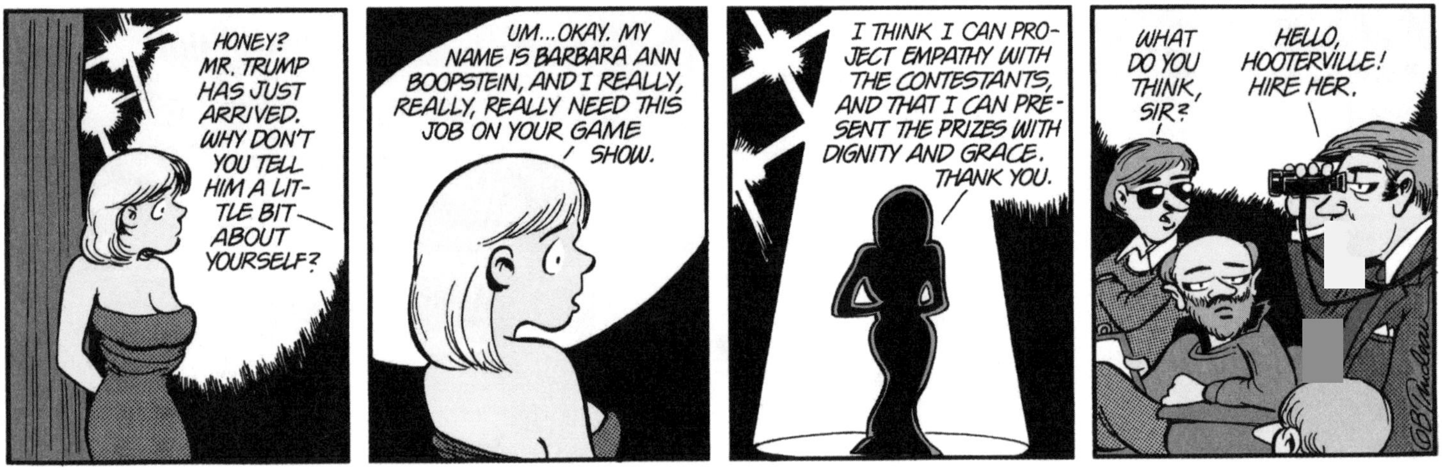
HONEY? MR. TRUMP HAS JUST ARRIVED. WHY DON'T YOU TELL HIM A LITTLE BIT ABOUT YOURSELF?
UM...OKAY. MY NAME IS BARBARA ANN BOOPSTEIN, AND I REALLY, REALLY, REALLY NEED THIS JOB ON YOUR GAME SHOW.
I THINK I CAN PROJECT EMPATHY WITH THE CONTESTANTS, AND THAT I CAN PRESENT THE PRIZES WITH DIGNITY AND GRACE. THANK YOU.
WHAT DO YOU THINK, SIR?
HELLO, HOOTERVILLE! HIRE HER.
GB Trudeau

September 23, 1989

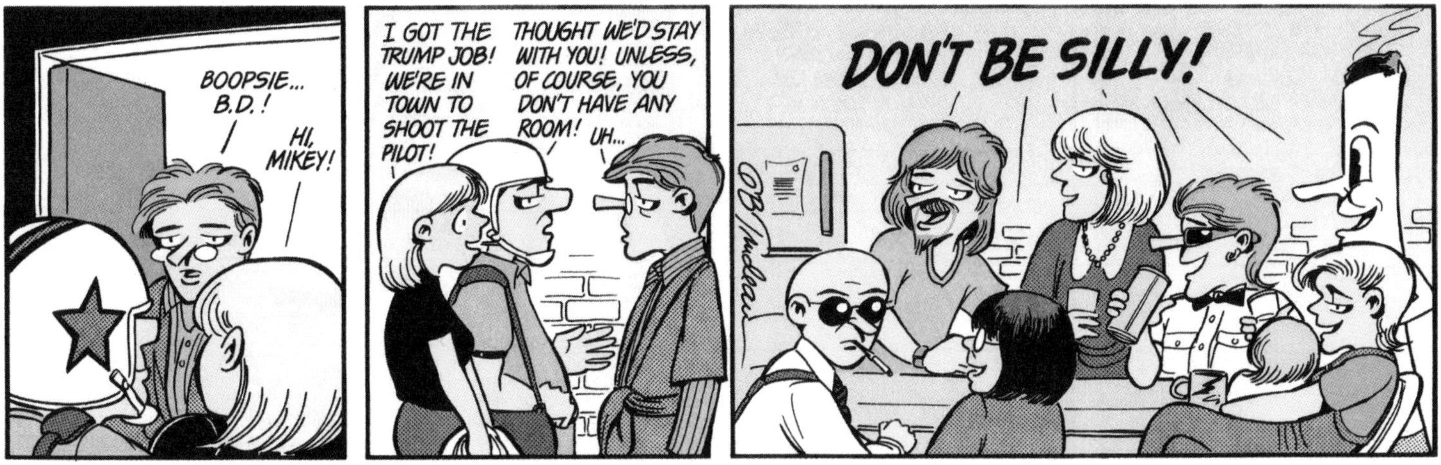
BOOPSIE... B.D.!
HI, MIKEY!
I GOT THE TRUMP JOB! WE'RE IN TOWN TO SHOOT THE PILOT!
THOUGHT WE'D STAY WITH YOU! UNLESS, OF COURSE, YOU DON'T HAVE ANY ROOM!
UH...
DON'T BE SILLY!

October 2, 1989

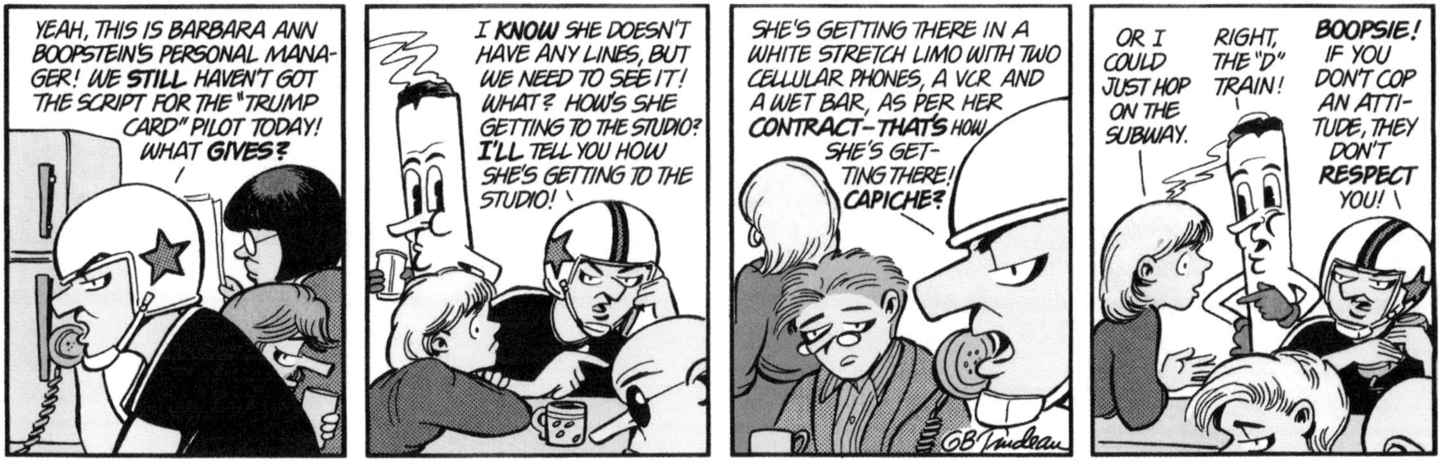
YEAH, THIS IS BARBARA ANN BOOPSTEIN'S PERSONAL MANAGER! WE STILL HAVEN'T GOT THE SCRIPT FOR THE "TRUMP CARD" PILOT TODAY! WHAT GIVES?
I KNOW SHE DOESN'T HAVE ANY LINES, BUT WE NEED TO SEE IT! WHAT? HOW'S SHE GETTING TO THE STUDIO? I'LL TELL YOU HOW SHE'S GETTING TO THE STUDIO!
SHE'S GETTING THERE IN A WHITE STRETCH LIMO WITH TWO CELLULAR PHONES, A VCR AND A WET BAR, AS PER HER CONTRACT–THAT'S HOW SHE'S GETTING THERE! CAPICHE?
OR I COULD JUST HOP ON THE SUBWAY.
RIGHT, THE "D" TRAIN!
BOOPSIE! IF YOU DON'T COP AN ATTITUDE, THEY DON'T RESPECT YOU!

October 3, 1989

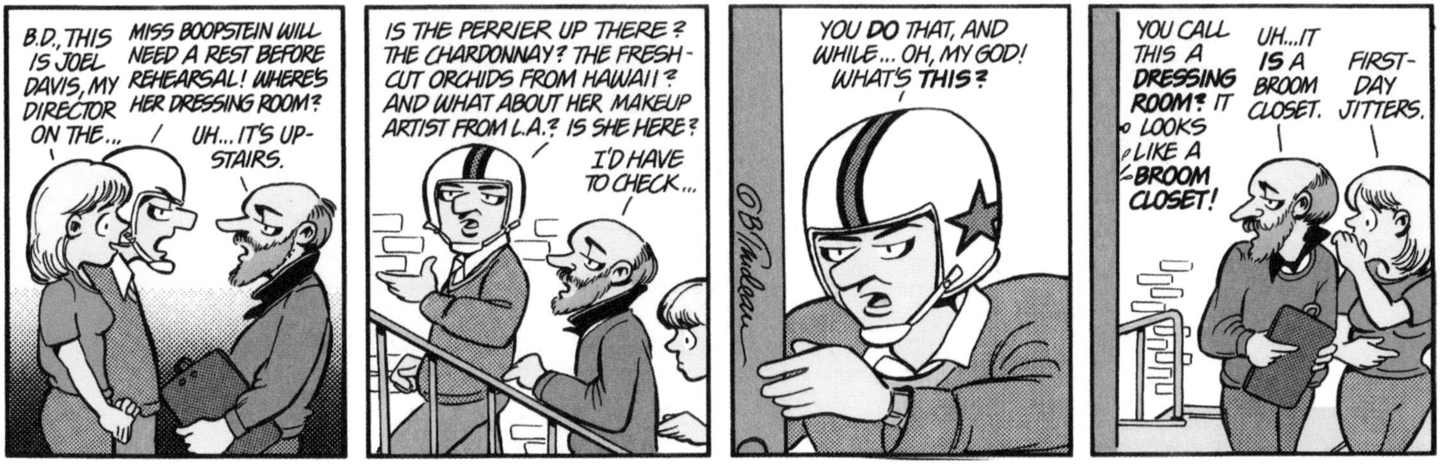
B.D., THIS IS JOEL DAVIS, MY DIRECTOR ON THE...
MISS BOOPSTEIN WILL NEED A REST BEFORE REHEARSAL! WHERE'S HER DRESSING ROOM?
UH... IT'S UPSTAIRS.
IS THE PERRIER UP THERE? THE CHARDONNAY? THE FRESH-CUT ORCHIDS FROM HAWAII? AND WHAT ABOUT HER MAKEUP ARTIST FROM L.A.? IS SHE HERE?
I'D HAVE TO CHECK...
YOU DO THAT, AND WHILE... OH, MY GOD! WHAT'S THIS?
YOU CALL THIS A DRESSING ROOM? IT LOOKS LIKE A BROOM CLOSET!
UH...IT IS A BROOM CLOSET.
FIRST-DAY JITTERS.

October 4, 1989

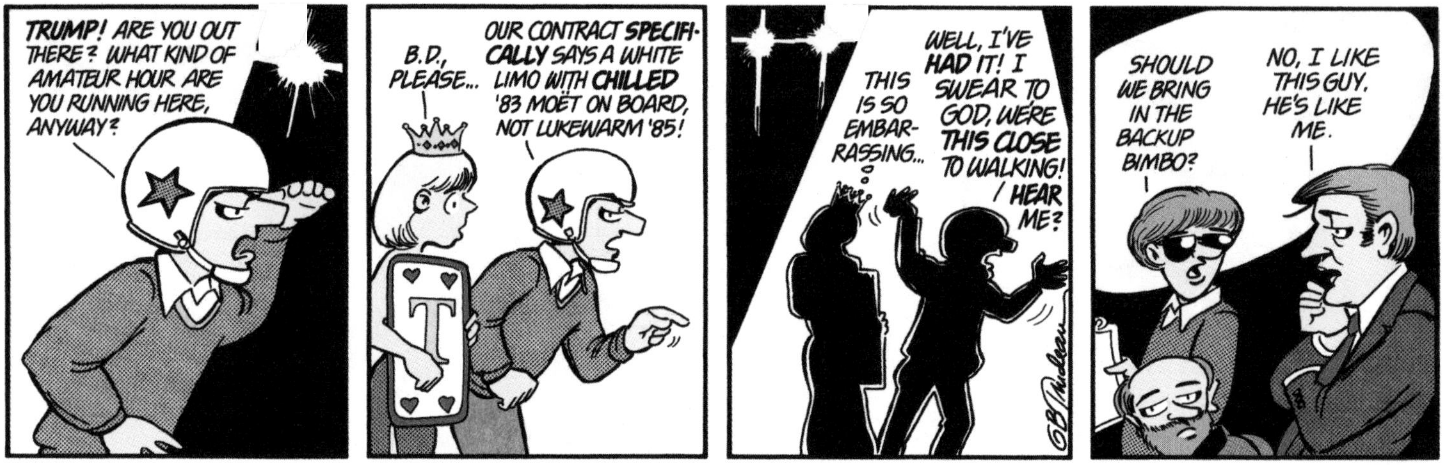
TRUMP! ARE YOU OUT THERE? WHAT KIND OF AMATEUR HOUR ARE YOU RUNNING HERE, ANYWAY?
B.D., PLEASE...
OUR CONTRACT SPECIFICALLY SAYS A WHITE LIMO WITH CHILLED '83 MOËT ON BOARD, NOT LUKEWARM '85!
THIS IS SO EMBARRASSING...
WELL, I'VE HAD IT! I SWEAR TO GOD, WE'RE THIS CLOSE TO WALKING! HEAR ME?
SHOULD WE BRING IN THE BACKUP BIMBO?
NO, I LIKE THIS GUY. HE'S LIKE ME.

October 5, 1989

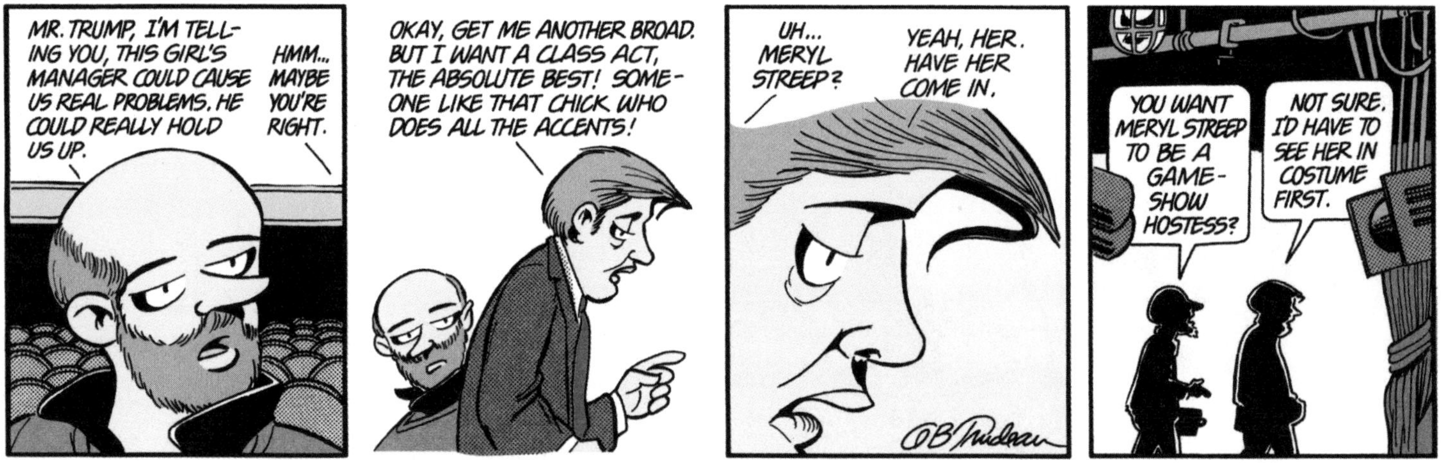
MR. TRUMP, I'M TELLING YOU, THIS GIRL'S MANAGER COULD CAUSE US REAL PROBLEMS. HE COULD REALLY HOLD US UP.
HMM... MAYBE YOU'RE RIGHT.
OKAY, GET ME ANOTHER BROAD. BUT I WANT A CLASS ACT, THE ABSOLUTE BEST! SOMEONE LIKE THAT CHICK WHO DOES ALL THE ACCENTS!
UH... MERYL STREEP?
YEAH, HER. HAVE HER COME IN.
YOU WANT MERYL STREEP TO BE A GAME-SHOW HOSTESS?
NOT SURE. I'D HAVE TO SEE HER IN COSTUME FIRST.

October 6, 1989

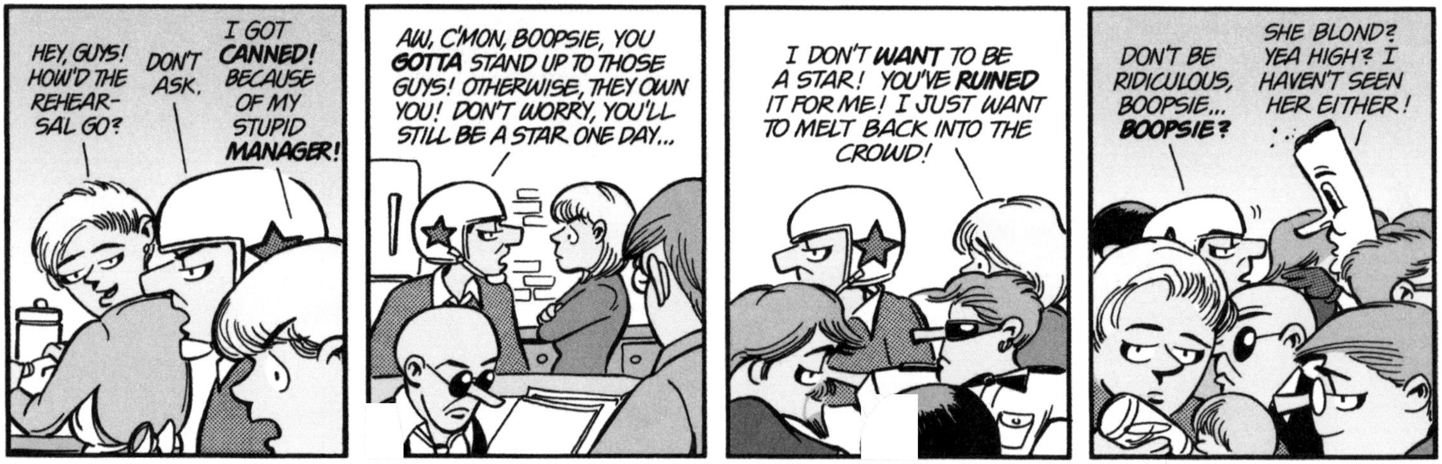
HEY, GUYS! HOW'D THE REHEARSAL GO?
DON'T ASK.
I GOT CANNED! BECAUSE OF MY STUPID MANAGER!
AW, C'MON, BOOPSIE, YOU GOTTA STAND UP TO THOSE GUYS! OTHERWISE, THEY OWN YOU! DON'T WORRY, YOU'LL STILL BE A STAR ONE DAY...
I DON'T WANT TO BE A STAR! YOU'VE RUINED IT FOR ME! I JUST WANT TO MELT BACK INTO THE CROWD!
DON'T BE RIDICULOUS, BOOPSIE... BOOPSIE?
SHE BLOND? YEA HIGH? I HAVEN'T SEEN HER EITHER!

October 7, 1989

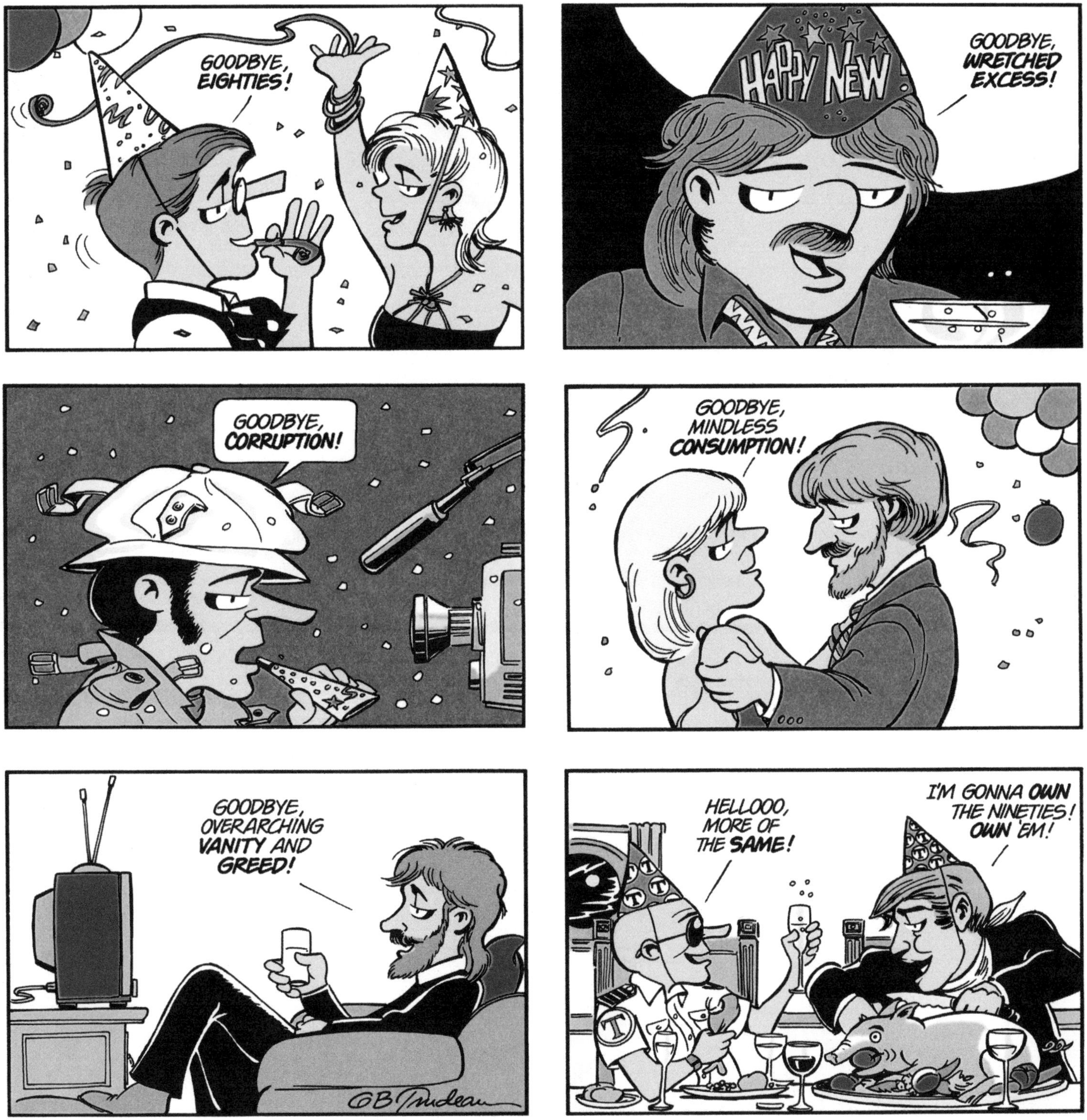
GOODBYE, EIGHTIES!
HAPPY NEW
GOODBYE, WRETCHED EXCESS!
GOODBYE, CORRUPTION!
GOODBYE, MINDLESS CONSUMPTION!
GOODBYE, OVERARCHING VANITY AND GREED!
GB Trudeau
HELLOOO, MORE OF THE SAME!
I'M GONNA OWN THE NINETIES! OWN 'EM!

December 31, 1989

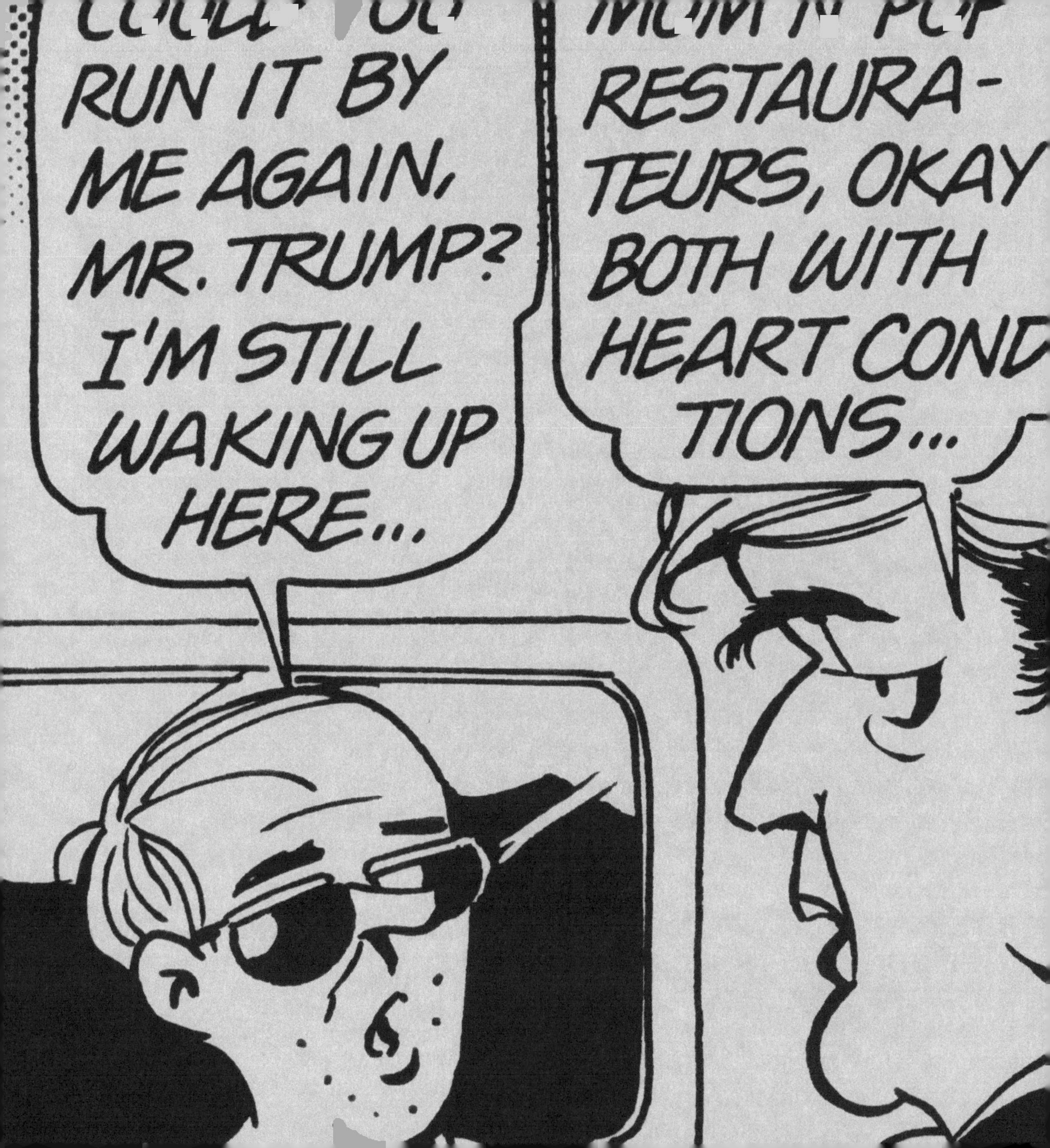
RUN IT BY ME AGAIN, MR. TRUMP? I'M STILL WAKING UP HERE...
RESTAURA-TEURS, OKAY BOTH WITH HEART COND TIONS...

1990s

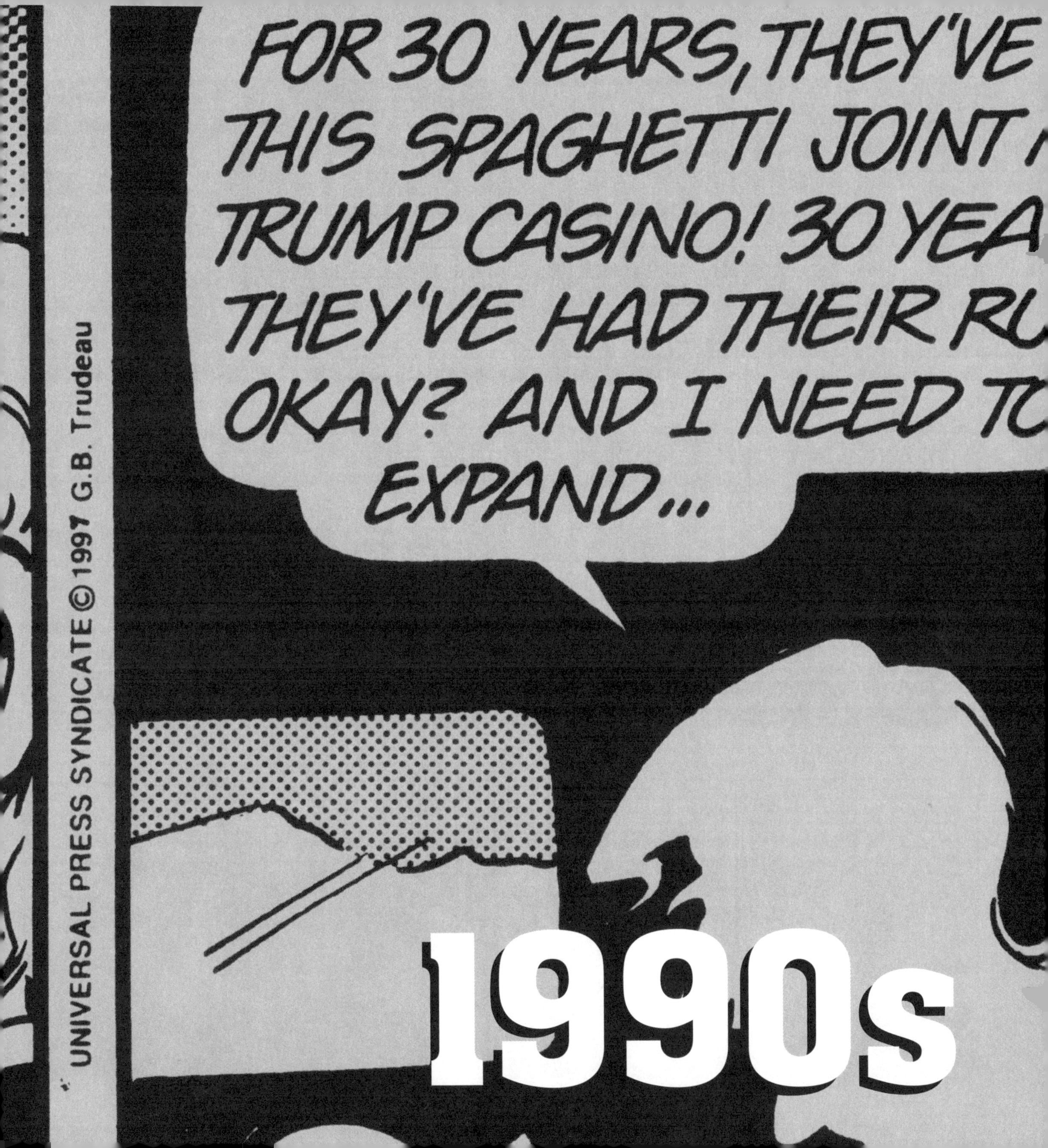
FOR 30 YEARS, THEY'VE
THIS SPAGHETTI JOINT
TRUMP CASINO! 30 YEA
THEY'VE HAD THEIR
OKAY? AND I NEED
EXPAND...
UNIVERSAL PRESS SYNDICATE © 1997 G.B. Trudeau

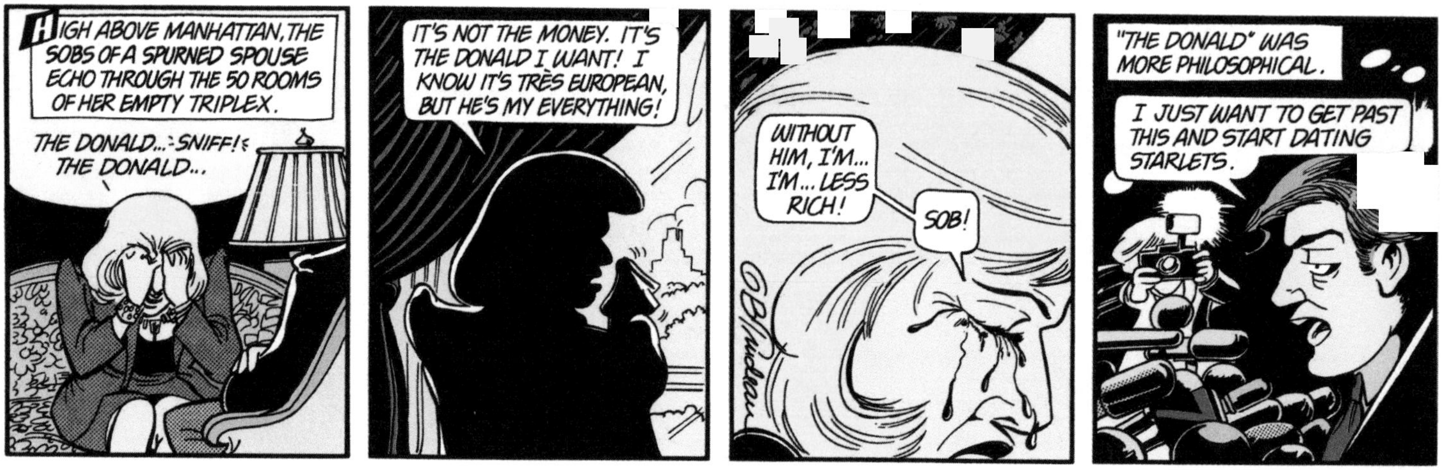
HIGH ABOVE MANHATTAN, THE SOBS OF A SPURNED SPOUSE ECHO THROUGH THE 50 ROOMS OF HER EMPTY TRIPLEX.
THE DONALD... SNIFF! THE DONALD...
IT'S NOT THE MONEY. IT'S THE DONALD I WANT! I KNOW IT'S TRÈS EUROPEAN, BUT HE'S MY EVERYTHING!
WITHOUT HIM, I'M... I'M... LESS RICH!
SOB!
"THE DONALD" WAS MORE PHILOSOPHICAL.
I JUST WANT TO GET PAST THIS AND START DATING STARLETS.

February 26, 1990

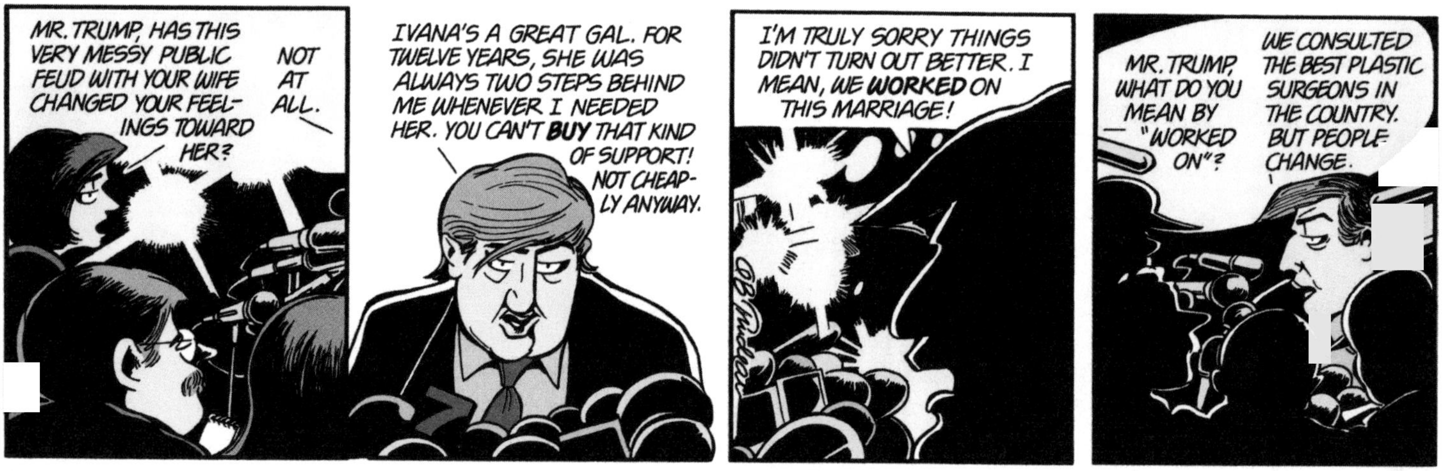
MR. TRUMP, HAS THIS VERY MESSY PUBLIC FEUD WITH YOUR WIFE CHANGED YOUR FEELINGS TOWARD HER?
NOT AT ALL.
IVANA'S A GREAT GAL. FOR TWELVE YEARS, SHE WAS ALWAYS TWO STEPS BEHIND ME WHENEVER I NEEDED HER. YOU CAN'T BUY THAT KIND OF SUPPORT! NOT CHEAPLY ANYWAY.
I'M TRULY SORRY THINGS DIDN'T TURN OUT BETTER. I MEAN, WE WORKED ON THIS MARRIAGE!
MR. TRUMP, WHAT DO YOU MEAN BY "WORKED ON"?
WE CONSULTED THE BEST PLASTIC SURGEONS IN THE COUNTRY. BUT PEOPLE CHANGE.

February 27, 1990

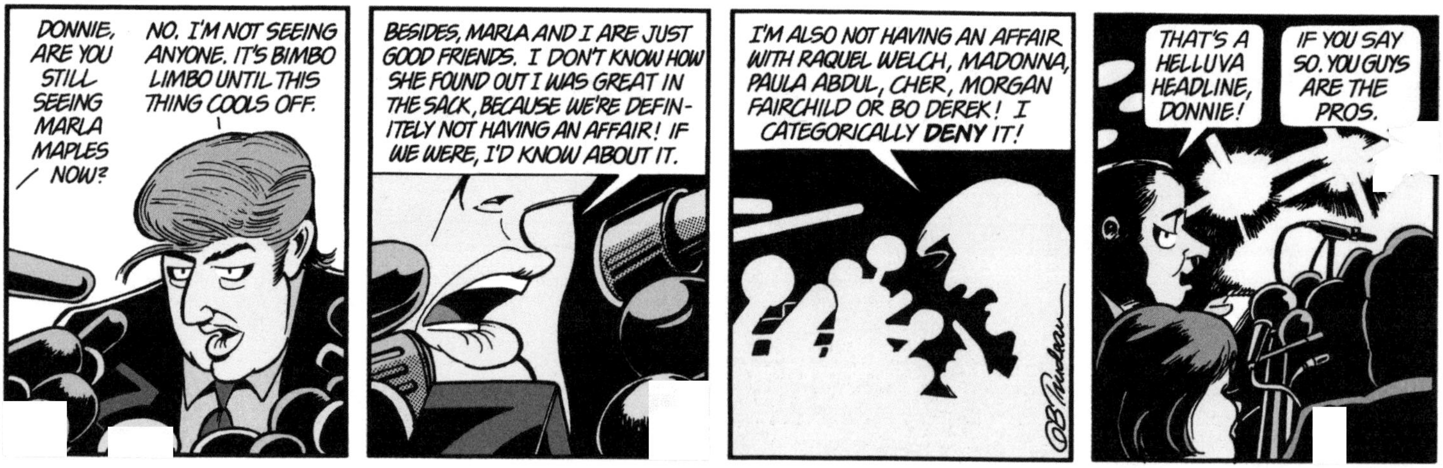
DONNIE, ARE YOU STILL SEEING MARLA MAPLES NOW?
NO. I'M NOT SEEING ANYONE. IT'S BIMBO LIMBO UNTIL THIS THING COOLS OFF.
BESIDES, MARLA AND I ARE JUST GOOD FRIENDS. I DON'T KNOW HOW SHE FOUND OUT I WAS GREAT IN THE SACK, BECAUSE WE'RE DEFINITELY NOT HAVING AN AFFAIR! IF WE WERE, I'D KNOW ABOUT IT.
I'M ALSO NOT HAVING AN AFFAIR WITH RAQUEL WELCH, MADONNA, PAULA ABDUL, CHER, MORGAN FAIRCHILD OR BO DEREK! I CATEGORICALLY DENY IT!
THAT'S A HELLUVA HEADLINE, DONNIE!
IF YOU SAY SO. YOU GUYS ARE THE PROS.

February 28, 1990

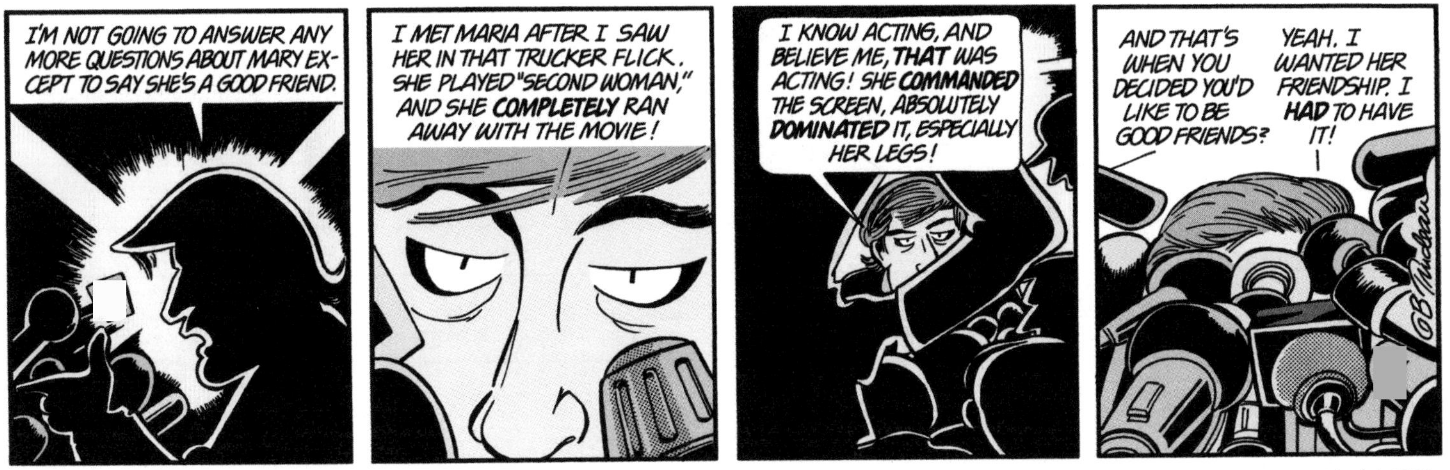
I'M NOT GOING TO ANSWER ANY MORE QUESTIONS ABOUT MARY EXCEPT TO SAY SHE'S A GOOD FRIEND.
I MET MARIA AFTER I SAW HER IN THAT TRUCKER FLICK. SHE PLAYED "SECOND WOMAN," AND SHE COMPLETELY RAN AWAY WITH THE MOVIE!
I KNOW ACTING, AND BELIEVE ME, THAT WAS ACTING! SHE COMMANDED THE SCREEN, ABSOLUTELY DOMINATED IT, ESPECIALLY HER LEGS!
AND THAT'S WHEN YOU DECIDED YOU'D LIKE TO BE GOOD FRIENDS?
YEAH. I WANTED HER FRIENDSHIP. I HAD TO HAVE IT!

March 1, 1990

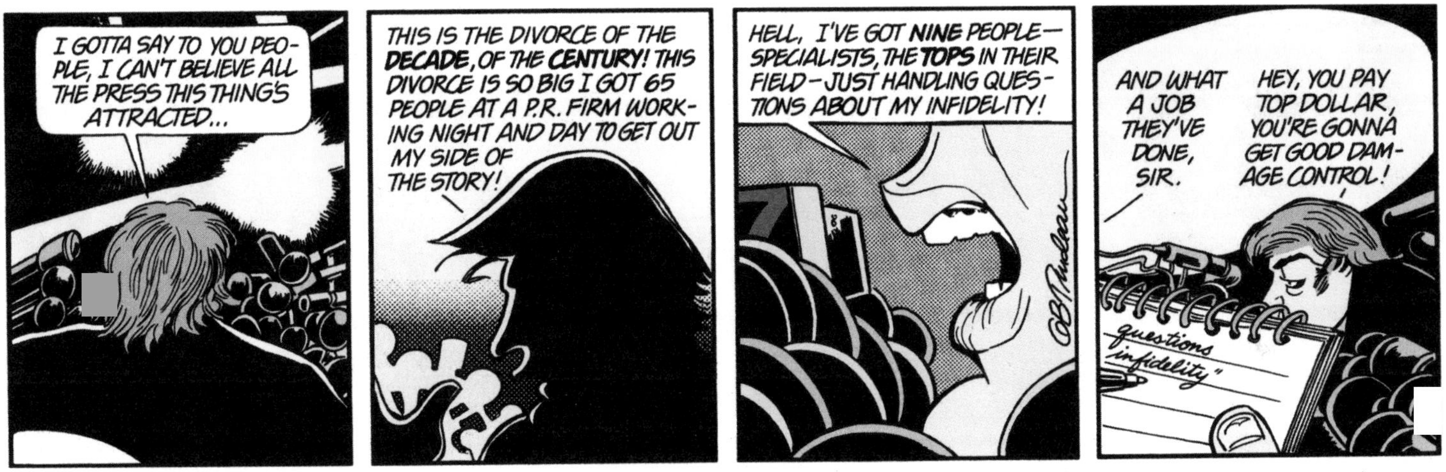
I GOTTA SAY TO YOU PEOPLE, I CAN'T BELIEVE ALL THE PRESS THIS THING'S ATTRACTED...
THIS IS THE DIVORCE OF THE DECADE, OF THE CENTURY! THIS DIVORCE IS SO BIG I GOT 65 PEOPLE AT A P.R. FIRM WORKING NIGHT AND DAY TO GET OUT MY SIDE OF THE STORY!
HELL, I'VE GOT NINE PEOPLE— SPECIALISTS, THE TOPS IN THEIR FIELD—JUST HANDLING QUESTIONS ABOUT MY INFIDELITY!
AND WHAT A JOB THEY'VE DONE, SIR.
HEY, YOU PAY TOP DOLLAR, YOU'RE GONNA GET GOOD DAMAGE CONTROL!
questions
infidelity"

March 2, 1990

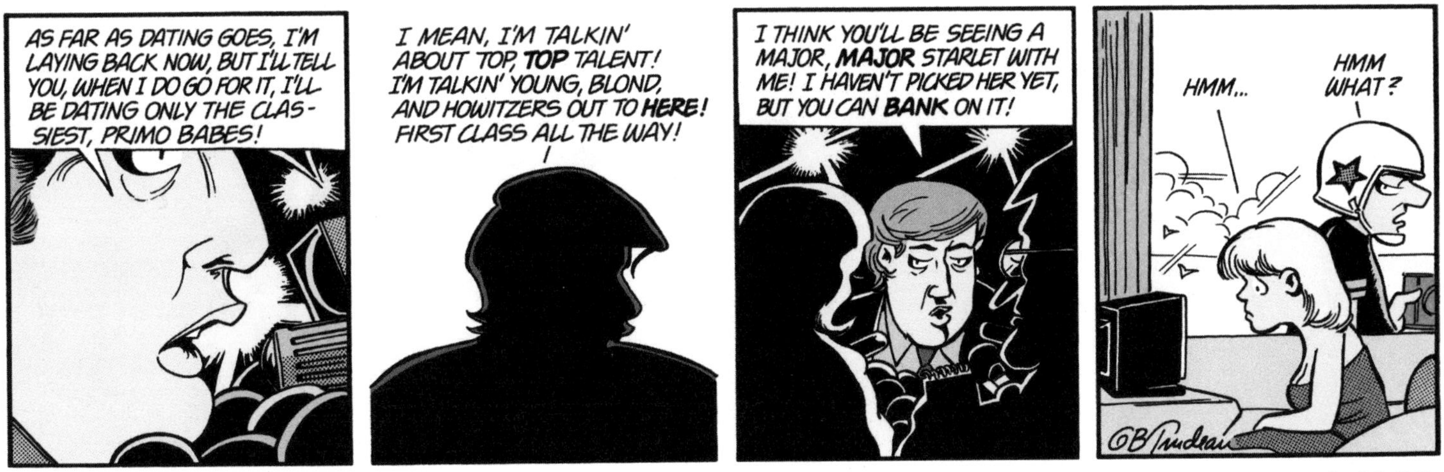
AS FAR AS DATING GOES, I'M LAYING BACK NOW, BUT I'LL TELL YOU, WHEN I DO GO FOR IT, I'LL BE DATING ONLY THE CLASSIEST, PRIMO BABES!
I MEAN, I'M TALKIN' ABOUT TOP, TOP TALENT! I'M TALKIN' YOUNG, BLOND, AND HOWITZERS OUT TO HERE! FIRST CLASS ALL THE WAY!
I THINK YOU'LL BE SEEING A MAJOR, MAJOR STARLET WITH ME! I HAVEN'T PICKED HER YET, BUT YOU CAN BANK ON IT!
HMM...
HMM WHAT?

March 3, 1990

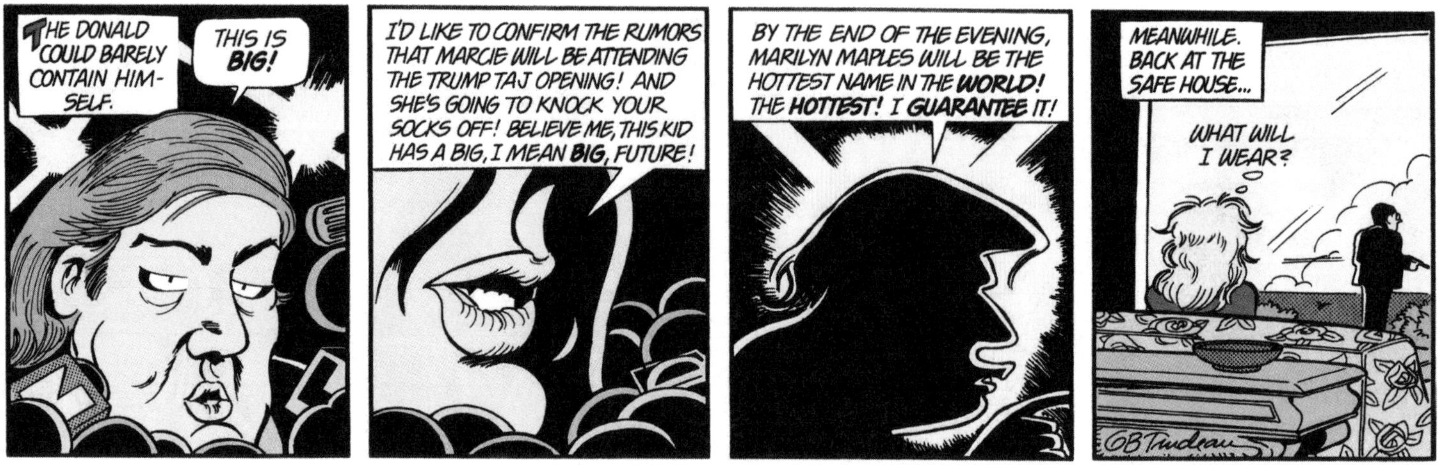
THE DONALD COULD BARELY CONTAIN HIMSELF.
THIS IS BIG!
I'D LIKE TO CONFIRM THE RUMORS THAT MARCIE WILL BE ATTENDING THE TRUMP TAJ OPENING! AND SHE'S GOING TO KNOCK YOUR SOCKS OFF! BELIEVE ME, THIS KID HAS A BIG, I MEAN BIG, FUTURE!
BY THE END OF THE EVENING, MARILYN MAPLES WILL BE THE HOTTEST NAME IN THE WORLD! THE HOTTEST! I GUARANTEE IT!
MEANWHILE. BACK AT THE SAFE HOUSE...
WHAT WILL I WEAR?
©B Trudeau

March 12, 1990

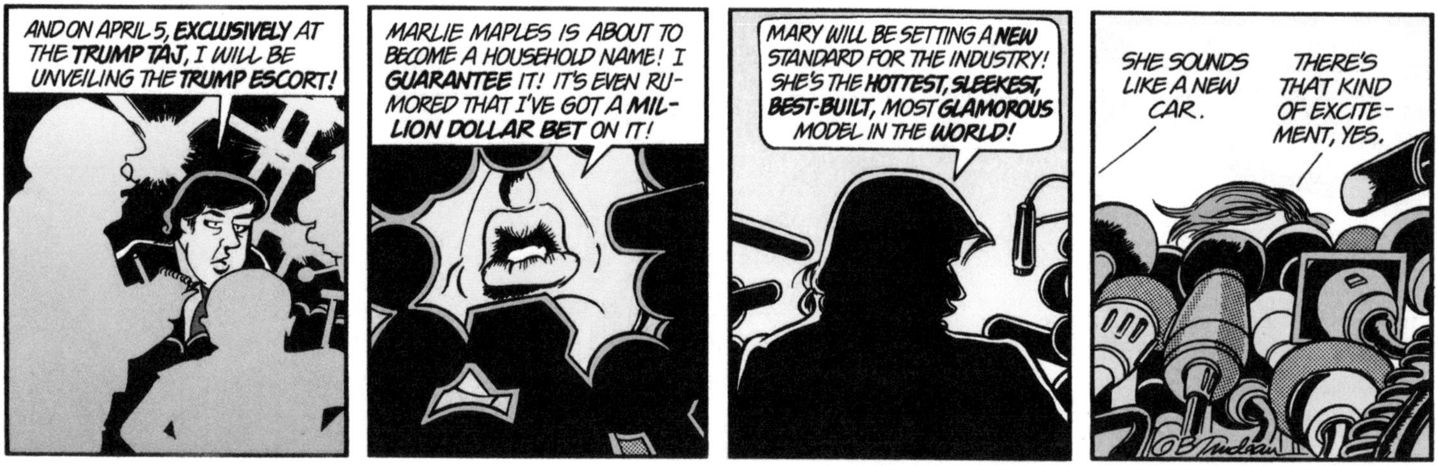
AND ON APRIL 5, EXCLUSIVELY AT THE TRUMP TAJ, I WILL BE UNVEILING THE TRUMP ESCORT!
MARLIE MAPLES IS ABOUT TO BECOME A HOUSEHOLD NAME! I GUARANTEE IT! IT'S EVEN RUMORED THAT I'VE GOT A MILLION DOLLAR BET ON IT!
MARY WILL BE SETTING A NEW STANDARD FOR THE INDUSTRY! SHE'S THE HOTTEST, SLEEKEST, BEST-BUILT, MOST GLAMOROUS MODEL IN THE WORLD!
SHE SOUNDS LIKE A NEW CAR.
THERE'S THAT KIND OF EXCITEMENT, YES.
©B Trudeau

March 13, 1990

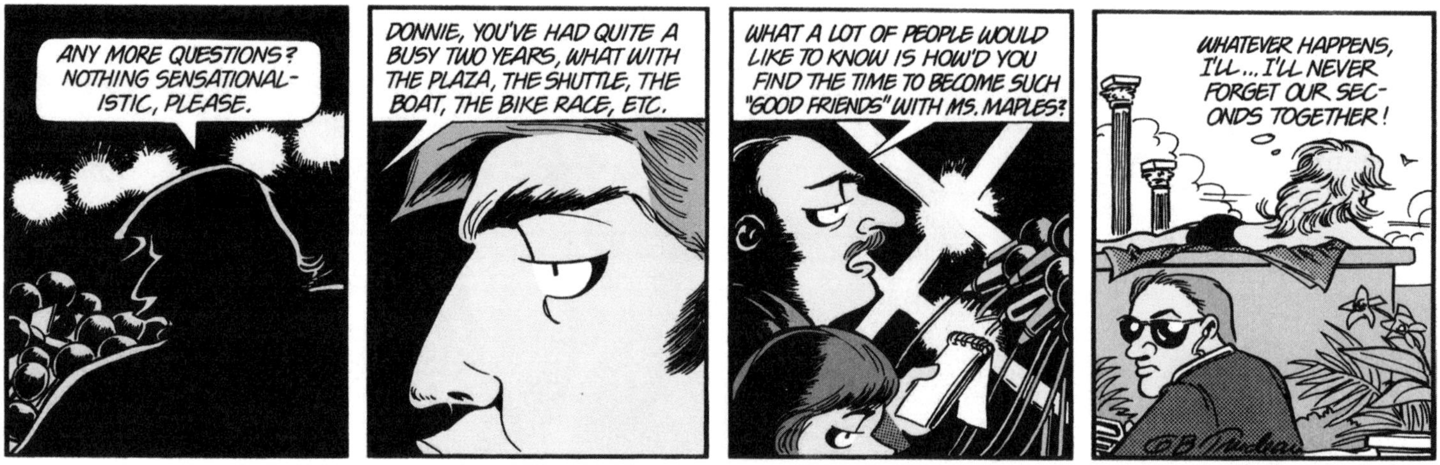
ANY MORE QUESTIONS? NOTHING SENSATIONALISTIC, PLEASE.
DONNIE, YOU'VE HAD QUITE A BUSY TWO YEARS, WHAT WITH THE PLAZA, THE SHUTTLE, THE BOAT, THE BIKE RACE, ETC.
WHAT A LOT OF PEOPLE WOULD LIKE TO KNOW IS HOW'D YOU FIND THE TIME TO BECOME SUCH "GOOD FRIENDS" WITH MS. MAPLES?
WHATEVER HAPPENS, I'LL... I'LL NEVER FORGET OUR SECONDS TOGETHER!
©B Trudeau

March 14, 1990

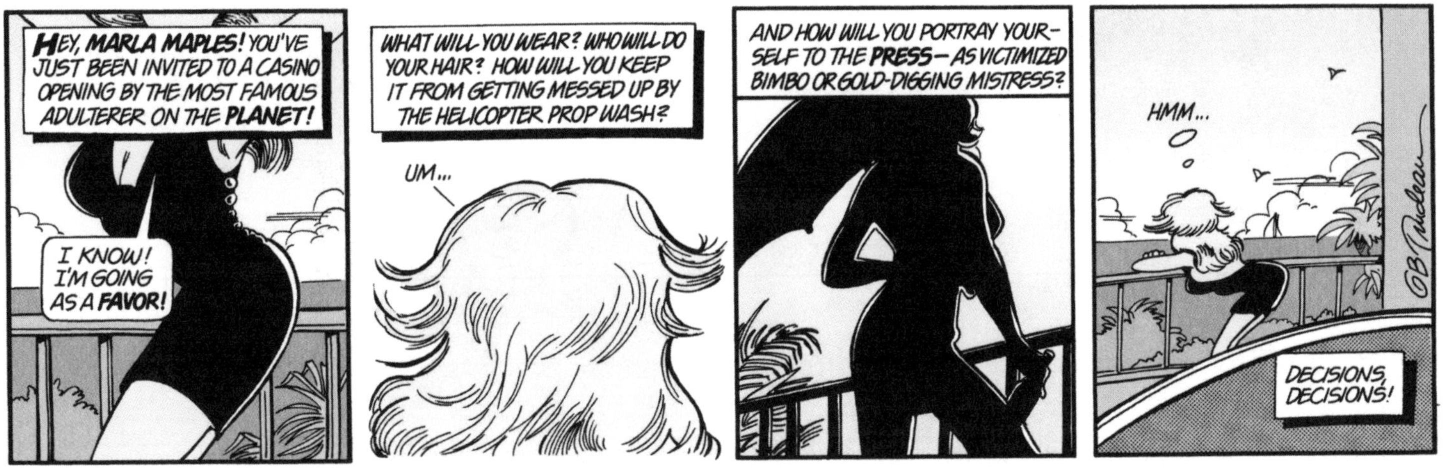
HEY, MARLA MAPLES! YOU'VE JUST BEEN INVITED TO A CASINO OPENING BY THE MOST FAMOUS ADULTERER ON THE PLANET!
I KNOW! I'M GOING AS A FAVOR!
WHAT WILL YOU WEAR? WHO WILL DO YOUR HAIR? HOW WILL YOU KEEP IT FROM GETTING MESSED UP BY THE HELICOPTER PROP WASH?
UM...
AND HOW WILL YOU PORTRAY YOURSELF TO THE PRESS—AS VICTIMIZED BIMBO OR GOLD-DIGGING MISTRESS?
HMM...
DECISIONS, DECISIONS!

March 15, 1990

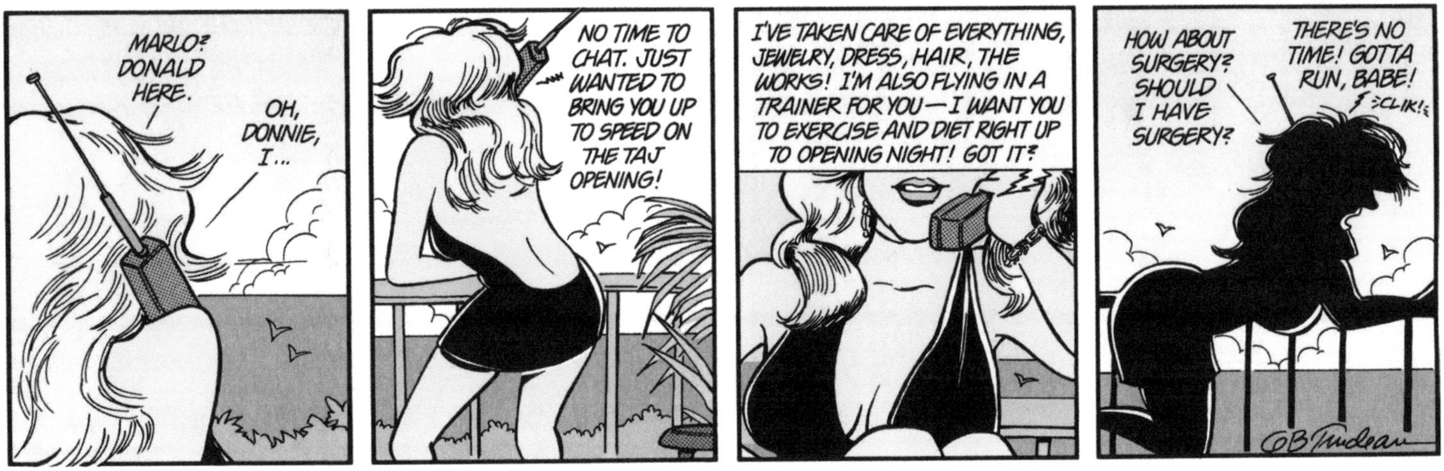
MARLO? DONALD HERE.
OH, DONNIE, I...
NO TIME TO CHAT. JUST WANTED TO BRING YOU UP TO SPEED ON THE TAJ OPENING!
I'VE TAKEN CARE OF EVERYTHING, JEWELRY, DRESS, HAIR, THE WORKS! I'M ALSO FLYING IN A TRAINER FOR YOU—I WANT YOU TO EXERCISE AND DIET RIGHT UP TO OPENING NIGHT! GOT IT?
HOW ABOUT SURGERY? SHOULD I HAVE SURGERY?
THERE'S NO TIME! GOTTA RUN, BABE!
CLIK!

March 16, 1990

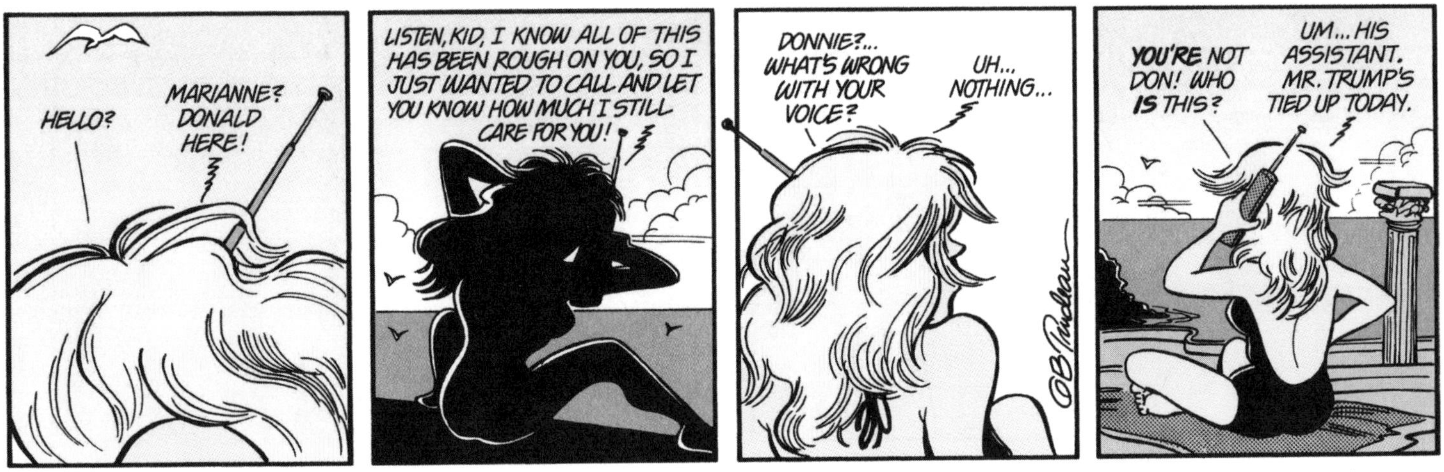
HELLO?
MARIANNE? DONALD HERE!
LISTEN, KID, I KNOW ALL OF THIS HAS BEEN ROUGH ON YOU, SO I JUST WANTED TO CALL AND LET YOU KNOW HOW MUCH I STILL CARE FOR YOU!
DONNIE?... WHAT'S WRONG WITH YOUR VOICE?
UH... NOTHING...
YOU'RE NOT DON! WHO IS THIS?
UM... HIS ASSISTANT. MR. TRUMP'S TIED UP TODAY.

March 17, 1990

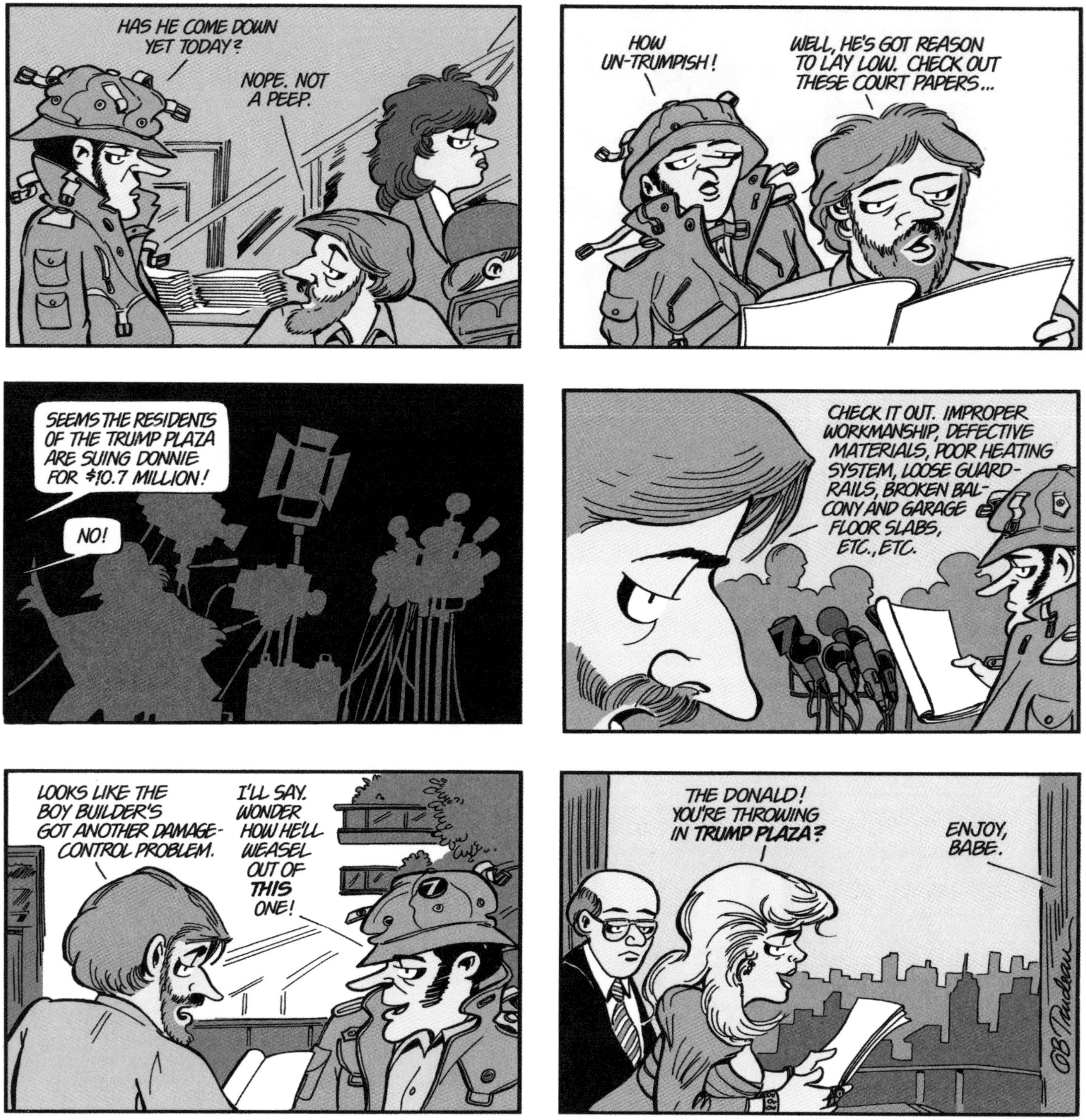
HAS HE COME DOWN YET TODAY?
NOPE. NOT A PEEP.
HOW UN-TRUMPISH!
WELL, HE'S GOT REASON TO LAY LOW. CHECK OUT THESE COURT PAPERS...
SEEMS THE RESIDENTS OF THE TRUMP PLAZA ARE SUING DONNIE FOR $10.7 MILLION!
NO!
CHECK IT OUT. IMPROPER WORKMANSHIP, DEFECTIVE MATERIALS, POOR HEATING SYSTEM, LOOSE GUARD-RAILS, BROKEN BAL-CONY AND GARAGE FLOOR SLABS, ETC., ETC.
LOOKS LIKE THE BOY BUILDER'S GOT ANOTHER DAMAGE-CONTROL PROBLEM.
I'LL SAY. WONDER HOW HE'LL WEASEL OUT OF THIS ONE!
THE DONALD! YOU'RE THROWING IN TRUMP PLAZA?
ENJOY, BABE.

April 1, 1990

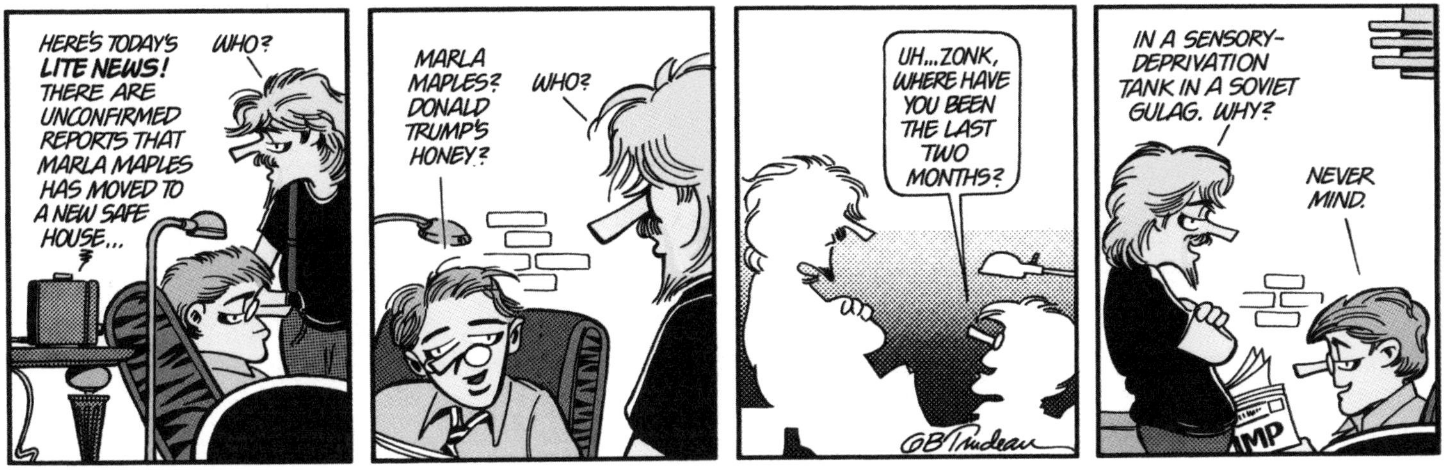
HERE'S TODAY'S **LITE NEWS!** THERE ARE UNCONFIRMED REPORTS THAT MARLA MAPLES HAS MOVED TO A NEW SAFE HOUSE...
WHO?
MARLA MAPLES? DONALD TRUMP'S HONEY?
WHO?
UH...ZONK, WHERE HAVE YOU BEEN THE LAST TWO MONTHS?
IN A SENSORY-DEPRIVATION TANK IN A SOVIET GULAG. WHY?
NEVER MIND.

March 24, 1990

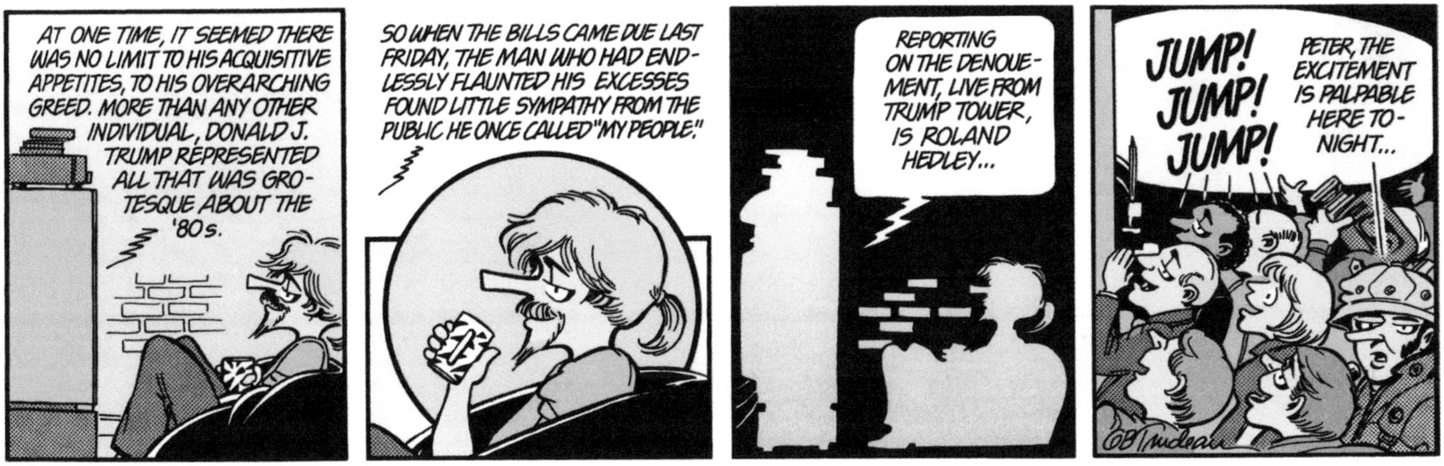
AT ONE TIME, IT SEEMED THERE WAS NO LIMIT TO HIS ACQUISITIVE APPETITES, TO HIS OVERARCHING GREED. MORE THAN ANY OTHER INDIVIDUAL, DONALD J. TRUMP REPRESENTED ALL THAT WAS GROTESQUE ABOUT THE '80s.
SO WHEN THE BILLS CAME DUE LAST FRIDAY, THE MAN WHO HAD ENDLESSLY FLAUNTED HIS EXCESSES FOUND LITTLE SYMPATHY FROM THE PUBLIC HE ONCE CALLED "MY PEOPLE."
REPORTING ON THE DENOUEMENT, LIVE FROM TRUMP TOWER, IS ROLAND HEDLEY...
JUMP! JUMP! JUMP!
PETER, THE EXCITEMENT IS PALPABLE HERE TONIGHT...

June 18, 1990

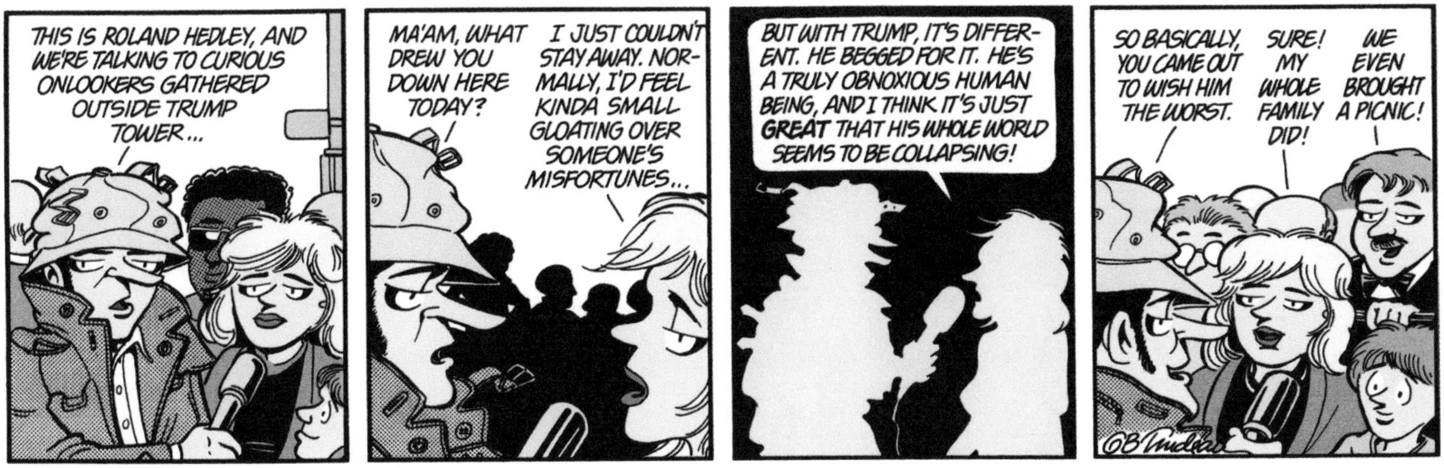
THIS IS ROLAND HEDLEY, AND WE'RE TALKING TO CURIOUS ONLOOKERS GATHERED OUTSIDE TRUMP TOWER...
MA'AM, WHAT DREW YOU DOWN HERE TODAY?
I JUST COULDN'T STAY AWAY. NORMALLY, I'D FEEL KINDA SMALL GLOATING OVER SOMEONE'S MISFORTUNES...
BUT WITH TRUMP, IT'S DIFFERENT. HE BEGGED FOR IT. HE'S A TRULY OBNOXIOUS HUMAN BEING, AND I THINK IT'S JUST **GREAT** THAT HIS WHOLE WORLD SEEMS TO BE COLLAPSING!
SO BASICALLY, YOU CAME OUT TO WISH HIM THE WORST.
SURE! MY WHOLE FAMILY DID!
WE EVEN BROUGHT A PICNIC!

June 19, 1990

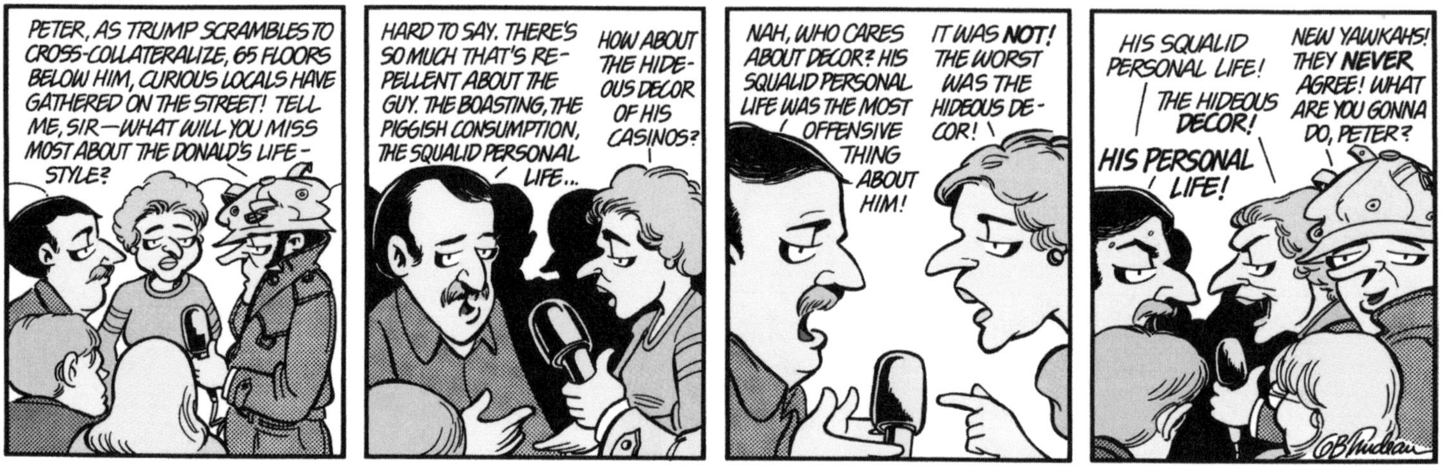
PETER, AS TRUMP SCRAMBLES TO CROSS-COLLATERALIZE, 65 FLOORS BELOW HIM, CURIOUS LOCALS HAVE GATHERED ON THE STREET! TELL ME, SIR—WHAT WILL YOU MISS MOST ABOUT THE DONALD'S LIFE-STYLE?
HARD TO SAY. THERE'S SO MUCH THAT'S RE-PELLENT ABOUT THE GUY. THE BOASTING, THE PIGGISH CONSUMPTION, THE SQUALID PERSONAL LIFE...
HOW ABOUT THE HIDE-OUS DECOR OF HIS CASINOS?
NAH, WHO CARES ABOUT DECOR? HIS SQUALID PERSONAL LIFE WAS THE MOST OFFENSIVE THING ABOUT HIM!
IT WAS NOT! THE WORST WAS THE HIDEOUS DE-COR!
HIS SQUALID PERSONAL LIFE!
THE HIDEOUS DECOR!
HIS PERSONAL LIFE!
NEW YAWKAHS! THEY NEVER AGREE! WHAT ARE YOU GONNA DO, PETER?
GBTrudeau

June 20, 1990

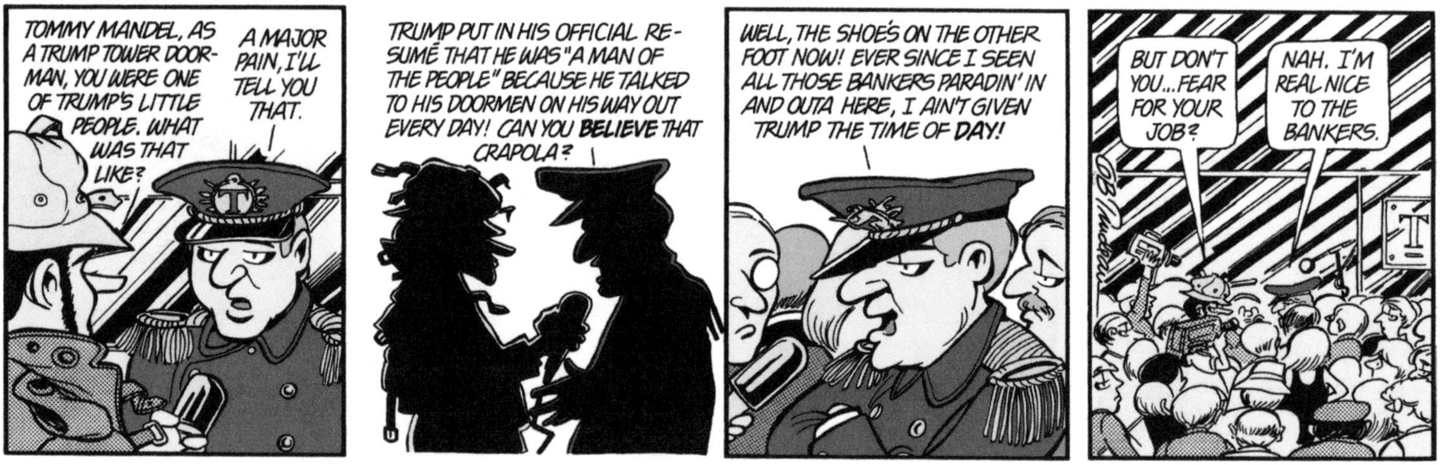
TOMMY MANDEL, AS A TRUMP TOWER DOOR-MAN, YOU WERE ONE OF TRUMP'S LITTLE PEOPLE. WHAT WAS THAT LIKE?
A MAJOR PAIN, I'LL TELL YOU THAT.
TRUMP PUT IN HIS OFFICIAL RE-SUMÉ THAT HE WAS "A MAN OF THE PEOPLE" BECAUSE HE TALKED TO HIS DOORMEN ON HIS WAY OUT EVERY DAY! CAN YOU BELIEVE THAT CRAPOLA?
WELL, THE SHOE'S ON THE OTHER FOOT NOW! EVER SINCE I SEEN ALL THOSE BANKERS PARADIN' IN AND OUTA HERE, I AIN'T GIVEN TRUMP THE TIME OF DAY!
BUT DON'T YOU...FEAR FOR YOUR JOB?
NAH. I'M REAL NICE TO THE BANKERS.
GBTrudeau

June 21, 1990

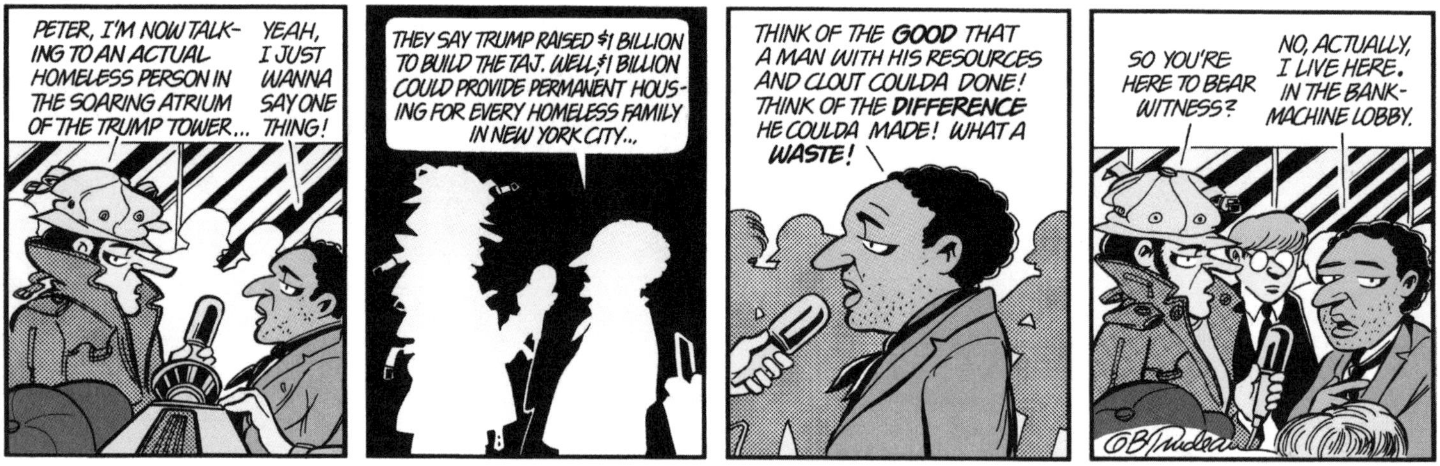
PETER, I'M NOW TALK-ING TO AN ACTUAL HOMELESS PERSON IN THE SOARING ATRIUM OF THE TRUMP TOWER...
YEAH, I JUST WANNA SAY ONE THING!
THEY SAY TRUMP RAISED $1 BILLION TO BUILD THE TAJ. WELL, $1 BILLION COULD PROVIDE PERMANENT HOUS-ING FOR EVERY HOMELESS FAMILY IN NEW YORK CITY...
THINK OF THE GOOD THAT A MAN WITH HIS RESOURCES AND CLOUT COULDA DONE! THINK OF THE DIFFERENCE HE COULDA MADE! WHAT A WASTE!
SO YOU'RE HERE TO BEAR WITNESS?
NO, ACTUALLY, I LIVE HERE. IN THE BANK-MACHINE LOBBY.
GBTrudeau

June 22, 1990

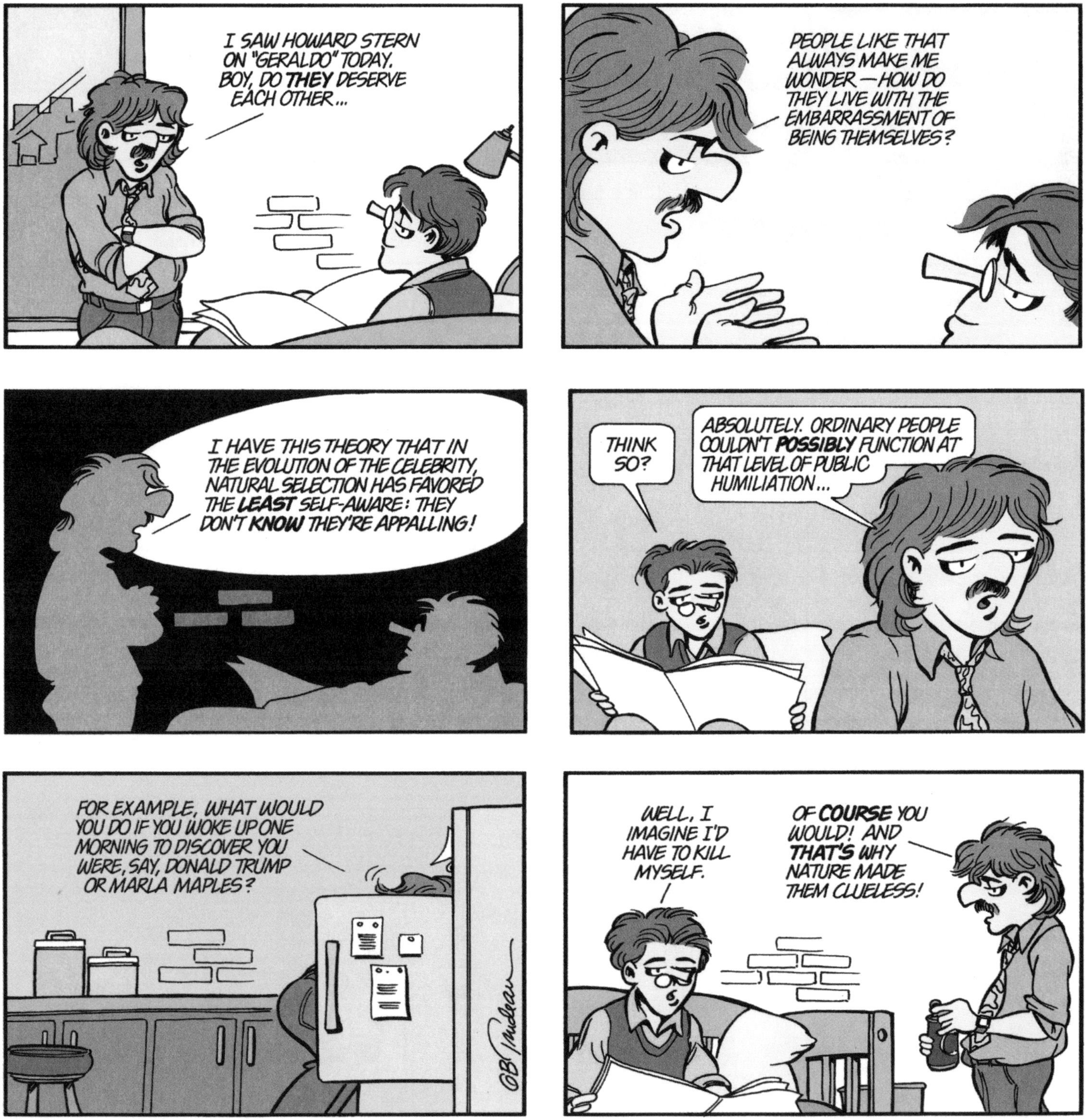
I SAW HOWARD STERN ON "GERALDO" TODAY. BOY, DO **THEY** DESERVE EACH OTHER...
PEOPLE LIKE THAT ALWAYS MAKE ME WONDER—HOW DO THEY LIVE WITH THE EMBARRASSMENT OF BEING THEMSELVES?
I HAVE THIS THEORY THAT IN THE EVOLUTION OF THE CELEBRITY, NATURAL SELECTION HAS FAVORED THE **LEAST** SELF-AWARE: THEY DON'T **KNOW** THEY'RE APPALLING!
THINK SO?
ABSOLUTELY. ORDINARY PEOPLE COULDN'T **POSSIBLY** FUNCTION AT THAT LEVEL OF PUBLIC HUMILIATION...
FOR EXAMPLE, WHAT WOULD YOU DO IF YOU WOKE UP ONE MORNING TO DISCOVER YOU WERE, SAY, DONALD TRUMP OR MARLA MAPLES?
WELL, I IMAGINE I'D HAVE TO KILL MYSELF.
OF **COURSE** YOU WOULD! AND **THAT'S** WHY NATURE MADE THEM CLUELESS!

May 1, 1994

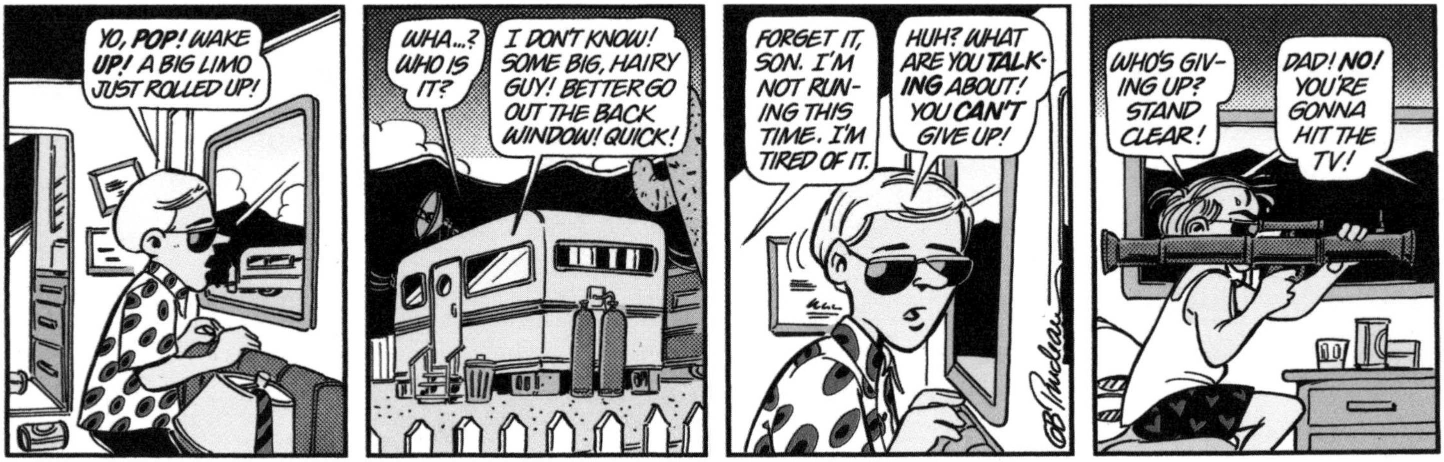

YO, POP! WAKE UP! A BIG LIMO JUST ROLLED UP!
WHA...? WHO IS IT?
I DON'T KNOW! SOME BIG, HAIRY GUY! BETTER GO OUT THE BACK WINDOW! QUICK!
FORGET IT, SON. I'M NOT RUNNING THIS TIME. I'M TIRED OF IT.
HUH? WHAT ARE YOU TALKING ABOUT! YOU CAN'T GIVE UP!
WHO'S GIVING UP? STAND CLEAR!
DAD! NO! YOU'RE GONNA HIT THE TV!

February 24, 1997

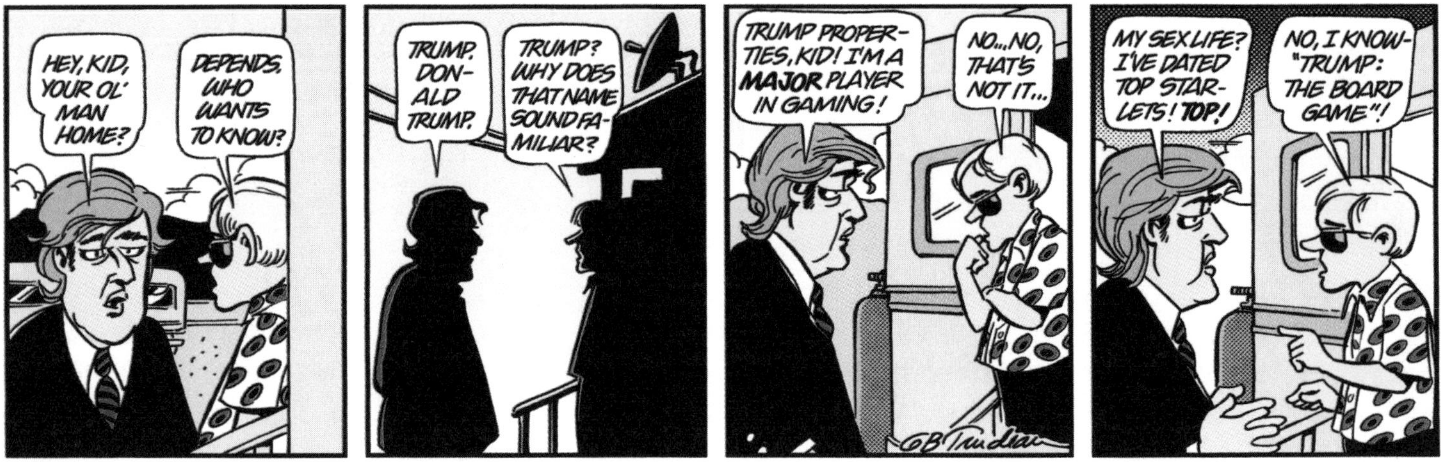

HEY, KID, YOUR OL' MAN HOME?
DEPENDS. WHO WANTS TO KNOW?
TRUMP. DONALD TRUMP.
TRUMP? WHY DOES THAT NAME SOUND FAMILIAR?
TRUMP PROPERTIES, KID! I'M A MAJOR PLAYER IN GAMING!
NO...NO, THAT'S NOT IT...
MY SEX LIFE? I'VE DATED TOP STARLETS! TOP!
NO, I KNOW— "TRUMP: THE BOARD GAME"!

February 25, 1997

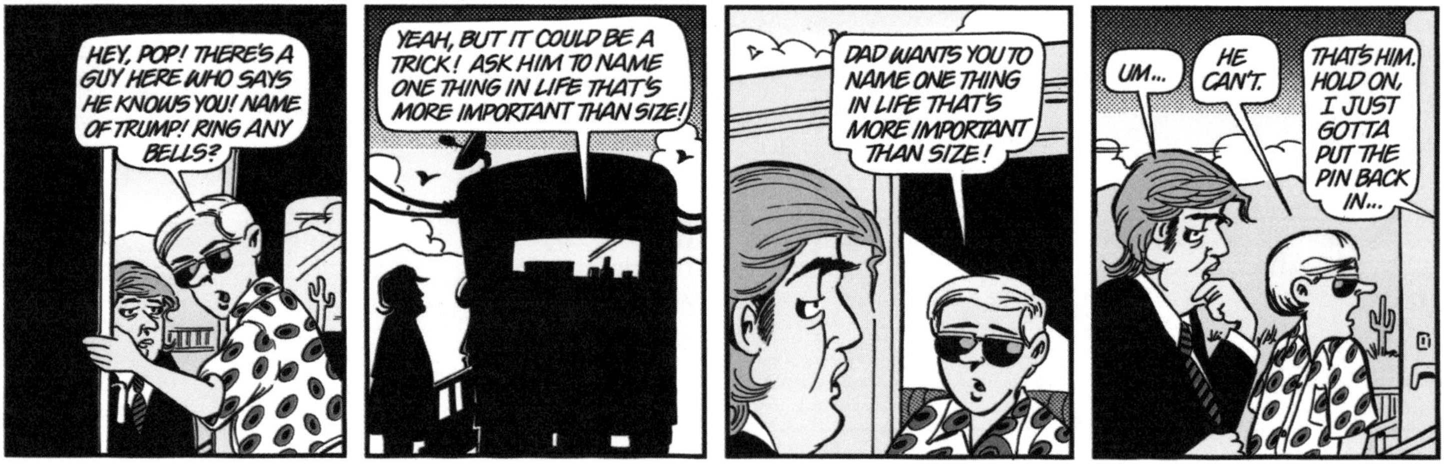

HEY, POP! THERE'S A GUY HERE WHO SAYS HE KNOWS YOU! NAME OF TRUMP! RING ANY BELLS?
YEAH, BUT IT COULD BE A TRICK! ASK HIM TO NAME ONE THING IN LIFE THAT'S MORE IMPORTANT THAN SIZE!
DAD WANTS YOU TO NAME ONE THING IN LIFE THAT'S MORE IMPORTANT THAN SIZE!
UM...
HE CAN'T.
THAT'S HIM. HOLD ON, I JUST GOTTA PUT THE PIN BACK IN...

February 26, 1997

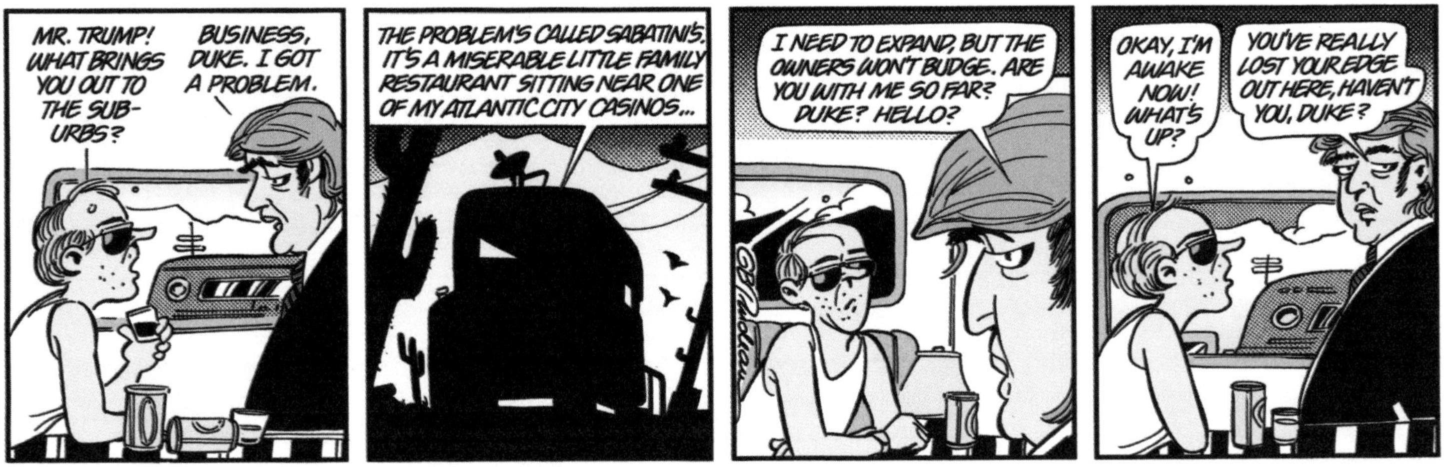
MR. TRUMP! WHAT BRINGS YOU OUT TO THE SUB-URBS?
BUSINESS, DUKE. I GOT A PROBLEM.
THE PROBLEM'S CALLED SABATINI'S. IT'S A MISERABLE LITTLE FAMILY RESTAURANT SITTING NEAR ONE OF MY ATLANTIC CITY CASINOS...
I NEED TO EXPAND, BUT THE OWNERS WON'T BUDGE. ARE YOU WITH ME SO FAR? DUKE? HELLO?
OKAY, I'M AWAKE NOW! WHAT'S UP?
YOU'VE REALLY LOST YOUR EDGE OUT HERE, HAVEN'T YOU, DUKE?

February 27, 1997

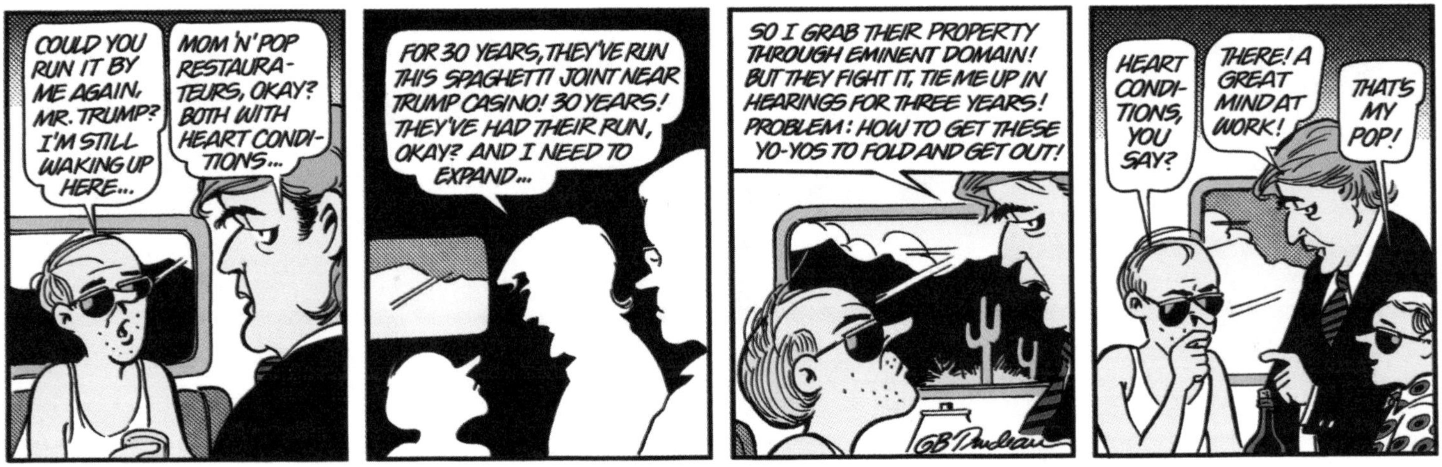
COULD YOU RUN IT BY ME AGAIN, MR. TRUMP? I'M STILL WAKING UP HERE...
MOM 'N' POP RESTAURA-TEURS, OKAY? BOTH WITH HEART CONDI-TIONS...
FOR 30 YEARS, THEY'VE RUN THIS SPAGHETTI JOINT NEAR TRUMP CASINO! 30 YEARS! THEY'VE HAD THEIR RUN, OKAY? AND I NEED TO EXPAND...
SO I GRAB THEIR PROPERTY THROUGH EMINENT DOMAIN! BUT THEY FIGHT IT, TIE ME UP IN HEARINGS FOR THREE YEARS! PROBLEM: HOW TO GET THESE YO-YOS TO FOLD AND GET OUT!
HEART CONDI-TIONS, YOU SAY?
THERE! A GREAT MIND AT WORK!
THAT'S MY POP!

February 28, 1997

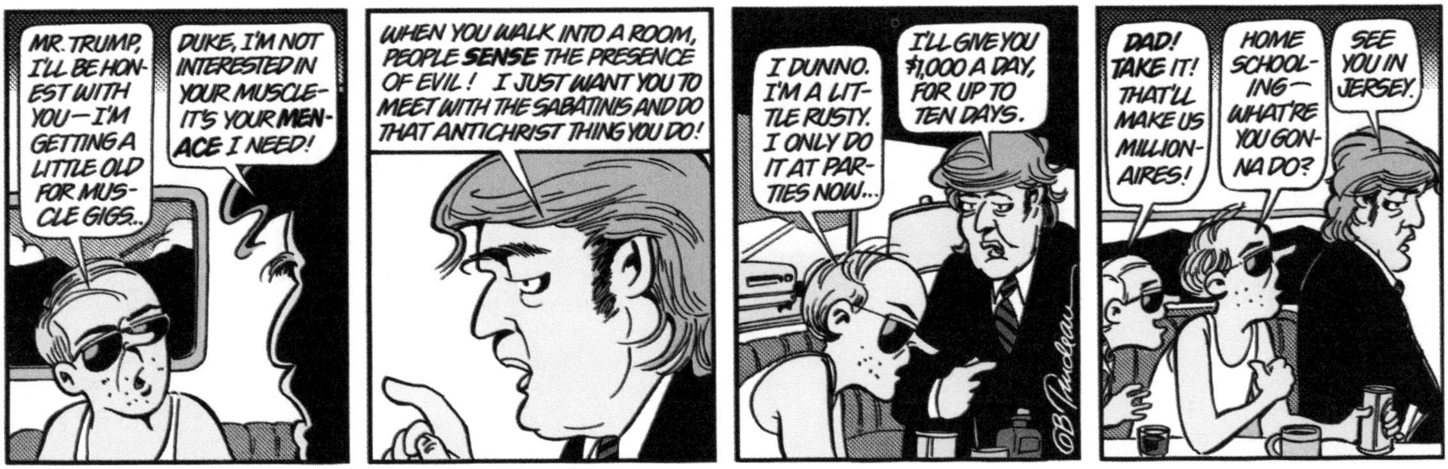
MR. TRUMP, I'LL BE HON-EST WITH YOU—I'M GETTING A LITTLE OLD FOR MUS-CLE GIGS...
DUKE, I'M NOT INTERESTED IN YOUR MUSCLE-IT'S YOUR MEN-ACE I NEED!
WHEN YOU WALK INTO A ROOM, PEOPLE SENSE THE PRESENCE OF EVIL! I JUST WANT YOU TO MEET WITH THE SABATINIS AND DO THAT ANTICHRIST THING YOU DO!
I DUNNO. I'M A LIT-TLE RUSTY. I ONLY DO IT AT PAR-TIES NOW...
I'LL GIVE YOU $1,000 A DAY, FOR UP TO TEN DAYS.
DAD! TAKE IT! THAT'LL MAKE US MILLION-AIRES!
HOME SCHOOL-ING—WHAT'RE YOU GON-NA DO?
SEE YOU IN JERSEY.

March 1, 1997

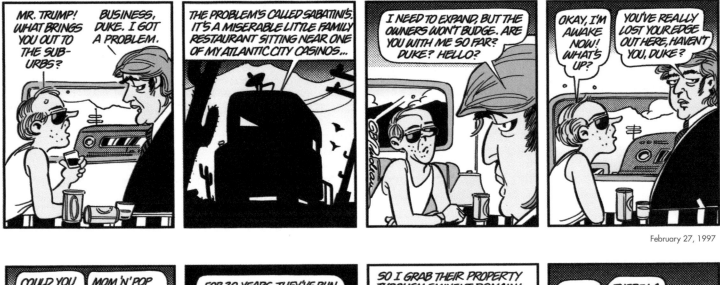

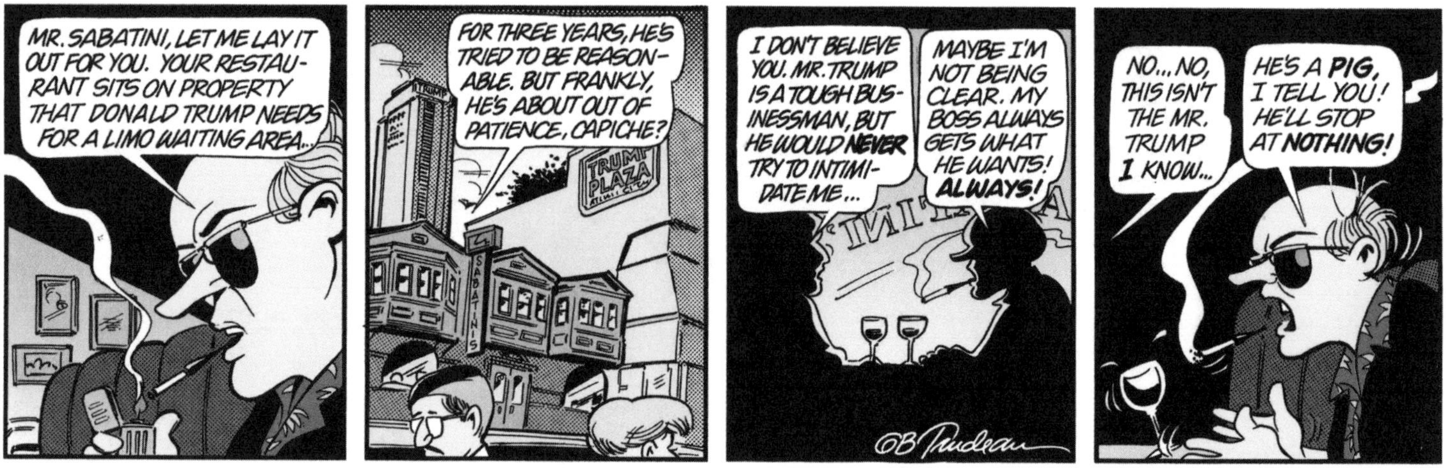
MR. SABATINI, LET ME LAY IT OUT FOR YOU. YOUR RESTAURANT SITS ON PROPERTY THAT DONALD TRUMP NEEDS FOR A LIMO WAITING AREA...
FOR THREE YEARS, HE'S TRIED TO BE REASONABLE. BUT FRANKLY, HE'S ABOUT OUT OF PATIENCE, CAPICHE?
TRUMP PLAZA
SABATINI'S
I DON'T BELIEVE YOU. MR. TRUMP IS A TOUGH BUSINESSMAN, BUT HE WOULD **NEVER** TRY TO INTIMIDATE ME...
MAYBE I'M NOT BEING CLEAR. MY BOSS ALWAYS GETS WHAT HE WANTS! **ALWAYS!**
©B Trudeau
NO... NO, THIS ISN'T THE MR. TRUMP **I** KNOW...
HE'S A **PIG**, I TELL YOU! HE'LL STOP AT **NOTHING!**

March 10, 1997

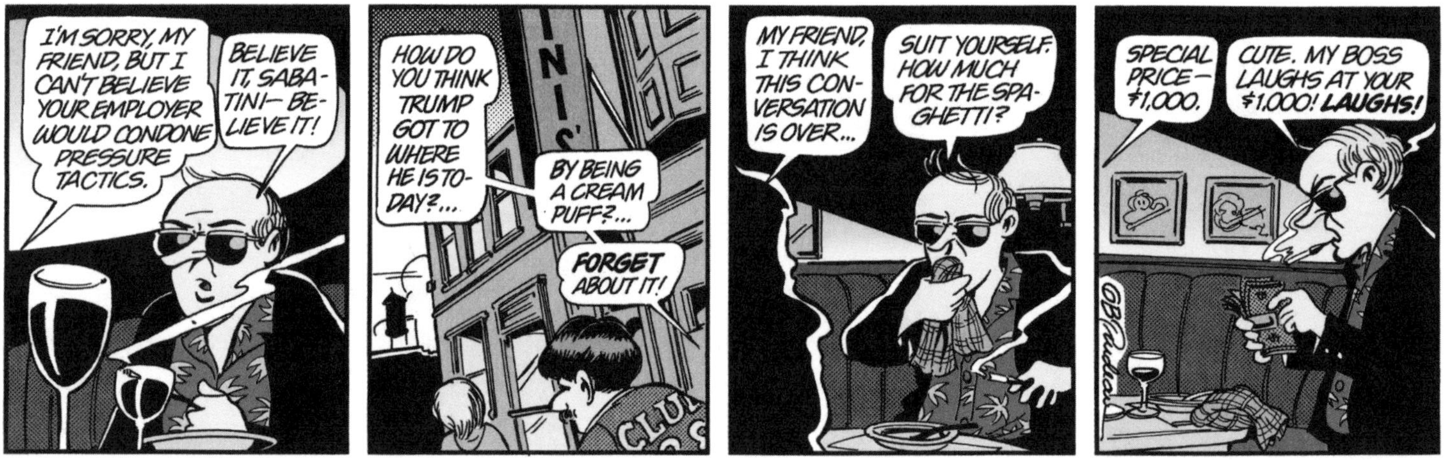
I'M SORRY, MY FRIEND, BUT I CAN'T BELIEVE YOUR EMPLOYER WOULD CONDONE PRESSURE TACTICS.
BELIEVE IT, SABATINI— BELIEVE IT!
HOW DO YOU THINK TRUMP GOT TO WHERE HE IS TODAY?...
BY BEING A CREAM PUFF?...
FORGET ABOUT IT!
MY FRIEND, I THINK THIS CONVERSATION IS OVER...
SUIT YOURSELF. HOW MUCH FOR THE SPAGHETTI?
SPECIAL PRICE— $1,000.
CUTE. MY BOSS LAUGHS AT YOUR $1,000! **LAUGHS!**
©B Trudeau

March 11, 1997

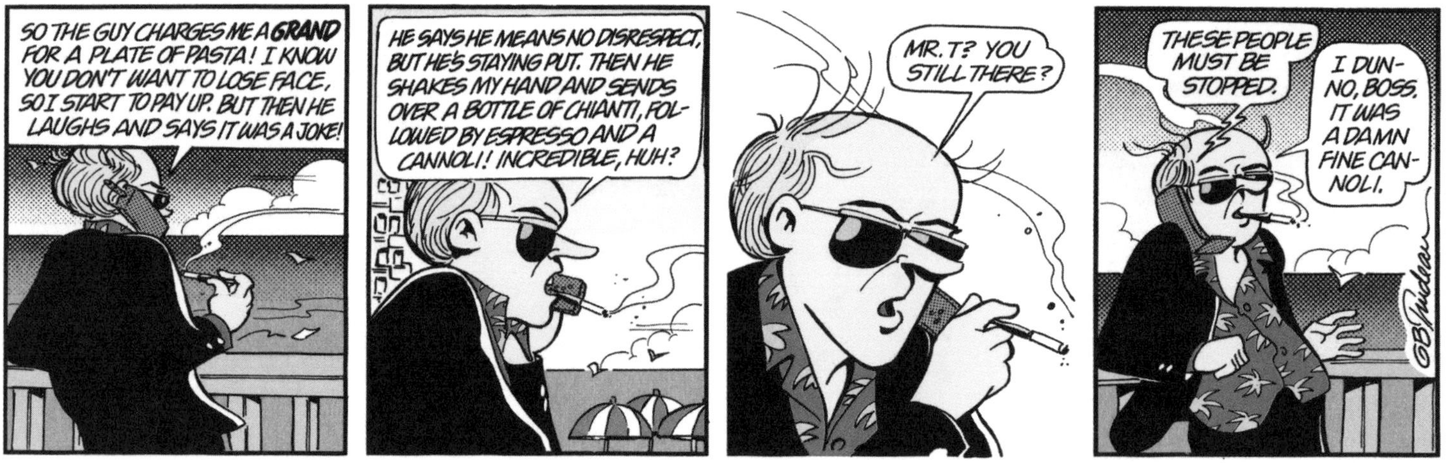
SO THE GUY CHARGES ME A **GRAND** FOR A PLATE OF PASTA! I KNOW YOU DON'T WANT TO LOSE FACE, SO I START TO PAY UP. BUT THEN HE LAUGHS AND SAYS IT WAS A JOKE!
HE SAYS HE MEANS NO DISRESPECT, BUT HE'S STAYING PUT. THEN HE SHAKES MY HAND AND SENDS OVER A BOTTLE OF CHIANTI, FOLLOWED BY ESPRESSO AND A CANNOLI! INCREDIBLE, HUH?
MR. T? YOU STILL THERE?
THESE PEOPLE MUST BE STOPPED.
I DUNNO, BOSS. IT WAS A DAMN FINE CANNOLI.
©B Trudeau

March 12, 1997

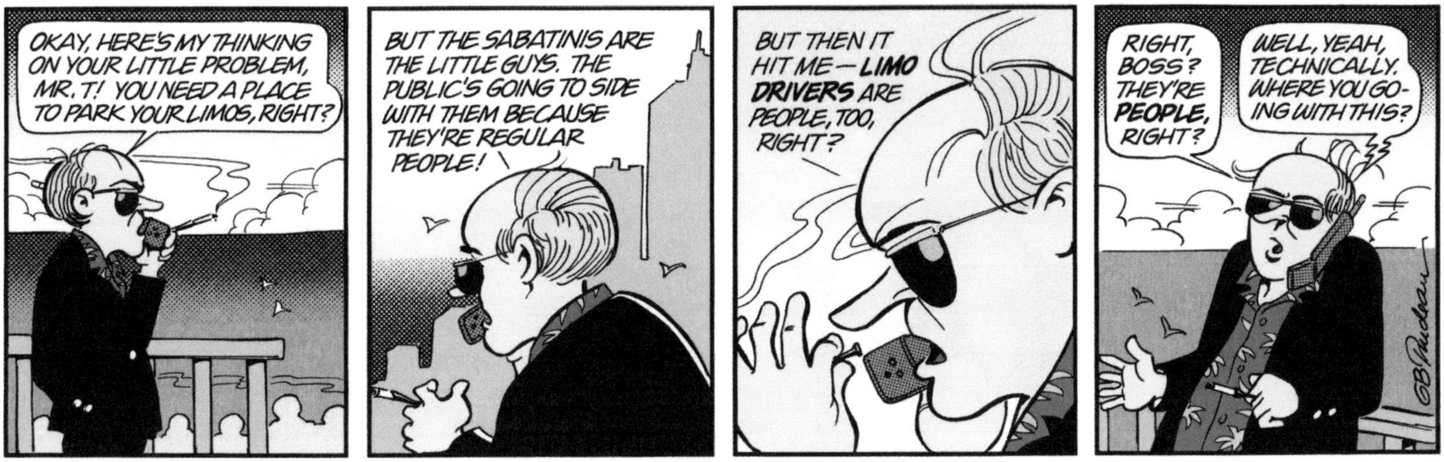
OKAY, HERE'S MY THINKING ON YOUR LITTLE PROBLEM, MR. T! YOU NEED A PLACE TO PARK YOUR LIMOS, RIGHT?
BUT THE SABATINIS ARE THE LITTLE GUYS. THE PUBLIC'S GOING TO SIDE WITH THEM BECAUSE THEY'RE REGULAR PEOPLE!
BUT THEN IT HIT ME — **LIMO DRIVERS** ARE PEOPLE, TOO, RIGHT?
RIGHT, BOSS? THEY'RE **PEOPLE,** RIGHT?
WELL, YEAH, TECHNICALLY. WHERE YOU GOING WITH THIS?

March 13, 1997

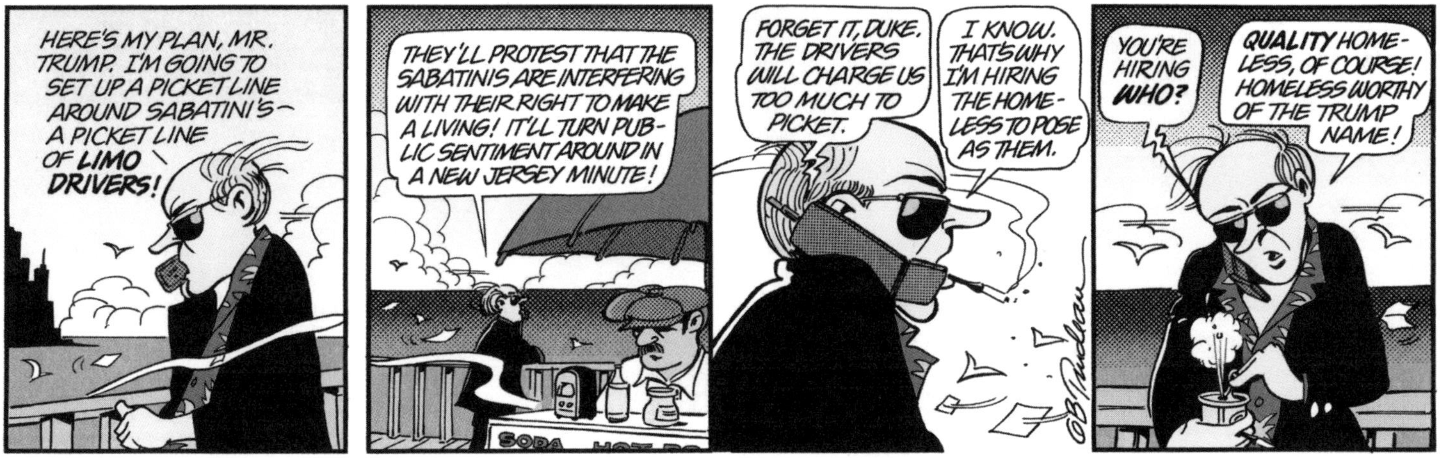
HERE'S MY PLAN, MR. TRUMP. I'M GOING TO SET UP A PICKET LINE AROUND SABATINI'S — A PICKET LINE OF **LIMO DRIVERS!**
THEY'LL PROTEST THAT THE SABATINIS ARE INTERFERING WITH THEIR RIGHT TO MAKE A LIVING! IT'LL TURN PUBLIC SENTIMENT AROUND IN A NEW JERSEY MINUTE!
SODA
FORGET IT, DUKE. THE DRIVERS WILL CHARGE US TOO MUCH TO PICKET.
I KNOW. THAT'S WHY I'M HIRING THE HOMELESS TO POSE AS THEM.
YOU'RE HIRING **WHO?**
QUALITY HOMELESS, OF COURSE! HOMELESS WORTHY OF THE TRUMP NAME!

March 14, 1997

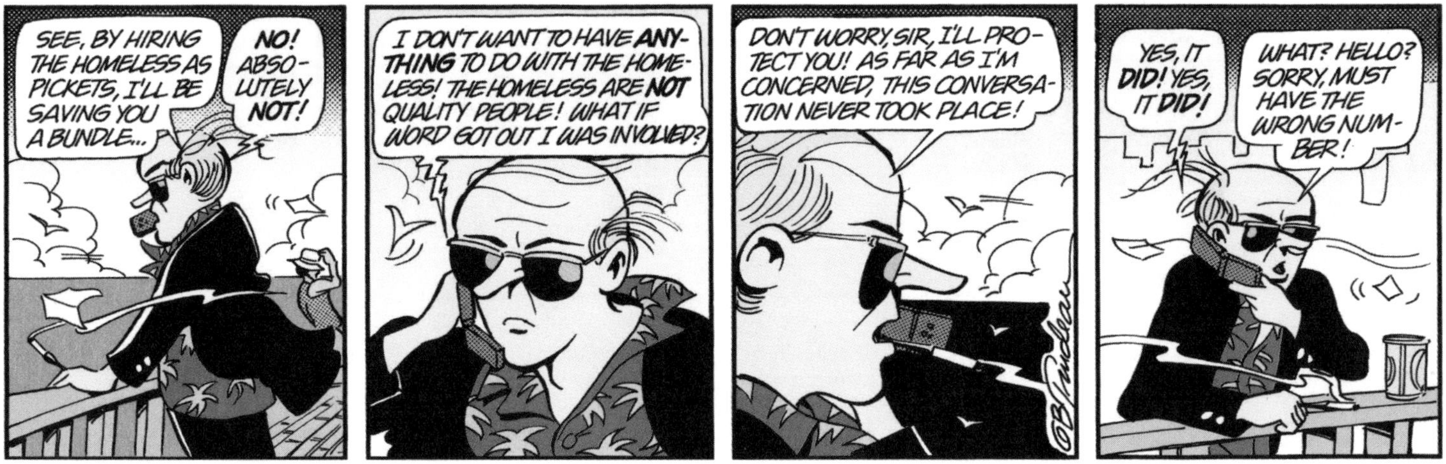
SEE, BY HIRING THE HOMELESS AS PICKETS, I'LL BE SAVING YOU A BUNDLE...
NO! ABSOLUTELY **NOT!**
I DON'T WANT TO HAVE **ANYTHING** TO DO WITH THE HOMELESS! THE HOMELESS ARE **NOT** QUALITY PEOPLE! WHAT IF WORD GOT OUT I WAS INVOLVED?
DON'T WORRY, SIR, I'LL PROTECT YOU! AS FAR AS I'M CONCERNED, THIS CONVERSATION NEVER TOOK PLACE!
YES, IT **DID!** YES, IT **DID!**
WHAT? HELLO? SORRY, MUST HAVE THE WRONG NUMBER!

March 15, 1997

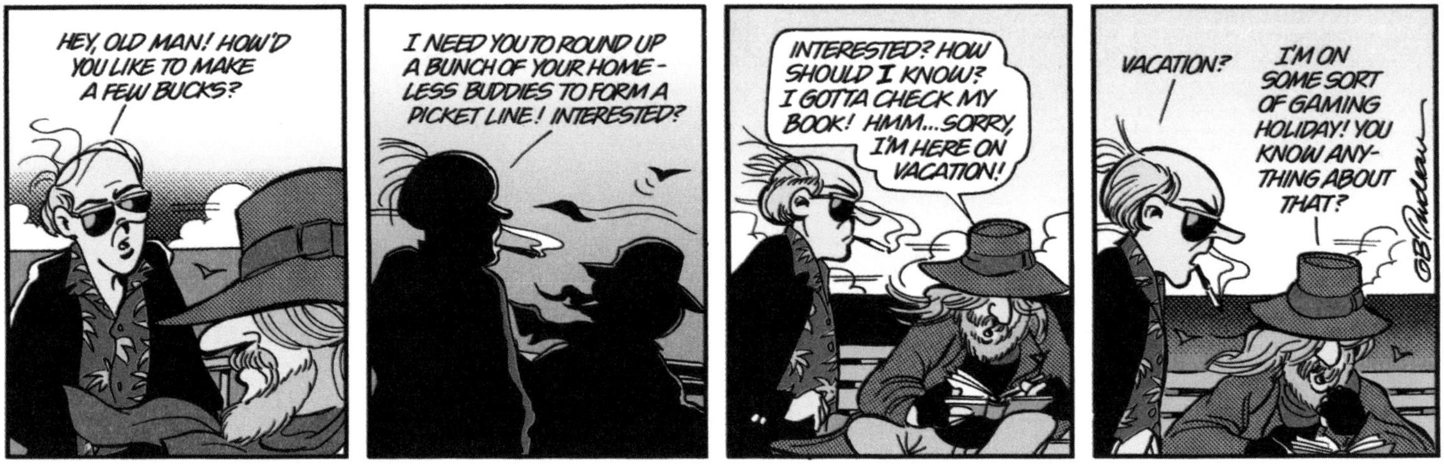
HEY, OLD MAN! HOW'D YOU LIKE TO MAKE A FEW BUCKS?
I NEED YOU TO ROUND UP A BUNCH OF YOUR HOME-LESS BUDDIES TO FORM A PICKET LINE! INTERESTED?
INTERESTED? HOW SHOULD I KNOW? I GOTTA CHECK MY BOOK! HMM... SORRY, I'M HERE ON VACATION!
VACATION?
I'M ON SOME SORT OF GAMING HOLIDAY! YOU KNOW ANY-THING ABOUT THAT?

March 17, 1997

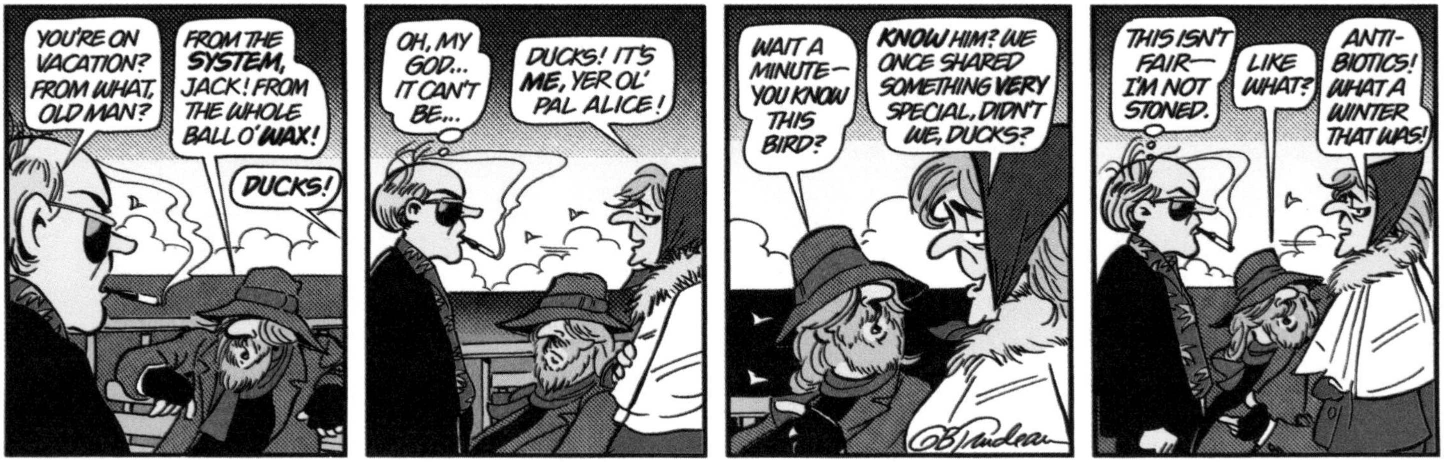
YOU'RE ON VACATION? FROM WHAT, OLD MAN?
FROM THE SYSTEM, JACK! FROM THE WHOLE BALL O' WAX!
DUCKS!
OH, MY GOD... IT CAN'T BE...
DUCKS! IT'S ME, YER OL' PAL ALICE!
WAIT A MINUTE-YOU KNOW THIS BIRD?
KNOW HIM? WE ONCE SHARED SOMETHING VERY SPECIAL, DIDN'T WE, DUCKS?
THIS ISN'T FAIR— I'M NOT STONED.
LIKE WHAT?
ANTI-BIOTICS! WHAT A WINTER THAT WAS!

March 18, 1997

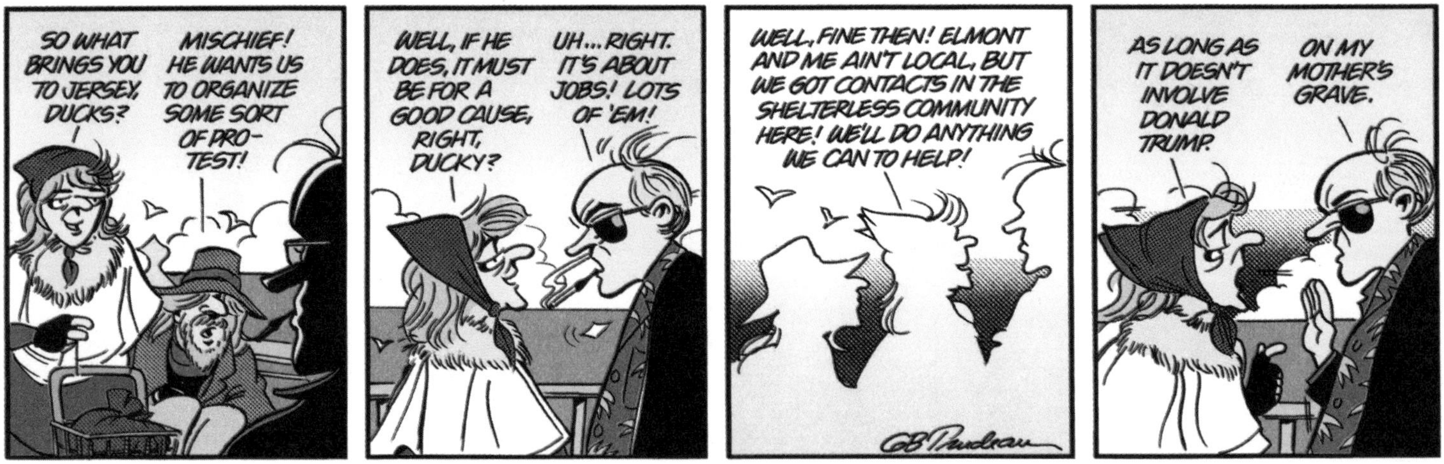
SO WHAT BRINGS YOU TO JERSEY, DUCKS?
MISCHIEF! HE WANTS US TO ORGANIZE SOME SORT OF PRO-TEST!
WELL, IF HE DOES, IT MUST BE FOR A GOOD CAUSE, RIGHT, DUCKY?
UH... RIGHT. IT'S ABOUT JOBS! LOTS OF 'EM!
WELL, FINE THEN! ELMONT AND ME AIN'T LOCAL, BUT WE GOT CONTACTS IN THE SHELTERLESS COMMUNITY HERE! WE'LL DO ANYTHING WE CAN TO HELP!
AS LONG AS IT DOESN'T INVOLVE DONALD TRUMP.
ON MY MOTHER'S GRAVE.

March 19, 1997

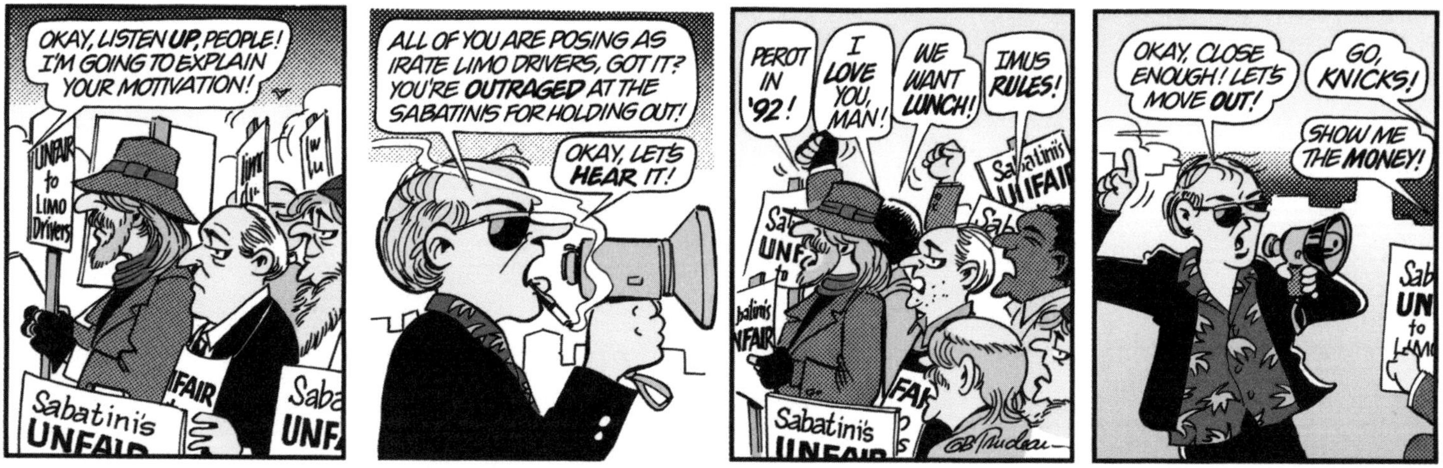
OKAY, LISTEN UP, PEOPLE! I'M GOING TO EXPLAIN YOUR MOTIVATION!
UNFAIR to LIMO Drivers
Sabatini's UNFAIR
ALL OF YOU ARE POSING AS IRATE LIMO DRIVERS, GOT IT? YOU'RE OUTRAGED AT THE SABATINIS FOR HOLDING OUT!
OKAY, LET'S HEAR IT!
PEROT IN '92!
I LOVE YOU, MAN!
WE WANT LUNCH!
IMUS RULES!
OKAY, CLOSE ENOUGH! LET'S MOVE OUT!
GO, KNICKS!
SHOW ME THE MONEY!

March 20, 1997

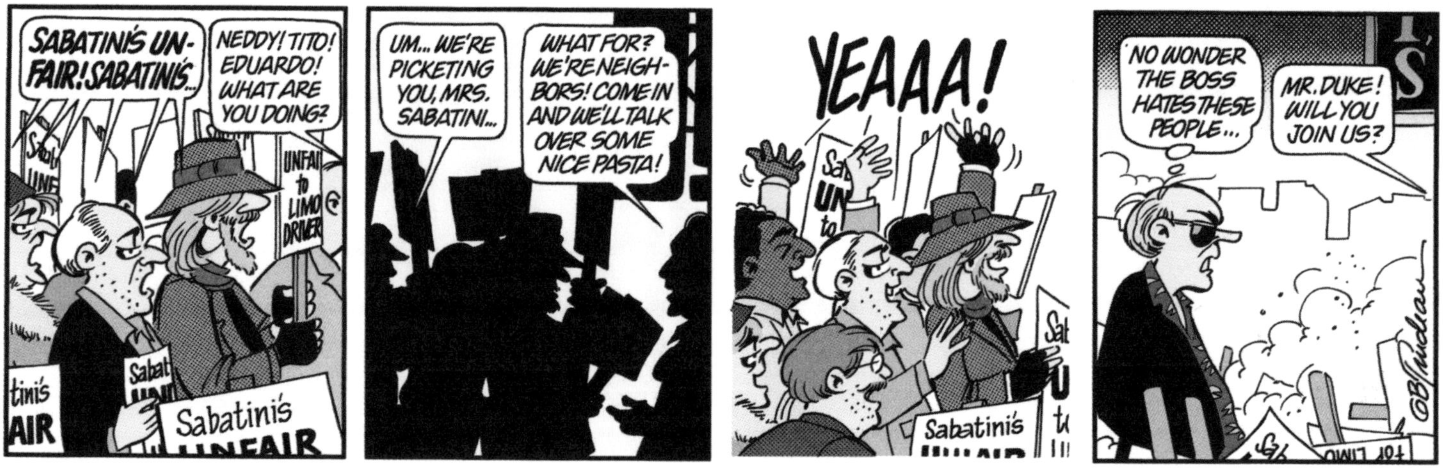
SABATINI'S UNFAIR! SABATINI'S...
NEDDY! TITO! EDUARDO! WHAT ARE YOU DOING?
UNFAIR to LIMO DRIVER
UM... WE'RE PICKETING YOU, MRS. SABATINI...
WHAT FOR? WE'RE NEIGHBORS! COME IN AND WE'LL TALK OVER SOME NICE PASTA!
YEAAA!
NO WONDER THE BOSS HATES THESE PEOPLE...
MR. DUKE! WILL YOU JOIN US?

March 21, 1997

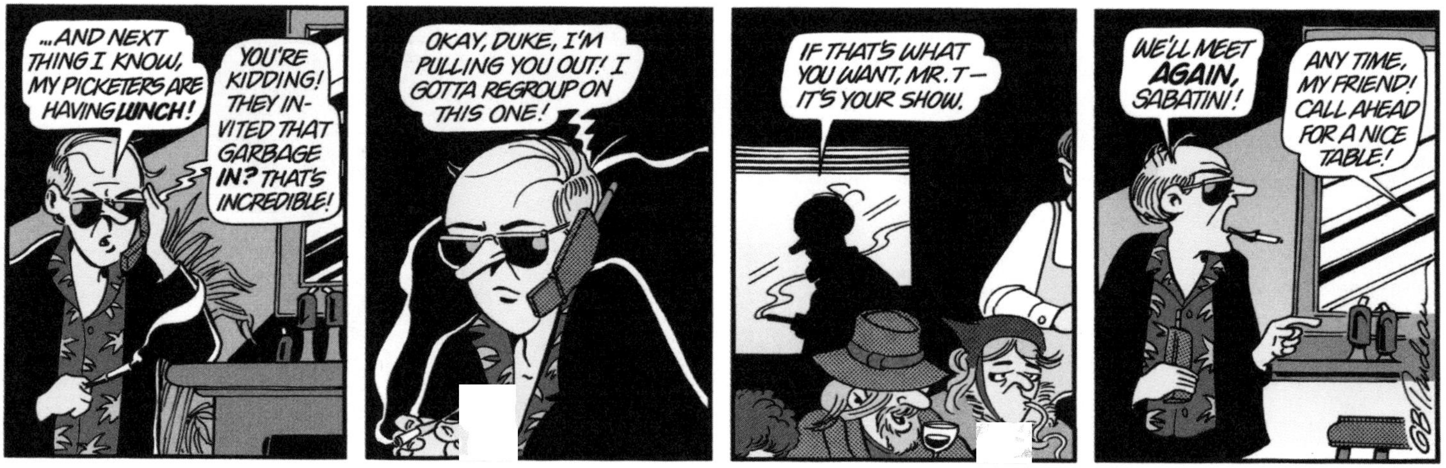
...AND NEXT THING I KNOW, MY PICKETERS ARE HAVING LUNCH!
YOU'RE KIDDING! THEY INVITED THAT GARBAGE IN? THAT'S INCREDIBLE!
OKAY, DUKE, I'M PULLING YOU OUT! I GOTTA REGROUP ON THIS ONE!
IF THAT'S WHAT YOU WANT, MR. T— IT'S YOUR SHOW.
WE'LL MEET AGAIN, SABATINI!
ANY TIME, MY FRIEND! CALL AHEAD FOR A NICE TABLE!

March 22, 1997

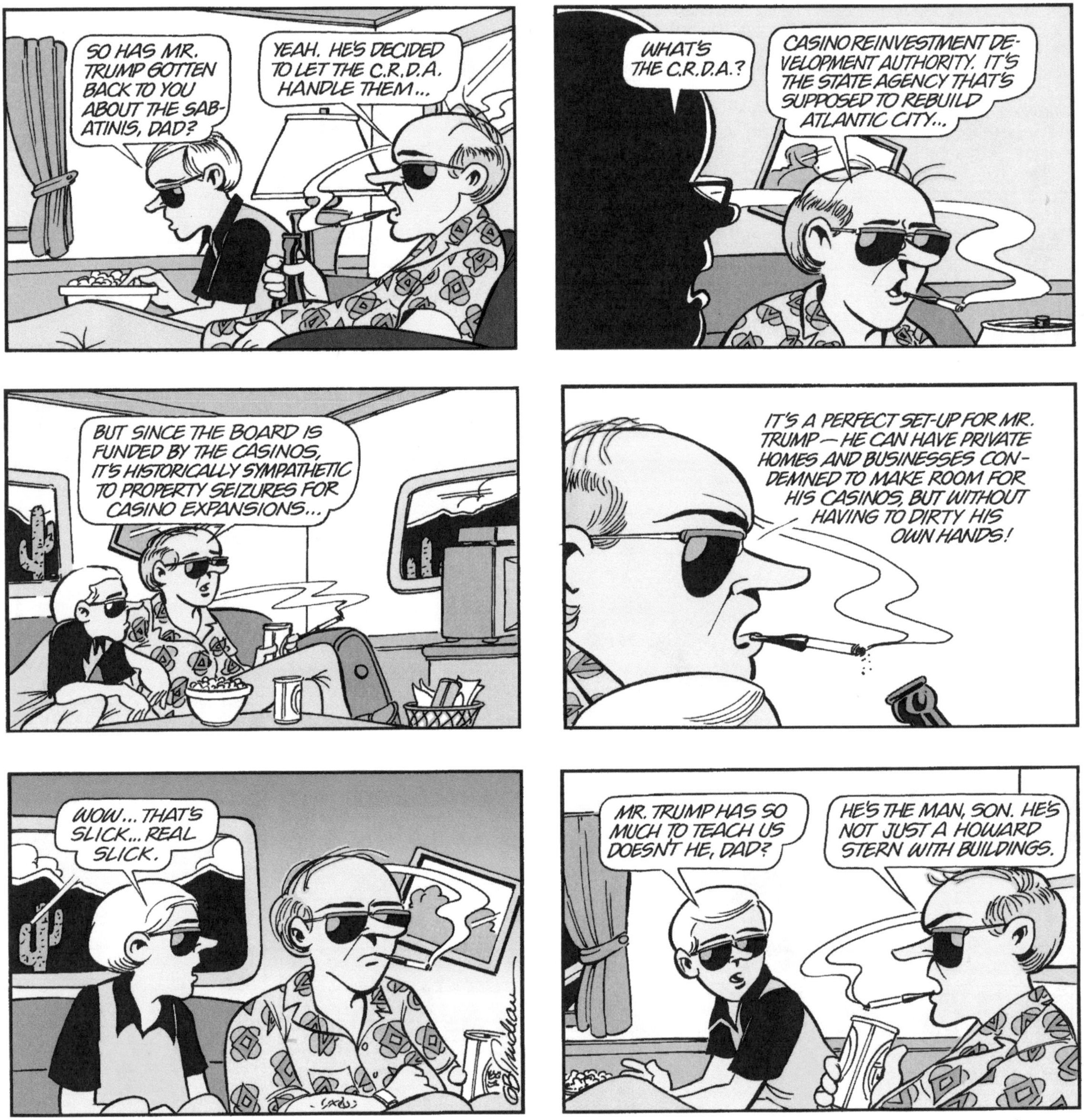
SO HAS MR. TRUMP GOTTEN BACK TO YOU ABOUT THE SABATINIS, DAD?
YEAH. HE'S DECIDED TO LET THE C.R.D.A. HANDLE THEM...
WHAT'S THE C.R.D.A.?
CASINO REINVESTMENT DEVELOPMENT AUTHORITY. IT'S THE STATE AGENCY THAT'S SUPPOSED TO REBUILD ATLANTIC CITY...
BUT SINCE THE BOARD IS FUNDED BY THE CASINOS, IT'S HISTORICALLY SYMPATHETIC TO PROPERTY SEIZURES FOR CASINO EXPANSIONS...
IT'S A PERFECT SET-UP FOR MR. TRUMP — HE CAN HAVE PRIVATE HOMES AND BUSINESSES CONDEMNED TO MAKE ROOM FOR HIS CASINOS, BUT WITHOUT HAVING TO DIRTY HIS OWN HANDS!
WOW... THAT'S SLICK... REAL SLICK.
MR. TRUMP HAS SO MUCH TO TEACH US DOESN'T HE, DAD?
HE'S THE MAN, SON. HE'S NOT JUST A HOWARD STERN WITH BUILDINGS.

April 20, 1997

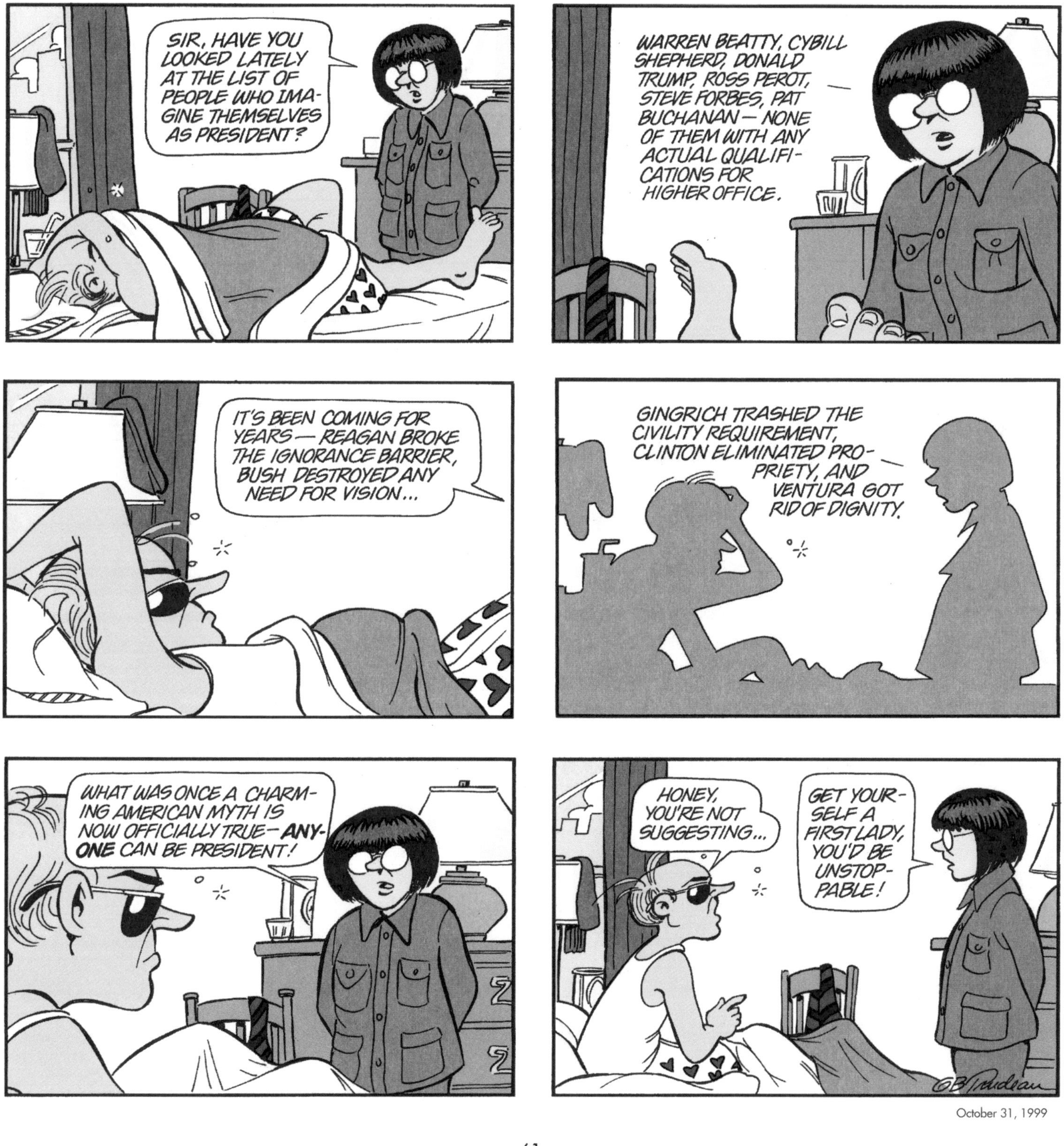
SIR, HAVE YOU LOOKED LATELY AT THE LIST OF PEOPLE WHO IMAGINE THEMSELVES AS PRESIDENT?
WARREN BEATTY, CYBILL SHEPHERD, DONALD TRUMP, ROSS PEROT, STEVE FORBES, PAT BUCHANAN — NONE OF THEM WITH ANY ACTUAL QUALIFICATIONS FOR HIGHER OFFICE.
IT'S BEEN COMING FOR YEARS — REAGAN BROKE THE IGNORANCE BARRIER, BUSH DESTROYED ANY NEED FOR VISION...
GINGRICH TRASHED THE CIVILITY REQUIREMENT, CLINTON ELIMINATED PROPRIETY, AND VENTURA GOT RID OF DIGNITY.
WHAT WAS ONCE A CHARMING AMERICAN MYTH IS NOW OFFICIALLY TRUE — **ANYONE** CAN BE PRESIDENT!
HONEY, YOU'RE NOT SUGGESTING...
GET YOURSELF A FIRST LADY, YOU'D BE UNSTOPPABLE!
©B Trudeau

October 31, 1999

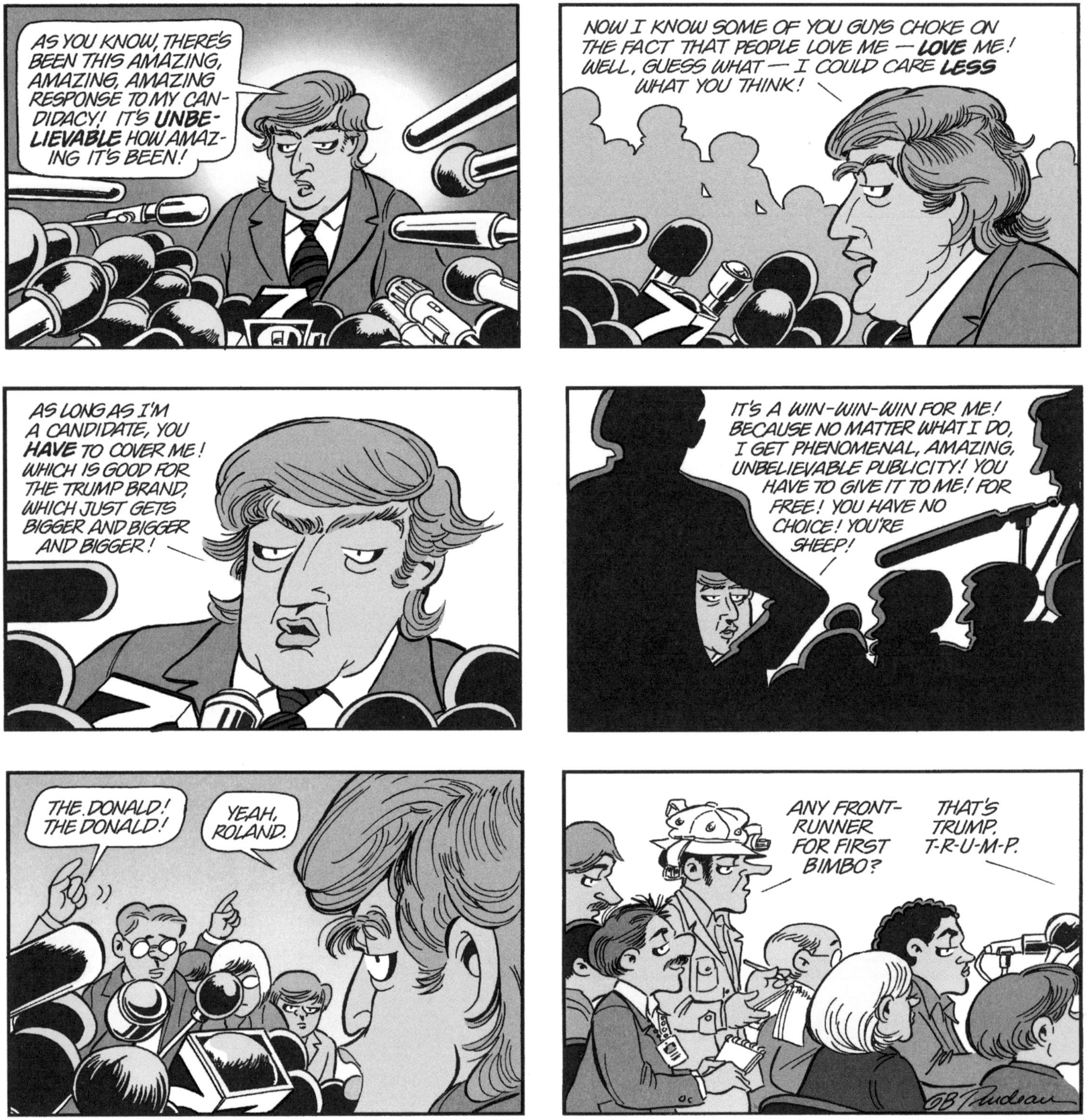
AS YOU KNOW, THERE'S BEEN THIS AMAZING, AMAZING, AMAZING RESPONSE TO MY CANDIDACY! IT'S UNBELIEVABLE HOW AMAZING IT'S BEEN!
NOW I KNOW SOME OF YOU GUYS CHOKE ON THE FACT THAT PEOPLE LOVE ME — LOVE ME! WELL, GUESS WHAT — I COULD CARE LESS WHAT YOU THINK!
AS LONG AS I'M A CANDIDATE, YOU HAVE TO COVER ME! WHICH IS GOOD FOR THE TRUMP BRAND, WHICH JUST GETS BIGGER AND BIGGER AND BIGGER!
IT'S A WIN-WIN-WIN FOR ME! BECAUSE NO MATTER WHAT I DO, I GET PHENOMENAL, AMAZING, UNBELIEVABLE PUBLICITY! YOU HAVE TO GIVE IT TO ME! FOR FREE! YOU HAVE NO CHOICE! YOU'RE SHEEP!
THE DONALD! THE DONALD!
YEAH, ROLAND.
ANY FRONT-RUNNER FOR FIRST BIMBO?
THAT'S TRUMP, T-R-U-M-P.
GB Trudeau

November 14, 1999

Panel 1: MIKE, HOW COME YOU'RE SUPPORTING McCAIN INSTEAD OF FORBES AGAIN?

Panel 2: I DUNNO, I GUESS I JUST ADMIRE HIM MORE. HE SEEMS TO BE THE ONLY ONE OUT THERE WHO'S HOLDING ON TO HIS DIGNITY...

Panel 3: WHICH AIN'T EASY IN A FIELD THAT INCLUDES DONALD TRUMP, JESSE VENTURA, PAT BUCHANAN, WARREN BEATTY, AND GOD KNOWS WHO ELSE.

Panel 4: WHY NOT, SIR? EVERY *OTHER* CARTOON CHARACTER IS RUNNING!

HOW MUCH DOES IT PAY AGAIN?

November 22, 1999

Panel 1: SIR, I'VE GIVEN THIS A LOT OF THOUGHT — THIS IS YOUR YEAR! YOU COULD GO ALL THE WAY!

Panel 2: THE ONLY SERIOUS COMPETITION YOU'D FACE IS PAT BUCHANAN, AND HE'S A BIGOTED, MISOGYNIST, GAY-BASHING, ISOLATIONIST BROWNSHIRT!

Panel 3: BUCHANAN'S A BIGOTED, MISOGYNIST, GAY-BASHING, ISOLATIONIST BROWNSHIRT?

PRETTY MUCH.

Panel 4: SO WHAT THE HELL AM I SUPPOSED TO RUN ON?

THERE'S SOME OVERLAP, IT'S TRUE.

November 23, 1999

Panel 1: THE POINT IS, SIR, THE BAR HAS NEVER BEEN LOWER! IT'S NOT ABOUT CREDENTIALING ANYMORE — IT'S ABOUT BRANDING!

Panel 2: BESIDES, JESSE NEEDS A CANDIDATE FOR THE REFORM PARTY NOMINATION, AND ALL HE'S GOT NOW IS TRUMP!

Panel 3: TRUMP IS RUNNING? *DONALD* TRUMP?

YES, SIR.

Panel 4: WHAT JOB IS THIS AGAIN?

PRESIDENT. DON'T LET THE CANDIDATES THROW YOU.

November 24, 1999

63

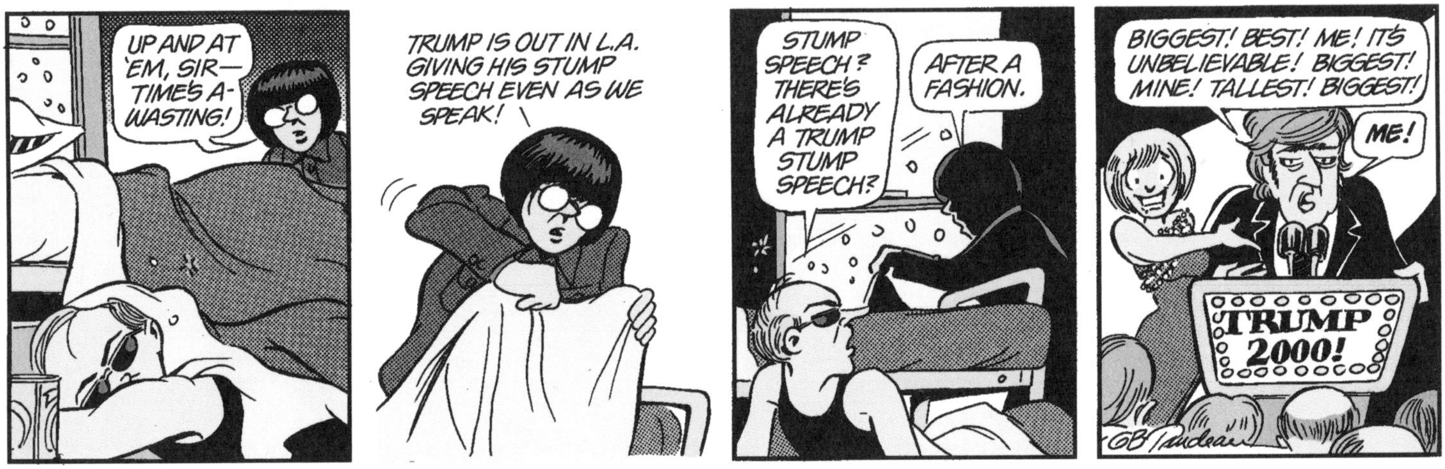

UP AND AT 'EM, SIR— TIME'S A-WASTING!
TRUMP IS OUT IN L.A. GIVING HIS STUMP SPEECH EVEN AS WE SPEAK!
STUMP SPEECH? THERE'S ALREADY A TRUMP STUMP SPEECH?
AFTER A FASHION.
BIGGEST! BEST! ME! IT'S UNBELIEVABLE! BIGGEST! MINE! TALLEST! BIGGEST!
ME!
TRUMP 2000!

December 6, 1999

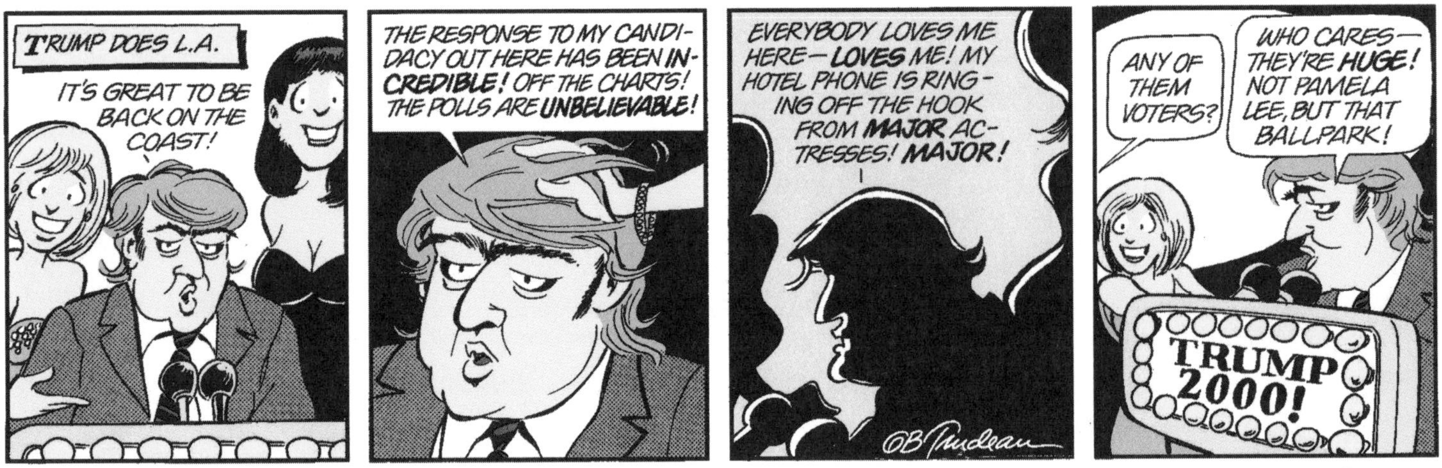

TRUMP DOES L.A.
IT'S GREAT TO BE BACK ON THE COAST!
THE RESPONSE TO MY CANDIDACY OUT HERE HAS BEEN INCREDIBLE! OFF THE CHARTS! THE POLLS ARE UNBELIEVABLE!
EVERYBODY LOVES ME HERE—LOVES ME! MY HOTEL PHONE IS RINGING OFF THE HOOK FROM MAJOR ACTRESSES! MAJOR!
ANY OF THEM VOTERS?
WHO CARES—THEY'RE HUGE! NOT PAMELA LEE, BUT THAT BALLPARK!
TRUMP 2000!

December 7, 1999

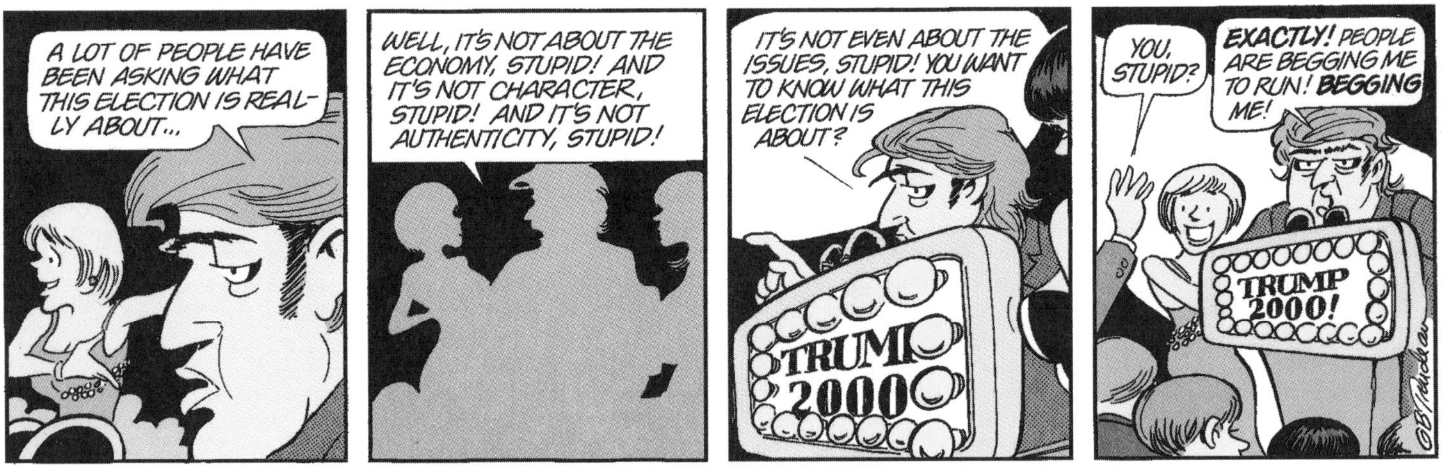

A LOT OF PEOPLE HAVE BEEN ASKING WHAT THIS ELECTION IS REALLY ABOUT...
WELL, IT'S NOT ABOUT THE ECONOMY, STUPID! AND IT'S NOT CHARACTER, STUPID! AND IT'S NOT AUTHENTICITY, STUPID!
IT'S NOT EVEN ABOUT THE ISSUES, STUPID! YOU WANT TO KNOW WHAT THIS ELECTION IS ABOUT?
YOU, STUPID?
EXACTLY! PEOPLE ARE BEGGING ME TO RUN! BEGGING ME!
TRUMP 2000!

December 8, 1999

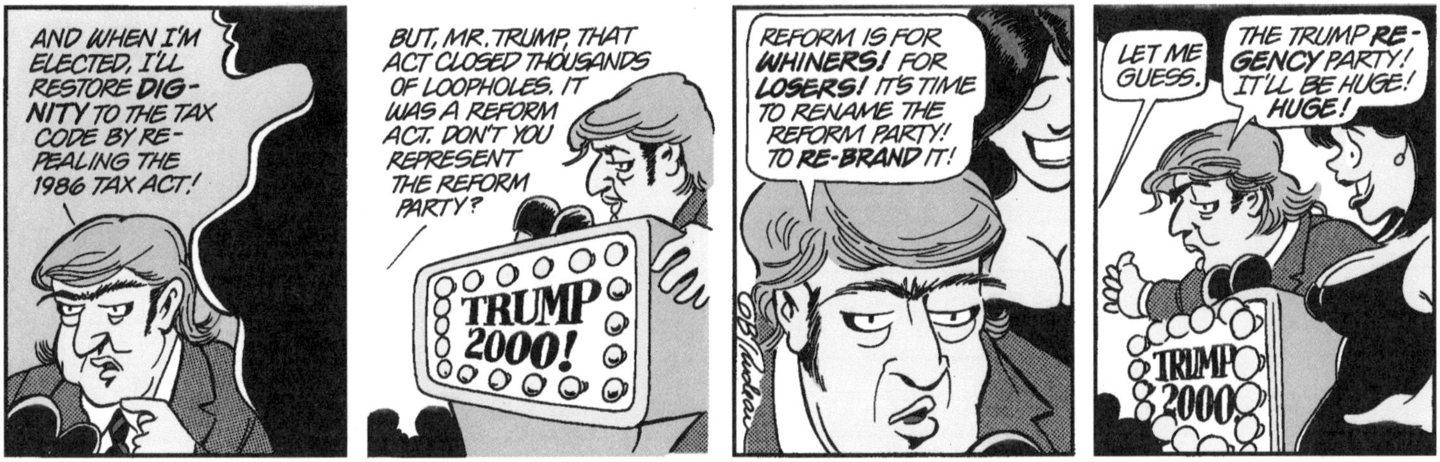
AND WHEN I'M ELECTED, I'LL RESTORE **DIGNITY** TO THE TAX CODE BY REPEALING THE 1986 TAX ACT!
BUT, MR. TRUMP, THAT ACT CLOSED THOUSANDS OF LOOPHOLES. IT WAS A REFORM ACT. DON'T YOU REPRESENT THE REFORM PARTY?
TRUMP 2000!
REFORM IS FOR **WHINERS!** FOR **LOSERS!** IT'S TIME TO RENAME THE REFORM PARTY! TO **RE-BRAND** IT!
LET ME GUESS.
THE TRUMP **REGENCY** PARTY! IT'LL BE HUGE! **HUGE!**
TRUMP 2000

December 9, 1999

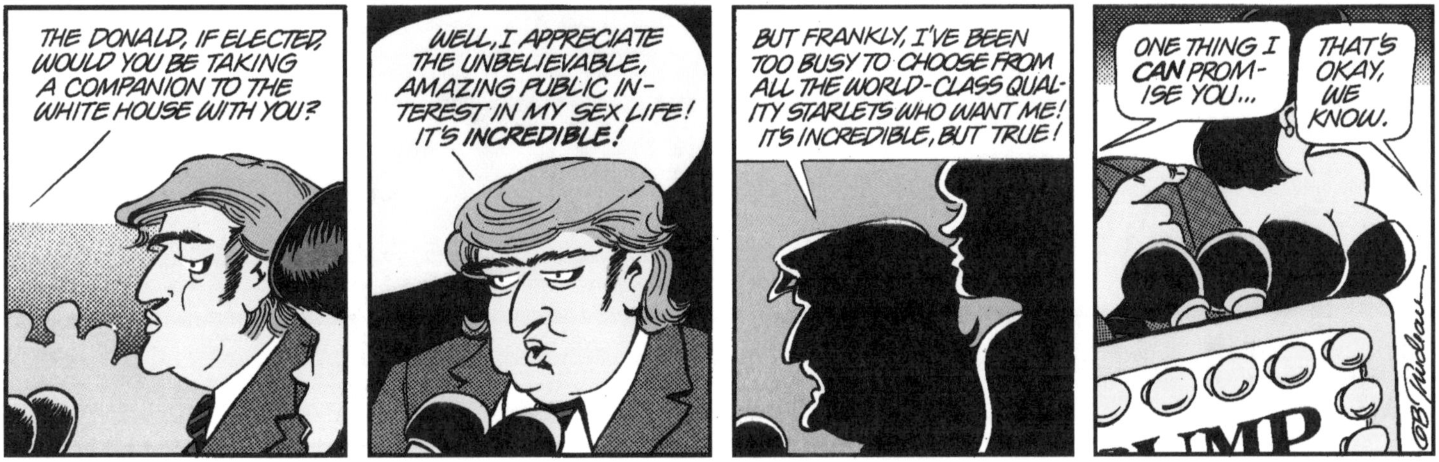
THE DONALD, IF ELECTED, WOULD YOU BE TAKING A COMPANION TO THE WHITE HOUSE WITH YOU?
WELL, I APPRECIATE THE UNBELIEVABLE, AMAZING PUBLIC INTEREST IN MY SEX LIFE! IT'S **INCREDIBLE!**
BUT FRANKLY, I'VE BEEN TOO BUSY TO CHOOSE FROM ALL THE WORLD-CLASS QUALITY STARLETS WHO WANT ME! IT'S INCREDIBLE, BUT TRUE!
ONE THING I **CAN** PROMISE YOU...
THAT'S OKAY, WE KNOW.

December 10, 1999

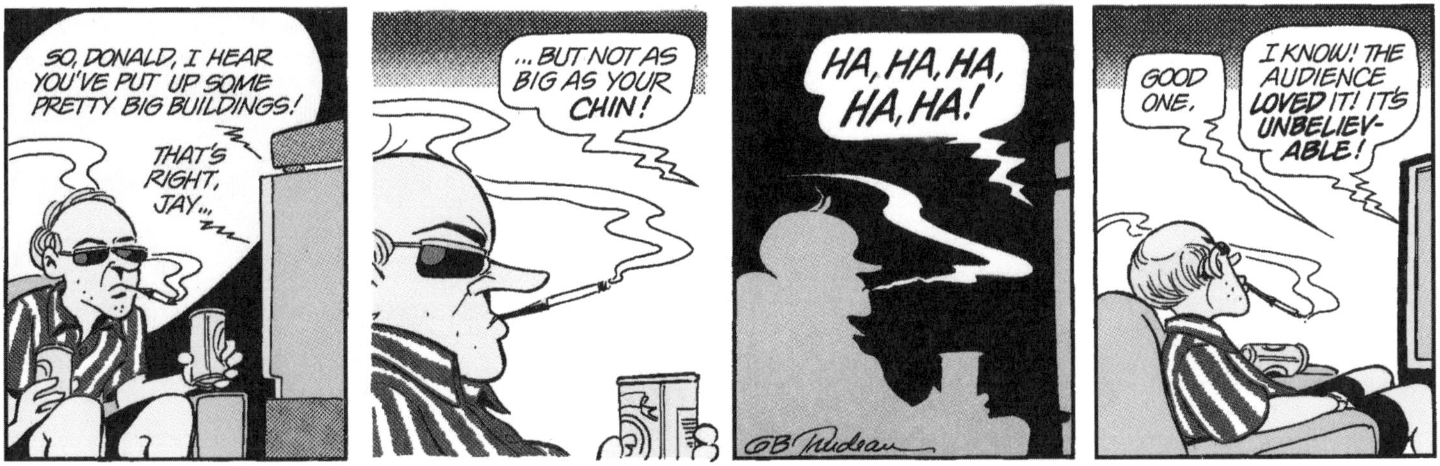
SO, DONALD, I HEAR YOU'VE PUT UP SOME PRETTY BIG BUILDINGS!
THAT'S RIGHT, JAY...
...BUT NOT AS BIG AS YOUR **CHIN!**
HA, HA, HA, HA, HA!
GOOD ONE.
I KNOW! THE AUDIENCE **LOVED** IT! IT'S **UNBELIEVABLE!**

December 11, 1999

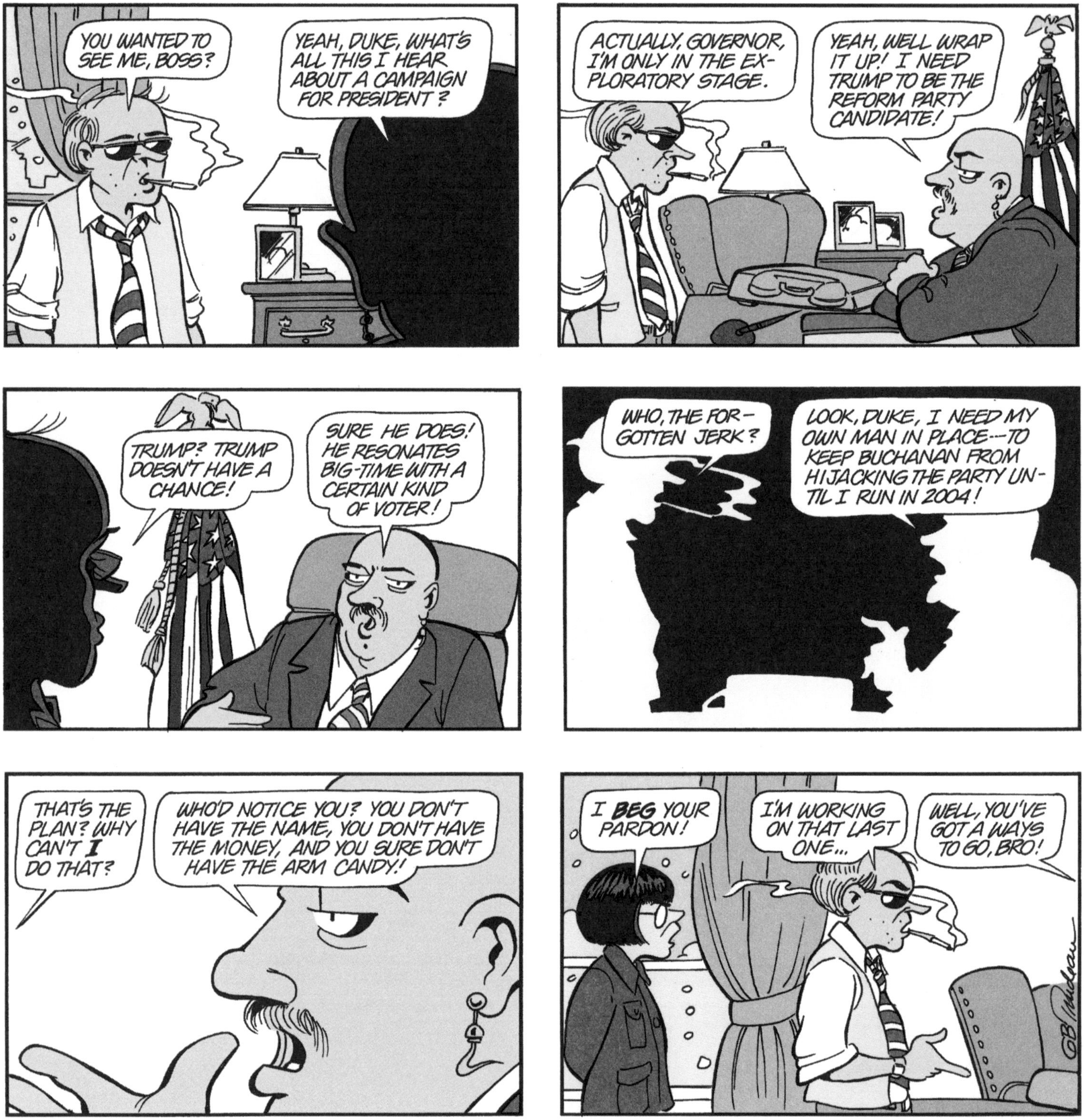
YOU WANTED TO SEE ME, BOSS?
YEAH, DUKE, WHAT'S ALL THIS I HEAR ABOUT A CAMPAIGN FOR PRESIDENT?
ACTUALLY, GOVERNOR, I'M ONLY IN THE EXPLORATORY STAGE.
YEAH, WELL WRAP IT UP! I NEED TRUMP TO BE THE REFORM PARTY CANDIDATE!
TRUMP? TRUMP DOESN'T HAVE A CHANCE!
SURE HE DOES! HE RESONATES BIG-TIME WITH A CERTAIN KIND OF VOTER!
WHO, THE FORGOTTEN JERK?
LOOK, DUKE, I NEED MY OWN MAN IN PLACE--TO KEEP BUCHANAN FROM HIJACKING THE PARTY UNTIL I RUN IN 2004!
THAT'S THE PLAN? WHY CAN'T **I** DO THAT?
WHO'D NOTICE YOU? YOU DON'T HAVE THE NAME, YOU DON'T HAVE THE MONEY, AND YOU SURE DON'T HAVE THE ARM CANDY!
I **BEG** YOUR PARDON!
I'M WORKING ON THAT LAST ONE...
WELL, YOU'VE GOT A WAYS TO GO, BRO!
GBTrudeau

December 26, 1999

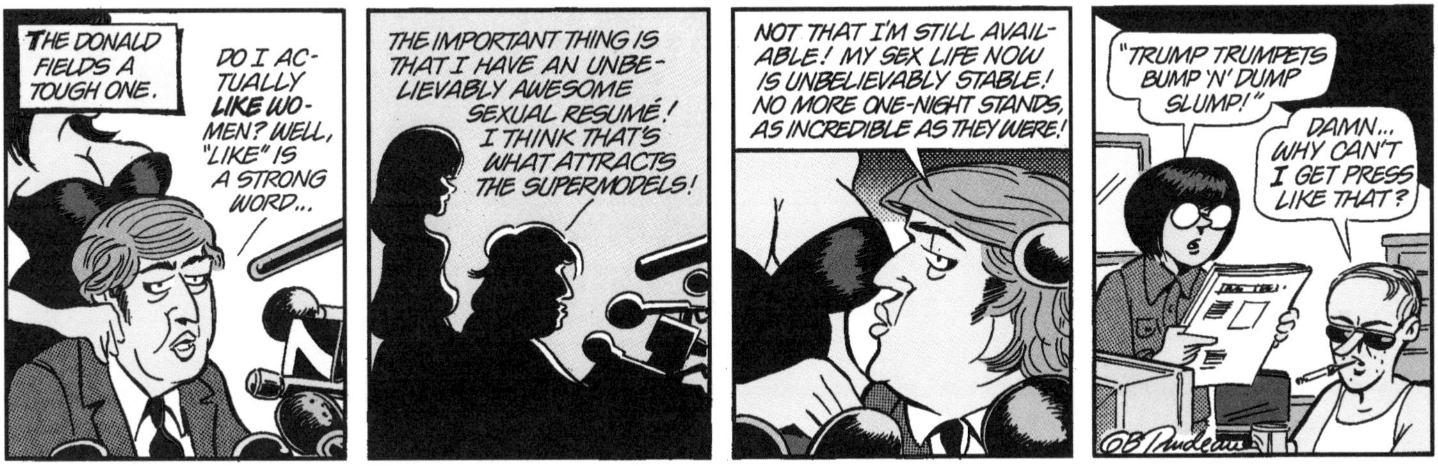
THE DONALD FIELDS A TOUGH ONE.
DO I ACTUALLY LIKE WOMEN? WELL, "LIKE" IS A STRONG WORD...
THE IMPORTANT THING IS THAT I HAVE AN UNBELIEVABLY AWESOME SEXUAL RESUMÉ! I THINK THAT'S WHAT ATTRACTS THE SUPERMODELS!
NOT THAT I'M STILL AVAILABLE! MY SEX LIFE NOW IS UNBELIEVABLY STABLE! NO MORE ONE-NIGHT STANDS, AS INCREDIBLE AS THEY WERE!
"TRUMP TRUMPETS BUMP 'N' DUMP SLUMP!"
DAMN... WHY CAN'T I GET PRESS LIKE THAT?

December 27, 1999

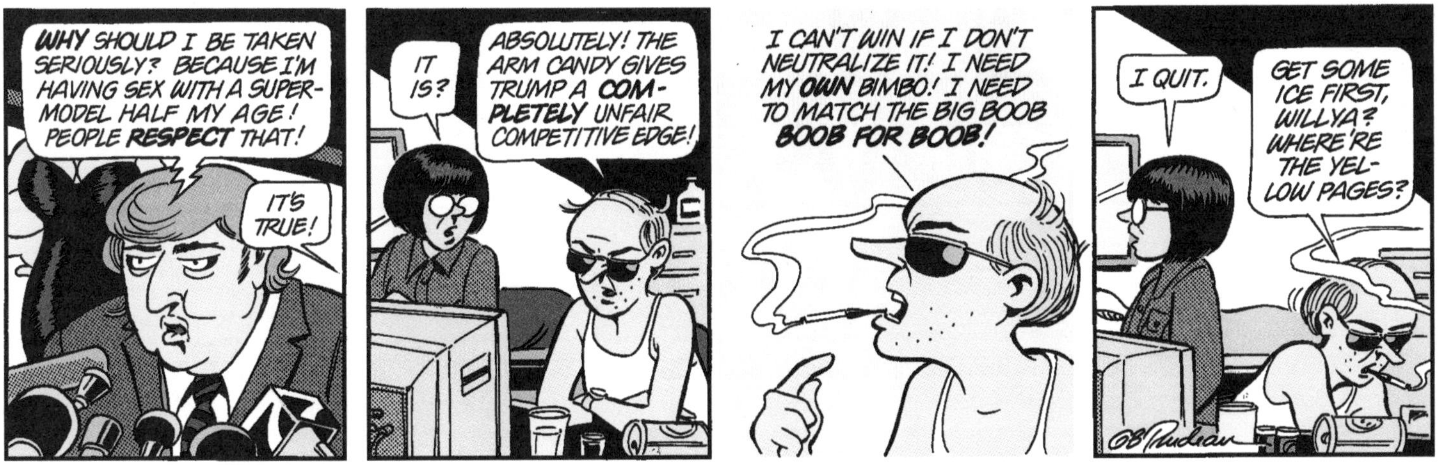
WHY SHOULD I BE TAKEN SERIOUSLY? BECAUSE I'M HAVING SEX WITH A SUPERMODEL HALF MY AGE! PEOPLE RESPECT THAT!
IT'S TRUE!
IT IS?
ABSOLUTELY! THE ARM CANDY GIVES TRUMP A COMPLETELY UNFAIR COMPETITIVE EDGE!
I CAN'T WIN IF I DON'T NEUTRALIZE IT! I NEED MY OWN BIMBO! I NEED TO MATCH THE BIG BOOB BOOB FOR BOOB!
I QUIT.
GET SOME ICE FIRST, WILLYA? WHERE'RE THE YELLOW PAGES?

December 28, 1999

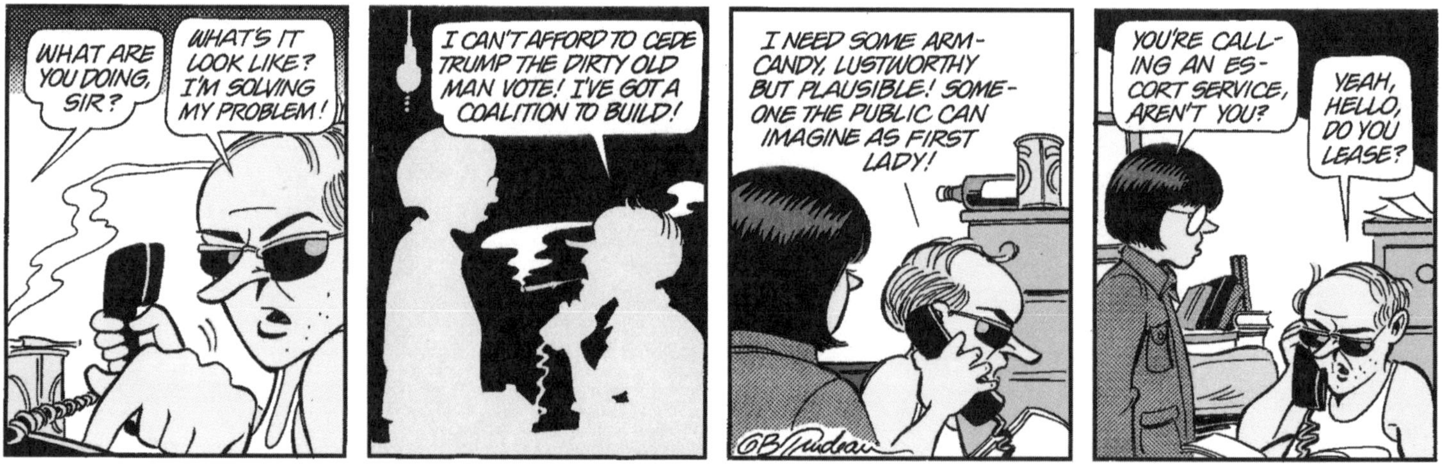
WHAT ARE YOU DOING, SIR?
WHAT'S IT LOOK LIKE? I'M SOLVING MY PROBLEM!
I CAN'T AFFORD TO CEDE TRUMP THE DIRTY OLD MAN VOTE! I'VE GOT A COALITION TO BUILD!
I NEED SOME ARM-CANDY, LUSTWORTHY BUT PLAUSIBLE! SOMEONE THE PUBLIC CAN IMAGINE AS FIRST LADY!
©B Trudeau
YOU'RE CALLING AN ESCORT SERVICE, AREN'T YOU?
YEAH, HELLO, DO YOU LEASE?

December 29, 1999

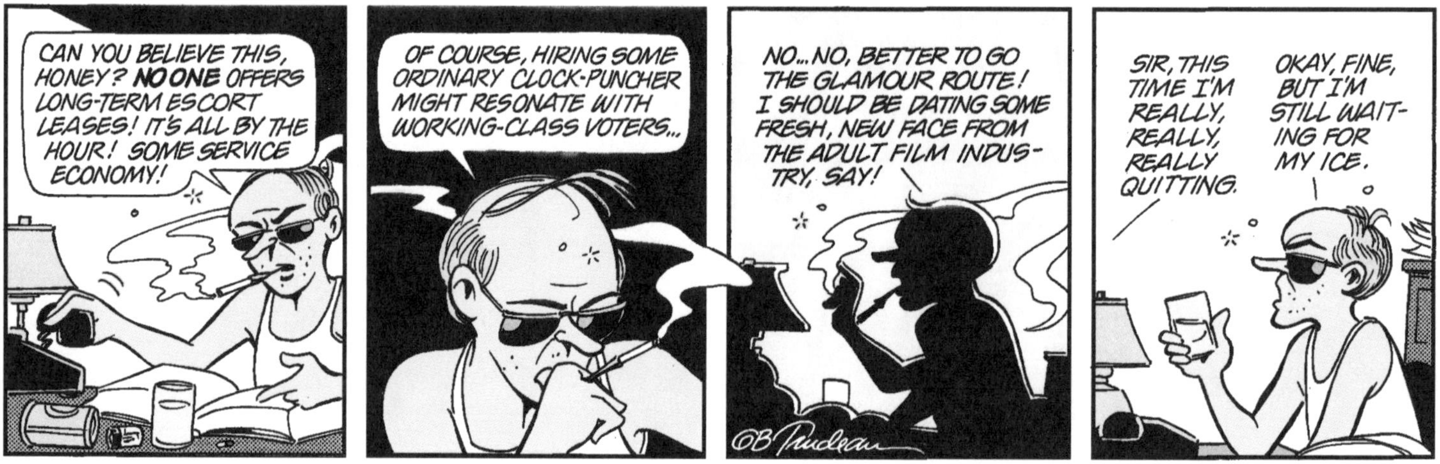
CAN YOU BELIEVE THIS, HONEY? **NO ONE** OFFERS LONG-TERM ESCORT LEASES! IT'S ALL BY THE HOUR! SOME SERVICE ECONOMY!
OF COURSE, HIRING SOME ORDINARY CLOCK-PUNCHER MIGHT RESONATE WITH WORKING-CLASS VOTERS...
NO... NO, BETTER TO GO THE GLAMOUR ROUTE! I SHOULD BE DATING SOME FRESH, NEW FACE FROM THE ADULT FILM INDUSTRY, SAY!
©B Trudeau
SIR, THIS TIME I'M REALLY, REALLY, REALLY QUITTING.
OKAY, FINE, BUT I'M STILL WAITING FOR MY ICE.

December 30, 1999

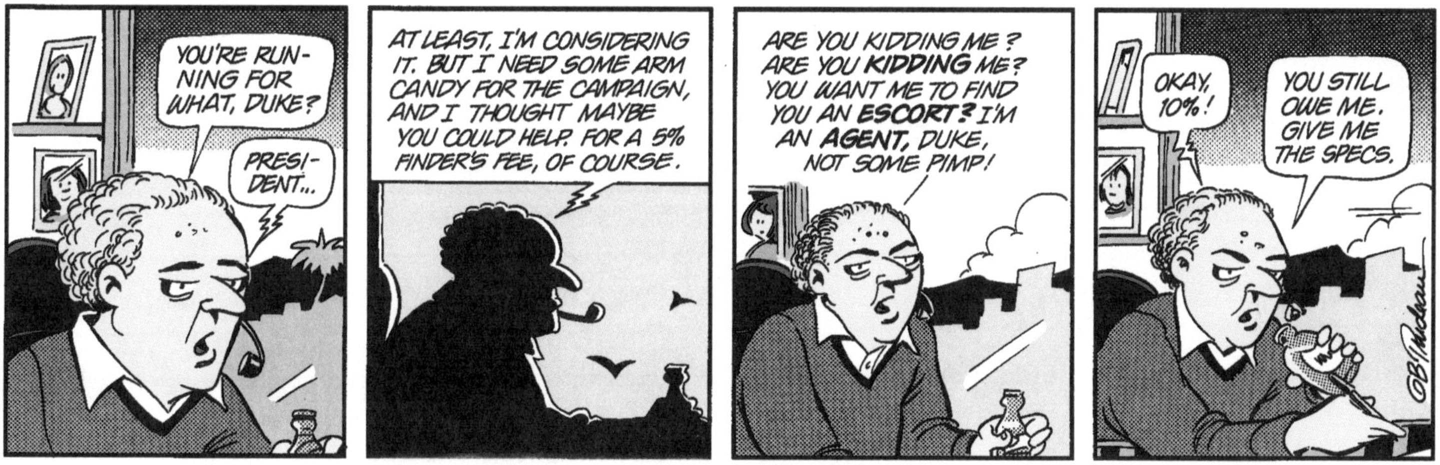
YOU'RE RUN-NING FOR WHAT, DUKE?
PRESI-DENT...
AT LEAST, I'M CONSIDERING IT. BUT I NEED SOME ARM CANDY FOR THE CAMPAIGN, AND I THOUGHT MAYBE YOU COULD HELP. FOR A 5% FINDER'S FEE, OF COURSE.
ARE YOU KIDDING ME? ARE YOU **KIDDING** ME? YOU WANT ME TO FIND YOU AN **ESCORT?** I'M AN **AGENT,** DUKE, NOT SOME PIMP!
OKAY, 10%!
YOU STILL OWE ME. GIVE ME THE SPECS.

December 31, 1999

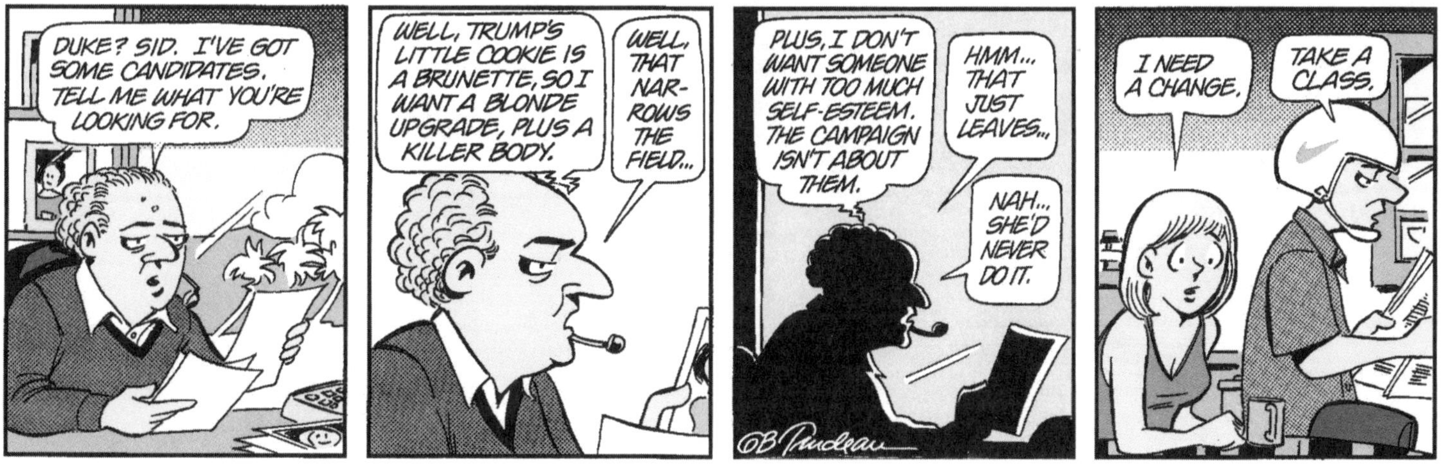
DUKE? SID. I'VE GOT SOME CANDIDATES. TELL ME WHAT YOU'RE LOOKING FOR.
WELL, TRUMP'S LITTLE COOKIE IS A BRUNETTE, SO I WANT A BLONDE UPGRADE, PLUS A KILLER BODY.
WELL, THAT NAR-ROWS THE FIELD...
PLUS, I DON'T WANT SOMEONE WITH TOO MUCH SELF-ESTEEM. THE CAMPAIGN ISN'T ABOUT THEM.
HMM... THAT JUST LEAVES...
NAH... SHE'D NEVER DO IT.
I NEED A CHANGE.
TAKE A CLASS.

January 1, 2000

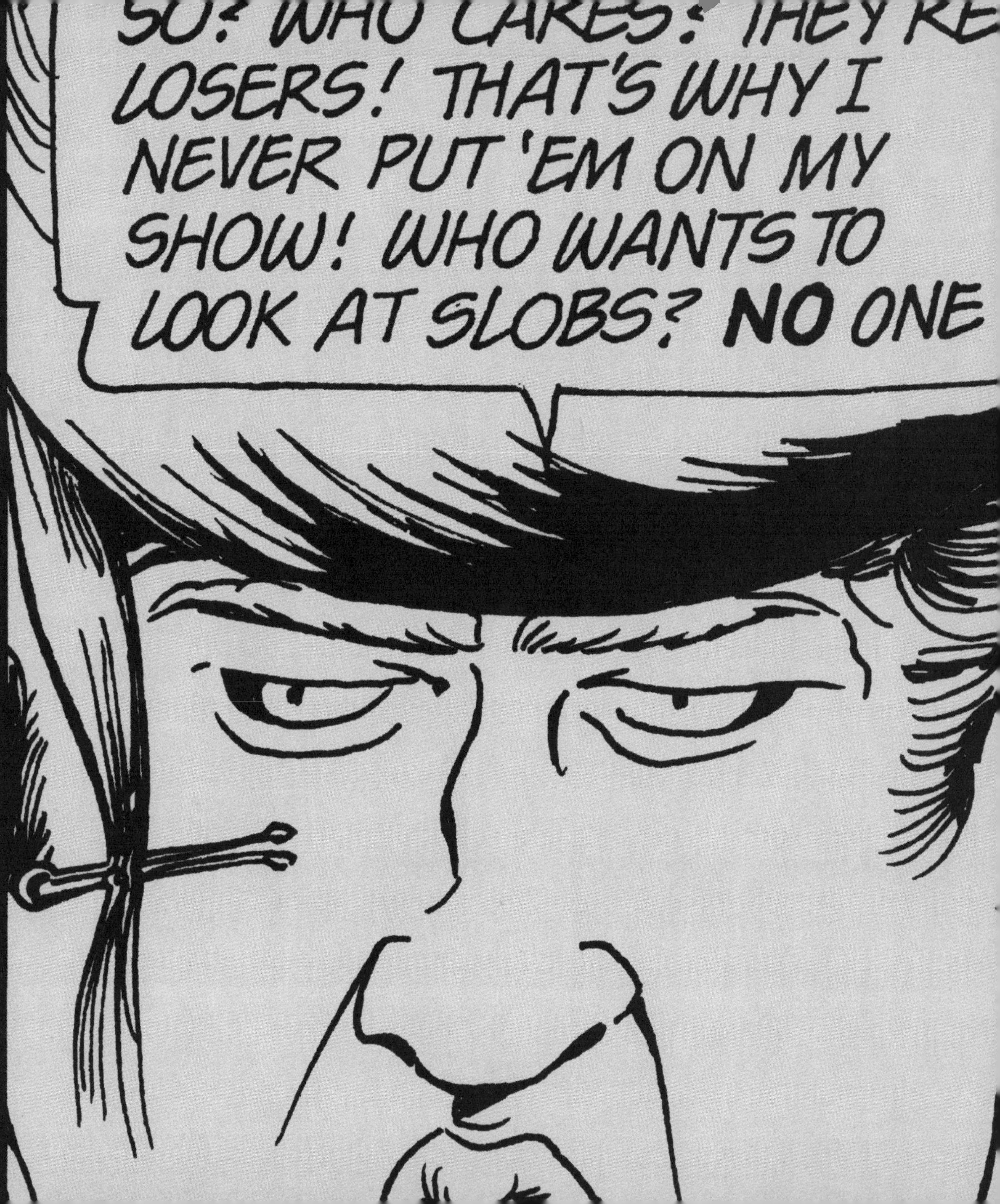
SO? WHO CARES? THEY'RE
LOSERS! THAT'S WHY I
NEVER PUT 'EM ON MY
SHOW! WHO WANTS TO
LOOK AT SLOBS? NO ONE

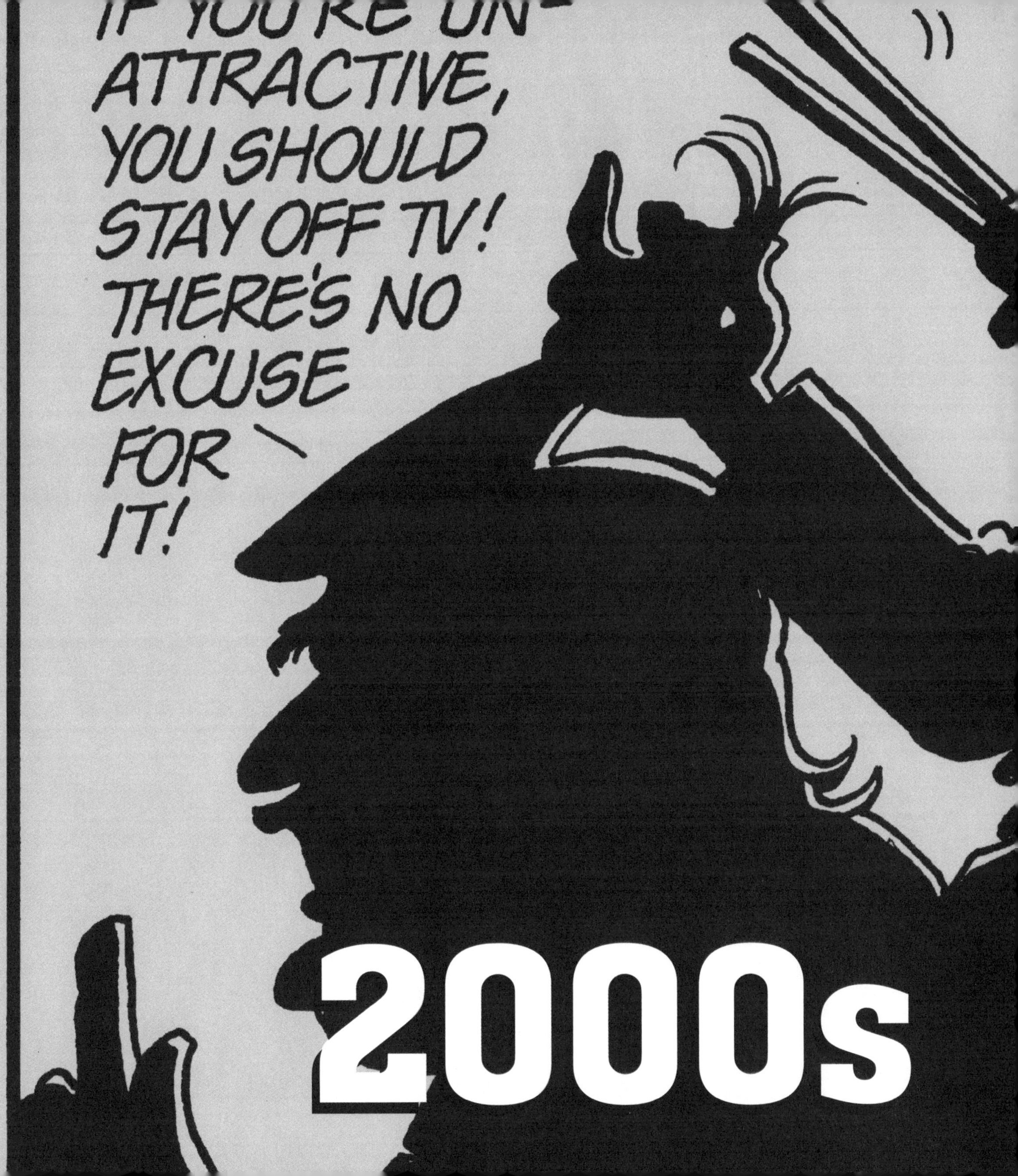
IF YOU'RE UN-ATTRACTIVE, YOU SHOULD STAY OFF TV! THERE'S NO EXCUSE FOR IT!

2000s

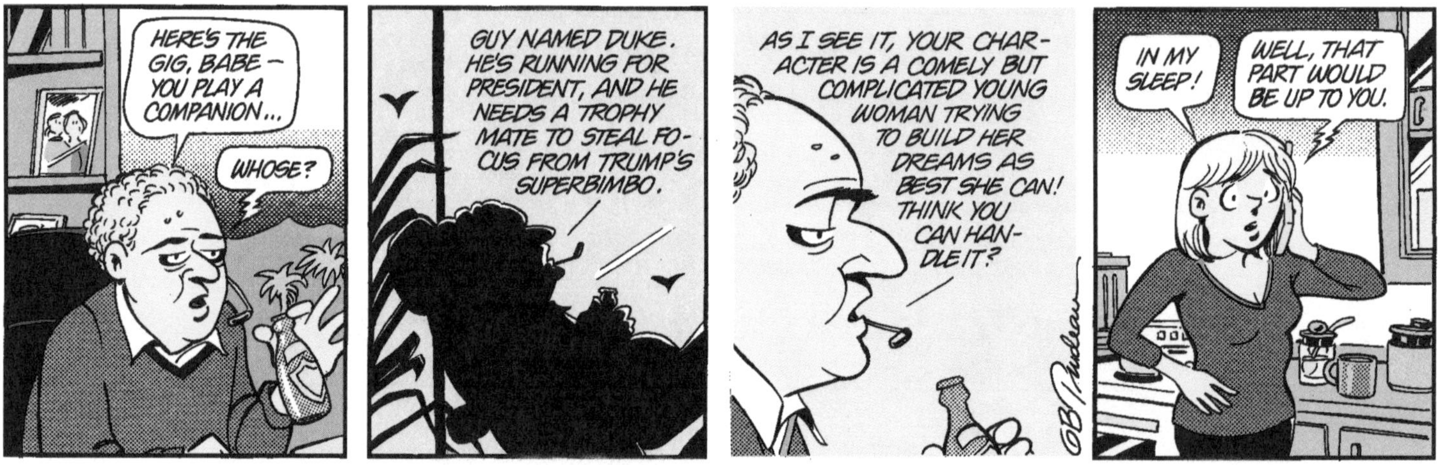
HERE'S THE GIG, BABE — YOU PLAY A COMPANION...
WHOSE?
GUY NAMED DUKE. HE'S RUNNING FOR PRESIDENT, AND HE NEEDS A TROPHY MATE TO STEAL FOCUS FROM TRUMP'S SUPERBIMBO.
AS I SEE IT, YOUR CHARACTER IS A COMELY BUT COMPLICATED YOUNG WOMAN TRYING TO BUILD HER DREAMS AS BEST SHE CAN! THINK YOU CAN HANDLE IT?
IN MY SLEEP!
WELL, THAT PART WOULD BE UP TO YOU.

January 10, 2000

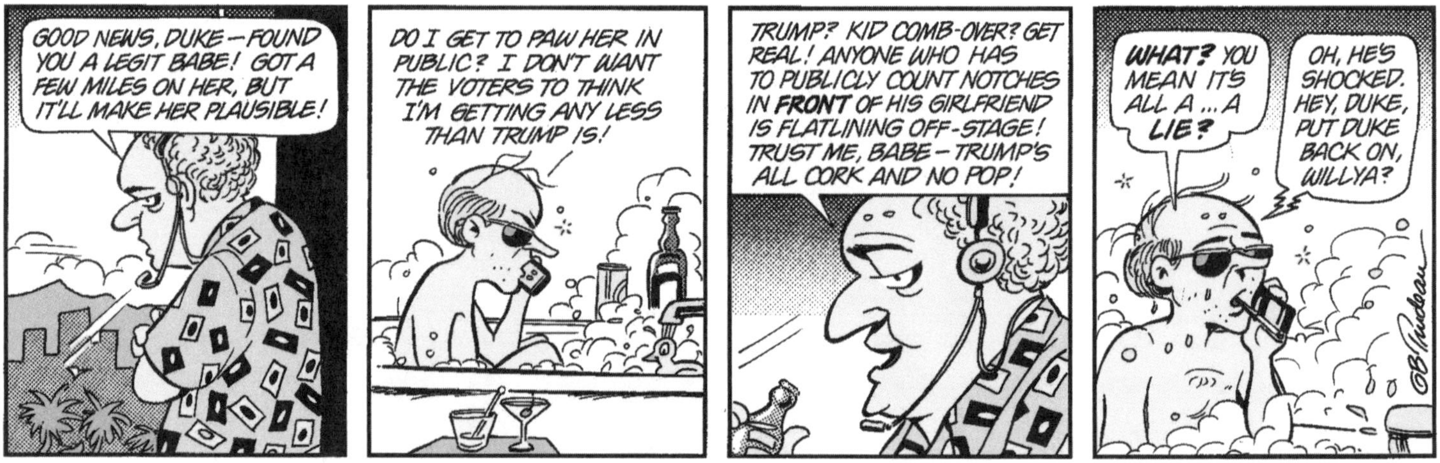
GOOD NEWS, DUKE — FOUND YOU A LEGIT BABE! GOT A FEW MILES ON HER, BUT IT'LL MAKE HER PLAUSIBLE!
DO I GET TO PAW HER IN PUBLIC? I DON'T WANT THE VOTERS TO THINK I'M GETTING ANY LESS THAN TRUMP IS!
TRUMP? KID COMB-OVER? GET REAL! ANYONE WHO HAS TO PUBLICLY COUNT NOTCHES IN **FRONT** OF HIS GIRLFRIEND IS FLATLINING OFF-STAGE! TRUST ME, BABE — TRUMP'S ALL CORK AND NO POP!
WHAT? YOU MEAN IT'S ALL A ... A **LIE?**
OH, HE'S SHOCKED. HEY, DUKE, PUT DUKE BACK ON, WILLYA?

January 11, 2000

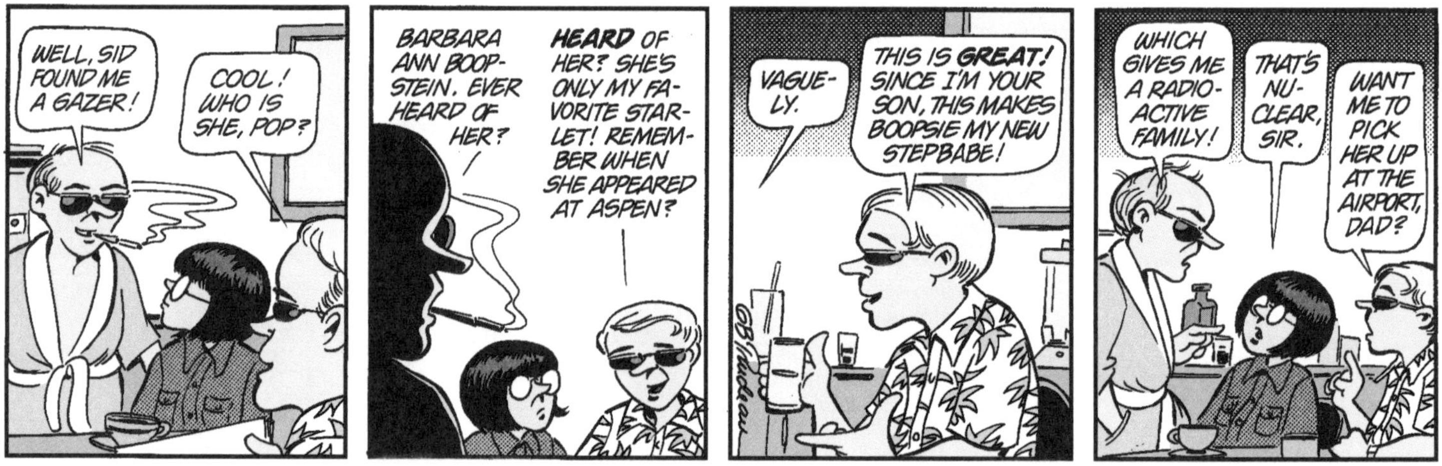
WELL, SID FOUND ME A GAZER!
COOL! WHO IS SHE, POP?
BARBARA ANN BOOPSTEIN. EVER HEARD OF HER?
HEARD OF HER? SHE'S ONLY MY FAVORITE STARLET! REMEMBER WHEN SHE APPEARED AT ASPEN?
VAGUELY.
THIS IS **GREAT!** SINCE I'M YOUR SON, THIS MAKES BOOPSIE MY NEW STEPBABE!
WHICH GIVES ME A RADIOACTIVE FAMILY!
THAT'S NUCLEAR, SIR.
WANT ME TO PICK HER UP AT THE AIRPORT, DAD?

January 12, 2000

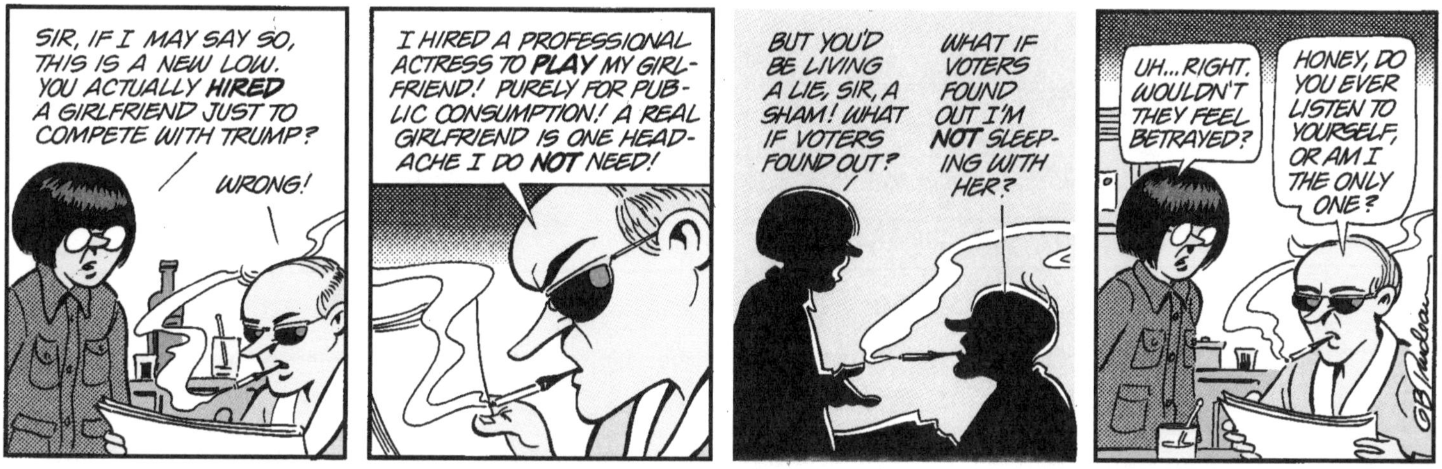
SIR, IF I MAY SAY SO, THIS IS A NEW LOW. YOU ACTUALLY **HIRED** A GIRLFRIEND JUST TO COMPETE WITH TRUMP?
WRONG!
I HIRED A PROFESSIONAL ACTRESS TO **PLAY** MY GIRLFRIEND! PURELY FOR PUBLIC CONSUMPTION! A REAL GIRLFRIEND IS ONE HEADACHE I DO **NOT** NEED!
BUT YOU'D BE LIVING A LIE, SIR, A SHAM! WHAT IF VOTERS FOUND OUT?
WHAT IF VOTERS FOUND OUT I'M **NOT** SLEEPING WITH HER?
UH... RIGHT. WOULDN'T THEY FEEL BETRAYED?
HONEY, DO YOU EVER LISTEN TO YOURSELF, OR AM I THE ONLY ONE?

January 13, 2000

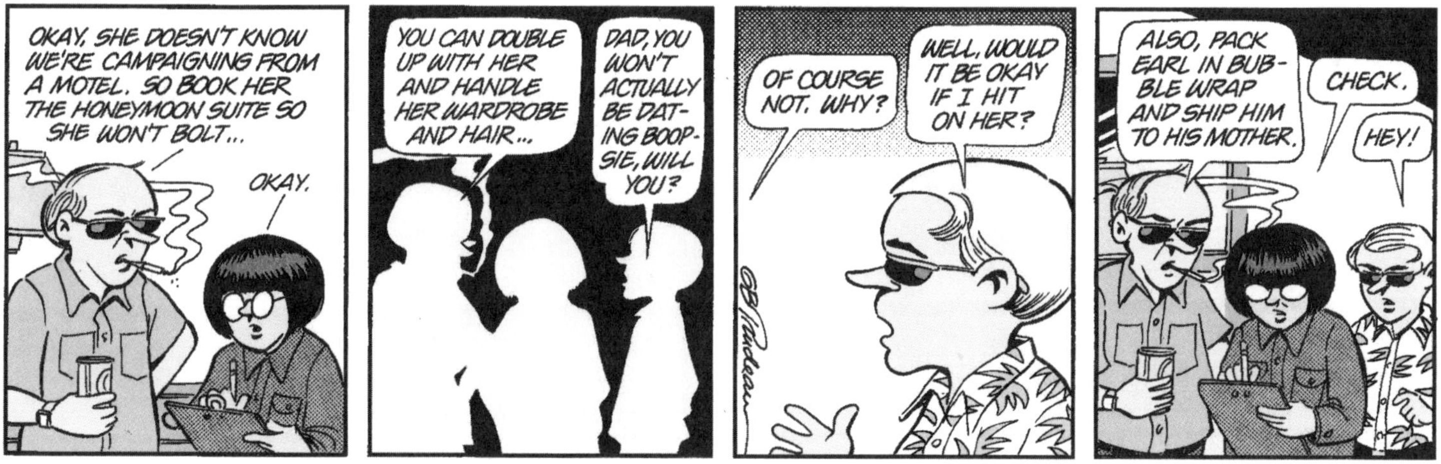
OKAY, SHE DOESN'T KNOW WE'RE CAMPAIGNING FROM A MOTEL. SO BOOK HER THE HONEYMOON SUITE SO SHE WON'T BOLT...
OKAY.
YOU CAN DOUBLE UP WITH HER AND HANDLE HER WARDROBE AND HAIR...
DAD, YOU WON'T ACTUALLY BE DATING BOOPSIE, WILL YOU?
OF COURSE NOT. WHY?
WELL, WOULD IT BE OKAY IF I HIT ON HER?
ALSO, PACK EARL IN BUBBLE WRAP AND SHIP HIM TO HIS MOTHER.
CHECK.
HEY!

January 14, 2000

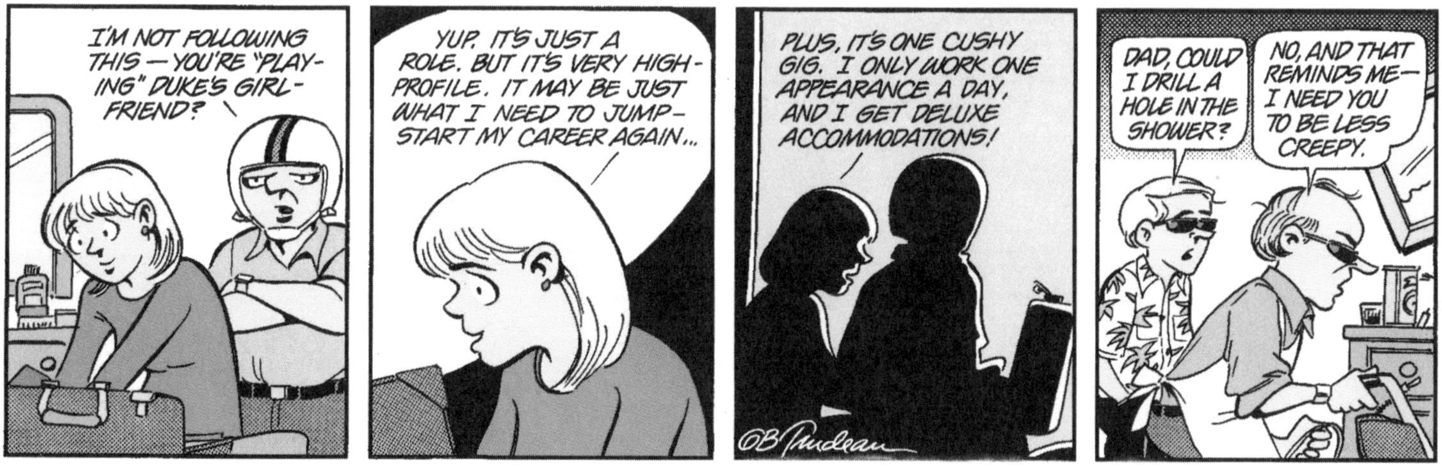
I'M NOT FOLLOWING THIS — YOU'RE "PLAYING" DUKE'S GIRLFRIEND?
YUP. IT'S JUST A ROLE. BUT IT'S VERY HIGH-PROFILE. IT MAY BE JUST WHAT I NEED TO JUMP-START MY CAREER AGAIN...
PLUS, IT'S ONE CUSHY GIG. I ONLY WORK ONE APPEARANCE A DAY, AND I GET DELUXE ACCOMMODATIONS!
DAD, COULD I DRILL A HOLE IN THE SHOWER?
NO, AND THAT REMINDS ME— I NEED YOU TO BE LESS CREEPY.

January 15, 2000

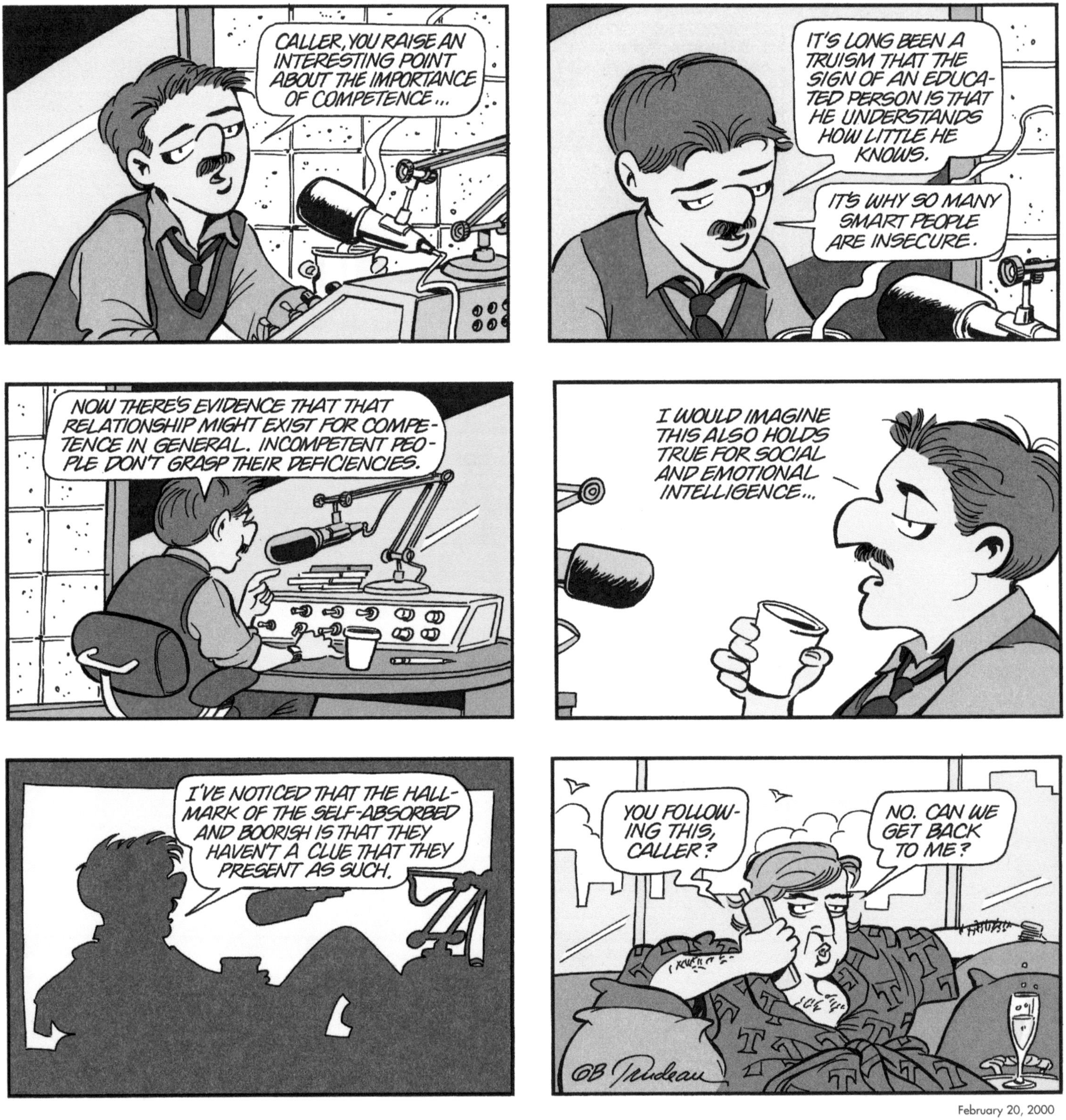
CALLER, YOU RAISE AN INTERESTING POINT ABOUT THE IMPORTANCE OF COMPETENCE...
IT'S LONG BEEN A TRUISM THAT THE SIGN OF AN EDUCATED PERSON IS THAT HE UNDERSTANDS HOW LITTLE HE KNOWS.
IT'S WHY SO MANY SMART PEOPLE ARE INSECURE.
NOW THERE'S EVIDENCE THAT THAT RELATIONSHIP MIGHT EXIST FOR COMPETENCE IN GENERAL. INCOMPETENT PEOPLE DON'T GRASP THEIR DEFICIENCIES.
I WOULD IMAGINE THIS ALSO HOLDS TRUE FOR SOCIAL AND EMOTIONAL INTELLIGENCE...
I'VE NOTICED THAT THE HALLMARK OF THE SELF-ABSORBED AND BOORISH IS THAT THEY HAVEN'T A CLUE THAT THEY PRESENT AS SUCH.
YOU FOLLOWING THIS, CALLER?
NO. CAN WE GET BACK TO ME?
GB Trudeau

February 20, 2000

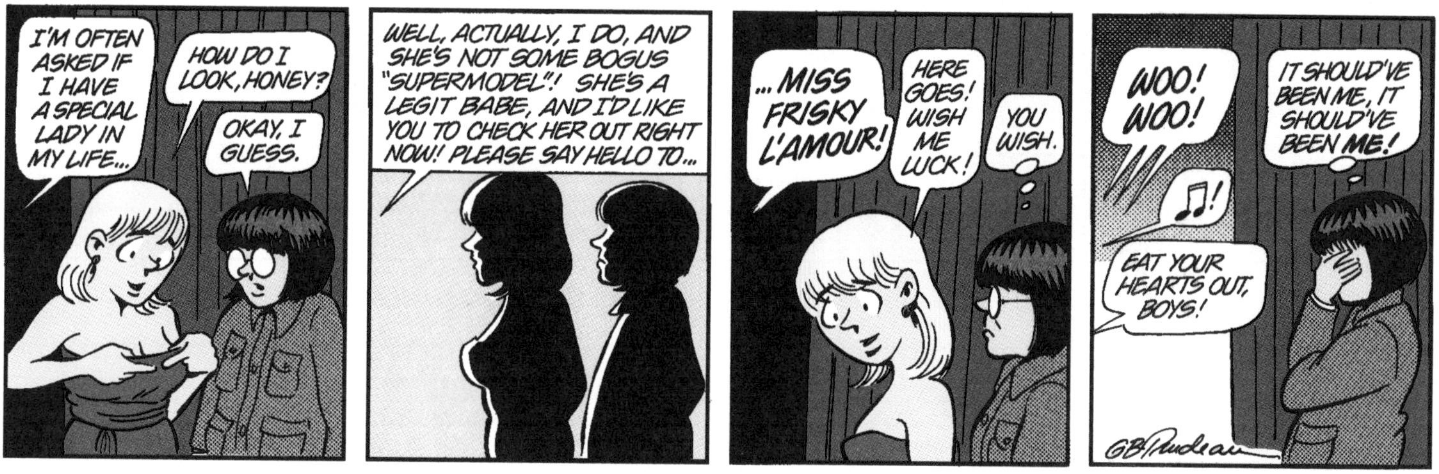
I'M OFTEN ASKED IF I HAVE A SPECIAL LADY IN MY LIFE...
HOW DO I LOOK, HONEY?
OKAY, I GUESS.
WELL, ACTUALLY, I DO, AND SHE'S NOT SOME BOGUS "SUPERMODEL"! SHE'S A LEGIT BABE, AND I'D LIKE YOU TO CHECK HER OUT RIGHT NOW! PLEASE SAY HELLO TO...
...MISS FRISKY L'AMOUR!
HERE GOES! WISH ME LUCK!
YOU WISH.
WOO! WOO!
♫!
EAT YOUR HEARTS OUT, BOYS!
IT SHOULD'VE BEEN ME, IT SHOULD'VE BEEN ME!

February 21, 2000

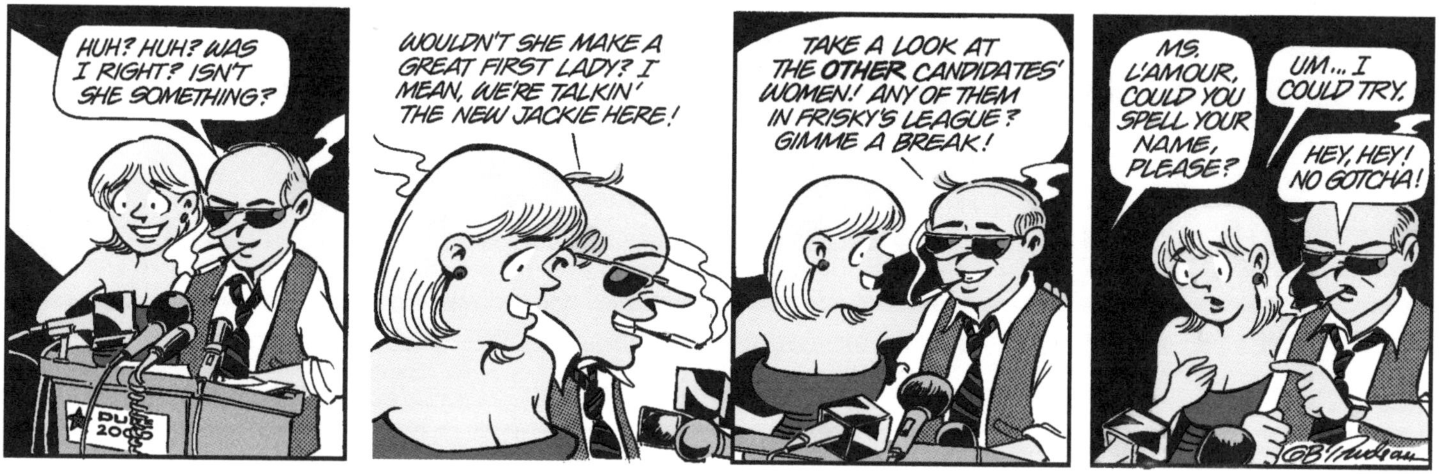
HUH? HUH? WAS I RIGHT? ISN'T SHE SOMETHING?
WOULDN'T SHE MAKE A GREAT FIRST LADY? I MEAN, WE'RE TALKIN' THE NEW JACKIE HERE!
TAKE A LOOK AT THE OTHER CANDIDATES' WOMEN! ANY OF THEM IN FRISKY'S LEAGUE? GIMME A BREAK!
MS. L'AMOUR, COULD YOU SPELL YOUR NAME, PLEASE?
UM... I COULD TRY.
HEY, HEY! NO GOTCHA!

February 22, 2000

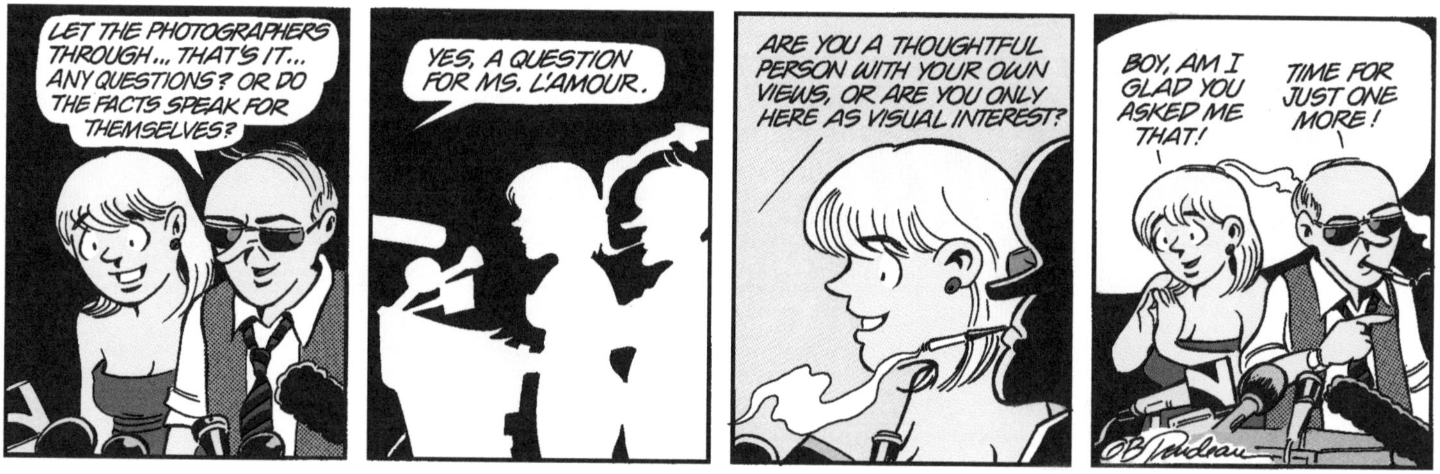
LET THE PHOTOGRAPHERS THROUGH... THAT'S IT... ANY QUESTIONS? OR DO THE FACTS SPEAK FOR THEMSELVES?
YES, A QUESTION FOR MS. L'AMOUR.
ARE YOU A THOUGHTFUL PERSON WITH YOUR OWN VIEWS, OR ARE YOU ONLY HERE AS VISUAL INTEREST?
BOY, AM I GLAD YOU ASKED ME THAT!
TIME FOR JUST ONE MORE!

February 23, 2000

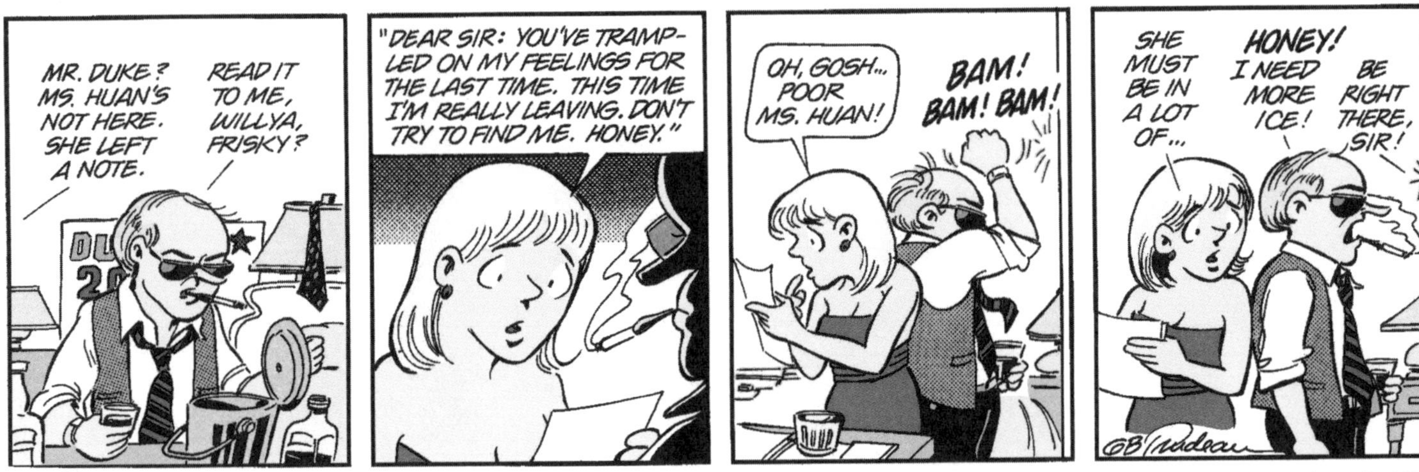
MR. DUKE? MS. HUAN'S NOT HERE. SHE LEFT A NOTE.
READ IT TO ME, WILLYA, FRISKY?
"DEAR SIR: YOU'VE TRAMPLED ON MY FEELINGS FOR THE LAST TIME. THIS TIME I'M REALLY LEAVING. DON'T TRY TO FIND ME. HONEY."
OH, GOSH... POOR MS. HUAN!
BAM! BAM! BAM!
SHE MUST BE IN A LOT OF...
HONEY! I NEED MORE ICE!
BE RIGHT THERE, SIR!

February 24, 2000

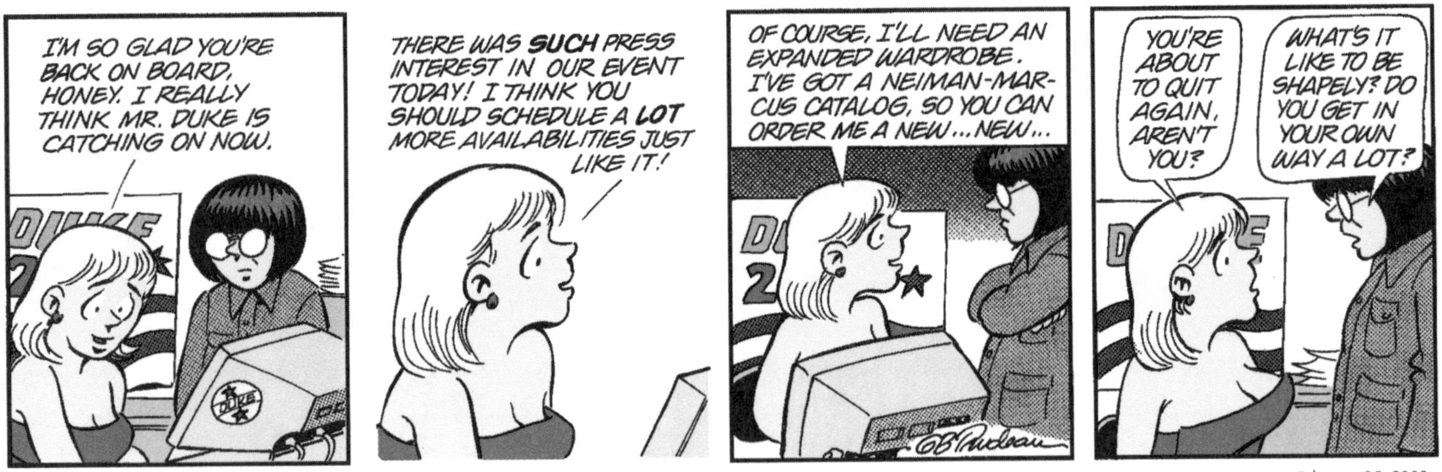
I'M SO GLAD YOU'RE BACK ON BOARD, HONEY. I REALLY THINK MR. DUKE IS CATCHING ON NOW.
THERE WAS SUCH PRESS INTEREST IN OUR EVENT TODAY! I THINK YOU SHOULD SCHEDULE A LOT MORE AVAILABILITIES JUST LIKE IT!
OF COURSE, I'LL NEED AN EXPANDED WARDROBE. I'VE GOT A NEIMAN-MARCUS CATALOG, SO YOU CAN ORDER ME A NEW... NEW...
YOU'RE ABOUT TO QUIT AGAIN, AREN'T YOU?
WHAT'S IT LIKE TO BE SHAPELY? DO YOU GET IN YOUR OWN WAY A LOT?

February 25, 2000

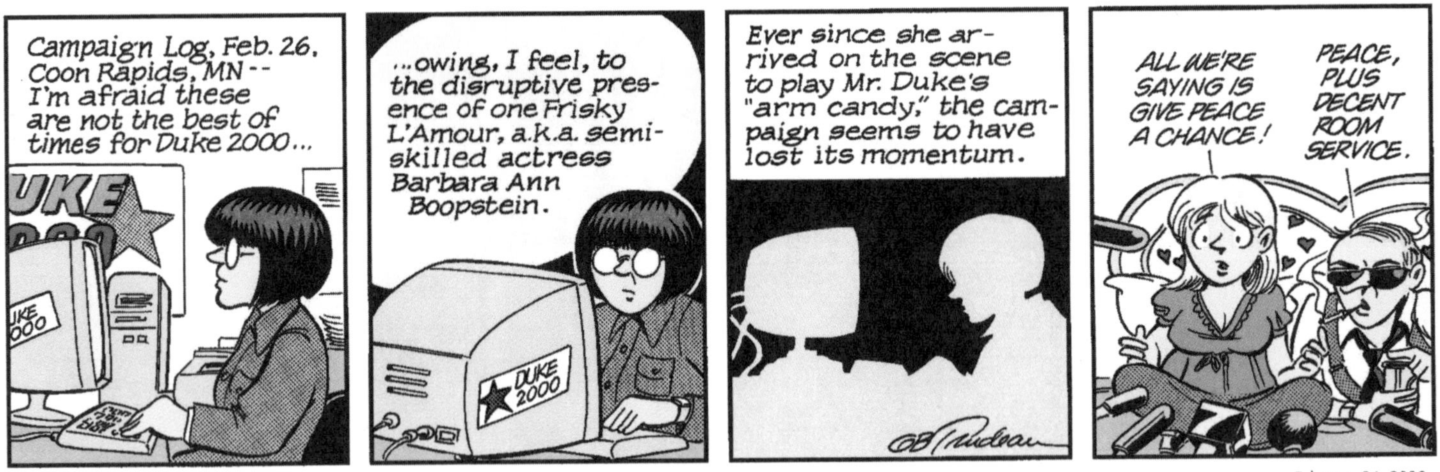
Campaign Log, Feb. 26. Coon Rapids, MN -- I'm afraid these are not the best of times for Duke 2000...
...owing, I feel, to the disruptive presence of one Frisky L'Amour, a.k.a. semi-skilled actress Barbara Ann Boopstein.
Ever since she arrived on the scene to play Mr. Duke's "arm candy," the campaign seems to have lost its momentum.
ALL WE'RE SAYING IS GIVE PEACE A CHANCE!
PEACE, PLUS DECENT ROOM SERVICE.

February 26, 2000

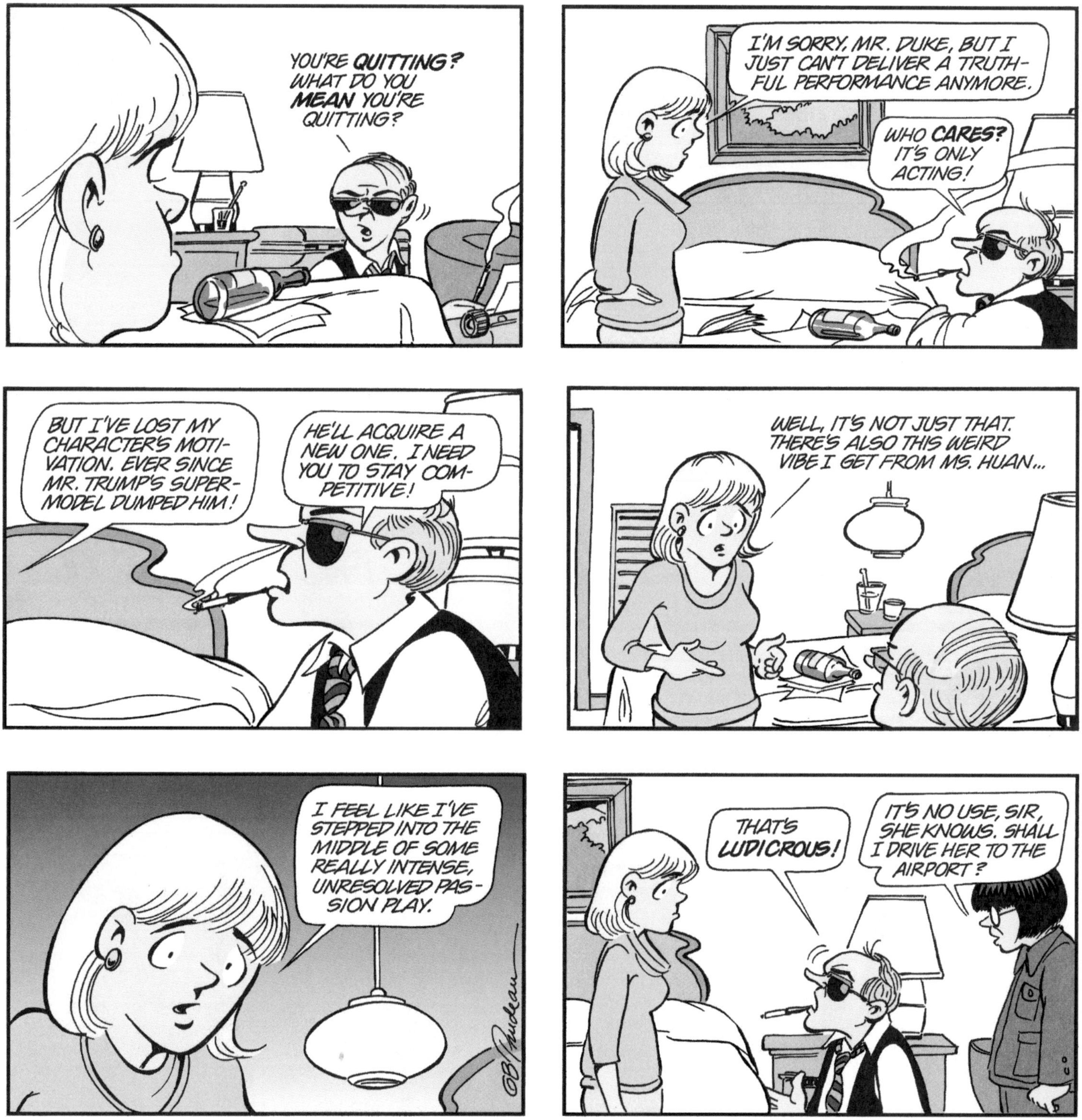
YOU'RE QUITTING? WHAT DO YOU MEAN YOU'RE QUITTING?
I'M SORRY, MR. DUKE, BUT I JUST CAN'T DELIVER A TRUTHFUL PERFORMANCE ANYMORE.
WHO CARES? IT'S ONLY ACTING!
BUT I'VE LOST MY CHARACTER'S MOTIVATION. EVER SINCE MR. TRUMP'S SUPERMODEL DUMPED HIM!
HE'LL ACQUIRE A NEW ONE. I NEED YOU TO STAY COMPETITIVE!
WELL, IT'S NOT JUST THAT. THERE'S ALSO THIS WEIRD VIBE I GET FROM MS. HUAN...
I FEEL LIKE I'VE STEPPED INTO THE MIDDLE OF SOME REALLY INTENSE, UNRESOLVED PASSION PLAY.
©B. Trudeau
THAT'S LUDICROUS!
IT'S NO USE, SIR, SHE KNOWS. SHALL I DRIVE HER TO THE AIRPORT?

February 27, 2000

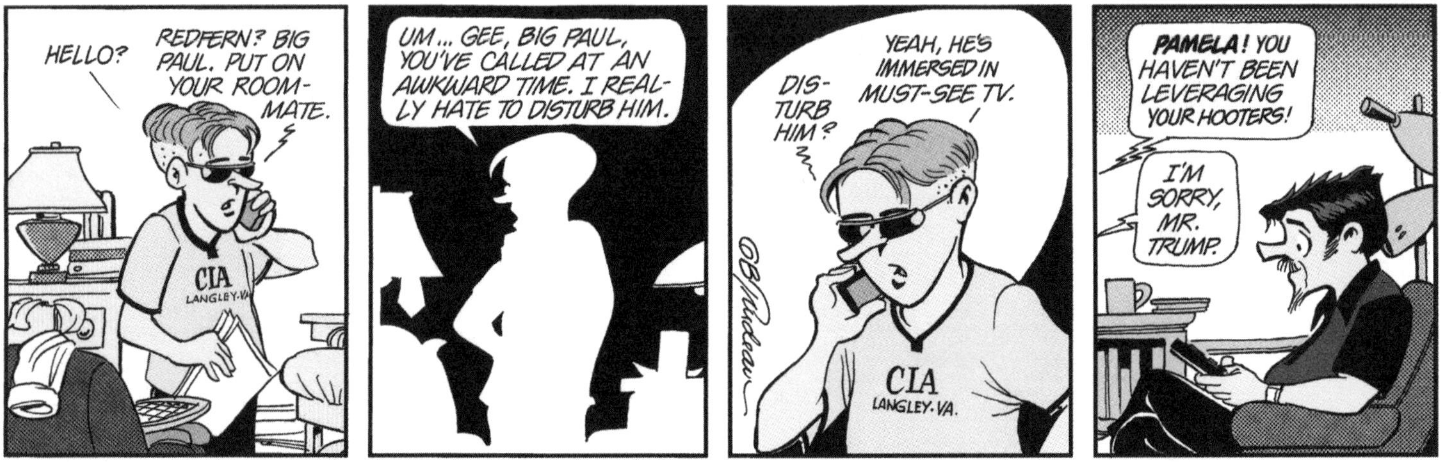
HELLO?
REDFERN? BIG PAUL. PUT ON YOUR ROOM-MATE.
CIA LANGLEY·VA
UM... GEE, BIG PAUL, YOU'VE CALLED AT AN AWKWARD TIME. I REALLY HATE TO DISTURB HIM.
DISTURB HIM?
YEAH, HE'S IMMERSED IN MUST-SEE TV.
CIA LANGLEY·VA.
PAMELA! YOU HAVEN'T BEEN LEVERAGING YOUR HOOTERS!
I'M SORRY, MR. TRUMP.

September 27, 2004

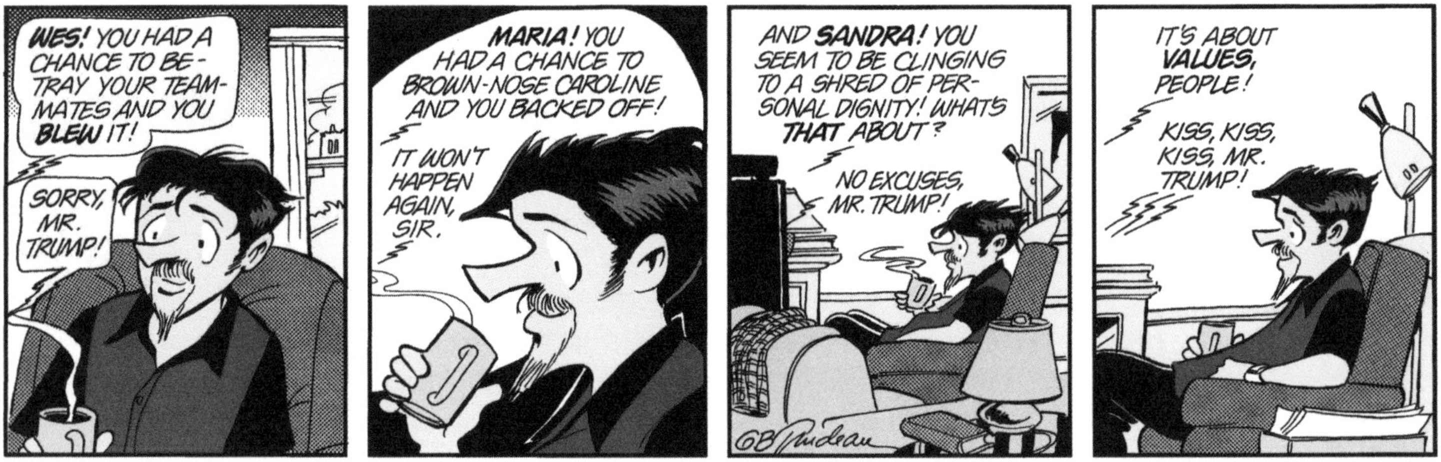
WES! YOU HAD A CHANCE TO BETRAY YOUR TEAMMATES AND YOU BLEW IT!
SORRY, MR. TRUMP!
MARIA! YOU HAD A CHANCE TO BROWN-NOSE CAROLINE AND YOU BACKED OFF!
IT WON'T HAPPEN AGAIN, SIR.
AND SANDRA! YOU SEEM TO BE CLINGING TO A SHRED OF PERSONAL DIGNITY! WHAT'S THAT ABOUT?
NO EXCUSES, MR. TRUMP!
IT'S ABOUT VALUES, PEOPLE!
KISS, KISS, KISS, MR. TRUMP!

September 28, 2004

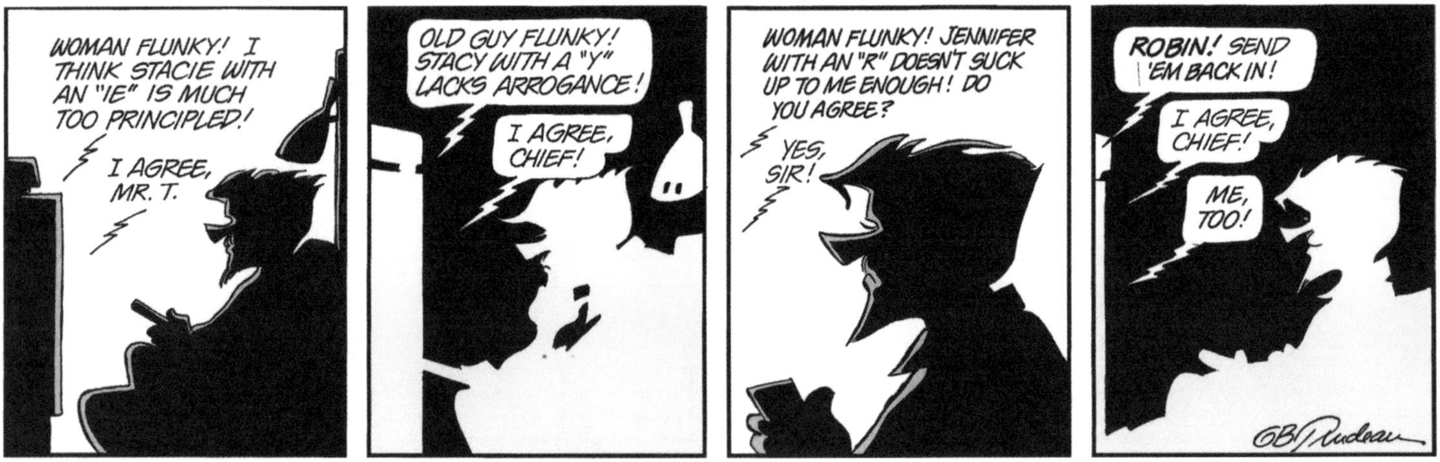
WOMAN FLUNKY! I THINK STACIE WITH AN "IE" IS MUCH TOO PRINCIPLED!
I AGREE, MR. T.
OLD GUY FLUNKY! STACY WITH A "Y" LACKS ARROGANCE!
I AGREE, CHIEF!
WOMAN FLUNKY! JENNIFER WITH AN "R" DOESN'T SUCK UP TO ME ENOUGH! DO YOU AGREE?
YES, SIR!
ROBIN! SEND 'EM BACK IN!
I AGREE, CHIEF!
ME, TOO!

September 29, 2004

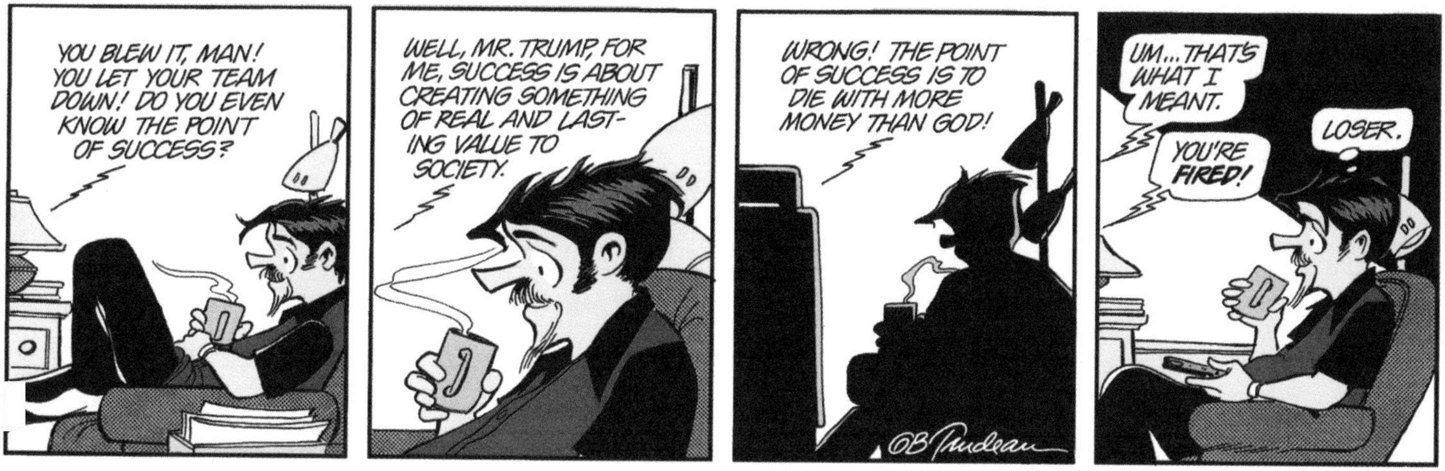

YOU BLEW IT, MAN! YOU LET YOUR TEAM DOWN! DO YOU EVEN KNOW THE POINT OF SUCCESS?
WELL, MR. TRUMP, FOR ME, SUCCESS IS ABOUT CREATING SOMETHING OF REAL AND LASTING VALUE TO SOCIETY.
WRONG! THE POINT OF SUCCESS IS TO DIE WITH MORE MONEY THAN GOD!
UM... THAT'S WHAT I MEANT.
YOU'RE **FIRED!**
LOSER.

September 30, 2004

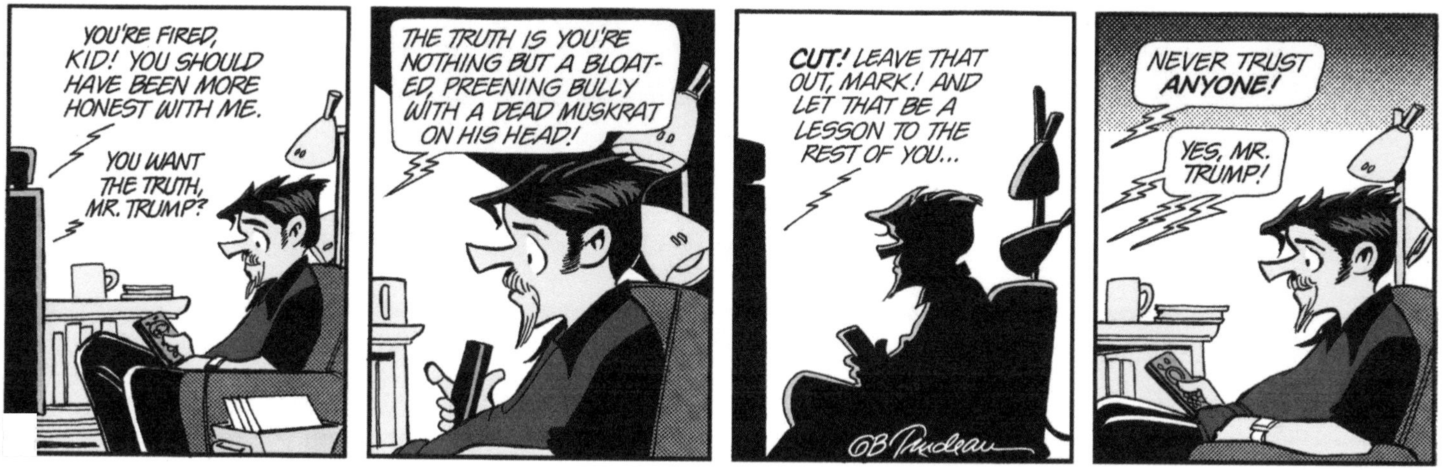

YOU'RE FIRED, KID! YOU SHOULD HAVE BEEN MORE HONEST WITH ME.
YOU WANT THE TRUTH, MR. TRUMP?
THE TRUTH IS YOU'RE NOTHING BUT A BLOATED, PREENING BULLY WITH A DEAD MUSKRAT ON HIS HEAD!
CUT! LEAVE THAT OUT, MARK! AND LET THAT BE A LESSON TO THE REST OF YOU...
NEVER TRUST **ANYONE!**
YES, MR. TRUMP!

October 1, 2004

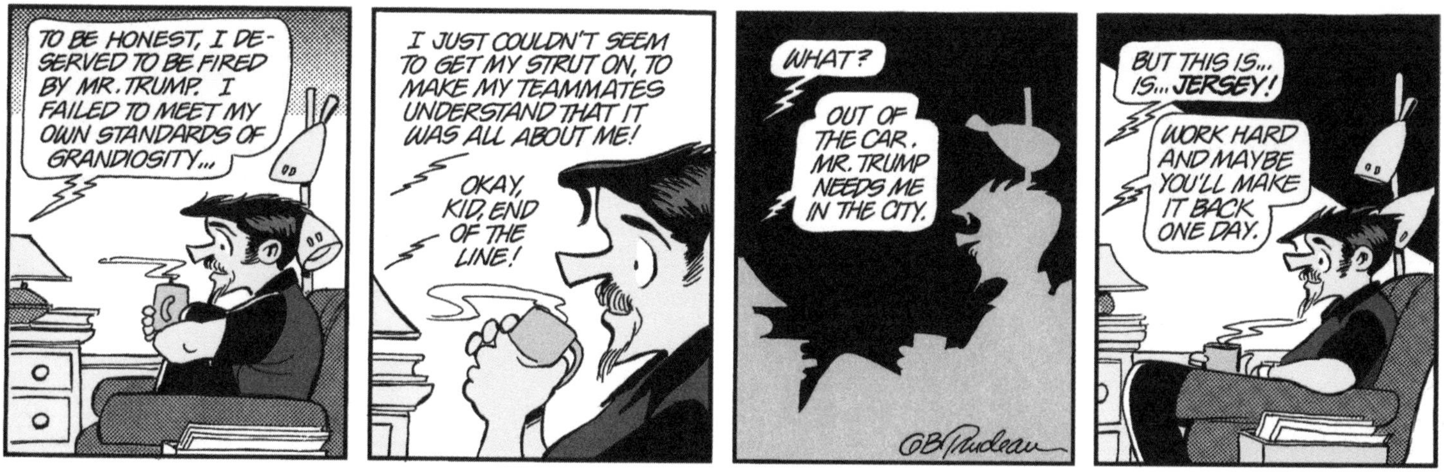

TO BE HONEST, I DESERVED TO BE FIRED BY MR. TRUMP. I FAILED TO MEET MY OWN STANDARDS OF GRANDIOSITY...
I JUST COULDN'T SEEM TO GET MY STRUT ON, TO MAKE MY TEAMMATES UNDERSTAND THAT IT WAS ALL ABOUT ME!
OKAY, KID, END OF THE LINE!
WHAT?
OUT OF THE CAR. MR. TRUMP NEEDS ME IN THE CITY.
BUT THIS IS... IS... **JERSEY!**
WORK HARD AND MAYBE YOU'LL MAKE IT BACK ONE DAY.

October 2, 2004

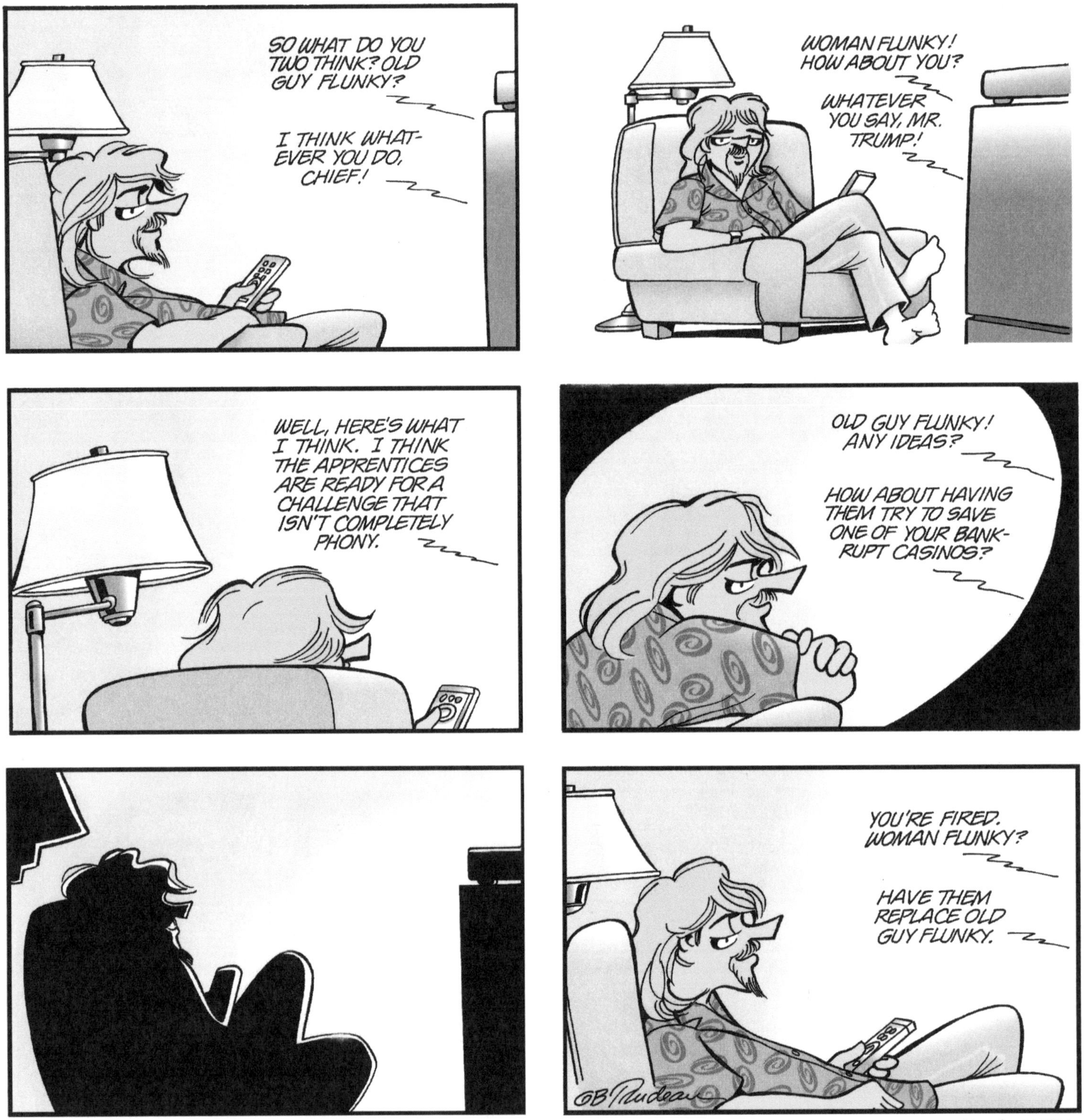
SO WHAT DO YOU TWO THINK? OLD GUY FLUNKY?
I THINK WHATEVER YOU DO, CHIEF!
WOMAN FLUNKY! HOW ABOUT YOU?
WHATEVER YOU SAY, MR. TRUMP!
WELL, HERE'S WHAT I THINK. I THINK THE APPRENTICES ARE READY FOR A CHALLENGE THAT ISN'T COMPLETELY PHONY.
OLD GUY FLUNKY! ANY IDEAS?
HOW ABOUT HAVING THEM TRY TO SAVE ONE OF YOUR BANKRUPT CASINOS?
YOU'RE FIRED. WOMAN FLUNKY?
HAVE THEM REPLACE OLD GUY FLUNKY.
GBTrudeau

November 14, 2004

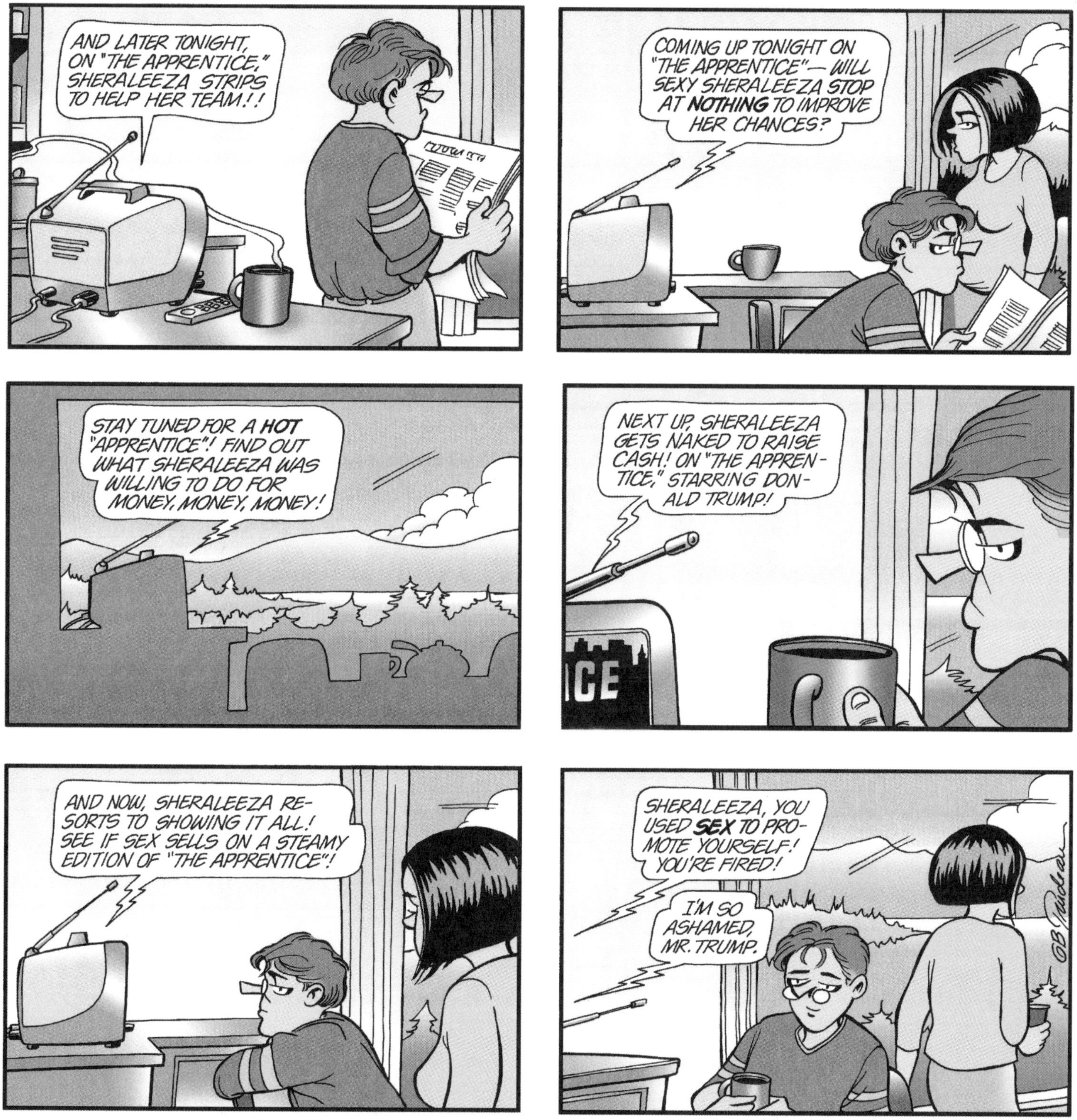
AND LATER TONIGHT, ON "THE APPRENTICE," SHERALEEZA STRIPS TO HELP HER TEAM!!
COMING UP TONIGHT ON "THE APPRENTICE"— WILL SEXY SHERALEEZA STOP AT **NOTHING** TO IMPROVE HER CHANCES?
STAY TUNED FOR A **HOT** "APPRENTICE"! FIND OUT WHAT SHERALEEZA WAS WILLING TO DO FOR MONEY, MONEY, MONEY!
NEXT UP, SHERALEEZA GETS NAKED TO RAISE CASH! ON "THE APPRENTICE," STARRING DONALD TRUMP!
ICE
AND NOW, SHERALEEZA RESORTS TO SHOWING IT ALL! SEE IF SEX SELLS ON A STEAMY EDITION OF "THE APPRENTICE"!
SHERALEEZA, YOU USED **SEX** TO PROMOTE YOURSELF! YOU'RE FIRED!
I'M SO ASHAMED, MR. TRUMP.
GB Trudeau

March 13, 2005

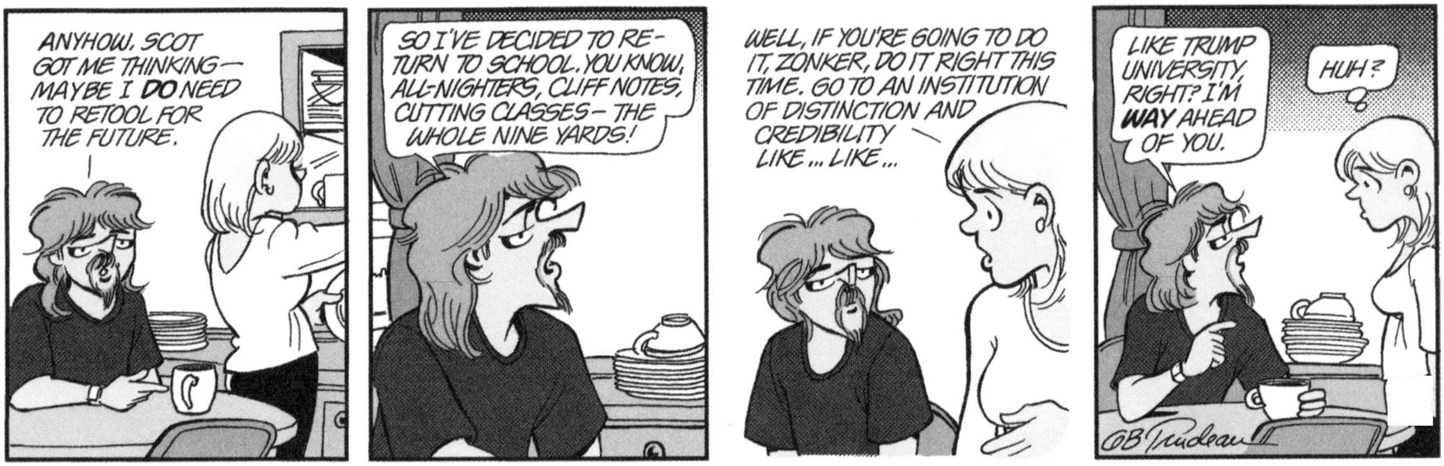
ANYHOW, SCOT GOT ME THINKING— MAYBE I DO NEED TO RETOOL FOR THE FUTURE.
SO I'VE DECIDED TO RETURN TO SCHOOL. YOU KNOW, ALL-NIGHTERS, CLIFF NOTES, CUTTING CLASSES— THE WHOLE NINE YARDS!
WELL, IF YOU'RE GOING TO DO IT, ZONKER, DO IT RIGHT THIS TIME. GO TO AN INSTITUTION OF DISTINCTION AND CREDIBILITY LIKE ... LIKE ...
LIKE TRUMP UNIVERSITY, RIGHT? I'M WAY AHEAD OF YOU.
HUH?
©B. Trudeau

June 6, 2005

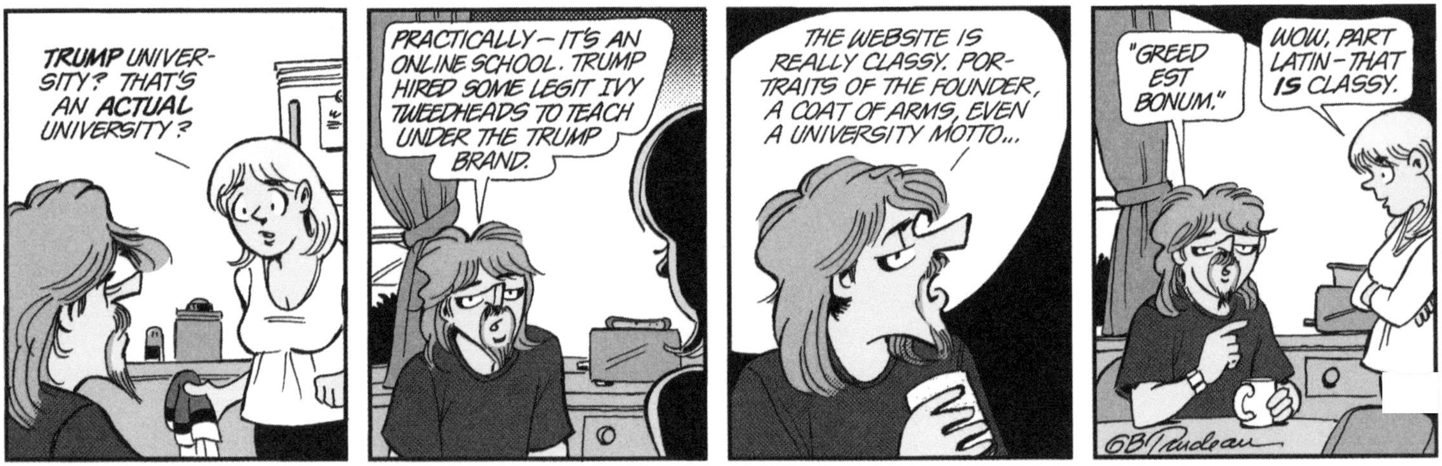
TRUMP UNIVERSITY? THAT'S AN ACTUAL UNIVERSITY?
PRACTICALLY— IT'S AN ONLINE SCHOOL. TRUMP HIRED SOME LEGIT IVY TWEEDHEADS TO TEACH UNDER THE TRUMP BRAND.
THE WEBSITE IS REALLY CLASSY. PORTRAITS OF THE FOUNDER, A COAT OF ARMS, EVEN A UNIVERSITY MOTTO...
"GREED EST BONUM."
WOW, PART LATIN— THAT IS CLASSY.
©B. Trudeau

June 7, 2005

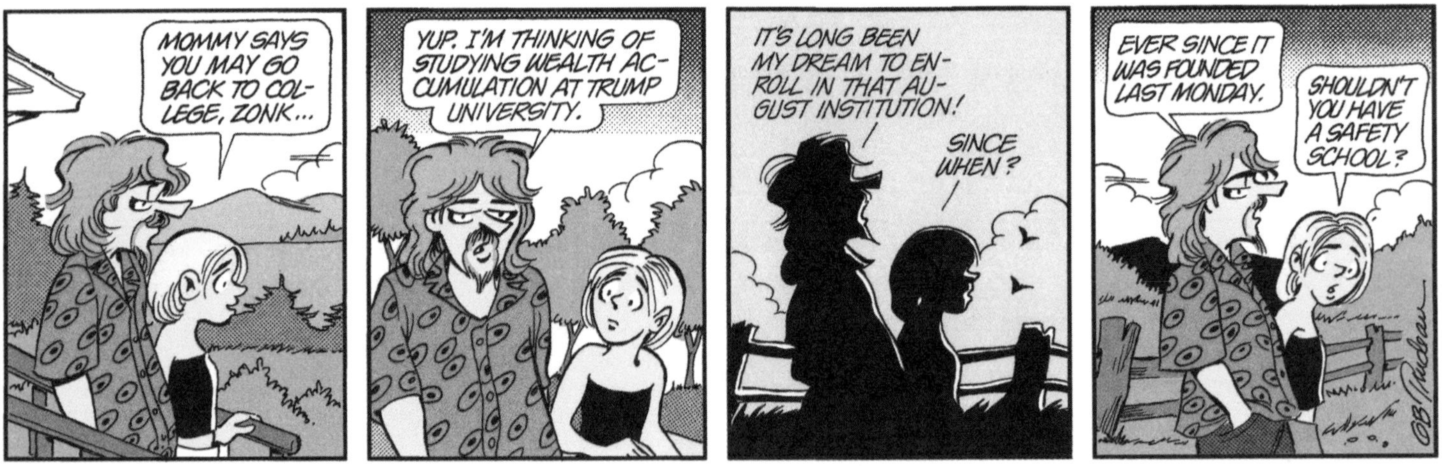
MOMMY SAYS YOU MAY GO BACK TO COLLEGE, ZONK...
YUP. I'M THINKING OF STUDYING WEALTH ACCUMULATION AT TRUMP UNIVERSITY.
IT'S LONG BEEN MY DREAM TO ENROLL IN THAT AUGUST INSTITUTION!
SINCE WHEN?
EVER SINCE IT WAS FOUNDED LAST MONDAY.
SHOULDN'T YOU HAVE A SAFETY SCHOOL?
©B. Trudeau

June 8, 2005

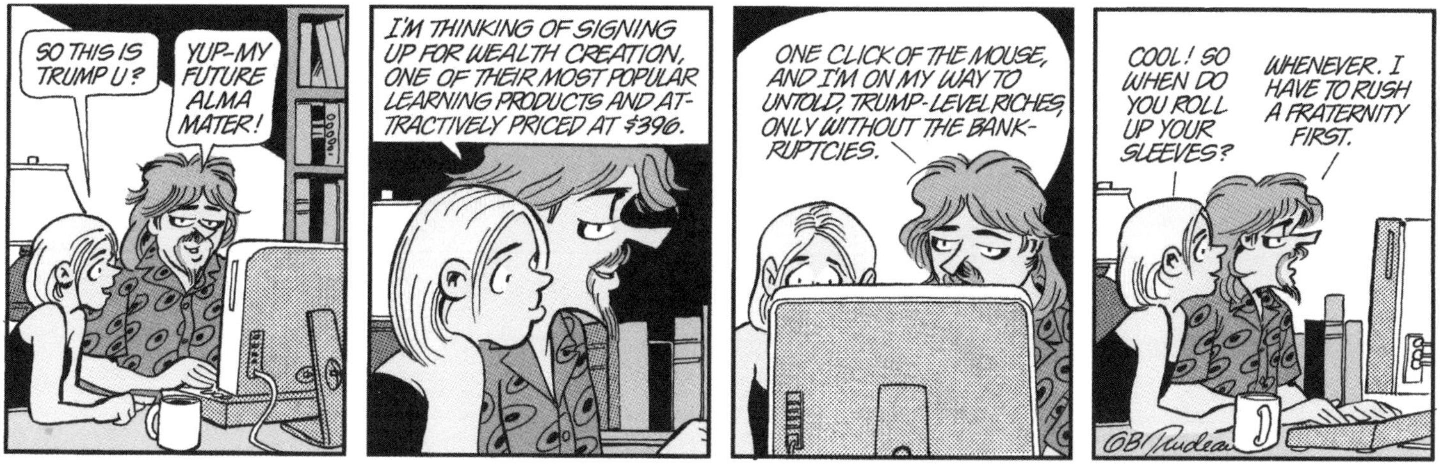
SO THIS IS TRUMP U?
YUP–MY FUTURE ALMA MATER!
I'M THINKING OF SIGNING UP FOR WEALTH CREATION, ONE OF THEIR MOST POPULAR LEARNING PRODUCTS AND ATTRACTIVELY PRICED AT $396.
ONE CLICK OF THE MOUSE, AND I'M ON MY WAY TO UNTOLD, TRUMP-LEVEL RICHES, ONLY WITHOUT THE BANKRUPTCIES.
COOL! SO WHEN DO YOU ROLL UP YOUR SLEEVES?
WHENEVER. I HAVE TO RUSH A FRATERNITY FIRST.

June 9, 2005

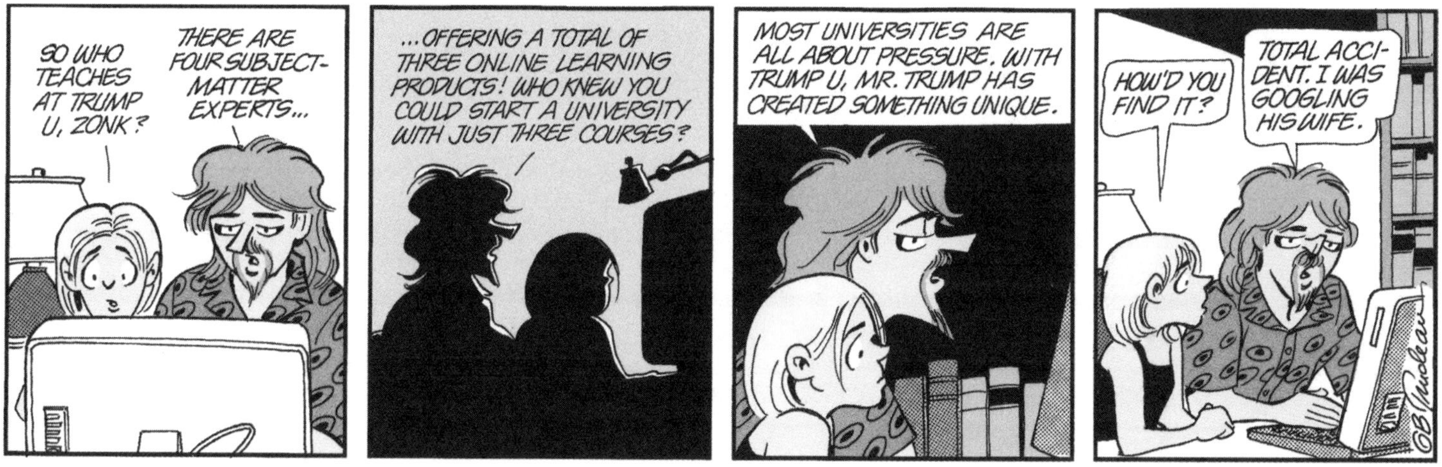
SO WHO TEACHES AT TRUMP U, ZONK?
THERE ARE FOUR SUBJECT-MATTER EXPERTS...
...OFFERING A TOTAL OF THREE ONLINE LEARNING PRODUCTS! WHO KNEW YOU COULD START A UNIVERSITY WITH JUST THREE COURSES?
MOST UNIVERSITIES ARE ALL ABOUT PRESSURE. WITH TRUMP U, MR. TRUMP HAS CREATED SOMETHING UNIQUE.
HOW'D YOU FIND IT?
TOTAL ACCIDENT. I WAS GOOGLING HIS WIFE.

June 10, 2005

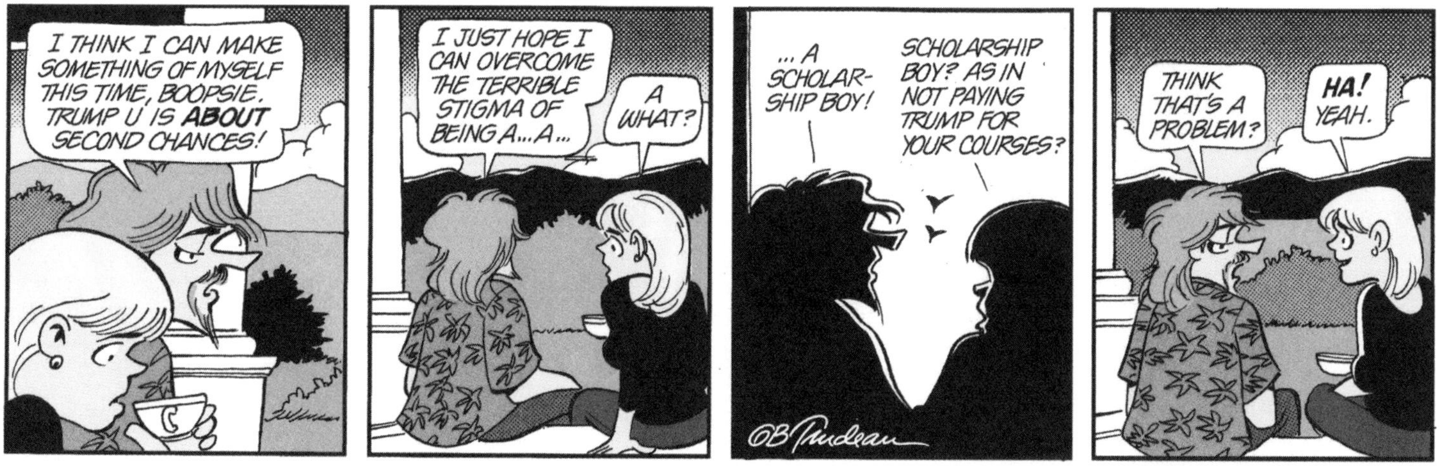
I THINK I CAN MAKE SOMETHING OF MYSELF THIS TIME, BOOPSIE. TRUMP U IS ABOUT SECOND CHANCES!
I JUST HOPE I CAN OVERCOME THE TERRIBLE STIGMA OF BEING A...A...
A WHAT?
...A SCHOLARSHIP BOY!
SCHOLARSHIP BOY? AS IN NOT PAYING TRUMP FOR YOUR COURSES?
THINK THAT'S A PROBLEM?
HA! YEAH.

June 11, 2005

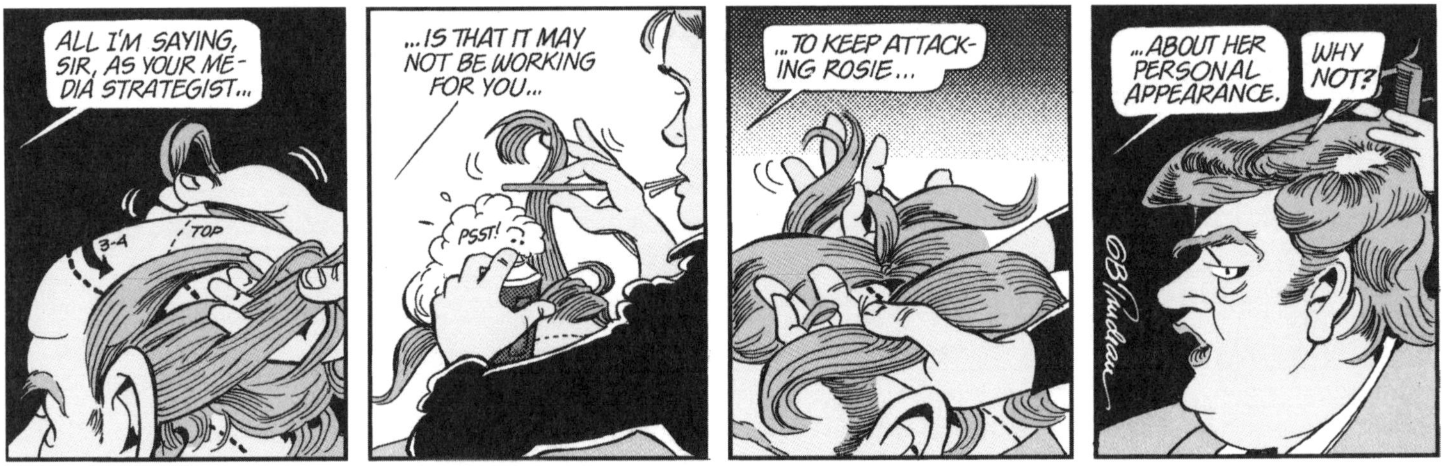
ALL I'M SAYING, SIR, AS YOUR MEDIA STRATEGIST...
3-4
TOP
...IS THAT IT MAY NOT BE WORKING FOR YOU...
PSST!
...TO KEEP ATTACKING ROSIE...
...ABOUT HER PERSONAL APPEARANCE.
WHY NOT?

January 22, 2007

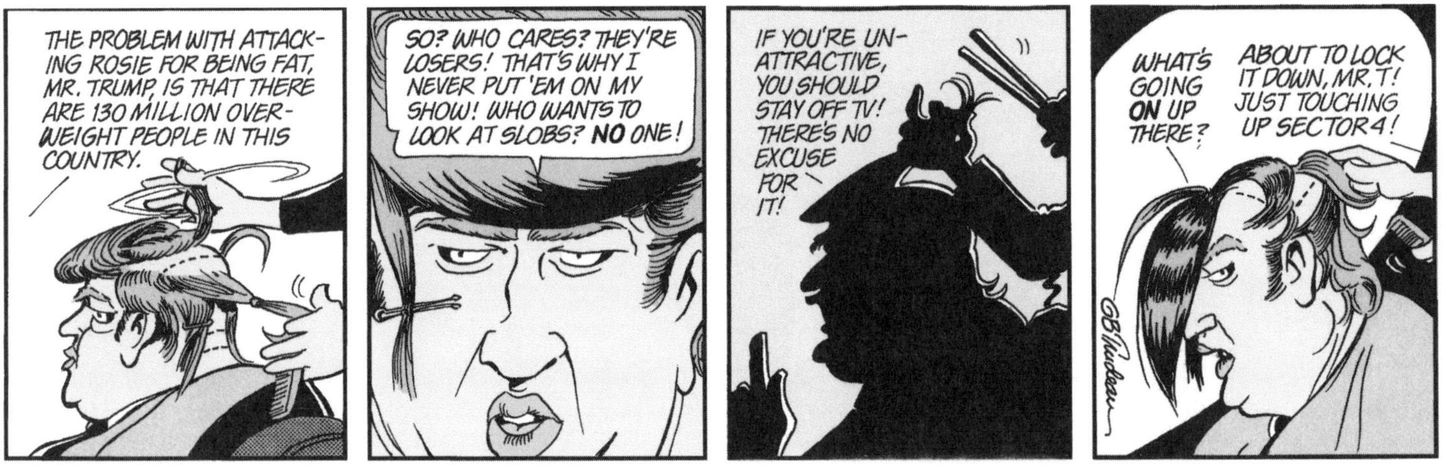
THE PROBLEM WITH ATTACKING ROSIE FOR BEING FAT, MR. TRUMP, IS THAT THERE ARE 130 MILLION OVERWEIGHT PEOPLE IN THIS COUNTRY.
SO? WHO CARES? THEY'RE LOSERS! THAT'S WHY I NEVER PUT 'EM ON MY SHOW! WHO WANTS TO LOOK AT SLOBS? NO ONE!
IF YOU'RE UNATTRACTIVE, YOU SHOULD STAY OFF TV! THERE'S NO EXCUSE FOR IT!
WHAT'S GOING ON UP THERE?
ABOUT TO LOCK IT DOWN, MR. T! JUST TOUCHING UP SECTOR 4!

January 23, 2007

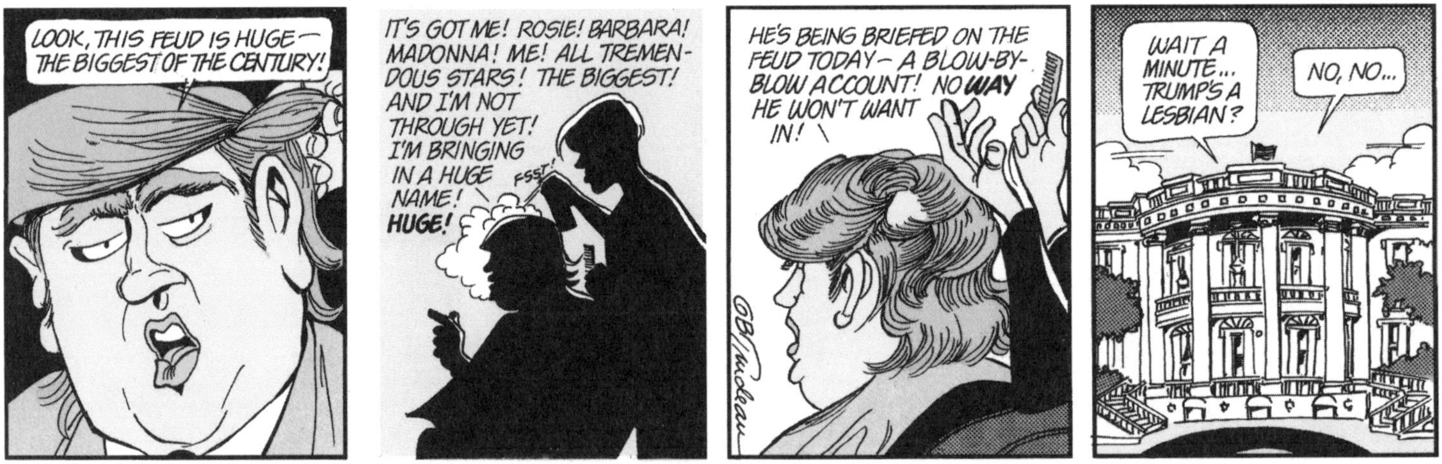
LOOK, THIS FEUD IS HUGE— THE BIGGEST OF THE CENTURY!
IT'S GOT ME! ROSIE! BARBARA! MADONNA! ME! ALL TREMENDOUS STARS! THE BIGGEST! AND I'M NOT THROUGH YET! I'M BRINGING IN A HUGE NAME! HUGE!
FSST!
HE'S BEING BRIEFED ON THE FEUD TODAY— A BLOW-BY-BLOW ACCOUNT! NO WAY HE WON'T WANT IN!
WAIT A MINUTE... TRUMP'S A LESBIAN?
NO, NO...

January 24, 2007

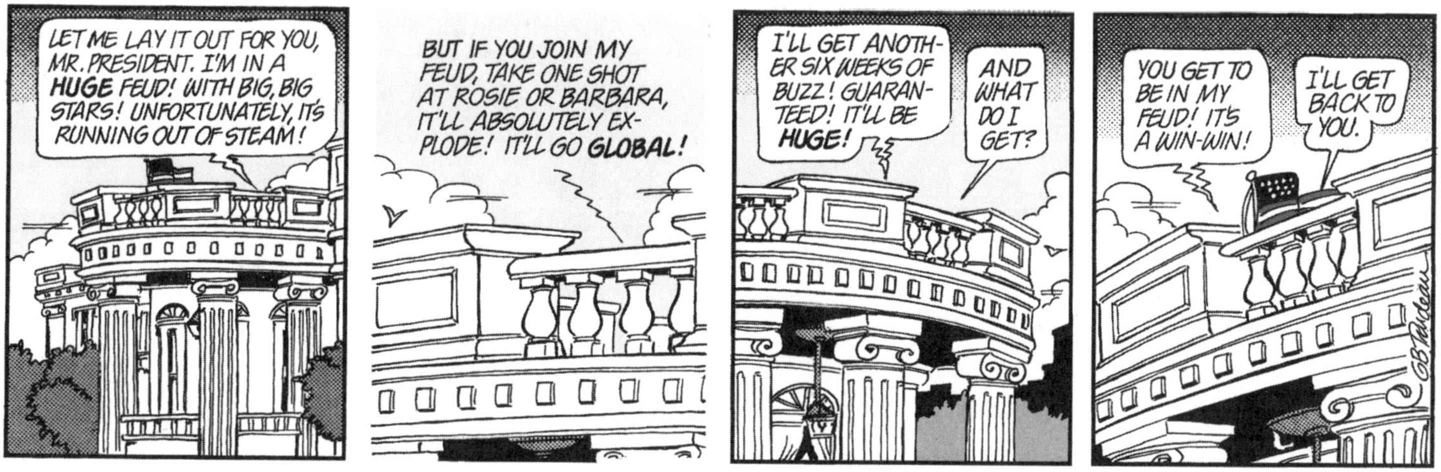
LET ME LAY IT OUT FOR YOU, MR. PRESIDENT. I'M IN A HUGE FEUD! WITH BIG, BIG STARS! UNFORTUNATELY, IT'S RUNNING OUT OF STEAM!
BUT IF YOU JOIN MY FEUD, TAKE ONE SHOT AT ROSIE OR BARBARA, IT'LL ABSOLUTELY EXPLODE! IT'LL GO GLOBAL!
I'LL GET ANOTHER SIX WEEKS OF BUZZ! GUARANTEED! IT'LL BE HUGE!
AND WHAT DO I GET?
YOU GET TO BE IN MY FEUD! IT'S A WIN-WIN!
I'LL GET BACK TO YOU.

January 25, 2007

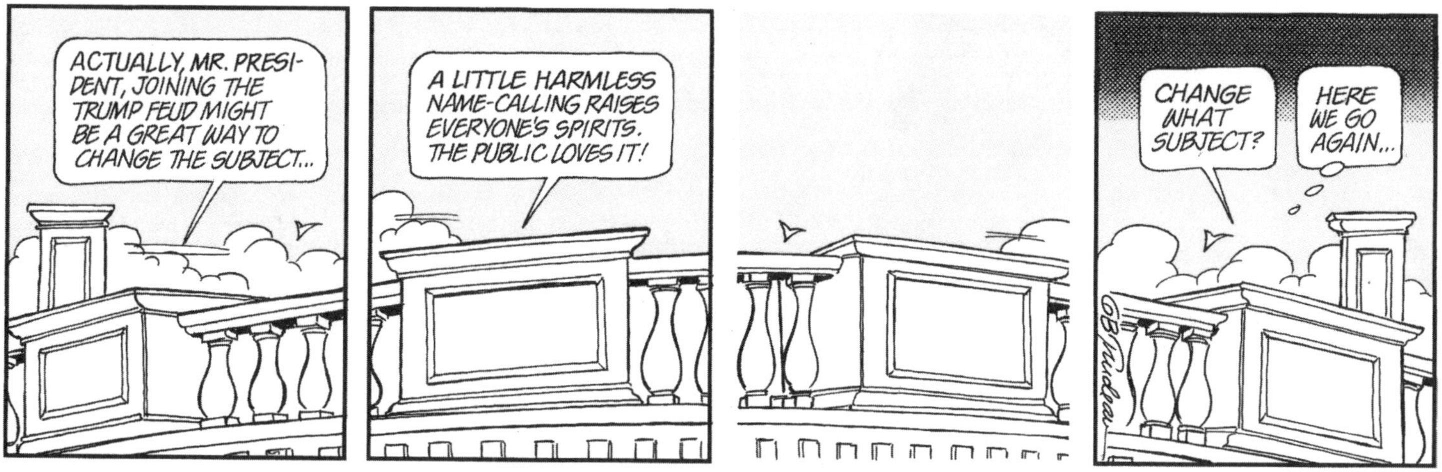
ACTUALLY, MR. PRESIDENT, JOINING THE TRUMP FEUD MIGHT BE A GREAT WAY TO CHANGE THE SUBJECT...
A LITTLE HARMLESS NAME-CALLING RAISES EVERYONE'S SPIRITS. THE PUBLIC LOVES IT!
CHANGE WHAT SUBJECT?
HERE WE GO AGAIN...

January 26, 2007

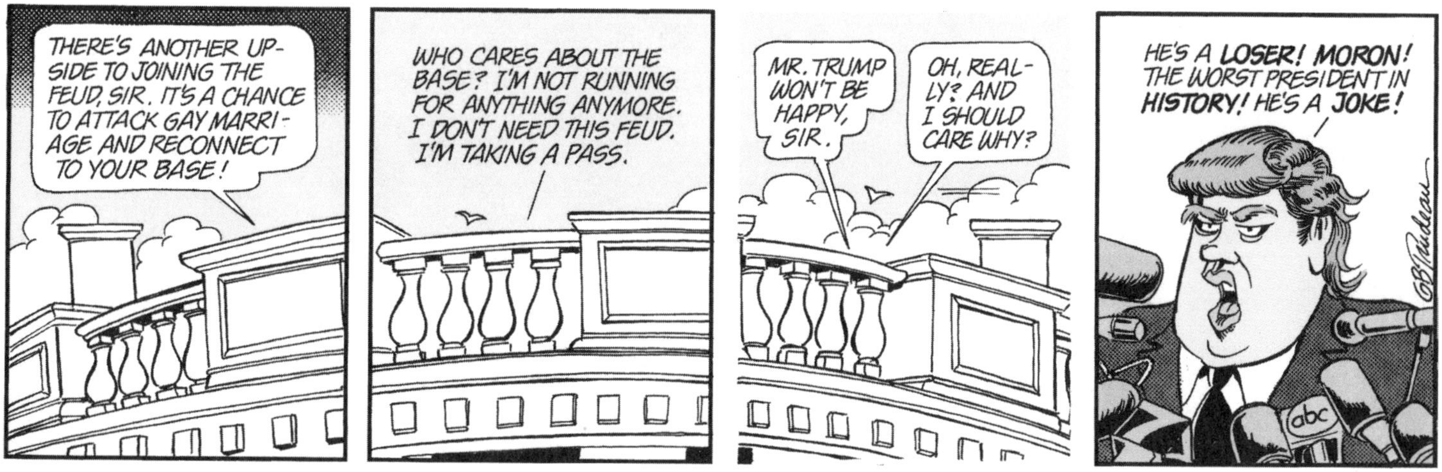
THERE'S ANOTHER UPSIDE TO JOINING THE FEUD, SIR. IT'S A CHANCE TO ATTACK GAY MARRIAGE AND RECONNECT TO YOUR BASE!
WHO CARES ABOUT THE BASE? I'M NOT RUNNING FOR ANYTHING ANYMORE. I DON'T NEED THIS FEUD. I'M TAKING A PASS.
MR. TRUMP WON'T BE HAPPY, SIR.
OH, REALLY? AND I SHOULD CARE WHY?
HE'S A LOSER! MORON! THE WORST PRESIDENT IN HISTORY! HE'S A JOKE!
abc

January 27, 2007

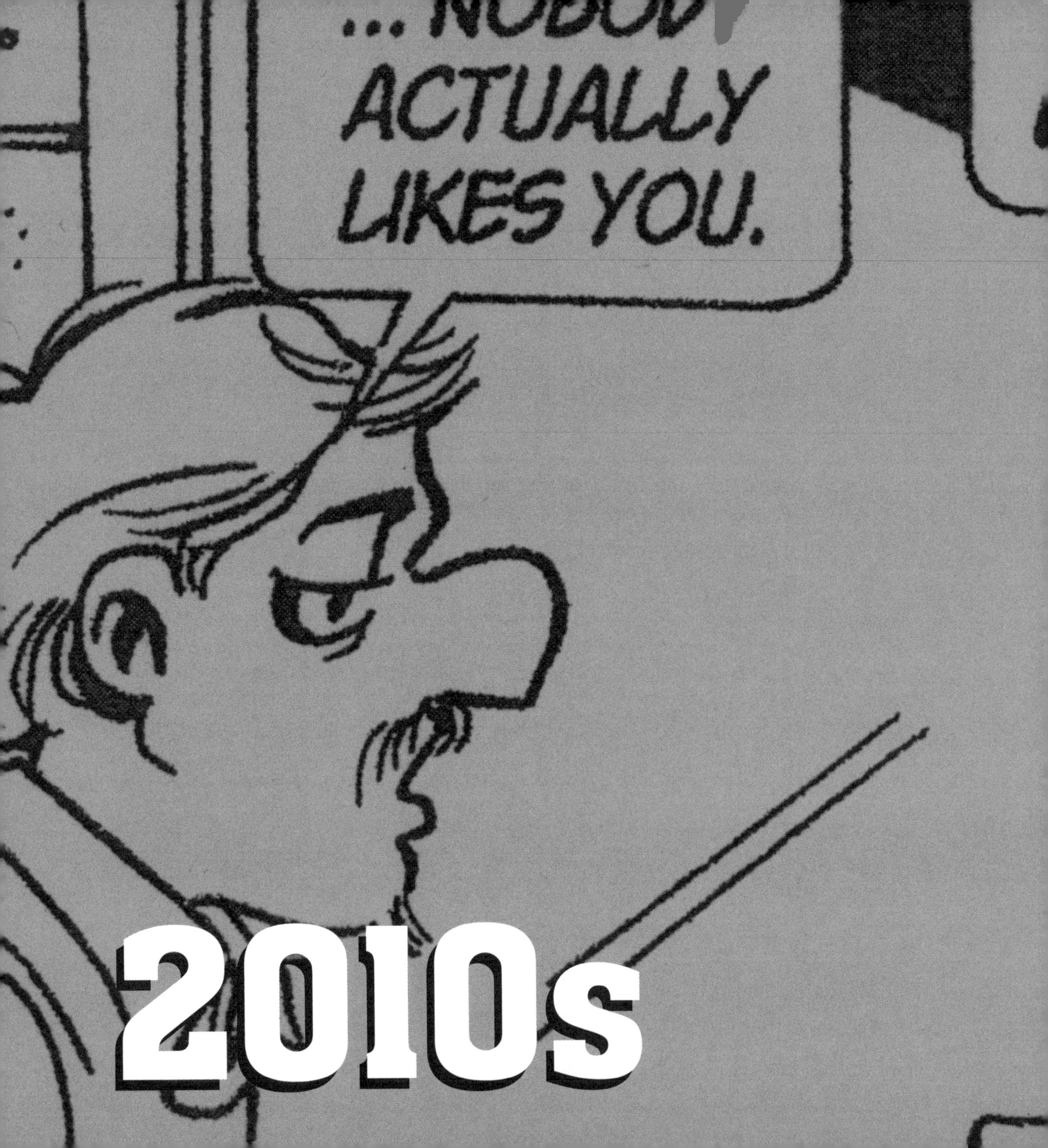
ACTUALLY LIKES YOU.

2010s

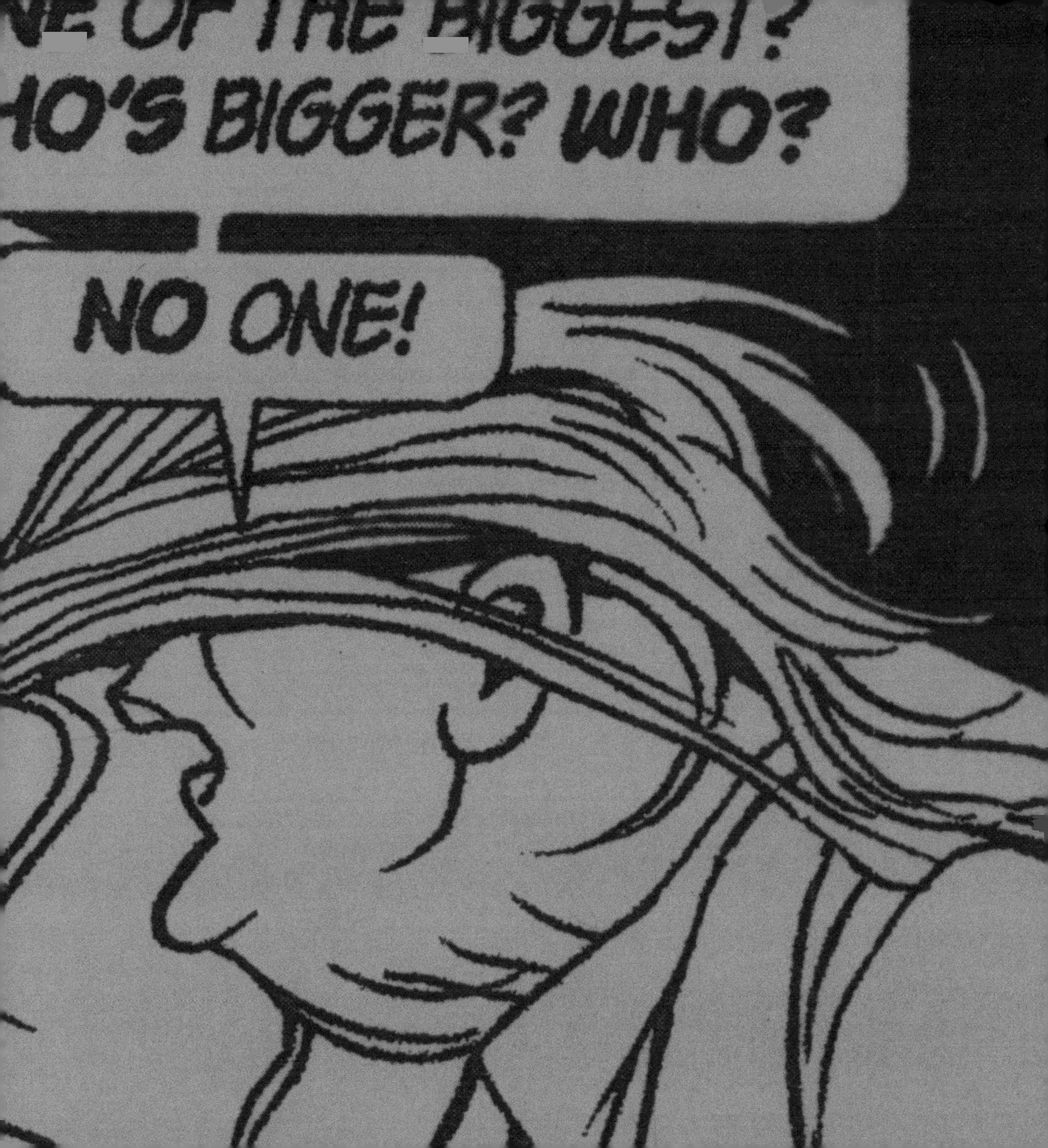

OF THE BIGGEST?
BIGGER? WHO?
NO ONE!

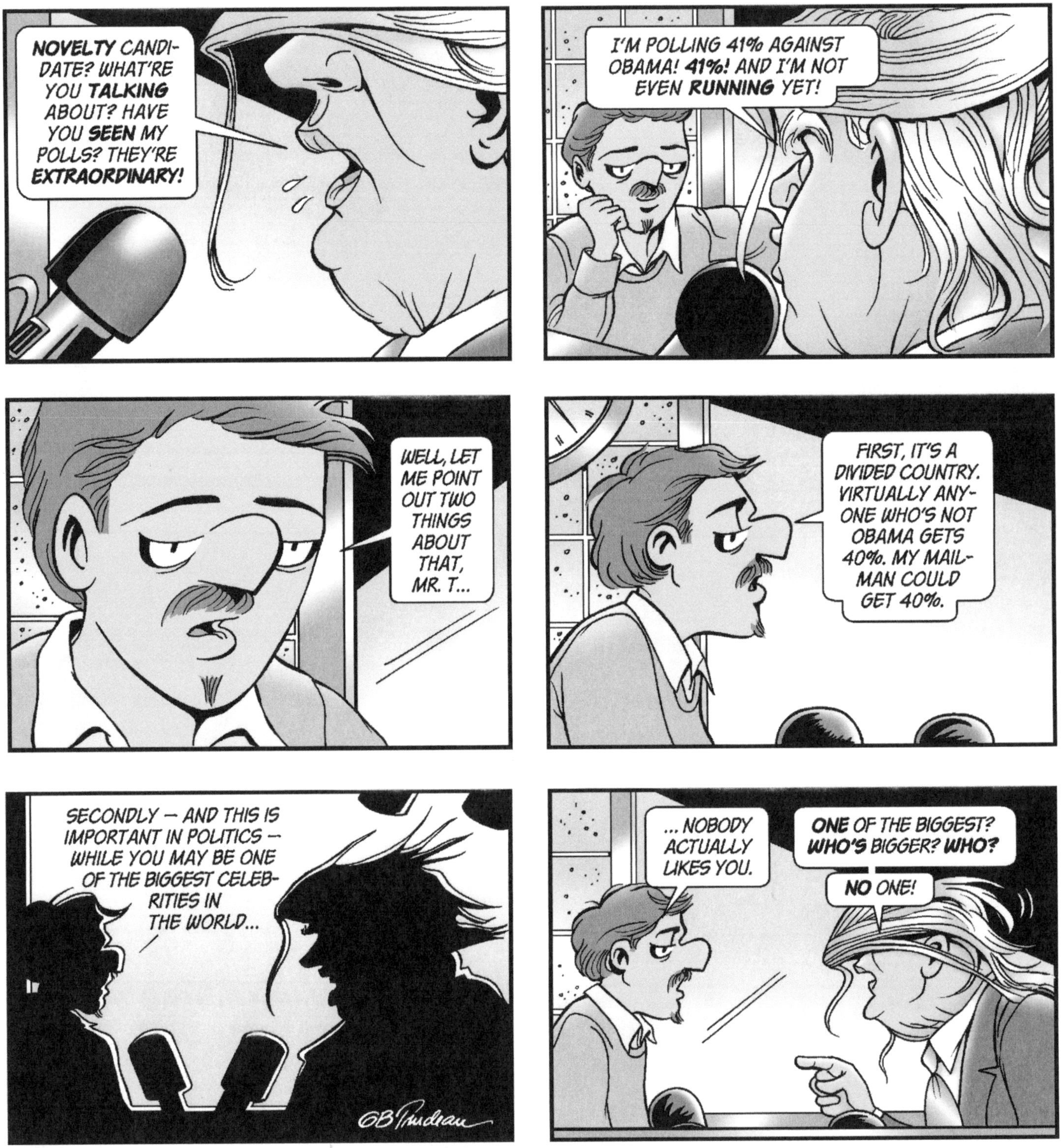
NOVELTY CANDIDATE? WHAT'RE YOU TALKING ABOUT? HAVE YOU SEEN MY POLLS? THEY'RE EXTRAORDINARY!
I'M POLLING 41% AGAINST OBAMA! 41%! AND I'M NOT EVEN RUNNING YET!
WELL, LET ME POINT OUT TWO THINGS ABOUT THAT, MR. T...
FIRST, IT'S A DIVIDED COUNTRY. VIRTUALLY ANYONE WHO'S NOT OBAMA GETS 40%. MY MAILMAN COULD GET 40%.
SECONDLY — AND THIS IS IMPORTANT IN POLITICS — WHILE YOU MAY BE ONE OF THE BIGGEST CELEBRITIES IN THE WORLD...
GB Trudeau
... NOBODY ACTUALLY LIKES YOU.
ONE OF THE BIGGEST? WHO'S BIGGER? WHO?
NO ONE!

April 17, 2011

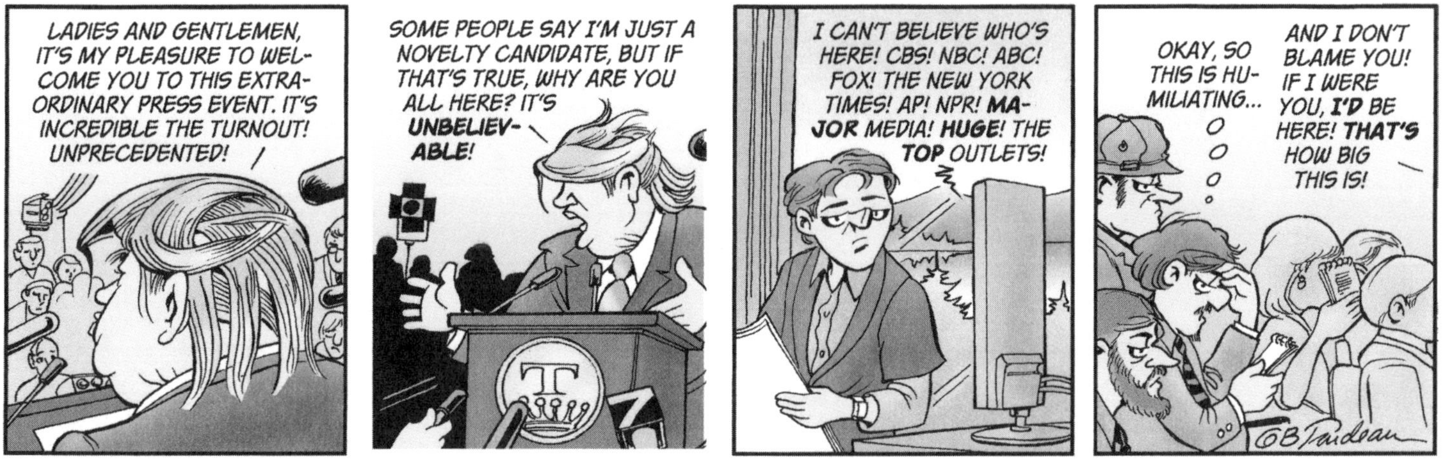
LADIES AND GENTLEMEN, IT'S MY PLEASURE TO WELCOME YOU TO THIS EXTRAORDINARY PRESS EVENT. IT'S INCREDIBLE THE TURNOUT! UNPRECEDENTED!
SOME PEOPLE SAY I'M JUST A NOVELTY CANDIDATE, BUT IF THAT'S TRUE, WHY ARE YOU ALL HERE? IT'S **UNBELIEVABLE**!
I CAN'T BELIEVE WHO'S HERE! CBS! NBC! ABC! FOX! THE NEW YORK TIMES! AP! NPR! **MAJOR** MEDIA! **HUGE**! THE **TOP** OUTLETS!
OKAY, SO THIS IS HUMILIATING...
AND I DON'T BLAME YOU! IF I WERE YOU, **I'D** BE HERE! **THAT'S** HOW BIG THIS IS!
GBTrudeau

April 18, 2011

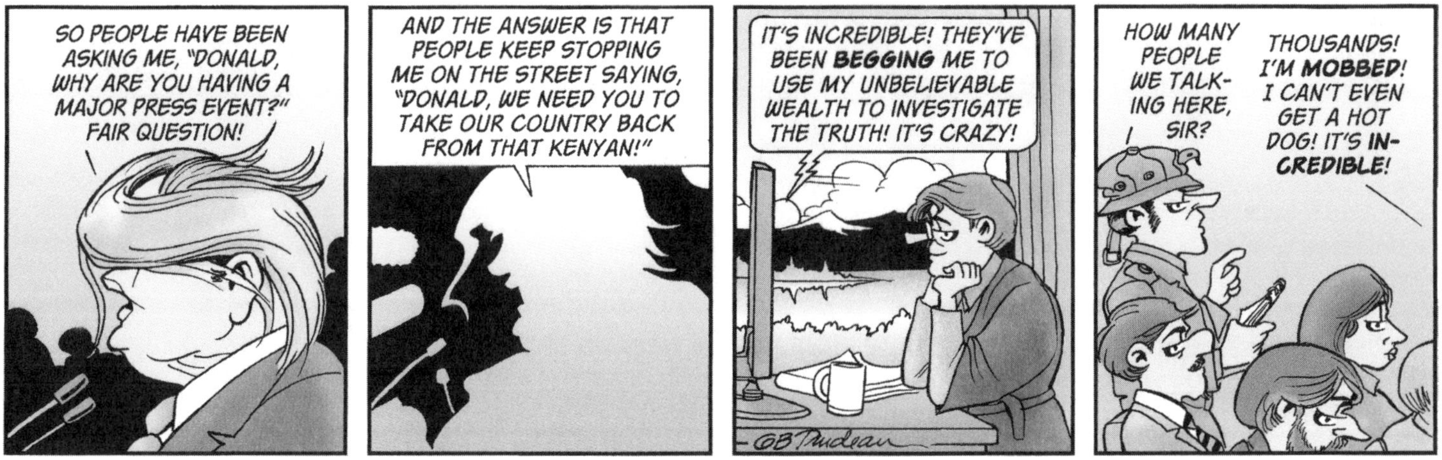
SO PEOPLE HAVE BEEN ASKING ME, "DONALD, WHY ARE YOU HAVING A MAJOR PRESS EVENT?" FAIR QUESTION!
AND THE ANSWER IS THAT PEOPLE KEEP STOPPING ME ON THE STREET SAYING, "DONALD, WE NEED YOU TO TAKE OUR COUNTRY BACK FROM THAT KENYAN!"
IT'S INCREDIBLE! THEY'VE BEEN **BEGGING** ME TO USE MY UNBELIEVABLE WEALTH TO INVESTIGATE THE TRUTH! IT'S CRAZY!
GBTrudeau
HOW MANY PEOPLE WE TALKING HERE, SIR?
THOUSANDS! I'M **MOBBED**! I CAN'T EVEN GET A HOT DOG! IT'S **INCREDIBLE**!

April 19, 2011

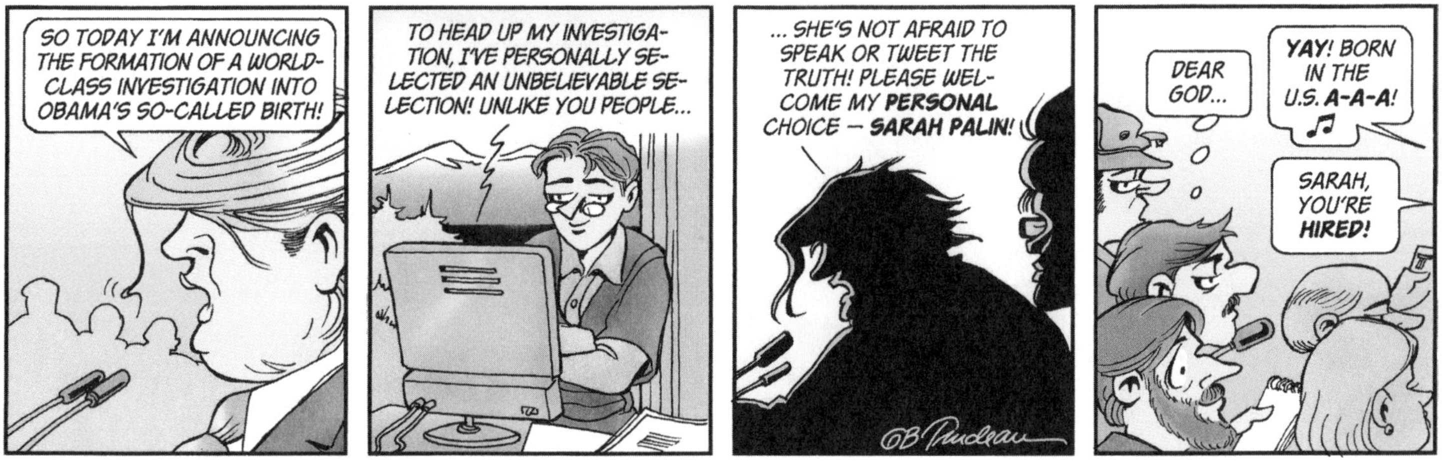
SO TODAY I'M ANNOUNCING THE FORMATION OF A WORLD-CLASS INVESTIGATION INTO OBAMA'S SO-CALLED BIRTH!
TO HEAD UP MY INVESTIGATION, I'VE PERSONALLY SELECTED AN UNBELIEVABLE SELECTION! UNLIKE YOU PEOPLE...
... SHE'S NOT AFRAID TO SPEAK OR TWEET THE TRUTH! PLEASE WELCOME MY **PERSONAL** CHOICE — **SARAH PALIN**!
GBTrudeau
DEAR GOD...
YAY! BORN IN THE U.S. **A-A-A**! ♫
SARAH, YOU'RE **HIRED**!

April 20, 2011

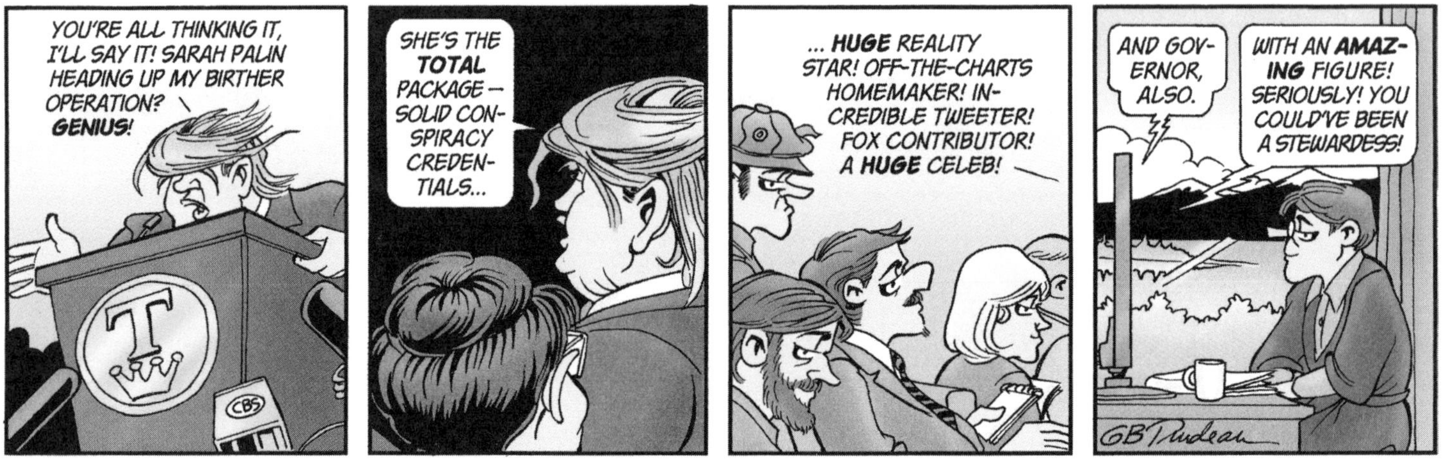
YOU'RE ALL THINKING IT, I'LL SAY IT! SARAH PALIN HEADING UP MY BIRTHER OPERATION? GENIUS!
CBS
SHE'S THE TOTAL PACKAGE — SOLID CONSPIRACY CREDENTIALS...
... HUGE REALITY STAR! OFF-THE-CHARTS HOMEMAKER! INCREDIBLE TWEETER! FOX CONTRIBUTOR! A HUGE CELEB!
AND GOVERNOR, ALSO.
WITH AN AMAZING FIGURE! SERIOUSLY! YOU COULD'VE BEEN A STEWARDESS!
GB Trudeau

April 21, 2011

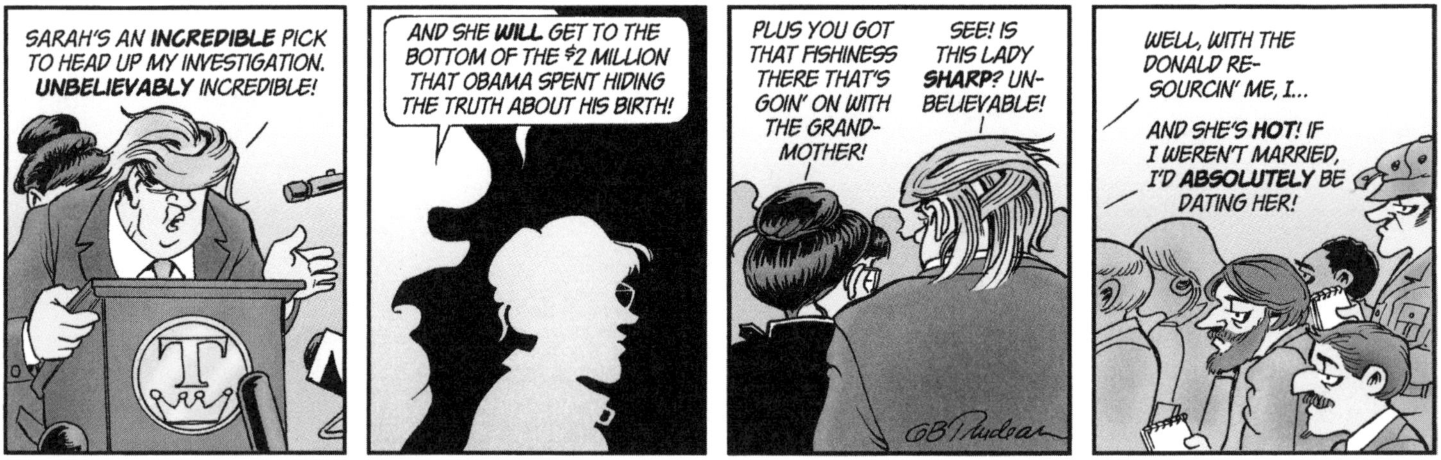
SARAH'S AN INCREDIBLE PICK TO HEAD UP MY INVESTIGATION. UNBELIEVABLY INCREDIBLE!
AND SHE WILL GET TO THE BOTTOM OF THE $2 MILLION THAT OBAMA SPENT HIDING THE TRUTH ABOUT HIS BIRTH!
PLUS YOU GOT THAT FISHINESS THERE THAT'S GOIN' ON WITH THE GRANDMOTHER!
SEE! IS THIS LADY SHARP? UNBELIEVABLE!
GB Trudeau
WELL, WITH THE DONALD RESOURCIN' ME, I...
AND SHE'S HOT! IF I WEREN'T MARRIED, I'D ABSOLUTELY BE DATING HER!

April 22, 2011

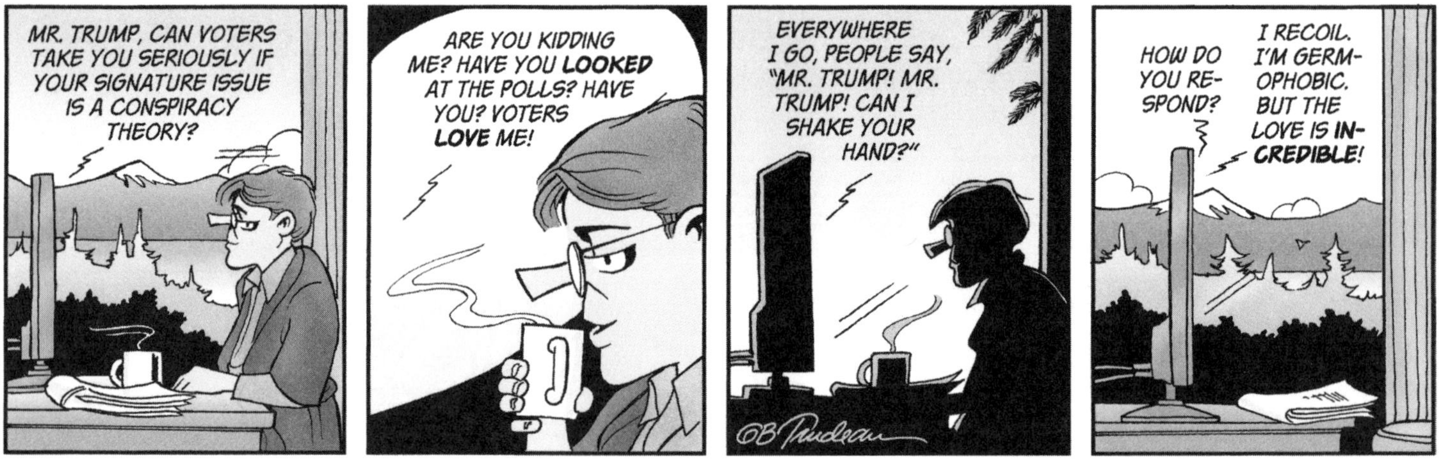
MR. TRUMP, CAN VOTERS TAKE YOU SERIOUSLY IF YOUR SIGNATURE ISSUE IS A CONSPIRACY THEORY?
ARE YOU KIDDING ME? HAVE YOU LOOKED AT THE POLLS? HAVE YOU? VOTERS LOVE ME!
EVERYWHERE I GO, PEOPLE SAY, "MR. TRUMP! MR. TRUMP! CAN I SHAKE YOUR HAND?"
GB Trudeau
HOW DO YOU RESPOND?
I RECOIL. I'M GERMOPHOBIC. BUT THE LOVE IS INCREDIBLE!

April 23, 2011

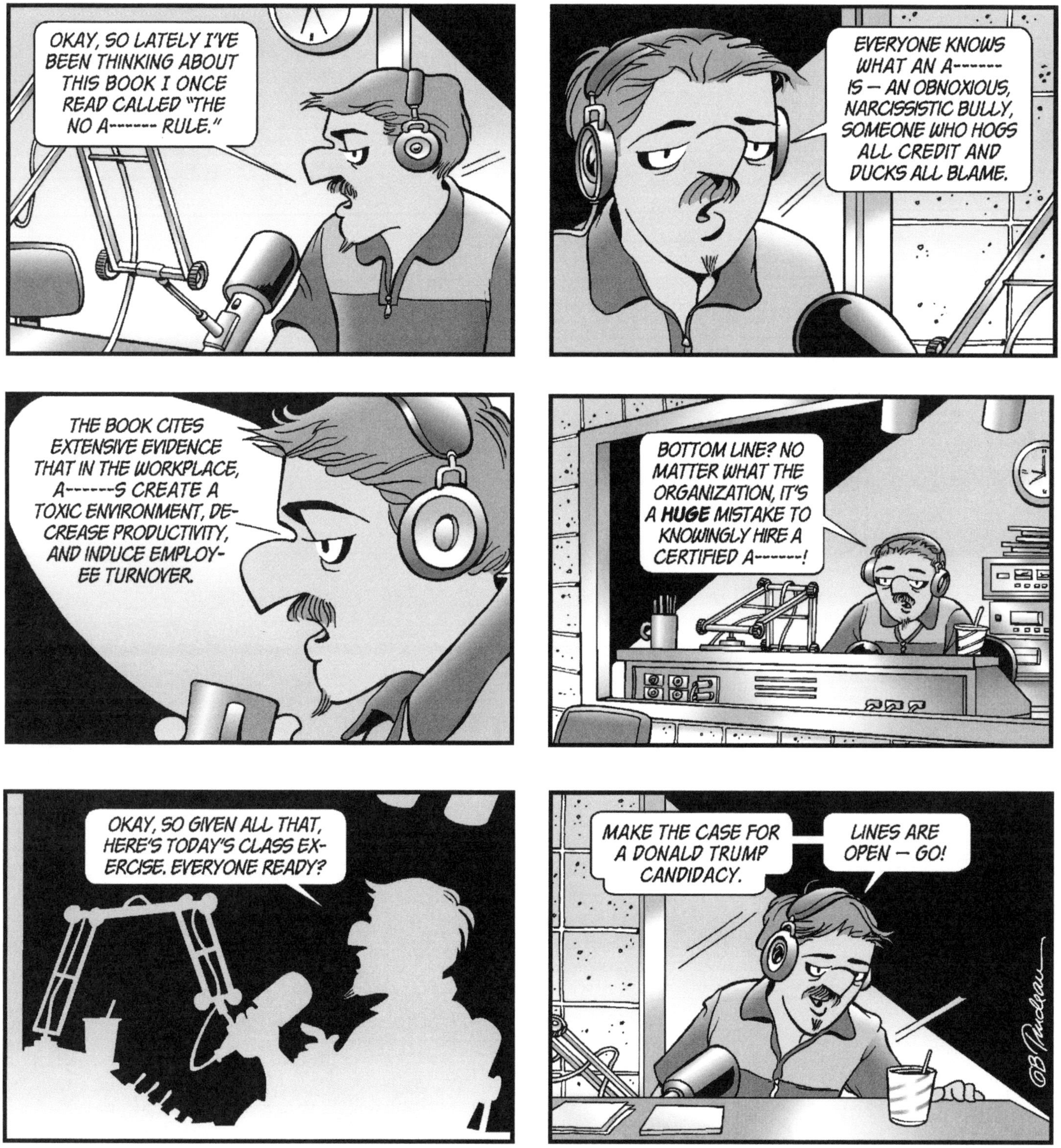
OKAY, SO LATELY I'VE BEEN THINKING ABOUT THIS BOOK I ONCE READ CALLED "THE NO A------- RULE."
EVERYONE KNOWS WHAT AN A------- IS — AN OBNOXIOUS, NARCISSISTIC BULLY, SOMEONE WHO HOGS ALL CREDIT AND DUCKS ALL BLAME.
THE BOOK CITES EXTENSIVE EVIDENCE THAT IN THE WORKPLACE, A-------S CREATE A TOXIC ENVIRONMENT, DECREASE PRODUCTIVITY, AND INDUCE EMPLOYEE TURNOVER.
BOTTOM LINE? NO MATTER WHAT THE ORGANIZATION, IT'S A **HUGE** MISTAKE TO KNOWINGLY HIRE A CERTIFIED A-------!
OKAY, SO GIVEN ALL THAT, HERE'S TODAY'S CLASS EXERCISE. EVERYONE READY?
MAKE THE CASE FOR A DONALD TRUMP CANDIDACY.
LINES ARE OPEN — GO!
©B Trudeau

May 22, 2011

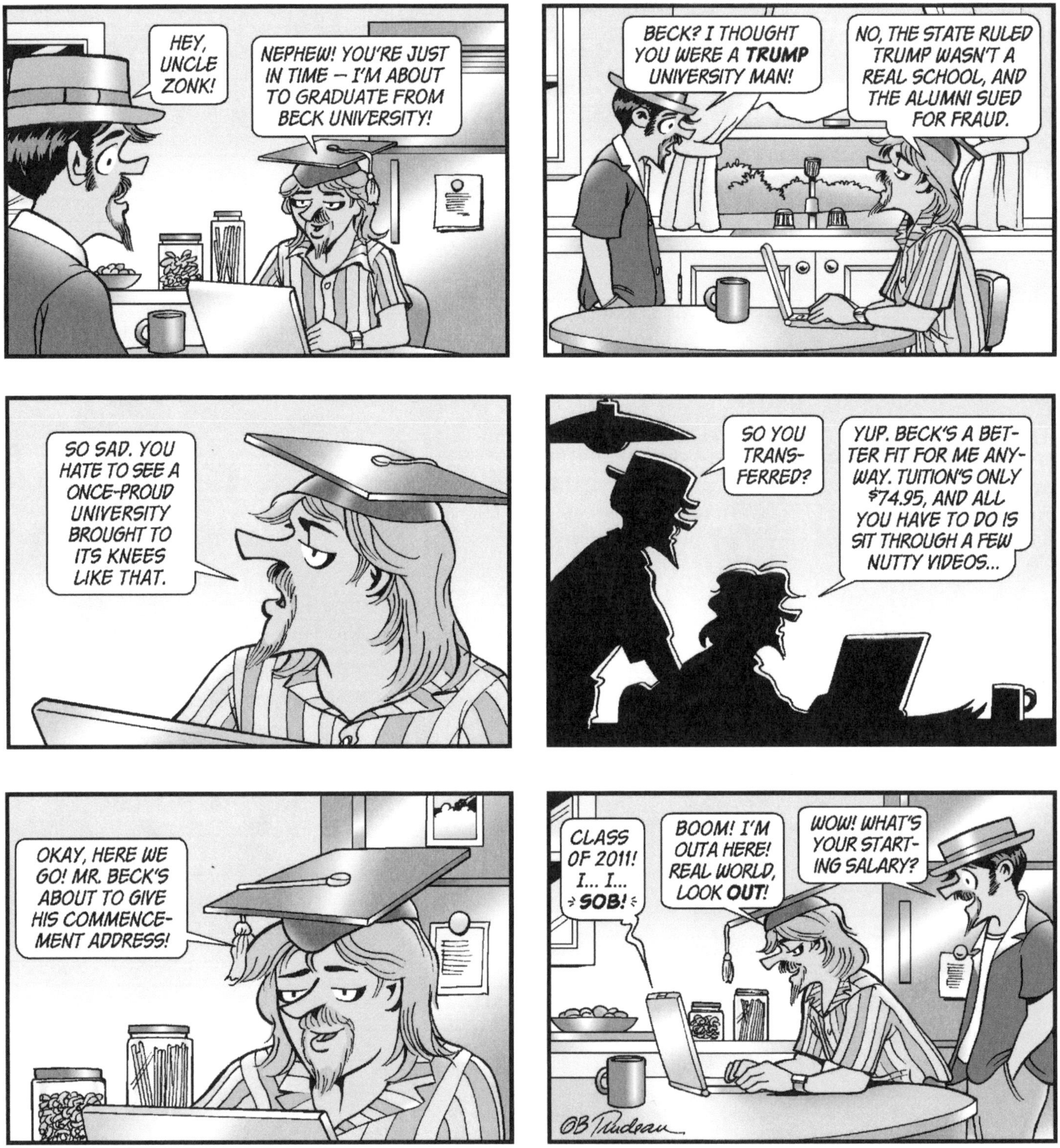
HEY, UNCLE ZONK!
NEPHEW! YOU'RE JUST IN TIME — I'M ABOUT TO GRADUATE FROM BECK UNIVERSITY!
BECK? I THOUGHT YOU WERE A **TRUMP** UNIVERSITY MAN!
NO, THE STATE RULED TRUMP WASN'T A REAL SCHOOL, AND THE ALUMNI SUED FOR FRAUD.
SO SAD. YOU HATE TO SEE A ONCE-PROUD UNIVERSITY BROUGHT TO ITS KNEES LIKE THAT.
SO YOU TRANS-FERRED?
YUP. BECK'S A BET-TER FIT FOR ME ANY-WAY. TUITION'S ONLY $74.95, AND ALL YOU HAVE TO DO IS SIT THROUGH A FEW NUTTY VIDEOS...
OKAY, HERE WE GO! MR. BECK'S ABOUT TO GIVE HIS COMMENCE-MENT ADDRESS!
CLASS OF 2011! I... I... **SOB!**
BOOM! I'M OUTA HERE! REAL WORLD, LOOK **OUT**!
WOW! WHAT'S YOUR START-ING SALARY?
GB Trudeau

July 17, 2011

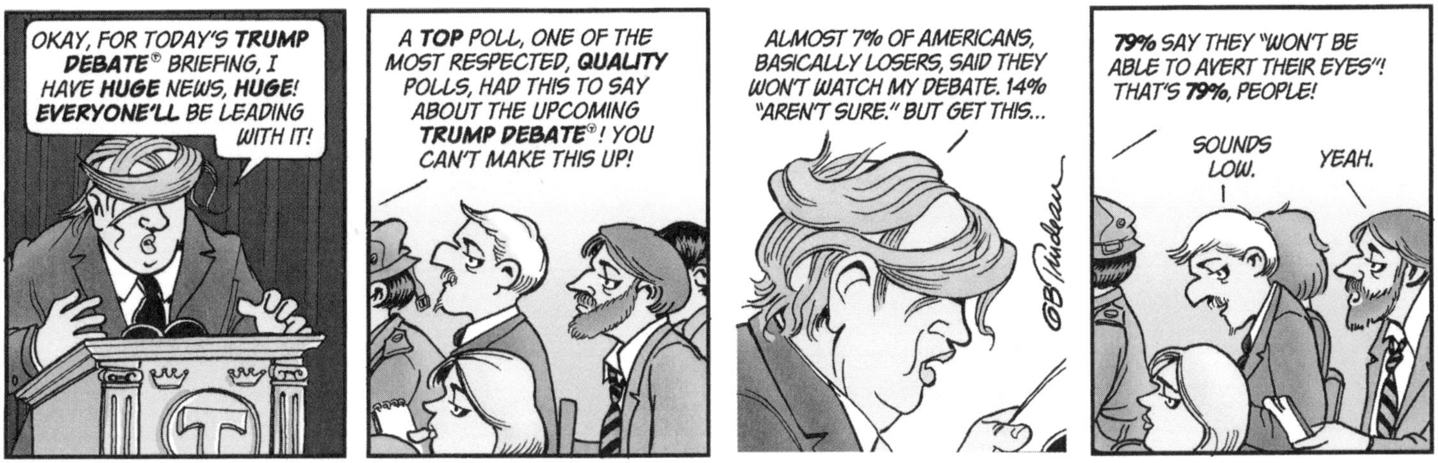
OKAY, FOR TODAY'S TRUMP DEBATE® BRIEFING, I HAVE HUGE NEWS, HUGE! EVERYONE'LL BE LEADING WITH IT!
A TOP POLL, ONE OF THE MOST RESPECTED, QUALITY POLLS, HAD THIS TO SAY ABOUT THE UPCOMING TRUMP DEBATE®! YOU CAN'T MAKE THIS UP!
ALMOST 7% OF AMERICANS, BASICALLY LOSERS, SAID THEY WON'T WATCH MY DEBATE. 14% "AREN'T SURE." BUT GET THIS...
79% SAY THEY "WON'T BE ABLE TO AVERT THEIR EYES"! THAT'S 79%, PEOPLE!
SOUNDS LOW.
YEAH.

December 12, 2011

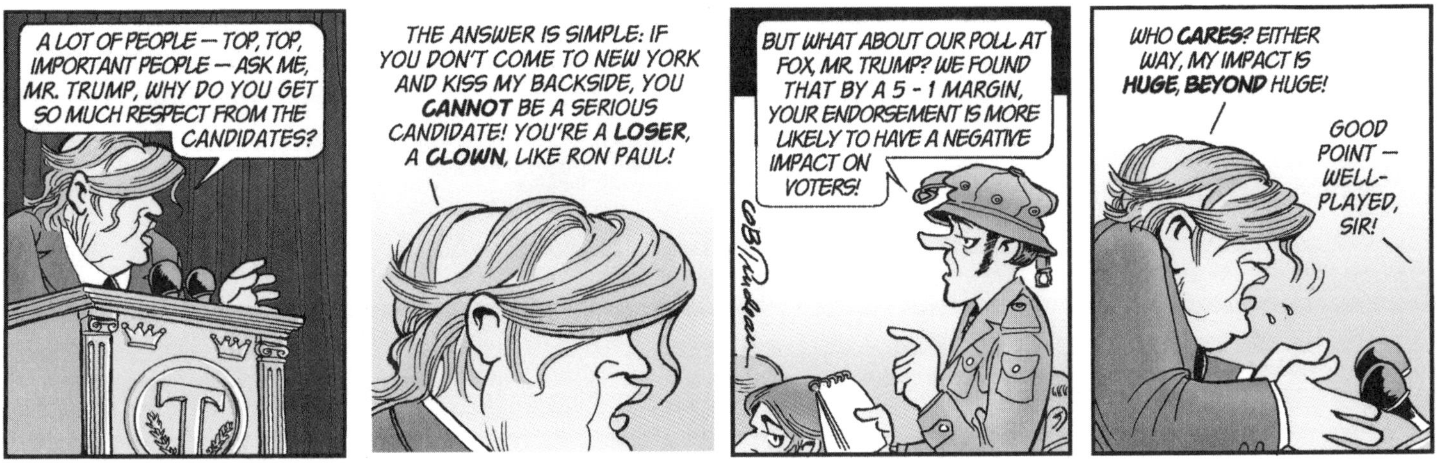
A LOT OF PEOPLE — TOP, TOP, IMPORTANT PEOPLE — ASK ME, MR. TRUMP, WHY DO YOU GET SO MUCH RESPECT FROM THE CANDIDATES?
THE ANSWER IS SIMPLE: IF YOU DON'T COME TO NEW YORK AND KISS MY BACKSIDE, YOU CANNOT BE A SERIOUS CANDIDATE! YOU'RE A LOSER, A CLOWN, LIKE RON PAUL!
BUT WHAT ABOUT OUR POLL AT FOX, MR. TRUMP? WE FOUND THAT BY A 5 - 1 MARGIN, YOUR ENDORSEMENT IS MORE LIKELY TO HAVE A NEGATIVE IMPACT ON VOTERS!
WHO CARES? EITHER WAY, MY IMPACT IS HUGE, BEYOND HUGE!
GOOD POINT — WELL-PLAYED, SIR!

December 13, 2011

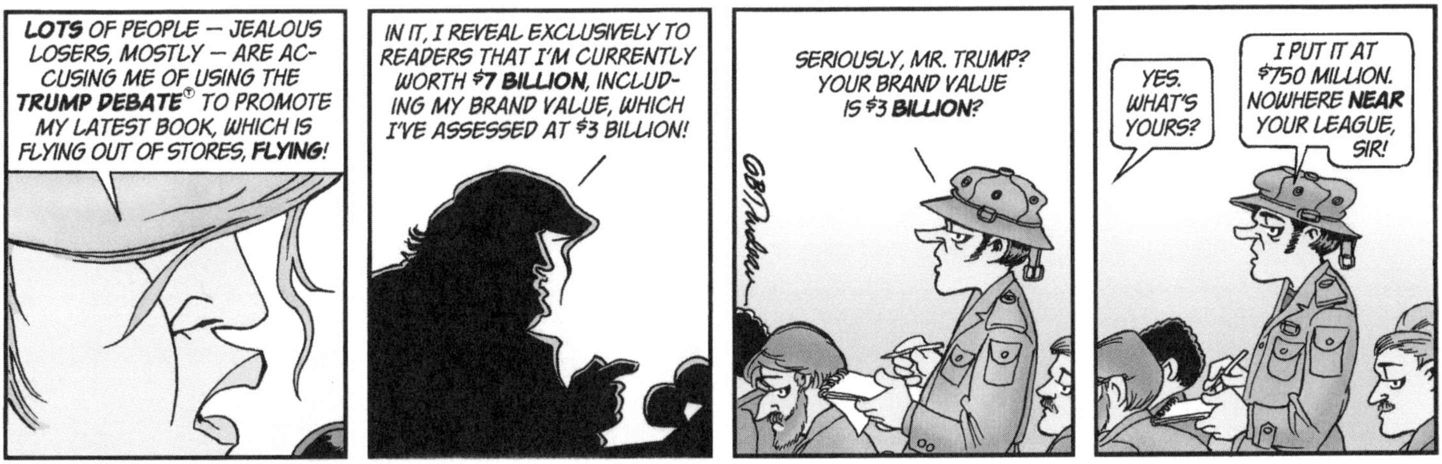
LOTS OF PEOPLE — JEALOUS LOSERS, MOSTLY — ARE ACCUSING ME OF USING THE TRUMP DEBATE® TO PROMOTE MY LATEST BOOK, WHICH IS FLYING OUT OF STORES, FLYING!
IN IT, I REVEAL EXCLUSIVELY TO READERS THAT I'M CURRENTLY WORTH $7 BILLION, INCLUDING MY BRAND VALUE, WHICH I'VE ASSESSED AT $3 BILLION!
SERIOUSLY, MR. TRUMP? YOUR BRAND VALUE IS $3 BILLION?
YES. WHAT'S YOURS?
I PUT IT AT $750 MILLION. NOWHERE NEAR YOUR LEAGUE, SIR!

December 14, 2011

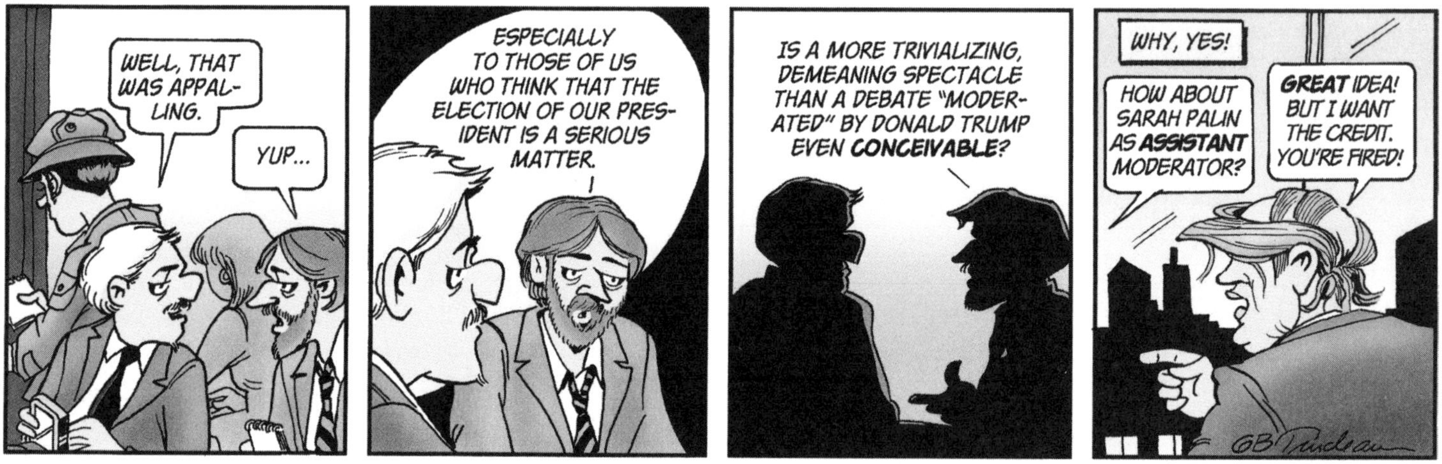
WELL, THAT WAS APPAL-LING.
YUP...
ESPECIALLY TO THOSE OF US WHO THINK THAT THE ELECTION OF OUR PRES-IDENT IS A SERIOUS MATTER.
IS A MORE TRIVIALIZING, DEMEANING SPECTACLE THAN A DEBATE "MODER-ATED" BY DONALD TRUMP EVEN **CONCEIVABLE**?
WHY, YES!
HOW ABOUT SARAH PALIN AS **ASSISTANT** MODERATOR?
GREAT IDEA! BUT I WANT THE CREDIT. YOU'RE FIRED!

December 15, 2011

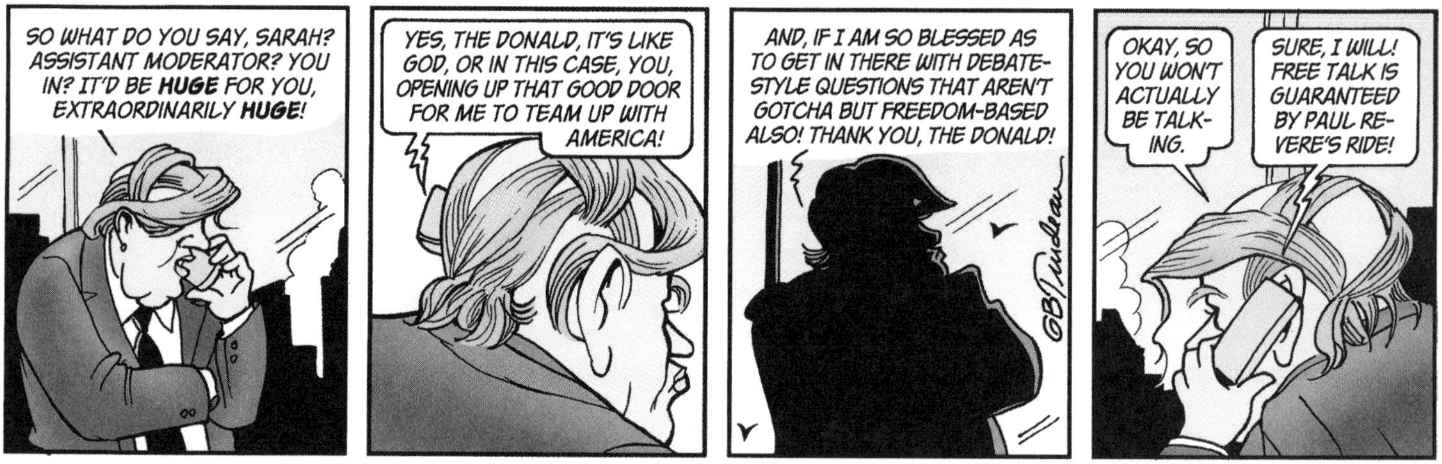
SO WHAT DO YOU SAY, SARAH? ASSISTANT MODERATOR? YOU IN? IT'D BE **HUGE** FOR YOU, EXTRAORDINARILY **HUGE**!
YES, THE DONALD, IT'S LIKE GOD, OR IN THIS CASE, YOU, OPENING UP THAT GOOD DOOR FOR ME TO TEAM UP WITH AMERICA!
AND, IF I AM SO BLESSED AS TO GET IN THERE WITH DEBATE-STYLE QUESTIONS THAT AREN'T GOTCHA BUT FREEDOM-BASED ALSO! THANK YOU, THE DONALD!
OKAY, SO YOU WON'T ACTUALLY BE TALK-ING.
SURE, I WILL! FREE TALK IS GUARANTEED BY PAUL RE-VERE'S RIDE!

December 16, 2011

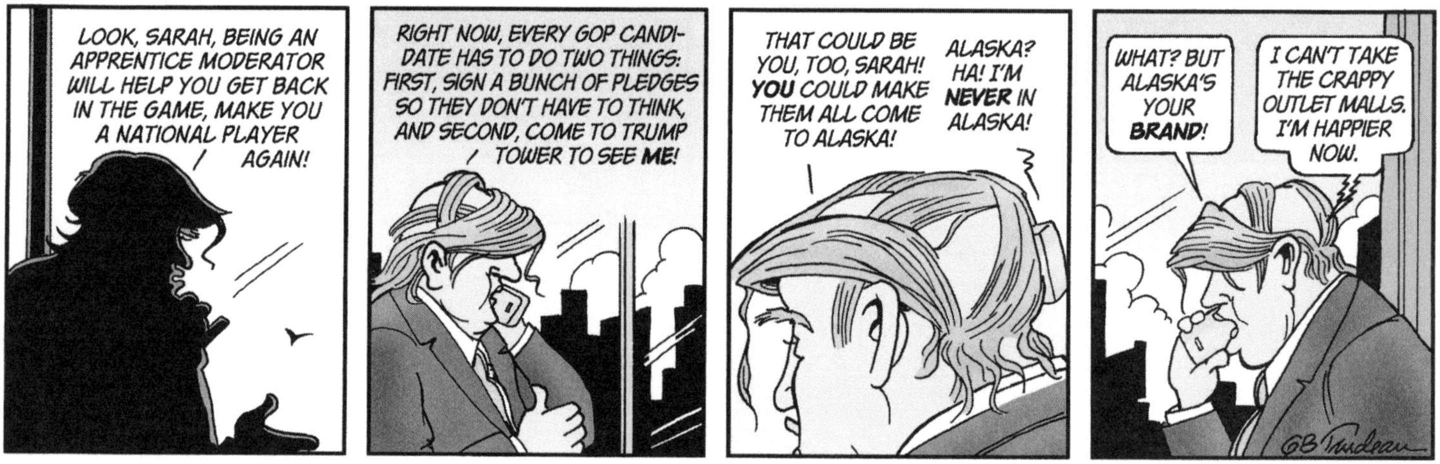
LOOK, SARAH, BEING AN APPRENTICE MODERATOR WILL HELP YOU GET BACK IN THE GAME, MAKE YOU A NATIONAL PLAYER AGAIN!
RIGHT NOW, EVERY GOP CANDI-DATE HAS TO DO TWO THINGS: FIRST, SIGN A BUNCH OF PLEDGES SO THEY DON'T HAVE TO THINK, AND SECOND, COME TO TRUMP TOWER TO SEE **ME**!
THAT COULD BE YOU, TOO, SARAH! **YOU** COULD MAKE THEM ALL COME TO ALASKA!
ALASKA? HA! I'M **NEVER** IN ALASKA!
WHAT? BUT ALASKA'S YOUR **BRAND**!
I CAN'T TAKE THE CRAPPY OUTLET MALLS. I'M HAPPIER NOW.

December 17, 2011

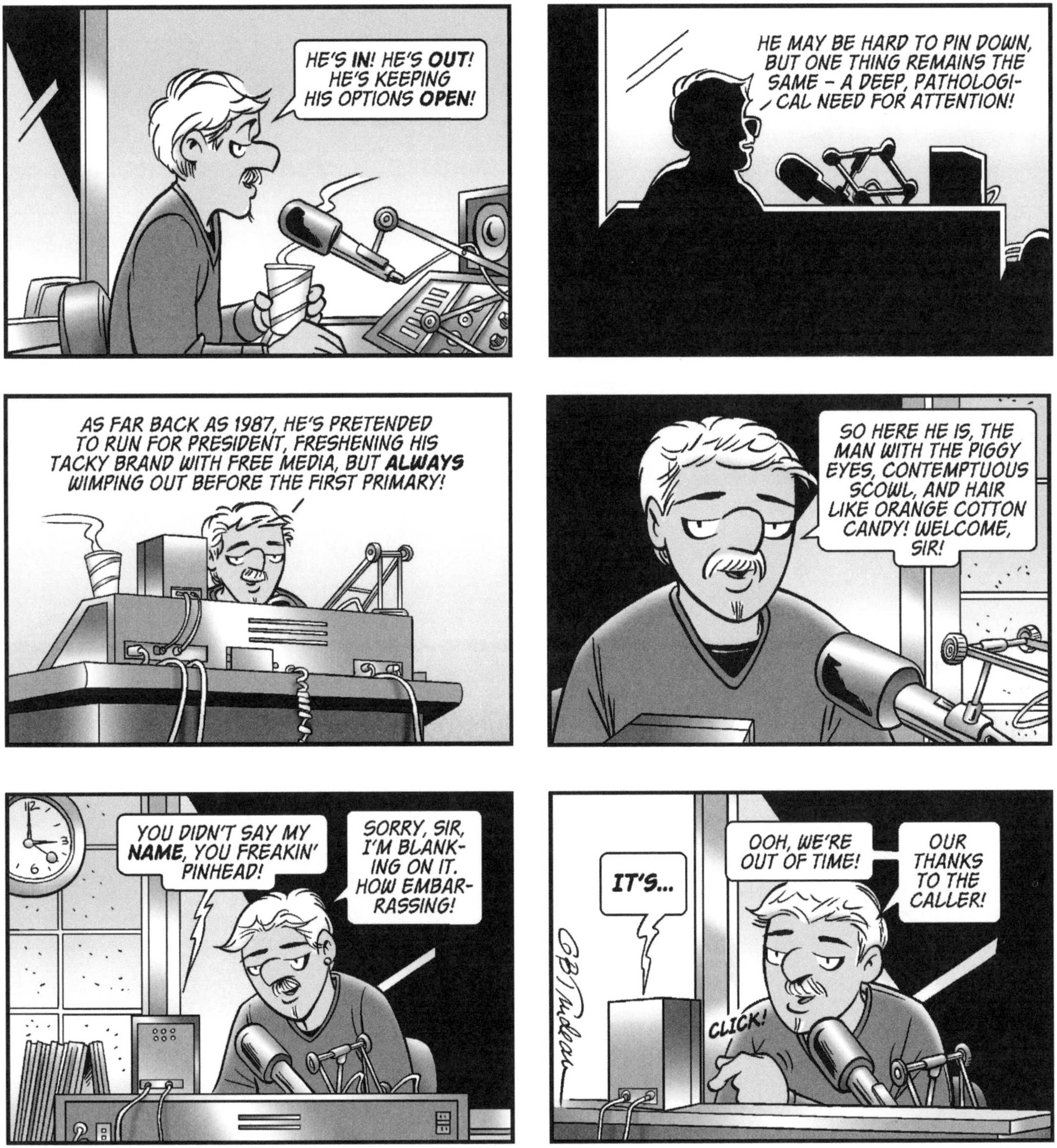
HE'S IN! HE'S OUT! HE'S KEEPING HIS OPTIONS OPEN!
HE MAY BE HARD TO PIN DOWN, BUT ONE THING REMAINS THE SAME – A DEEP, PATHOLOGICAL NEED FOR ATTENTION!
AS FAR BACK AS 1987, HE'S PRETENDED TO RUN FOR PRESIDENT, FRESHENING HIS TACKY BRAND WITH FREE MEDIA, BUT ALWAYS WIMPING OUT BEFORE THE FIRST PRIMARY!
SO HERE HE IS, THE MAN WITH THE PIGGY EYES, CONTEMPTUOUS SCOWL, AND HAIR LIKE ORANGE COTTON CANDY! WELCOME, SIR!
YOU DIDN'T SAY MY NAME, YOU FREAKIN' PINHEAD!
SORRY, SIR, I'M BLANKING ON IT. HOW EMBARRASSING!
IT'S...
OOH, WE'RE OUT OF TIME!
OUR THANKS TO THE CALLER!
CLICK!
GBTrudeau

April 5, 2015

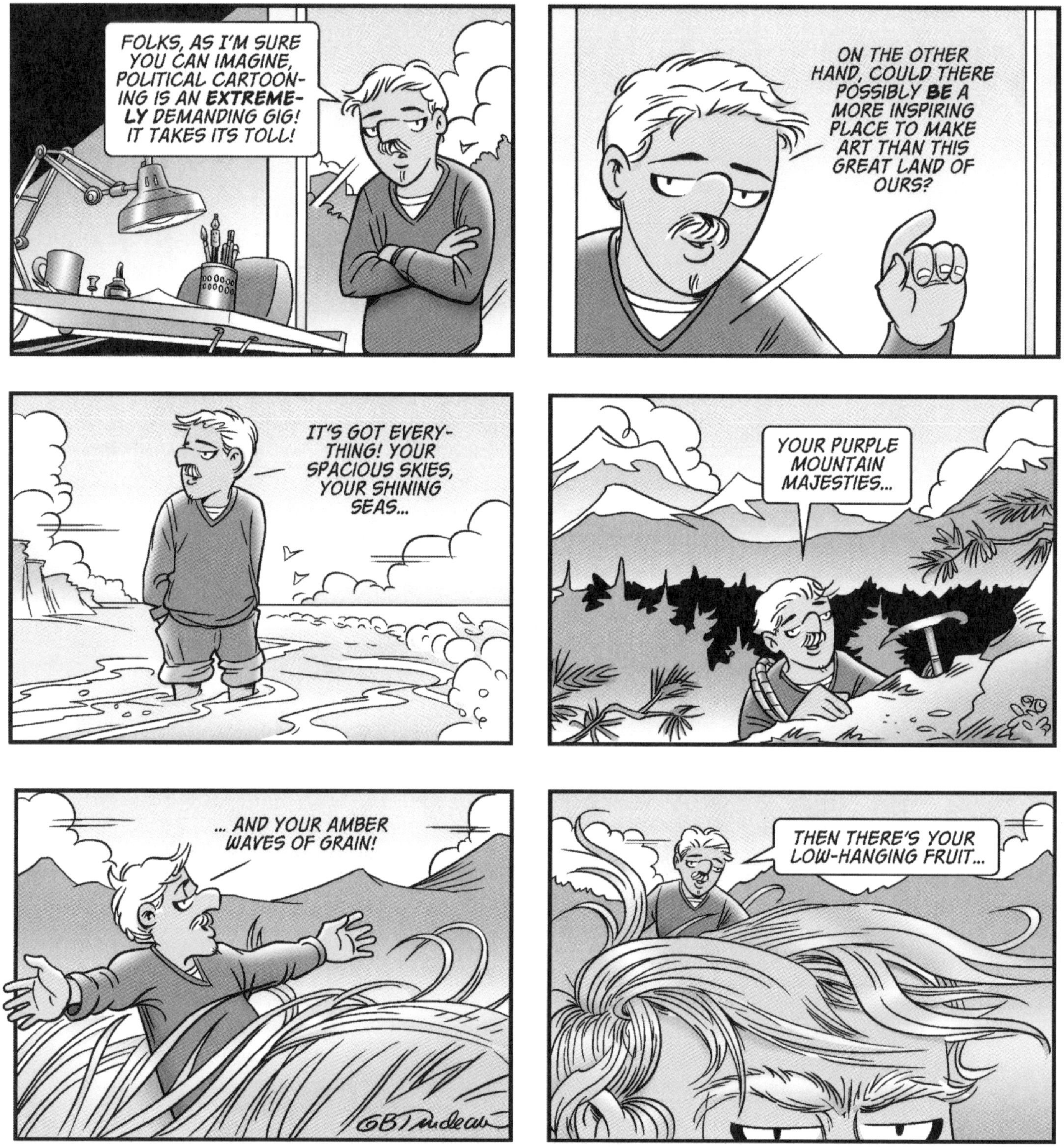
FOLKS, AS I'M SURE YOU CAN IMAGINE, POLITICAL CARTOONING IS AN **EXTREMELY** DEMANDING GIG! IT TAKES ITS TOLL!
ON THE OTHER HAND, COULD THERE POSSIBLY **BE** A MORE INSPIRING PLACE TO MAKE ART THAN THIS GREAT LAND OF OURS?
IT'S GOT EVERYTHING! YOUR SPACIOUS SKIES, YOUR SHINING SEAS...
YOUR PURPLE MOUNTAIN MAJESTIES...
... AND YOUR AMBER WAVES OF GRAIN!
THEN THERE'S YOUR LOW-HANGING FRUIT...
GBTrudeau

July 26, 2015

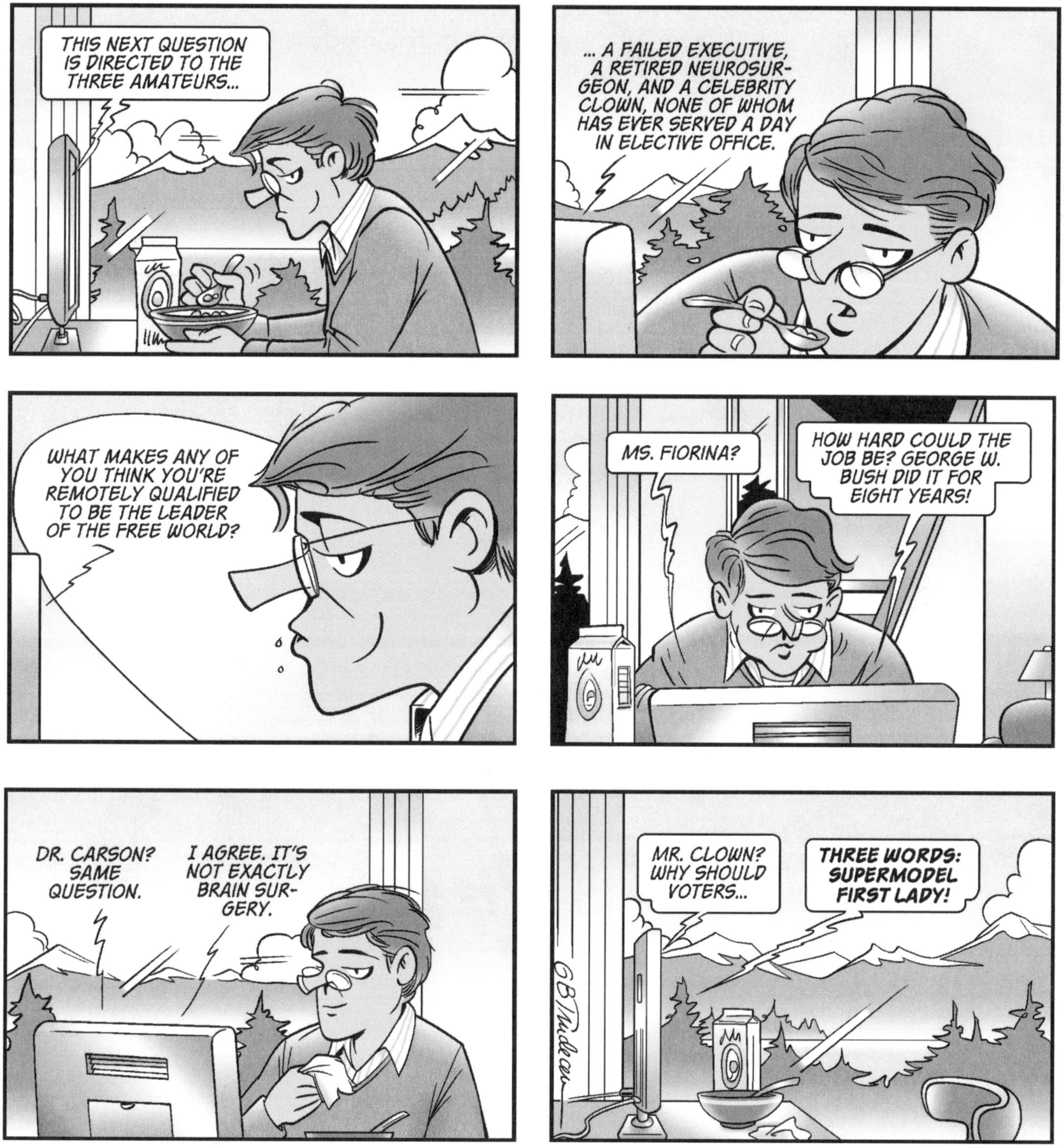
THIS NEXT QUESTION IS DIRECTED TO THE THREE AMATEURS...
... A FAILED EXECUTIVE, A RETIRED NEUROSURGEON, AND A CELEBRITY CLOWN, NONE OF WHOM HAS EVER SERVED A DAY IN ELECTIVE OFFICE.
WHAT MAKES ANY OF YOU THINK YOU'RE REMOTELY QUALIFIED TO BE THE LEADER OF THE FREE WORLD?
MS. FIORINA?
HOW HARD COULD THE JOB BE? GEORGE W. BUSH DID IT FOR EIGHT YEARS!
DR. CARSON? SAME QUESTION.
I AGREE. IT'S NOT EXACTLY BRAIN SURGERY.
MR. CLOWN? WHY SHOULD VOTERS...
THREE WORDS: SUPERMODEL FIRST LADY!

August 2, 2015

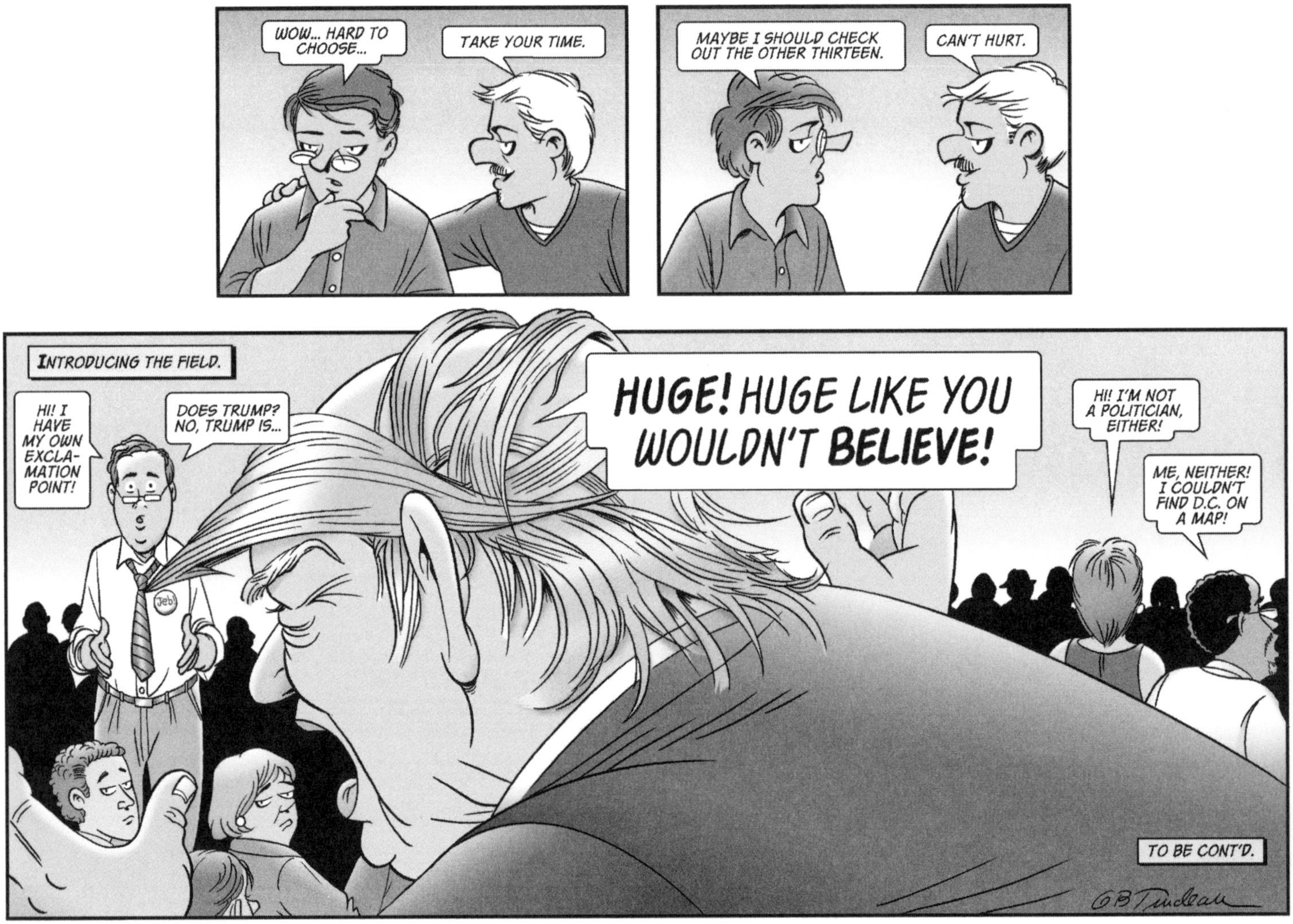
WOW... HARD TO CHOOSE...
TAKE YOUR TIME.
MAYBE I SHOULD CHECK OUT THE OTHER THIRTEEN.
CAN'T HURT.
INTRODUCING THE FIELD.
HI! I HAVE MY OWN EXCLA-MATION POINT!
DOES TRUMP? NO, TRUMP IS...
HUGE! HUGE LIKE YOU WOULDN'T BELIEVE!
HI! I'M NOT A POLITICIAN, EITHER!
ME, NEITHER! I COULDN'T FIND D.C. ON A MAP!
Jeb!
TO BE CONT'D.
GB Trudeau

September 27, 2015

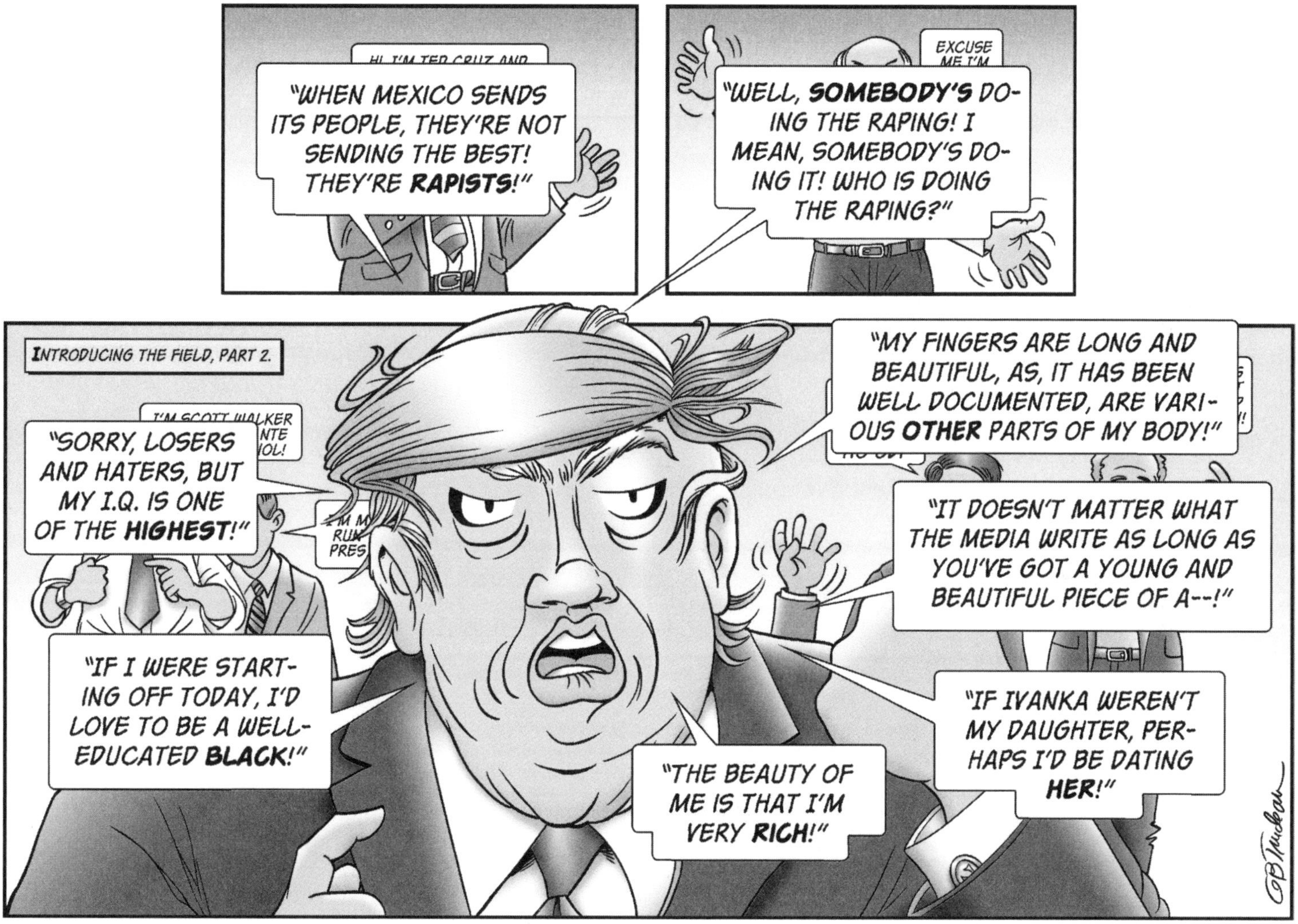
"WHEN MEXICO SENDS ITS PEOPLE, THEY'RE NOT SENDING THE BEST! THEY'RE **RAPISTS**!"
"WELL, **SOMEBODY'S** DO-ING THE RAPING! I MEAN, SOMEBODY'S DO-ING IT! WHO IS DOING THE RAPING?"
INTRODUCING THE FIELD, PART 2.
"MY FINGERS ARE LONG AND BEAUTIFUL, AS, IT HAS BEEN WELL DOCUMENTED, ARE VARI-OUS **OTHER** PARTS OF MY BODY!"
"SORRY, LOSERS AND HATERS, BUT MY I.Q. IS ONE OF THE **HIGHEST**!"
"IT DOESN'T MATTER WHAT THE MEDIA WRITE AS LONG AS YOU'VE GOT A YOUNG AND BEAUTIFUL PIECE OF A--!"
"IF I WERE START-ING OFF TODAY, I'D LOVE TO BE A WELL-EDUCATED **BLACK**!"
"IF IVANKA WEREN'T MY DAUGHTER, PER-HAPS I'D BE DATING **HER**!"
"THE BEAUTY OF ME IS THAT I'M VERY **RICH**!"

October 4, 2015

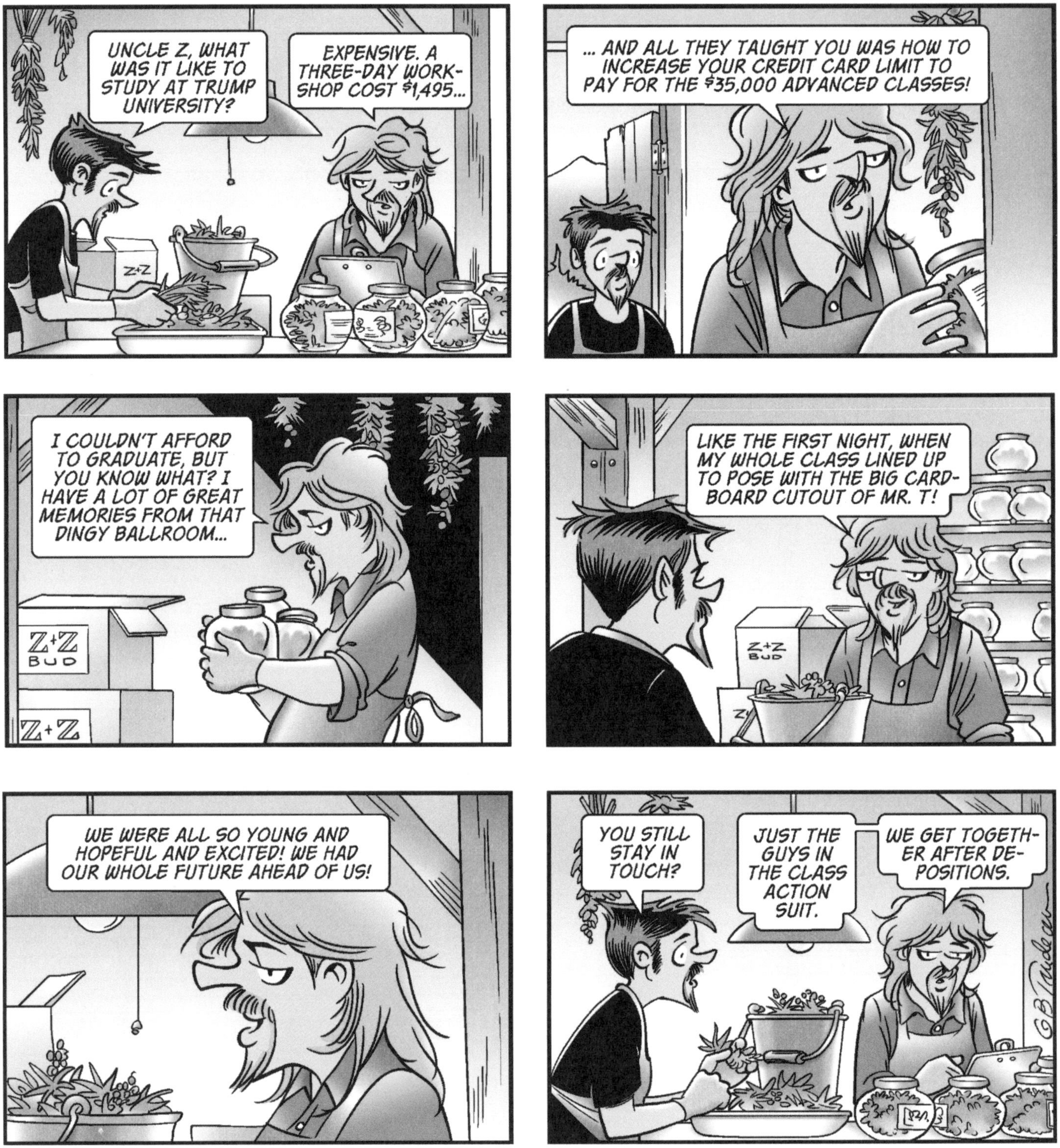
UNCLE Z, WHAT WAS IT LIKE TO STUDY AT TRUMP UNIVERSITY?
EXPENSIVE. A THREE-DAY WORK-SHOP COST $1,495...
... AND ALL THEY TAUGHT YOU WAS HOW TO INCREASE YOUR CREDIT CARD LIMIT TO PAY FOR THE $35,000 ADVANCED CLASSES!
I COULDN'T AFFORD TO GRADUATE, BUT YOU KNOW WHAT? I HAVE A LOT OF GREAT MEMORIES FROM THAT DINGY BALLROOM...
LIKE THE FIRST NIGHT, WHEN MY WHOLE CLASS LINED UP TO POSE WITH THE BIG CARD-BOARD CUTOUT OF MR. T!
WE WERE ALL SO YOUNG AND HOPEFUL AND EXCITED! WE HAD OUR WHOLE FUTURE AHEAD OF US!
YOU STILL STAY IN TOUCH?
JUST THE GUYS IN THE CLASS ACTION SUIT.
WE GET TOGETH-ER AFTER DE-POSITIONS.

October 18, 2015

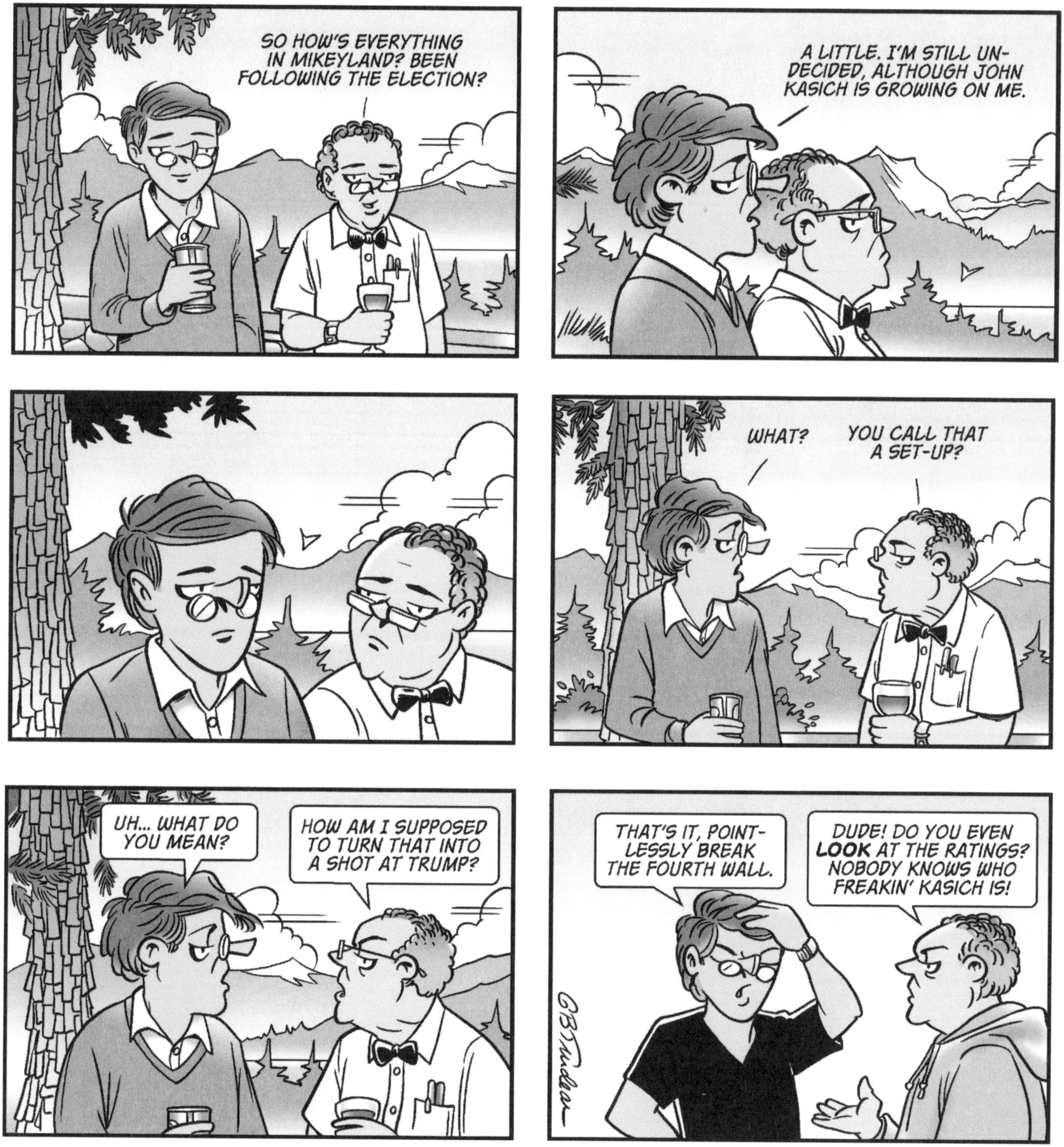
SO HOW'S EVERYTHING IN MIKEYLAND? BEEN FOLLOWING THE ELECTION?
A LITTLE. I'M STILL UN-DECIDED, ALTHOUGH JOHN KASICH IS GROWING ON ME.
WHAT?
YOU CALL THAT A SET-UP?
UH... WHAT DO YOU MEAN?
HOW AM I SUPPOSED TO TURN THAT INTO A SHOT AT TRUMP?
THAT'S IT, POINT-LESSLY BREAK THE FOURTH WALL.
DUDE! DO YOU EVEN **LOOK** AT THE RATINGS? NOBODY KNOWS WHO FREAKIN' KASICH IS!
GBTrudeau

November 1, 2015

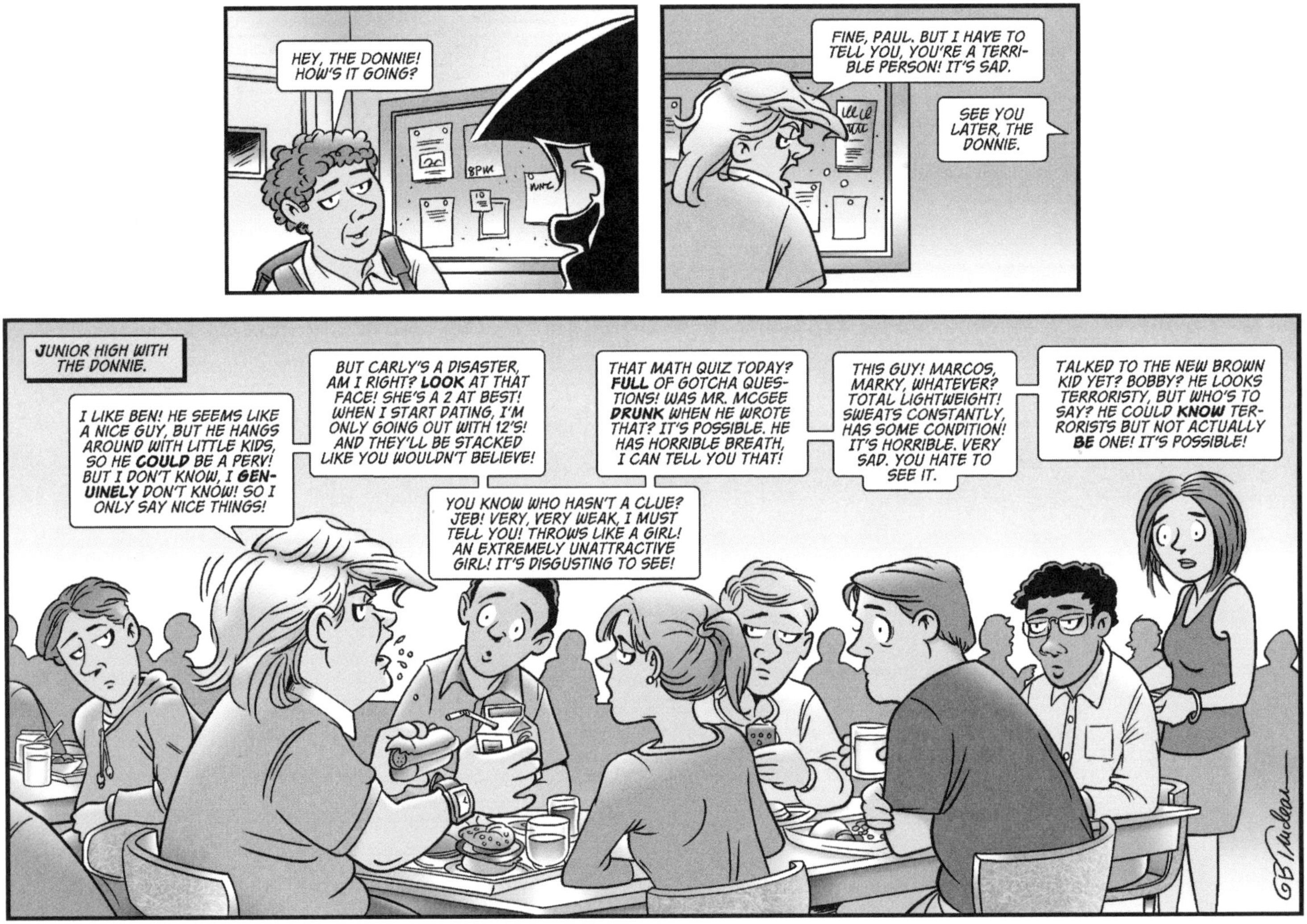
HEY, THE DONNIE! HOW'S IT GOING?
FINE, PAUL. BUT I HAVE TO TELL YOU, YOU'RE A TERRIBLE PERSON! IT'S SAD.
SEE YOU LATER, THE DONNIE.
JUNIOR HIGH WITH THE DONNIE.
I LIKE BEN! HE SEEMS LIKE A NICE GUY, BUT HE HANGS AROUND WITH LITTLE KIDS, SO HE **COULD** BE A PERV! BUT I DON'T KNOW, I **GENUINELY** DON'T KNOW! SO I ONLY SAY NICE THINGS!
BUT CARLY'S A DISASTER, AM I RIGHT? **LOOK** AT THAT FACE! SHE'S A 2 AT BEST! WHEN I START DATING, I'M ONLY GOING OUT WITH 12'S! AND THEY'LL BE STACKED LIKE YOU WOULDN'T BELIEVE!
YOU KNOW WHO HASN'T A CLUE? JEB! VERY, VERY WEAK, I MUST TELL YOU! THROWS LIKE A GIRL! AN EXTREMELY UNATTRACTIVE GIRL! IT'S DISGUSTING TO SEE!
THAT MATH QUIZ TODAY? **FULL** OF GOTCHA QUESTIONS! WAS MR. MCGEE **DRUNK** WHEN HE WROTE THAT? IT'S POSSIBLE. HE HAS HORRIBLE BREATH, I CAN TELL YOU THAT!
THIS GUY! MARCOS, MARKY, WHATEVER? TOTAL LIGHTWEIGHT! SWEATS CONSTANTLY, HAS SOME CONDITION! IT'S HORRIBLE. VERY SAD. YOU HATE TO SEE IT.
TALKED TO THE NEW BROWN KID YET? BOBBY? HE LOOKS TERRORISTY, BUT WHO'S TO SAY? HE COULD **KNOW** TERRORISTS BUT NOT ACTUALLY **BE** ONE! IT'S POSSIBLE!

December 27, 2015

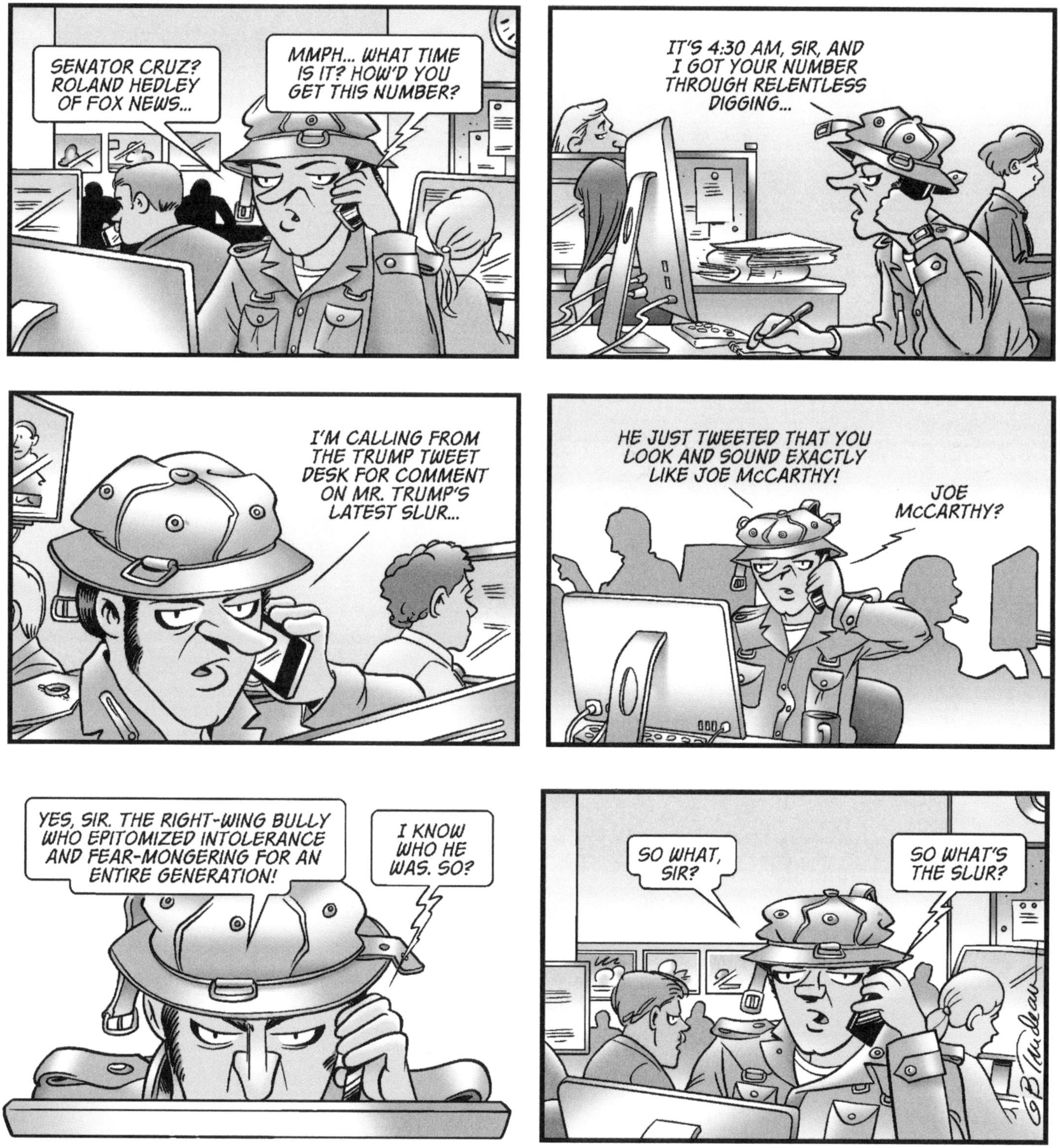
SENATOR CRUZ? ROLAND HEDLEY OF FOX NEWS...
MMPH... WHAT TIME IS IT? HOW'D YOU GET THIS NUMBER?
IT'S 4:30 AM, SIR, AND I GOT YOUR NUMBER THROUGH RELENTLESS DIGGING...
I'M CALLING FROM THE TRUMP TWEET DESK FOR COMMENT ON MR. TRUMP'S LATEST SLUR...
HE JUST TWEETED THAT YOU LOOK AND SOUND EXACTLY LIKE JOE McCARTHY!
JOE McCARTHY?
YES, SIR. THE RIGHT-WING BULLY WHO EPITOMIZED INTOLERANCE AND FEAR-MONGERING FOR AN ENTIRE GENERATION!
I KNOW WHO HE WAS. SO?
SO WHAT, SIR?
SO WHAT'S THE SLUR?
©B Trudeau

January 3, 2016

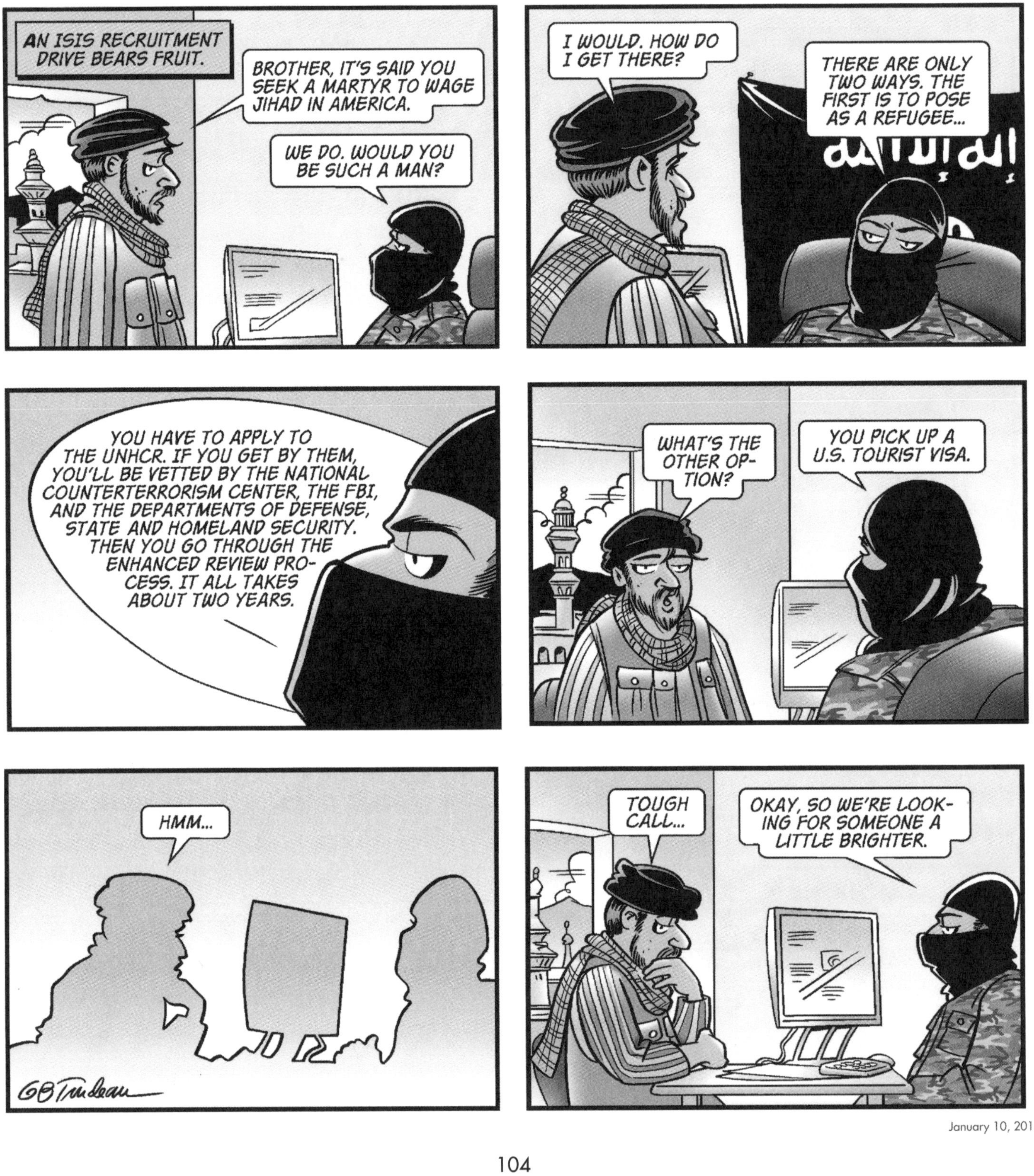
AN ISIS RECRUITMENT DRIVE BEARS FRUIT.
BROTHER, IT'S SAID YOU SEEK A MARTYR TO WAGE JIHAD IN AMERICA.
WE DO. WOULD YOU BE SUCH A MAN?
I WOULD. HOW DO I GET THERE?
THERE ARE ONLY TWO WAYS. THE FIRST IS TO POSE AS A REFUGEE...
YOU HAVE TO APPLY TO THE UNHCR. IF YOU GET BY THEM, YOU'LL BE VETTED BY THE NATIONAL COUNTERTERRORISM CENTER, THE FBI, AND THE DEPARTMENTS OF DEFENSE, STATE AND HOMELAND SECURITY. THEN YOU GO THROUGH THE ENHANCED REVIEW PROCESS. IT ALL TAKES ABOUT TWO YEARS.
WHAT'S THE OTHER OPTION?
YOU PICK UP A U.S. TOURIST VISA.
HMM...
TOUGH CALL...
OKAY, SO WE'RE LOOKING FOR SOMEONE A LITTLE BRIGHTER.
GBTrudeau

January 10, 2016

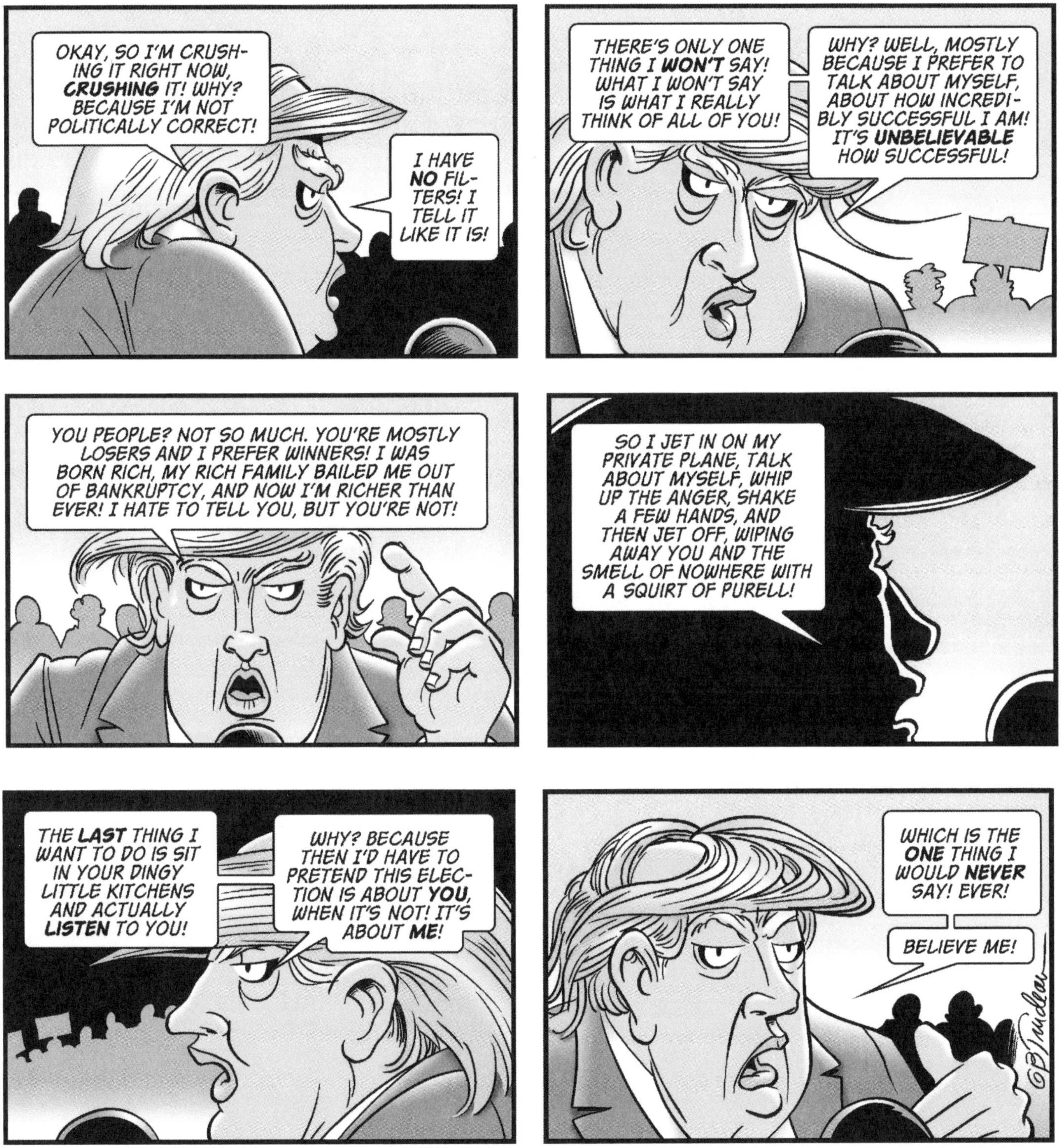
OKAY, SO I'M CRUSHING IT RIGHT NOW, **CRUSHING** IT! WHY? BECAUSE I'M NOT POLITICALLY CORRECT!
I HAVE **NO** FILTERS! I TELL IT LIKE IT IS!
THERE'S ONLY ONE THING I **WON'T** SAY! WHAT I WON'T SAY IS WHAT I REALLY THINK OF ALL OF YOU!
WHY? WELL, MOSTLY BECAUSE I PREFER TO TALK ABOUT MYSELF, ABOUT HOW INCREDIBLY SUCCESSFUL I AM! IT'S **UNBELIEVABLE** HOW SUCCESSFUL!
YOU PEOPLE? NOT SO MUCH. YOU'RE MOSTLY LOSERS AND I PREFER WINNERS! I WAS BORN RICH, MY RICH FAMILY BAILED ME OUT OF BANKRUPTCY, AND NOW I'M RICHER THAN EVER! I HATE TO TELL YOU, BUT YOU'RE NOT!
SO I JET IN ON MY PRIVATE PLANE, TALK ABOUT MYSELF, WHIP UP THE ANGER, SHAKE A FEW HANDS, AND THEN JET OFF, WIPING AWAY YOU AND THE SMELL OF NOWHERE WITH A SQUIRT OF PURELL!
THE **LAST** THING I WANT TO DO IS SIT IN YOUR DINGY LITTLE KITCHENS AND ACTUALLY **LISTEN** TO YOU!
WHY? BECAUSE THEN I'D HAVE TO PRETEND THIS ELECTION IS ABOUT **YOU**, WHEN IT'S NOT! IT'S ABOUT **ME**!
WHICH IS THE **ONE** THING I WOULD **NEVER** SAY! EVER!
BELIEVE ME!
©B Trudeau

February 14, 2016

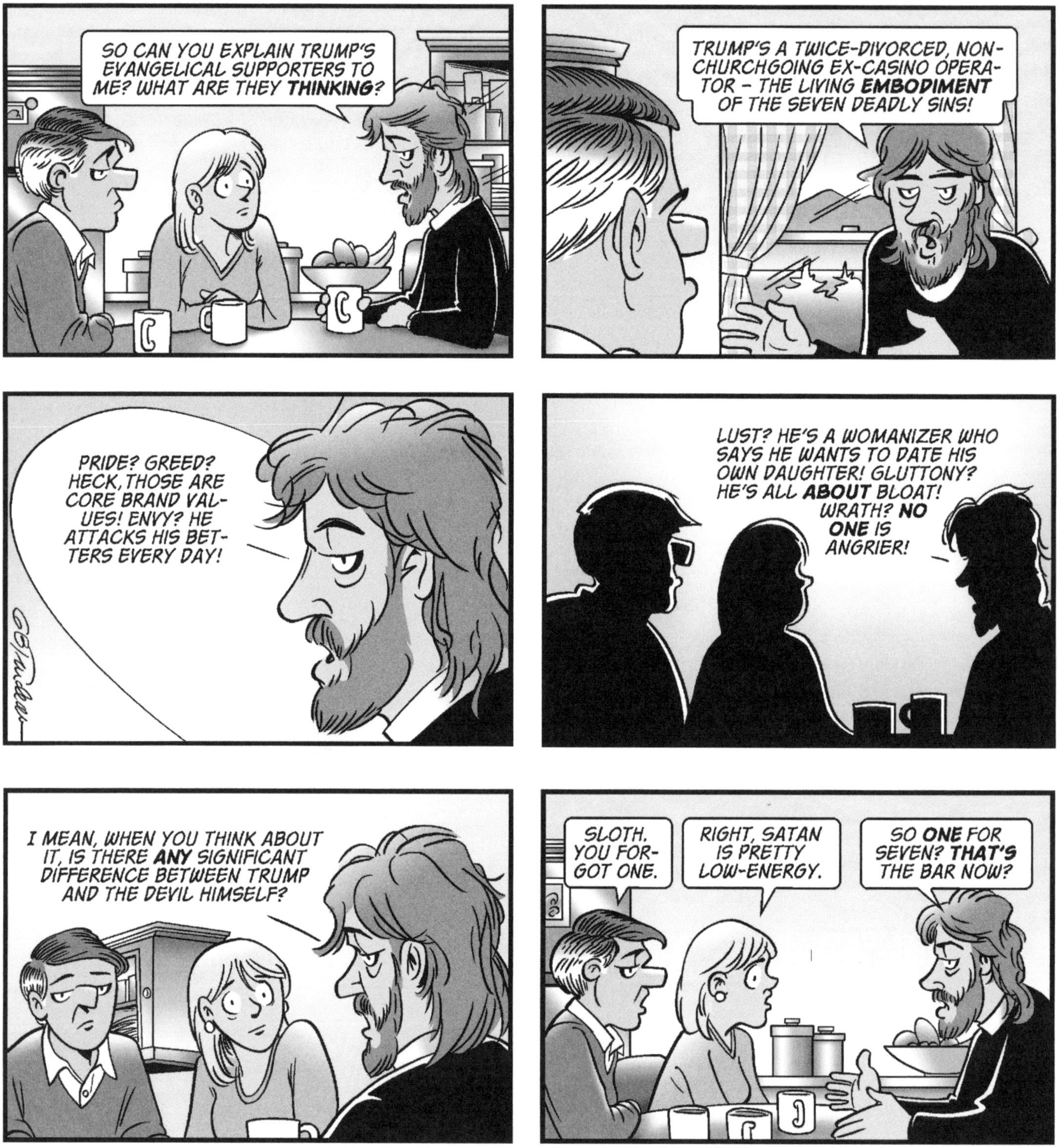
SO CAN YOU EXPLAIN TRUMP'S EVANGELICAL SUPPORTERS TO ME? WHAT ARE THEY **THINKING**?
TRUMP'S A TWICE-DIVORCED, NON-CHURCHGOING EX-CASINO OPERATOR – THE LIVING **EMBODIMENT** OF THE SEVEN DEADLY SINS!
PRIDE? GREED? HECK, THOSE ARE CORE BRAND VALUES! ENVY? HE ATTACKS HIS BETTERS EVERY DAY!
LUST? HE'S A WOMANIZER WHO SAYS HE WANTS TO DATE HIS OWN DAUGHTER! GLUTTONY? HE'S ALL **ABOUT** BLOAT!
WRATH? **NO ONE** IS ANGRIER!
I MEAN, WHEN YOU THINK ABOUT IT, IS THERE **ANY** SIGNIFICANT DIFFERENCE BETWEEN TRUMP AND THE DEVIL HIMSELF?
SLOTH. YOU FORGOT ONE.
RIGHT, SATAN IS PRETTY LOW-ENERGY.
SO **ONE** FOR SEVEN? **THAT'S** THE BAR NOW?

February 21, 2016

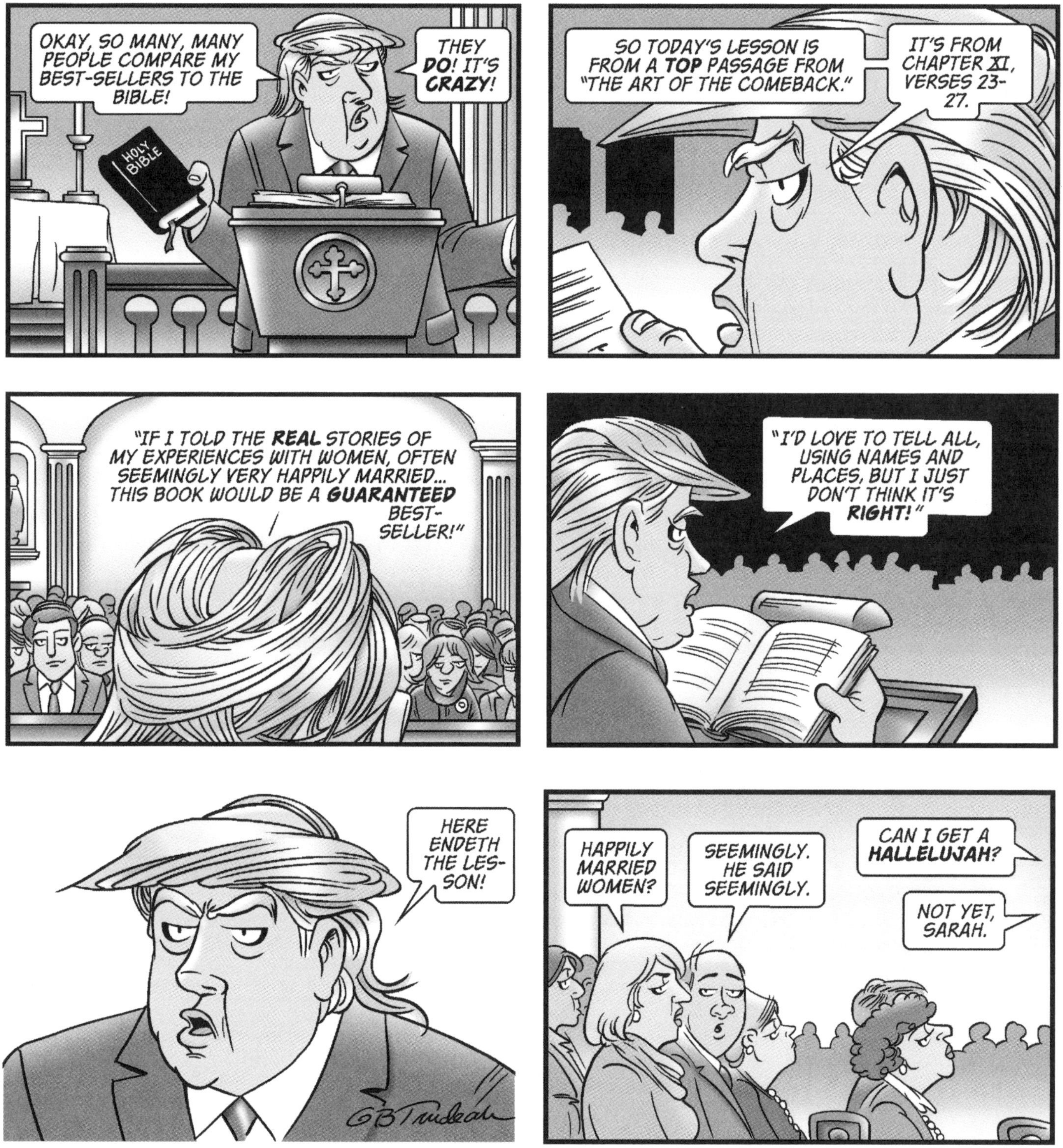
OKAY, SO MANY, MANY PEOPLE COMPARE MY BEST-SELLERS TO THE BIBLE!
THEY **DO**! IT'S **CRAZY**!
HOLY BIBLE
SO TODAY'S LESSON IS FROM A **TOP** PASSAGE FROM "THE ART OF THE COMEBACK."
IT'S FROM CHAPTER XI, VERSES 23-27.
"IF I TOLD THE **REAL** STORIES OF MY EXPERIENCES WITH WOMEN, OFTEN SEEMINGLY VERY HAPPILY MARRIED... THIS BOOK WOULD BE A **GUARANTEED** BEST-SELLER!"
"I'D LOVE TO TELL ALL, USING NAMES AND PLACES, BUT I JUST DON'T THINK IT'S **RIGHT!**"
HERE ENDETH THE LES-SON!
GBTrudeau
HAPPILY MARRIED WOMEN?
SEEMINGLY. HE SAID SEEMINGLY.
CAN I GET A **HALLELUJAH**?
NOT YET, SARAH.

February 28, 2016

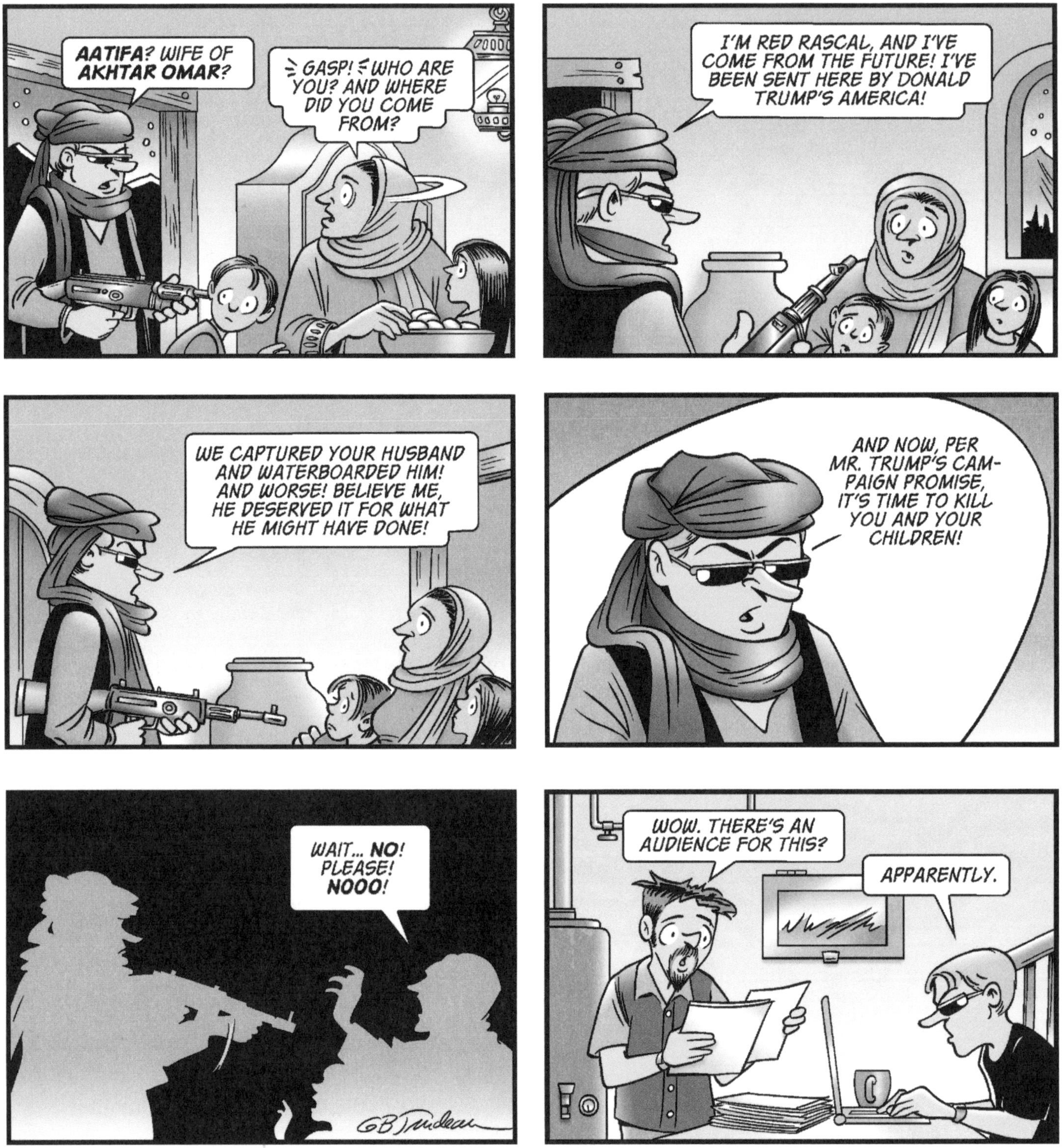
AATIFA? WIFE OF AKHTAR OMAR?
GASP! WHO ARE YOU? AND WHERE DID YOU COME FROM?
I'M RED RASCAL, AND I'VE COME FROM THE FUTURE! I'VE BEEN SENT HERE BY DONALD TRUMP'S AMERICA!
WE CAPTURED YOUR HUSBAND AND WATERBOARDED HIM! AND WORSE! BELIEVE ME, HE DESERVED IT FOR WHAT HE MIGHT HAVE DONE!
AND NOW, PER MR. TRUMP'S CAMPAIGN PROMISE, IT'S TIME TO KILL YOU AND YOUR CHILDREN!
WAIT... NO! PLEASE! NOOO!
GB Trudeau
WOW. THERE'S AN AUDIENCE FOR THIS?
APPARENTLY.

April 10, 2016

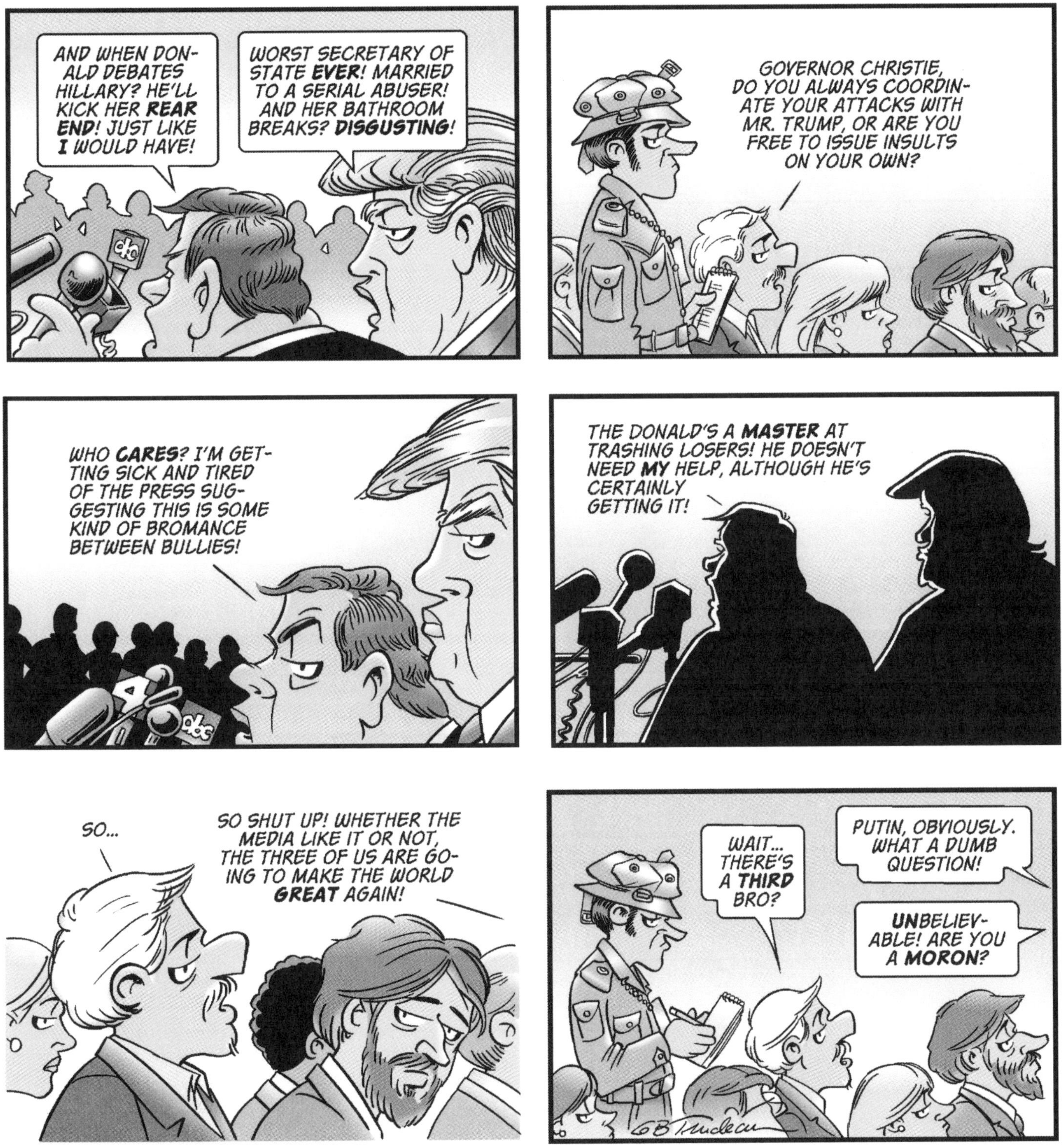
AND WHEN DONALD DEBATES HILLARY? HE'LL KICK HER **REAR END**! JUST LIKE **I** WOULD HAVE!
WORST SECRETARY OF STATE **EVER**! MARRIED TO A SERIAL ABUSER! AND HER BATHROOM BREAKS? **DISGUSTING**!
GOVERNOR CHRISTIE, DO YOU ALWAYS COORDINATE YOUR ATTACKS WITH MR. TRUMP, OR ARE YOU FREE TO ISSUE INSULTS ON YOUR OWN?
WHO **CARES**? I'M GETTING SICK AND TIRED OF THE PRESS SUGGESTING THIS IS SOME KIND OF BROMANCE BETWEEN BULLIES!
THE DONALD'S A **MASTER** AT TRASHING LOSERS! HE DOESN'T NEED **MY** HELP, ALTHOUGH HE'S CERTAINLY GETTING IT!
SO...
SO SHUT UP! WHETHER THE MEDIA LIKE IT OR NOT, THE THREE OF US ARE GOING TO MAKE THE WORLD **GREAT** AGAIN!
WAIT... THERE'S A **THIRD** BRO?
PUTIN, OBVIOUSLY. WHAT A DUMB QUESTION!
UNBELIEVABLE! ARE YOU A **MORON**?

April 3, 2016

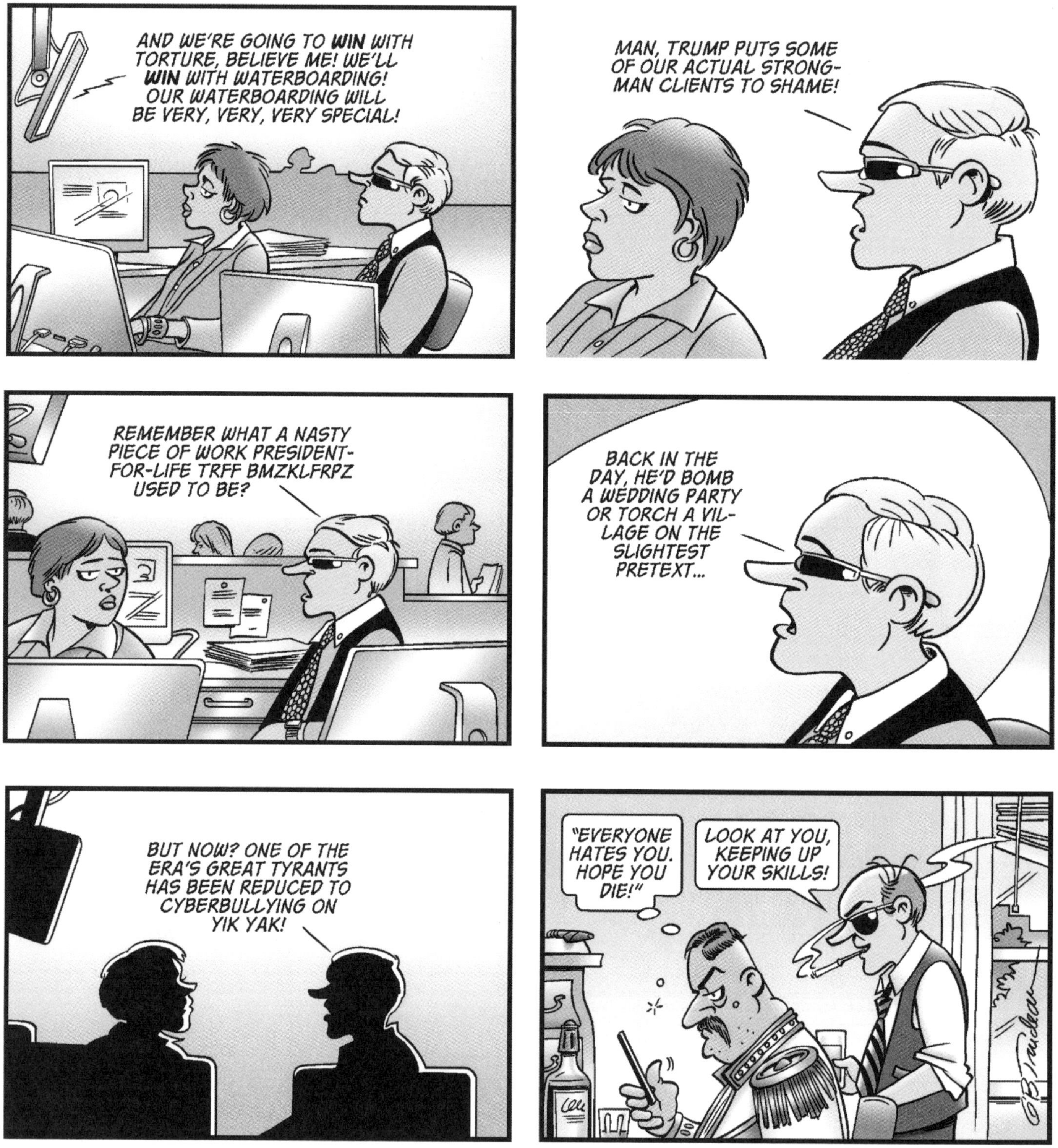
AND WE'RE GOING TO WIN WITH TORTURE, BELIEVE ME! WE'LL WIN WITH WATERBOARDING! OUR WATERBOARDING WILL BE VERY, VERY, VERY SPECIAL!
MAN, TRUMP PUTS SOME OF OUR ACTUAL STRONG-MAN CLIENTS TO SHAME!
REMEMBER WHAT A NASTY PIECE OF WORK PRESIDENT-FOR-LIFE TRFF BMZKLFRPZ USED TO BE?
BACK IN THE DAY, HE'D BOMB A WEDDING PARTY OR TORCH A VIL-LAGE ON THE SLIGHTEST PRETEXT...
BUT NOW? ONE OF THE ERA'S GREAT TYRANTS HAS BEEN REDUCED TO CYBERBULLYING ON YIK YAK!
"EVERYONE HATES YOU. HOPE YOU DIE!"
LOOK AT YOU, KEEPING UP YOUR SKILLS!
GBTrudeau

April 24, 2016

OH, YEAH? WELL, YOU'RE A...A...
A WHAT?
HEY, KIDS! TIRED OF GETTING KILLED ON INSULTS IN THE CAFETERIA?
THEN START FIGHTING BACK WITH MY QUALITY TRUMP® BRAND INSULTS!
CHOOSE FROM OVER 500 TREMENDOUS INSULTS I'VE TWEETED OUT SINCE LAST JUNE, INCLUDING...
"LIGHTWEIGHT!"
"EMBARRASSMENT!"
"CHOKER!"
"DISASTER!"
"PHONY!"
"HYPOCRITE!"
"DOPE!"
"FRAUD!"
"ARROGANT!"
"LOSER!"
"GRUBBY!"
"WACKO!"
"THIRD-RATE!"
"CLOWN!"
"DUMB!"
"CLUELESS!"
"NASTY!"
"FAILED!"
"TERRIBLE!"
"RIDICULOUS!"
"DECEPTIVE!"
"WEAK!"
"SAD!"
"CRAZY!"
"TOTALLY CORRUPT!"
"DUMB AS A ROCK!"
"RECKLESS!"
"TOTALLY FLAWED!"
"NOT NICE!"
"NERVOUS WRECK!"
"ZERO TALENT!"
"SLOPPY!"
"A REAL NUT JOB!"
"BLOWHARD!"
"OVERRATED!"
"TRULY WEIRD!"
"A JOKE!"
"UNATTRACTIVE!"
"DISGUSTING!"
"IRRELEVANT!"
"SPOILED BRAT!"
"LOW-CLASS SLOB!"
"GOOFBALL ATHEIST!"
"HATER AND RACIST!"
"FAILING!"
"FOOL!"
"WORTHLESS!"
"GARBAGE!"
"PURE SCUM!"
"CRUDE!"
"BIASED!"
"KOOKY!"
"AWKWARD!"
"DISHONEST!"
"HOPELESS!"
"DUMMY!"
"LIAR!"
"DISGRACE!"
"BASKET CASE!"
"DISLOYAL!"
"REALLY PATHETIC!"
SO STOP BEING A HUGE LOSER – USE TRUMP® BRAND INSULTS AND START WINNING TODAY!
PHONY! CLOWN! LIAR! GRUBBY! WACKO! DUMMY!

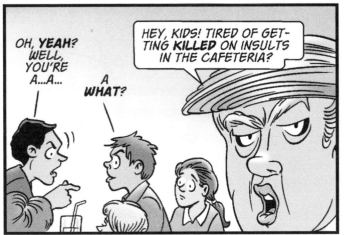

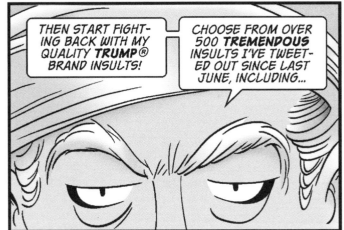

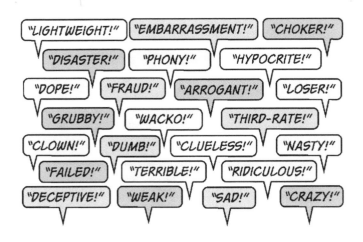

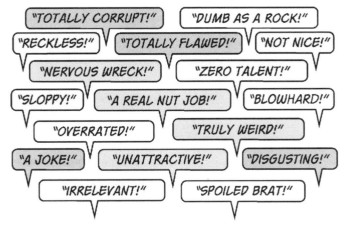

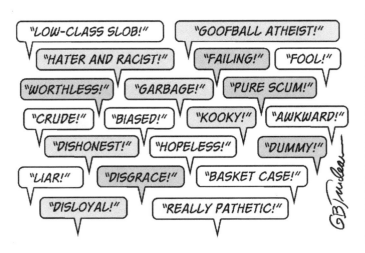

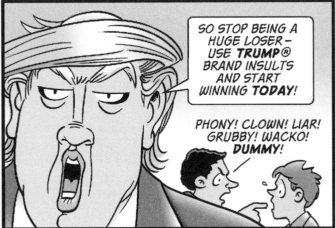

April 17, 2016

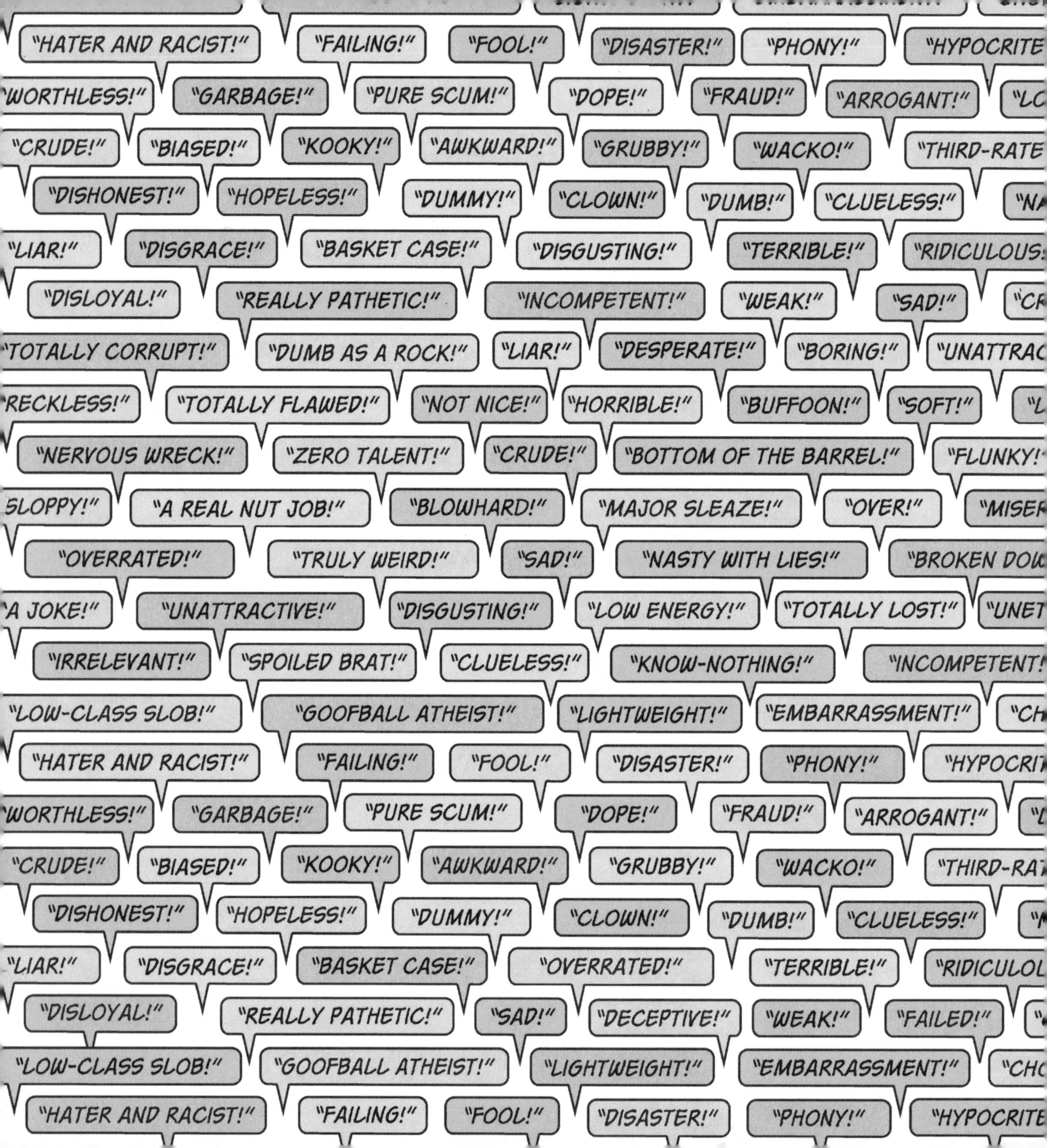
"HATER AND RACIST!"
"FAILING!"
"FOOL!"
"DISASTER!"
"PHONY!"
"HYPOCRITE
"WORTHLESS!"
"GARBAGE!"
"PURE SCUM!"
"DOPE!"
"FRAUD!"
"ARROGANT!"
"CRUDE!"
"BIASED!"
"KOOKY!"
"AWKWARD!"
"GRUBBY!"
"WACKO!"
"THIRD-RATE
"DISHONEST!"
"HOPELESS!"
"DUMMY!"
"CLOWN!"
"DUMB!"
"CLUELESS!"
"LIAR!"
"DISGRACE!"
"BASKET CASE!"
"DISGUSTING!"
"TERRIBLE!"
"RIDICULOUS
"DISLOYAL!"
"REALLY PATHETIC!"
"INCOMPETENT!"
"WEAK!"
"SAD!"
"TOTALLY CORRUPT!"
"DUMB AS A ROCK!"
"LIAR!"
"DESPERATE!"
"BORING!"
"RECKLESS!"
"TOTALLY FLAWED!"
"NOT NICE!"
"HORRIBLE!"
"BUFFOON!"
"SOFT!"
"NERVOUS WRECK!"
"ZERO TALENT!"
"CRUDE!"
"BOTTOM OF THE BARREL!"
"FLUNKY!
"SLOPPY!"
"A REAL NUT JOB!"
"BLOWHARD!"
"MAJOR SLEAZE!"
"OVER!"
"OVERRATED!"
"TRULY WEIRD!"
"SAD!"
"NASTY WITH LIES!"
"A JOKE!"
"UNATTRACTIVE!"
"DISGUSTING!"
"LOW ENERGY!"
"TOTALLY LOST!"
"IRRELEVANT!"
"SPOILED BRAT!"
"CLUELESS!"
"KNOW-NOTHING!"
"INCOMPETENT!
"LOW-CLASS SLOB!"
"GOOFBALL ATHEIST!"
"LIGHTWEIGHT!"
"EMBARRASSMENT!"
"HATER AND RACIST!"
"FAILING!"
"FOOL!"
"DISASTER!"
"PHONY!"
"WORTHLESS!"
"GARBAGE!"
"PURE SCUM!"
"DOPE!"
"FRAUD!"
"ARROGANT!"
"CRUDE!"
"BIASED!"
"KOOKY!"
"AWKWARD!"
"GRUBBY!"
"WACKO!"
"DISHONEST!"
"HOPELESS!"
"DUMMY!"
"CLOWN!"
"DUMB!"
"CLUELESS!"
"LIAR!"
"DISGRACE!"
"BASKET CASE!"
"OVERRATED!"
"TERRIBLE!"
"DISLOYAL!"
"REALLY PATHETIC!"
"SAD!"
"DECEPTIVE!"
"WEAK!"
"FAILED!"
"LOW-CLASS SLOB!"
"GOOFBALL ATHEIST!"
"LIGHTWEIGHT!"
"EMBARRASSMENT!"
"HATER AND RACIST!"
"FAILING!"
"FOOL!"
"DISASTER!"
"PHONY!"
"HYPOCRITE